I0901720

"The method of the Second Vatican Council in engaging every issue is dialogue. The issue of the relationship between the ordinary and extraordinary forms of the Roman Rite of eucharistic celebration is addressed in William Johnston's book by placing in dialogue all the partners in the liturgical reform, alive and dead. He does this to achieve a balance in the worship of the Church, not allowing it to be captured by a single viewpoint or argument. *Care for the Church and Its Liturgy* is a much-needed contribution to liturgical renewal."

Francis Cardinal George, OMI
Archbishop of Chicago

William H. Johnston

Care for the Church and Its Liturgy

A Study of *Summorum Pontificum* and the Extraordinary Form of the Roman Rite

A PUEBLO BOOK

Liturgical Press Collegeville, Minnesota
www.litpress.org

A Pueblo Book published by Liturgical Press

Cover design by Jodi Hendrickson.

1 2 3 4 5 6 7 8 9

Library of Congress Cataloging-in-Publication Data

Johnston, William H., 1950–
Care for the church and its liturgy : A Study of Summorum Pontificum and the Extraordinary Form of the Roman Rite / William H. Johnston.
pages cm
"A Pueblo Book."
Includes bibliographical references.
ISBN 978-0-8146-6269-4 — ISBN 978-0-8146-6294-6 (ebook)
1. Catholic Church. Pope (2005–2013 : Benedict XVI). Summorum Pontificum. 2. Catholic Church—Liturgy—History. I. Title.

BX1975.J64 2013
264'.02036—dc23 2013031523

MAGISTRO PRAECIPUO
WILLIAM G. STOREY, D.M.S.,
QUI ABHINC ANNOS
ERUDITIONE ATQUE EXEMPLO SUO
ME PARTICIPANDO ET INQUIRENDO
STUDIUM LITURGIAE INGENIUMQUE DOCUIT

Contents

Preface and Acknowledgments

My first impression on reading Pope Benedict XVI's *Summorum Pontificum* and *Con Grande Fiducia* in July 2007—whether on July 7 or a few days after I no longer remember—was amazement at how many different things this one liturgical-legislative initiative, expressed in these two documents, was doing all at once. I thought those many things both interesting and important and during that summer drafted an initial reflection on the documents. Apart from several more focused and short-term projects along the way, this book has been my main research preoccupation during the past six years, and it incorporates much of the results of that research.

Such a study remains relevant even after Pope Benedict's papacy, for *Summorum Pontificum* is still in force. In his 2013 interview with Antonio Spadaro, SJ, Pope Francis referred to his predecessor's action in allowing greater access to the traditional liturgy as "prudent" and "motivated by the desire to help people who have this sensitivity," that is, an appreciation and longing for the prior liturgical forms.[1] Pope Francis did voice some concern, but only for the misuse of *Summorum Pontificum*. He worried about "the risk of the ideologization of the *Vetus Ordo*, its exploitation."[2] This might indicate, for example, those who would intend and promote its use more as an act of church politics (e.g., to oppose Vatican II) than pastoral care, or, on the other hand, those who would misinterpret its genuinely pastoral implementation in solely political or ideological categories and resist it on those grounds. But the pope's words express no fundamental opposition to *Summorum Pontificum* and indicate no intention to revoke its provisions.

The core of this book is found in part 2, where chapters 4 and 5 offer analysis and commentary—by turns historical, liturgical, pastoral, canonical, and speculative—on the two documents issued by Pope Benedict. Part 1 prepares the way, with chapter 1 explaining the informed, appreciative, critical, and constructive

[1] Antonio Spadaro, "A Big Heart Open to God: The Exclusive Interview with Pope Francis," *America* 209, no. 8 (September 30, 2013): 30; available online at http://www.america magazine.org/pope-interview (accessed September 23, 2013).

[2] Ibid.

method of the study, chapter 2 addressing some objections that might hinder a fresh reading of part 2, and chapter 3 outlining the multiple purposes I think this liturgical initiative was meant and designed to serve. Part 3 selects for further exploration two features of the new situation created by these documents: in chapter 6, some pastoral implications and in chapter 7, the key process of mutual enrichment. A concluding chapter rounds out the study with a review of various potential beneficial effects that may follow from a predominantly appreciative reception and implementation of the new structure and dynamics of the Roman Rite as instantiated by Pope Benedict in *Summorum Pontificum,* along with an invitation to choose to adopt such an approach so as to give what positive potential may follow a chance to emerge.

The argument of the book can be found in the text proper. But that argument receives a more extended presentation and development in the footnotes, many of which serve to support, illustrate, explain, qualify, or draw out consequences of points made in the text. Reading the notes should make the meaning and force of what is said in the text clearer.

This book on the liturgy and the church is addressed to both academic and pastoral audiences and seeks to be relevant and helpful to both. It even hopes to bridge the divide and lessen the perception of separation between them, for each benefits when it listens to and takes into consideration the voice and perspective of the other, received and engaged as a legitimate and natural dialogue partner. I hope the book will be informative, illuminating, and helpful for all who have an interest in the Catholic Church, in particular its (Roman Rite) liturgy and the way that liturgy serves the worship of God and the holiness and building up of God's people in communion and mission. In view of the turmoil that has marked the liturgical and ecclesial scene over the past half century, and convinced Pope Benedict has with these two documents not (as it might be construed) entered the lists of the liturgy wars on one side but rather done a "new thing" that creates new possibilities, I have sought throughout to write in as balanced, open-minded, constructive, and irenic a spirit as possible, mindful of the different perspectives of different readers. With respect, I invite readers to consider the plausibility of that conviction, and to read in that same spirit.

I owe sincere thanks to those who provided assistance as this work was in progress. My colleagues Sandra Yocum and Dennis Doyle read those initial reflections in 2007 and responded with helpful comments and critique, and Bill Portier later read several chapters in draft form and offered further encouragement. Fred Jenkins (Latin) and Art Mosher (German) along with Martha Williams (Spanish) most kindly provided consultation and assistance regarding the translation of selected passages. Melissa Berry gave much appreciated commentary from the perspective of a social psychologist; though it was for the most part on material other than that in this book, it was most helpful to my learning and use of the categories of social psychology. John Huels and Chad Glendinning replied to some canonical questions and speculations; Glendinning and Lynda Robitaille helpfully recommended additional sources to research. Karen Kane read several chapters and offered insightful and useful observations that informed my sense of how best to present some of the material, especially in part 1. Jeremy Helmes read many of the chapters, on short notice no less, and replied in a timely and balanced fashion with comments that helped me judge my bearings. I offer my sincere thanks to each of them for their generous assistance—adding also the customary and very appropriate proviso, that while their assistance has improved what follows, any errors or shortcomings in the book are entirely my own responsibility.

In the summer of 2009 I received a University of Dayton Research Council seed grant—a summer research fellowship, under the rubric of the Forum for the Catholic Intellectual Tradition Today, coordinated by Una Cadegan. This fellowship allowed me to devote the summer to research and to writing the first drafts of several chapters. It was a fruitful three months, and I am grateful for the support.

Several persons deserve special mention. I originally voiced some ideas regarding *Summorum Pontificum* to Jeffrey Leo Gainey, then the editor of the University of Scranton Press; he replied, expressing interest in the ideas and offering me a contract. Without his initial and enthusiastic response, this project may never have been undertaken. I am most grateful to him for his support and his friendship over the years. After the University of Scranton Press ceased doing business, I sought another publisher. Sincere thanks to Hans Christoffersen and Liturgical Press for adopting the work-in-progress, agreeing to publish much of it, and waiting with kind patience for its completion.

Father David J. Tokarz generously read and made suggestions on the complete translations of both *Summorum Pontificum* and *Con Grande Fiducia*. His afternoon tutorial in Italian one summer day on the porch was invaluable. He also reviewed and critiqued selected chapters, and has responded thoughtfully to a range of issues and questions posed now and again. I am most grateful to him for his advice of several kinds and, as with Gainey, for his friendship over the years.

Sister Joyce Ann Zimmerman and I are both members of the advisory board of the Vital Worship Grants Program (formerly the Worship Renewal Grants Program) administered by the Calvin Institute of Christian Worship at Calvin College in Grand Rapids, Michigan. As we both live in Dayton, Ohio, whenever possible we have driven to the board meetings together. Before a number of these trips she willingly read drafts of chapters I was then working on, and during the drive we discussed at length those chapters and the wider issues they raised. Her comments and suggestions were invariably helpful. But I am particularly grateful for her encouragement and support for the work I was doing, especially in the early stages when my steps were tentative and exploratory. A special word of thanks to her.

During my undergraduate and graduate studies at the University of Notre Dame, William G. Storey served as my undergraduate advisor, the faculty member for whom I worked as graduate assistant (leading a small-group seminar in his Church Evolution course), and my dissertation director. His teaching, mentorship, and example taught me to love and study the liturgy. With gratitude, I dedicate this book to him.

While the manuscript was in press, Pope Francis announced his intention to canonize Blessed John XXIII. Since formal canonization is not scheduled to take place until April 27, 2014, after the book is published, and since Pope John is referred to as "Blessed" in *Summorum Pontificum*, we will retain that usage in what follows. But may I invoke already Pope Saint John XXIII to pray that this book, and the documents it studies, may serve the good of the liturgy and the church.

Finally, my wife, Maureen, has lived with this project for as long as I have. For her encouragement, support, patience, and love, which are constant, I am grateful—more than I can ever say.

October 4, 2013
The Feast of St. Francis of Assisi
in both the ordinary and
extraordinary forms of the
Roman Rite
Franciscus vir catholicus
et totus apostolicus . . .

Abbreviations

AA	*Apostolicam Actuositatem* (1965), the Second Vatican Council's Decree on the Laity
CGF	*Con Grande Fiducia* (2007), Pope Benedict XVI's Letter to Catholic Bishops accompanying publication of *Summorum Pontificum*
DOL	International Commission on English in the Liturgy, *Documents on the Liturgy 1963–1979: Conciliar, Papal, and Curial Texts* (Collegeville, MN: Liturgical Press, 1982)
ED	John Paul II, *Ecclesia Dei Adflicta* (1988)
FE	*Forma extraordinaria* ("extraordinary form"), the term designated by Pope Benedict XVI to name the permitted use of the Roman Missal of John XXIII (1962)—and certain other liturgical books in use in 1962—in the Roman Rite today, in accord with the provisions of his 2007 *motu proprio* on the liturgy, *Summorum Pontificum*
FO	*Forma ordinaria* ("ordinary form"), the term designated by Pope Benedict XVI to name the regular use of the current edition of the Roman Missal of Paul VI in the Roman Rite today, in accord with the provisions of his 2007 *motu proprio* on the liturgy, *Summorum Pontificum*
GIRM	*General Instruction of the Roman Missal*
LG	*Lumen Gentium* (1964), the Second Vatican Council's Dogmatic Constitution on the Church
PCED	Pontifical Commission *Ecclesia Dei*
QAA	*Quattuor Abhinc Annos* (1984)
SC	*Sacrosanctum Concilium* (1963), the Second Vatican Council's Constitution on the Sacred Liturgy
SCDW	Sacred Congregation for Divine Worship
SP	*Summorum Pontificum* (2007), Pope Benedict XVI's *motu proprio* establishing the "ordinary form" and the "extraordinary form" of the liturgy as the two usages of the Roman Rite
SSPX	Society of Saint Pius X
UE	*Universae Ecclesiae* (2011), the PCED instruction on SP

Part 1

Chapter 1

Introduction and Orientation

On July 7, 2007, Pope Benedict XVI issued *motu proprio* an apostolic letter, *Summorum Pontificum*, changing the liturgy of the Catholic Church in a unique and unprecedented way. He designated two *uses* or *forms* of the Roman Rite, declaring the Missal of Paul VI formally promulgated in 1970 and revised on several occasions since to be that Rite's ordinary form (*forma ordinaria*, hereafter FO), and the Missal of John XXIII published in 1962 to be its extraordinary form (*forma extraordinaria*, hereafter FE). The latter is the last preconciliar edition of the Roman Missal, designated by the Second Vatican Council for *instauratio* (restoration, or renewal); the former is the result of that renewal. On the same day Benedict also published a letter to bishops, *Con Grande Fiducia*, to accompany and offer commentary on *Summorum Pontificum*.[1]

[1] The official text of *Summorum Pontificum* (hereafter abbreviated SP) is published in *Acta Apostolicae Sedis* 99, no. 9 (2007): 777–81, and reprinted in the appendix of this book. Though the introductory paragraphs of SP are not numbered in AAS, for the purposes of this study they will be referred to by number. Thus, the first paragraph, beginning "Summorum Pontificum cura ad hoc tempus," will be designated SP 1. The second paragraph, beginning "Ab immemorabili tempore," will be SP 2. And so on. The legislative articles of SP are already numbered in the official text and will be referred to here as SP, article 1, and so on. The text of *Con Grande Fiducia* (hereafter abbreviated CGF) is published in *Acta Apostolicae Sedis* 99, no. 9 (2007): 795–99, and reprinted in the appendix of this book. Its paragraphs are not numbered, but in this study will be referred to by number. Thus, the first paragraph, beginning "con grande fiducia," will be designated CGF 1. The second paragraph, beginning "Notizie e giudizi," will be CGF 2. And so on, through to CGF 14, beginning "Affido alla potente intercessione di Maria." Subsequently, on April 20, 2011, the Pontifical Commission *Ecclesia Dei*, which has responsibility to oversee implementation of SP, issued an instruction, *Universae Ecclesiae* (hereafter abbreviated UE), containing directives regarding that implementation. Each paragraph of that instruction is numbered and will be referred to accordingly.

The central section of this book, part 2, offers analysis and commentary on these two documents, giving attention to their meaning, context, purposes, implementation, and potential effects, doing so with reference to other statements of Pope Benedict and to his body of work before becoming pope—his writings and addresses as theologian and as prefect of the Congregation for the Doctrine of the Faith, Cardinal Joseph Ratzinger. We will explore the meaning of the two documents paragraph by paragraph, situate their immediate context (the complexity of postconciliar dynamics in the Catholic Church) in a wider historical framework, look at the multiple purposes the documents aim to serve, and address various questions attendant on their implementation. In the course of our study we may even find reason to speculate that the long-range effects of these documents in reshaping the form and celebration of the church's liturgy are potentially so significant as to render July 7, 2007, one of the truly notable days in the history of the liturgy.

As we commence I should draw attention to a particular characteristic of this book, deriving from a double dynamic in the two principal documents to be studied. First and most obviously, in these documents the *usus antiquior* or "more ancient use," as the 1962 form of the Roman Rite is sometimes called, is understood positively, as a ritual form of historic status, inherent worth, and pastoral benefit. The second dynamic is that Pope Benedict XVI anticipated certain objections to his liturgical initiative and addressed them in his letter *Con Grande Fiducia*, responding to two in particular—that SP will undermine the authority of the Second Vatican Council and that it will prove divisive within parish communities. He thought both fears unfounded and devoted much of the letter to explaining why.

It is this double dynamic in the two documents—Pope Benedict's positive approach to the older liturgy and his disagreement with those who think wider use of that liturgy ill advised—that the present study seeks to understand, explain, and assess. A characteristic feature of this book is that it will do so in a predominantly appreciative way, within the context of a method that is fourfold: *informed*, *appreciative*, *critical*, and *constructive*.[2] A word about each feature of this method is in order.

[2] The trio *informed-appreciative-critical* is borrowed from the wording of several educational goals formulated in 2006 at my university, the University of

METHOD: INFORMED, APPRECIATIVE, CRITICAL, CONSTRUCTIVE

Informed simply means this study, as any other, has made use of relevant sources and disciplines to the extent possible within the inevitable limitations of time, ability, and competing responsibilities. Let me express thanks beforehand to commentators who can helpfully develop, improve, or correct what follows with further relevant information and interpretation.

Appreciative warrants more explanation, naming as it does the predominant approach of this study, guiding and governing the reading and interpretation of *Summorum Pontificum* and its accompanying letter, *Con Grande Fiducia*. Why make this method primary? First of all because it best promotes the kind of understanding this study seeks.

I find good sense in the request Joseph Ratzinger (Pope Benedict XVI) made of his readers in the foreword to the first published volume in his trilogy *Jesus of Nazareth*. Regarding the contents of that book he said "everyone is free, then, to contradict me. I would only ask my readers for that initial goodwill without which there can be no understanding."[3] A reasonable and appropriate request, for one is more likely to understand an interlocutor's meaning and intention by listening in a spirit of initial goodwill rather than initial mistrust or disagreement. Any communication process, scholarly or otherwise, stands to gain from at least some degree of willingness to set one's own perspectives, assumptions, and judgments aside

---

Dayton: for example, "All undergraduates will develop and demonstrate ability to engage in intellectually informed, appreciative, and critical inquiry regarding major faith traditions"; see the Marianist Education Working Group's "Habits of Inquiry and Reflection: A Report on Education in the Catholic and Marianist Traditions at the University of Dayton" (2006), 8, http://www.udayton.edu/artssciences/about/images/Habits_of_Inquiry.pdf. I decided to adopt the three named components, in that sequence, as a sound methodology for this work. The fourth component, constructive, seemed appropriate to round out the process. For a work using the trio *appreciative-critical-constructive* as its method, see *Reclaiming Catholicism: Treasures Old and New*, ed. Thomas H. Groome and Michael J. Daley (Maryknoll, NY: Orbis Books, 2010), with the explanation of the method given by Groome in his preface (xiii).

[3] Joseph Ratzinger / Pope Benedict XVI, *Jesus of Nazareth: From the Baptism in the Jordan to the Transfiguration* (New York: Doubleday, 2007), xxiv.

for a moment, methodologically, in the effort to see and appreciate more clearly what the other sees and values, and to the extent possible *as* the other sees and values it. Cultivating such a practice—from conviction, or courtesy, or simply as a thought experiment—widens the possibility of seeing new perspectives and helps lessen a tendency to hear and interpret the other from within or over against one's own existing categories and frame of reference. The present study seeks to read these two documents of Pope Benedict with this kind of goodwill, and I invite readers to do the same, the better to encounter and understand his thoughts and intentions on his own terms.

This approach is not unlike "appreciative awareness," a feature of the work of Bernard Meland as described by theologian and psychologist Michael A. Cowan. Appreciative awareness entails receptivity to the "stories of others' lives," and to "taking account of the symbols and meanings of our own and other cultures" in a mutually enriching way.[4] Doing so invites "taking off our shoes as we approach the others' holy places," so as more respectfully and fully to encounter, appreciate, and perhaps even to some extent to "internalize the breadth and depths of human experience in the world."[5] Here, this means turning with an appreciative awareness toward something *Summorum Pontificum* affirms: the "human experience" of those Catholics who find the celebration of the 1962 Missal a still valid and worthy form for worshiping God, an important and effective link with centuries of Catholic tradition and community, and a fruitful means of growth in holiness.

Let me add that, in this work addressing both scholarly and pastoral issues and audiences, and in addition to the foregoing considerations, I also adopt an appreciative approach to this papal *motu proprio* because the Second Vatican Council teaches me to, and so I will, "sincerely adhere to decisions made by [the Roman Pon-

[4] See Michael A. Cowan, "Sacramental Moments: Appreciative Awareness in the Iron Cage," in *Alternative Futures for Worship*, vol. 1, *General Introduction*, ed. Regis A. Duffy (Collegeville, MN: Liturgical Press, 1987), 35–61, here at 53.

[5] Ibid., 54. The "holy ground" citation echoes language Cowan had just cited from John V. Taylor, *Primal Vision* (New York: Oxford, 1963), referring ultimately to Exod 3:5.

tiff], conformably with his manifest mind and intention" (LG 25). Doing so also helps me toward a primary goal of this study—that is, to understand as fully and sympathetically as possible that papal mind and intention; it is also consistent in general with the ecclesial vocation of a theologian, and it does not preclude but is well balanced by the critical and constructive elements of the fourfold methodology used here.[6]

Critical and *constructive* are the other two components of this study. While predominantly appreciative, the stance taken toward aspects of Pope Benedict's liturgical initiative and his explanation of it is critical when I think there is sound reason for it; on such occasions I try to set forth the reasons as clearly as possible, to be judged on their merits. At times I also offer suggestions for alternate ways to think about or implement the *motu proprio*, intending these points of constructive criticism to serve the good of the church and its liturgy. When helpful, I hope they might be adopted, when not, let them be amended, and when matters remain unclear, let further discussion seek light, proceeding freely and charitably.

I have chosen this fourfold method so as to follow and promote the path the council set forth for the church, not only in *Lumen Gentium* as already noted, but also at the conclusion of *Gaudium et Spes*, the Pastoral Constitution on the Church in the Modern World. The constitution affirms that the path of the church—in fulfilling its mission to witness in the world to the light of the Gospel and unite all people in the one Spirit—both "allows and invigorates sincere dialogue," which in turn "requires us first of all to create in the Church itself mutual esteem, reverence, and harmony, and acknowledge all legitimate diversity" (GS 92).[7] The methodological intention to be informed and appreciative where possible serves well the present study's aim to explore one facet of that legitimate diversity in the liturgical life of the church today, in a way that

[6] See *Donum Veritatis* (Instruction on the Ecclesial Vocation of the Theologian) 21–31.

[7] The first phrase quoted is my translation (*sincerum dialogum permittit atque roborat*); the second phrase is from Flannery's translation. Except for the translation of *Sacrosanctum Concilium*, and unless otherwise noted, the Flannery translation of Vatican II documents is used throughout.

shows esteem for Catholics across an admittedly broad sweep of ecclesial identity and belonging; it also manifests reverence for sacred things both new and old and hopes to promote in doing so that desired spirit of harmony. Where this study is critical and constructive, it seeks to be so within the unity, freedom, and charity the council commended: "let there be unity in what is necessary, freedom in what is doubtful, and charity in everything" (GS 92).

Sincere dialogue, mutual esteem, reverence, harmony, diversity, unity, freedom, charity—these are the qualities I hope this study respects, embodies, and helps to promote in ongoing discussion of *Summorum Pontificum*, both pastoral and academic, as the church discerns its liturgical way forward.

Chapter 2

Addressing Some Objections

> Like a fish who cannot grasp the concept of "water" because it cannot imagine swimming in anything else, the partisans of each side have trouble understanding the other's model, because they have not cultivated sufficient objective distance from their own.
>
> —Peter Jeffery, *Translating Tradition* (2005)

> Mindlessness . . . is a state of mind overdetermined by the past, where the individual relies on distinctions and categories created in the past and is oblivious to novel (or simply other) aspects of the target information.
>
> —Ellen J. Langer, "Mindfulness/Mindlessness" (1995)[1]

With its designation of two legitimate and distinct usages of the Roman Rite, *Summorum Pontificum* represents a significant development in Roman Catholic liturgy, only a relatively short time after the dramatic liturgical reforms arising out of the Second Vatican Council. Such a new development would be striking and controversial under any circumstances, but especially so since one of those usages is the very liturgical form the council mandated be reformed. For many people that liturgy can generate strong feelings (whether positive or negative) and it has come to function for some as a prominent symbol of disagreement with or even opposition to

[1] Epigraph citations: Peter Jeffery, *Translating Tradition: A Chant Historian Reads* Liturgiam Authenticam (Collegeville, MN: Liturgical Press, 2005), 108; Ellen J. Langer, "Mindfulness/Mindlessness," in *The Blackwell Encyclopedia of Social Psychology*, ed. Anthony S. R. Manstead and Miles Hewstone (Oxford: Blackwell Reference, 1995), 389.

the council. All this places obstacles in the way of a calm reception and impartial interpretation of SP.

This chapter attempts to address a few of the difficulties, objections, and misunderstandings that may stand in the way of adopting a predominantly appreciative (while occasionally critical) reading of *Summorum Pontificum*. Such difficulties, objections, or misunderstandings include the following.

- A general sense of mistrust of Pope Benedict XVI—that his true leanings and ultimate intentions for the church and the liturgy were anticonciliar.
- Fundamental rejection of the 1962 liturgy—the understanding that it has no place in the church today because Pope Paul VI of set purpose forbade its use, because the bishops at Vatican II judged it in need of reform and mandated that reform, because its theology is problematic if not erroneous in view of conciliar developments in church teaching and its articulation, and because its presence together with the reformed liturgy creates in the same parish or local community simultaneously two liturgical worlds that are different, incompatible, and thus inherently divisive.
- A sense of frustration or resentment—that Pope Benedict accommodated liturgical sensibilities on the ecclesial *right* but criticized those on the *left*.
- Maximizing interpretations of SP—from the *right*.

These represent a sampling of difficulties that may impede an appreciative if sometimes critical reading of SP, and we will address each in turn. But let me suggest first that there is a common cause contributing to each and a common corrective helpful in responding to each. The common cause is a certain kind of continuing influence of the past; the common corrective is a certain mode of openness to a new situation.

The social psychological terms for these two factors are, respectively, *mindlessness* and *mindfulness*. Social psychology is a relevant field for us because the understanding, reception, and implementation of *Summorum Pontificum* involve the study not only of distinct ritual forms (the ordinary and extraordinary forms of the Roman Rite) but also of distinct ritual communities (the communities of persons favoring one or the other ritual form) and their relationships. As such, we are engaged in a study of human groups, the subject matter of social psychology. Moreover, some readers of this book may identify with one or the other ritual community or be in sympathy with its concerns. If so, then mindfulness about what such adherence may mean for one's perceptions and views of our subject matter—of the ritual forms (the form one favors, and the other) and ritual groups (the group one belongs to or sympathizes with, and the other)—mindfulness of this can aid in achieving some measure of the methodological "objective distance" that allows one to see, or at least try to see, the familiar in a new way, which is exactly what SP calls for.[2]

Mindfulness aids in this endeavor because it involves "the process of drawing novel distinctions" in familiar circumstances.[3] An individual in a condition of mindfulness "is open to novelty" and new ways of looking at things, is "aware of multiple perspectives," including legitimate multiple perspectives of the same thing at the same time, and is "sensitive to context" and the significance of changes in context over time.[4] *Mindlessness* (the term sounds a little harsh but is properly taken as neutral) involves "a state of mind overdetermined by the past, where the individual relies on distinctions and categories created in the past and is oblivious to novel (or simply other) aspects of the target information."[5]

[2] On "objective distance," see Peter Jeffery, *Translating Tradition: A Chant Historian Reads* Liturgiam Authenticam (Collegeville, MN: Liturgical Press, 2005), 108.

[3] Ellen J. Langer and Mihnea Moldoveanu, "The Construct of Mindfulness," *Journal of Social Issues* 56, no. 1 (2000): 1–9, here at 1; see also Ellen Langer, "Mindfulness Versus Positive Evaluation," in *Oxford Handbook of Positive Psychology*, ed. C. R. Snyder and Shane J. Lopez (Oxford: Oxford University Press, 2009), 279.

[4] Ellen J. Langer, "Mindfulness/Mindlessness," in *The Blackwell Encyclopedia of Social Psychology*, ed. Anthony S. R. Manstead and Miles Hewstone, 388–90 (Oxford: Blackwell Reference, 1995), 388–89. See also Langer, *The Power of Mindful Learning* (Reading, MA: Addison-Wesley Publishing Co., 1997), 4 and 23.

[5] Langer, "Mindfulness/Mindlessness," 389. Mindlessness keeps one "in a single perspective," rendering one "unaware of new or different views or uses to which [new] information," such as the provisions of SP and the perspectives of CGF, "could be put" (389).

The danger of mindlessness can beset both those who oppose and those who prefer the *usus antiquior*; individuals on either side can respond out of the habitual frames of reference that have held sway for the half century since the council. Each side views the liturgical forms of the other as flawed, inadequate, and even inimical to Catholic faith and life, best eliminated or, barring that, significantly revised. Some of the more high-intensity, single-minded proponents of the *usus antiquior* might interpret SP as supportive of and useful for their larger agenda (out with the new liturgy, back with the old); similar proponents of the reformed liturgy might agree, and on that basis oppose SP. Both groups would thus be closed to a more "mindful" reading of SP that would entertain an unforeseen possibility—that the document was Pope Benedict's invitation to envision the two liturgical forms and their possible roles and interrelationship in a new way, moving beyond the impasse of the long-familiar polarities by recognizing and valuing the respective riches each form has to offer for the sake of bringing about a liturgical, and thereby an ecclesial, reconciliation.

Here is an illustration of the two terms. At a liturgical conference in 1996, M. Francis Mannion spoke of the desire for a "new liturgical movement" that had been voiced from "various quarters" in the church over the preceding two decades; he then delineated the different features of what he maintained were in fact "not one but five identifiable liturgical movements in the English-speaking world."[6] The five movements are: (1) advancing the official reform, (2) promoting traditionalism and restoration of the preconciliar liturgy (and within this category he draws further distinctions), (3) reforming the reform, (4) taking the reform further through inculturation, and (5) what he calls "recatholicizing the reform." The ability to draw such distinctions among a wide range of positions

[6] M. Francis Mannion, "The Catholicity of the Liturgy: Shaping a New Agenda," in *Beyond the Prosaic: Renewing the Liturgical Movement*, ed. Stratford Caldecott (Edinburgh: T&T Clark, 1998), 11–48, here at 11; reprinted in a slightly edited version in Mannion, *Masterworks of God: Essays in Liturgical Theory and Practice* (Chicago: Hillenbrand Books, Liturgy Training Publications, 2004), 202–35, here at 202. Both versions offer extensive bibliography for each of the five types.

and agendas previously viewed under a single rubric illustrates a mindful approach to the subject.

Compare the following understanding of the term "new liturgical movement":

> The call to a "new liturgical movement" often heard within Catholicism means just and only a call to cast doubts and to reverse the liturgical reform of Vatican II. Fifty years from the event of Vatican II, "going back to the liturgical movement" does not mean anything but a return to the preconciliar mentality, with the nostalgia nourished by the desperation of those who no longer have any confidence in the future. These calls for a nostalgic "new liturgical movement" are nothing more than "a radical negation of every possible movement in the field of ritual and the emergence of a stagnation for a Church that is lifeless and without children."[7]

This analysis contrasts with the former chiefly in not drawing distinctions, but instead recognizing only one view, doing so in a way that interprets the present in terms of categories formed in the past. Here, the new liturgical movement "does not mean anything but" one thing, and in this case, "just and only" the most negative of Mannion's five categories, perhaps specifically the extreme wing of that category, those favoring full restoration of preconciliar forms and "revers[al of] the liturgical reform of Vatican II." The analysis in this passage, then, is limited and limiting. It hinders recognizing a range and diversity of perspectives among those who see value in a new liturgical movement and precludes finding merit in those positions.[8] This, and the ascription of only negative motives to the

[7] Massimo Faggioli, *True Reform: Liturgy and Ecclesiology in* Sacrosanctum Concilium (Collegeville, MN: Liturgical Press, 2012), 165; internal citation is to Marco Grillo and Andrea Grillo, "Il tempo giusto per leggere 'Il movimento liturgico' di Bernard Botte," preface to Bernard Botte, *Il movimento liturgico. Testimonianza e ricordi* (Cantalupa: Effatà, 2009), 13.

[8] Langer speaks to the limiting impact consequent upon the manner in which information is presented. Writing with the school setting in view but making pedagogical observations relevant for our context as well, she cites multiple studies "showing that conditionalized presentation of information ('x could be seen as y') to students leads to better 'performance' of the students on subsequent tests than does the unconditionalized presentation of information ('x is nothing but y,' or 'x is y'), lend[ing] support to the notion that successful

other and only negative consequences to their views, leaves the reader with no reason to engage in "sincere dialogue," for there is nothing to be learned, only something to be opposed. Such an approach, exemplifying the term mindlessness, seems destined to heighten tensions and perpetuate existing misunderstandings rather than foster respect and invite a new mutual understanding. Mannion's more mindful approach has already been found a fair, hermeneutically useful, and reliable description of the liturgical landscape, valued by those with diverse liturgical perspectives.[9] This—a taste of reconciliation amid diverse perspectives—is what mindfulness can bring about.

If, in view of these benefits, we intentionally sought to take a mindful look at potential difficulties or objections to a predominantly appreciative reading of SP and to engaging in the kind of dialogue this study hopes to engender, attempting to make new distinctions or seek modes of understanding and interpretation that cast new light on positions or perspectives long assumed to be well-grounded and still valid, what might we see? Let us explore this question, focusing on the difficulties, objections, or misunderstandings previously identified.

MISTRUST OF POPE BENEDICT'S INTENTIONS

One example illustrating concerns of those who mistrusted Pope Benedict's intentions regarding the liturgy can be found in Rita Ferrone's contribution to *Commonweal*'s series of essays of initial response and commentary published shortly after promulgation of

---

adaptive behavior depends on the 'loosening' of the grip that our cognitive commitments have on our minds"; Langer, "Mindfulness Versus Positive Evaluation," 281–82. Our interest is in how to receive and respond (or "adapt") to the new liturgical situation created by *Summorum Pontificum*. Langer and the studies she references would encourage on our part—even if simply as a kind of thought experiment—a loosening of prior "cognitive commitments" and liturgical convictions, and a willingness to speculate how SP could be seen as beneficial rather than harmful, if we wish the ecclesial reception and response to SP to be as positive and "successful" as it can be for the life of the church.

[9] Mark Drew, "The Spirit or the Letter? Vatican II and Liturgical Reform," in Caldecott, *Beyond the Prosaic*, 60; John F. Baldovin, *Reforming the Liturgy: A Response to the Critics* (Collegeville, MN: Liturgical Press, 2008), 4 and 148.

Summorum Pontificum in 2007. She referred then to Cardinal Ratzinger as having been "a champion and supporter" of the few but influential Catholics promoting not only "restoration of Tridentine liturgical forms" but also "the marginalization of the reformed liturgy."[10] As for Pope Benedict's long-term intentions, she speculated that a "plausible understanding of the present moment"—the moment he created by promulgating SP—"is that it marks another step toward a goal that the vast majority of Catholics would not countenance if it were openly acknowledged—namely, the gradual dismantling of the liturgical reform in its entirety."[11] Whether one reads this speculation as having suggested the eventual outcome of Benedict's actions, or his conscious liturgical agenda, or also his intention to pursue that agenda covertly, it exemplifies the deep-seated concern that on this matter he was fundamentally anticonciliar and thus untrustworthy.

Is it possible to understand Pope Benedict differently, as someone other than a champion of the Tridentine over against the postconciliar liturgy, or the would-be dismantler of the Vatican II liturgical reforms? What alternative lens might help us see this pope and this document in a different light? Let me propose three such lenses, drawn from a study of pastoral leadership. When used to view Pope Benedict these lenses allow us to envision a more positive interpretation of his intentions and actions.

Between 2001 and 2005, Lilly Endowment, Inc., funded a major research project on pastoral leadership that included a "Colloquium on Excellence in Ministry," conducted at Duke Divinity School.[12] *Resurrecting Excellence* by L. Gregory Jones and Kevin R. Armstrong was among the fruits of the colloquium. In a chapter on cultivating excellence in ministry, Jones and Armstrong's description of what pastoral leaders do offers us a way of understanding Pope Benedict's initiative in SP.[13] They propose three roles

[10] Rita Ferrone, "A Step Backward," *Commonweal* 134, no. 14 (August 17, 2007): 13–15, at 13.

[11] Ibid., 15.

[12] For more information on the various component programs of the Pulpit & Pew project, see http://pulpitandpew.org.

[13] L. Gregory Jones and Kevin R. Armstrong, *Resurrecting Excellence: Shaping Faithful Christian Ministry* (Grand Rapids, MI: Eerdmans, 2006). Chapter 5 is "Leading and Learning: The Cultivation of Excellent Ministry," 111–40.

or skills that pastoral leaders should cultivate to gain the competence needed "for the faithful and effective governance of [their] religious institutions"—namely, the skills of being "interpreters, visionaries, and reconcilers."[14] Let us view Pope Benedict in light of these three roles or lenses, reviewing each and giving particular attention to the third role, that of reconciler.

Interpreters

Jones and Armstrong describe interpreters as "a community's custodians of both memory and hope, people who help set the challenges and opportunities of the present within the much larger context of what God has done in the past and where God is leading in the future."[15] Ratzinger's sense of this "larger context" informed all his writings about the liturgy, seen as something that, most fundamentally, we inherit as a gift from the church through the ages rather than design or fabricate for ourselves in the present. His sense of positive appreciation for the preconciliar liturgical forms, his sense of dismay that they were prohibited upon introduction of the Missal of Paul VI, and his judgment that it would benefit the church to make those prior forms more available again to some degree, were all consistent with the interpreter's penchant "to nurture continuity with tradition."[16]

In Pope Benedict's judgment, steps today to foster a greater degree of continuity with the church's (recent) liturgical tradition could helpfully address two concerns: namely, the break he believed was made in the church's long liturgical tradition with the prohibition of the 1962 Missal upon publication of the Missal of Paul VI in 1970, as well as the difficulty or pain (CGF 4) that some experienced due to the degree of liturgical change that took place with the introduction of the new liturgy after the council, in particular through the kind of liturgical experimentation not un-

[14] Ibid., 128.

[15] Ibid., 130.

[16] Ibid. At the same time, of course, we do well to keep in mind that this same concern motivated and guided the liturgical reform itself, which purposefully drew upon and incorporated more of the church's liturgical tradition than did the Mass and other sacraments as they were celebrated in 1962 when the council began.

common in that era—an experimentation often critiqued at that time and once described by Ratzinger as "chaos," which, he said, "to some extent still continues."[17] Benedict's hope was that both matters could be improved through an increased measure of continuity with liturgical tradition, a continuity enacted informally through his own liturgical practice, and more formally via officially renewed sanction for contemporary use of and contact with prior liturgical forms—which was precisely what the provisions of SP were intended to foster.

Jones and Armstrong also take note of what might be considered the negative potential of tradition, what they call the "Back to Egypt" syndrome, a fearful response to the future that draws a community to return to prior ways, characterized as "slavery, oppression, and suffering—but it was familiar."[18] This represents a failure to embrace a trust that God's power will be at work in the future—the kind of trust cultivated by interpreters as custodians of *hope*, as well as memory. It might be thought that Pope Benedict was calling in SP for such a return to Egypt, to a liturgy that was for some Catholics familiar yet for others constituted a kind of unfreedom, a "slavery" to liturgical forms now deemed liturgically, theologically, and pastorally outmoded and indefensible. Pope Benedict would disagree with this assessment of the *usus antiquior* and with the view that he wished the church at large to return to it. He had no intention to replace the reformed liturgy, but to affirm its legitimacy, amend its shortcomings and develop more fully its inherent riches. His hope for the future, an aspect of the interpreter's role, was that the two "uses" of the Roman Rite, the ordinary and extraordinary forms, would mutually enrich each other, thereby fashioning in a patient, unforced, and natural way a liturgy more clearly continuous with its past, more faithful to the council's full range of principles and intentions, different from either usage in its present form, and better capable of expressing "the sacrality which attracts many people" (CGF 7) and in some way quenches their thirst for God.

[17] Ratzinger, "Um die Erneuerung der Liturgie. Antwort auf Reiner Kaczynski," *Stimmen der Zeit* 219, no. 12 (2001): 837–42, at 842.

[18] Jones and Armstrong, *Resurrecting Excellence*, 132.

Visionaries

Like interpreters, visionaries also look ahead and maintain a sense of patience for the long haul. According to Jones and Armstrong, visionaries recognize that their actions are, at times, a planting of seeds whose harvest will only be reaped in the future.[19] Benedict surely had this sense regarding SP; beyond whatever short-term benefit might enrich some members of the church now by allowing celebration of the FE as well as the FO in the present, the ultimate goal he had in view was the liturgy that would emerge as the fruit of a new liturgical movement that SP was intended to support, guide, and resource.

In addition, according to Jones and Armstrong, besides practicing patience, visionaries also "involve the whole community" in the process of discerning and moving into the future.[20] This Benedict also did quite directly by allowing—with no further permission needed from bishop or pope—priests and people who desire it a greater access to the preconciliar liturgy, while not requiring it for or imposing it upon anyone.[21] Under SP, Roman Catholics were intended to have freedom to worship according to the FO or (if they seek it) the FE, and the question of how widely the FE would be used or what role it would play in the church's present or future was in a real way to be wholly dependent on whether the faithful request it or attend it. If they do not, the FE will fade; if they do, it will thrive and have an impact correlative to the measure of its thriving.[22] Benedict took steps, in this

[19] Ibid.

[20] Ibid., 133.

[21] Requiring it of no one, that is, except the pastors and bishops whom the faithful petition for the FE, and who are to respond freely and generously. See, e.g., SP, art. 5.1 and 7; art. 5.1 calls pastors to respond *libenter* to requests for the FE.

[22] Alcuin Reid puts it this way: "Indeed, we may observe that [Pope Benedict] has now left the question of what role the *usus antiquior* of the Roman rite will play in the life of the Church to Providence. He has imposed nothing on anyone—he has merely permitted its use by those who desire it. If the more ancient rites have something to offer that Church of today and of tomorrow they will survive if not flourish (and I think it is already possible to say that we are already seeing the first green shoots of the new springtime of the *usus antiquior* in the Church)." Alcuin Reid, "The Liturgical Reform of Pope Benedict

unique way, to put the matter precisely in the hands of "the whole community."

Finally, visionaries also "have a capacity for the prophetic use of power in both cursing and blessing," or as we might put it, through critique and praise.[23] Benedict more naturally tended—perhaps after, but certainly before assuming the papacy—to search out misguided steps and propose corrections than to dwell on progress achieved and offer encouragement. Nonetheless we can say that, even if his style or charism ran more to constructive critique than to affirmative praise, Joseph Ratzinger—as theologian, curial official, and pope—gave serious attention to the liturgy over the course of many years, in writings intended to give expression to the visionary's prophetic voice in both its "cursing and blessing" capacities, with regard to both the present and the prior liturgy, all with a view to enriching the forms and the manner in which the church today and in the future "offers worship to the eternal Father" (SC 7).[24]

In these ways, then, Pope Benedict manifested qualities that Jones and Armstrong associate with pastoral leaders in their roles as interpreters and visionaries. But Benedict made a point of identifying his key motivation for issuing his *motu proprio* as the desire to foster "an interior reconciliation in the heart of the church" (CGF 8). So let us take a closer look at Jones and Armstrong's description of pastoral leaders as reconcilers.

Reconcilers

Two key skills of reconcilers are counterweighting and overaccepting. Counterweighting is an image the authors borrow from Seamus Heaney, who borrowed it from Simon Weil.[25] It recognizes

---

XVI," in *Benedict XVI and the Sacred Liturgy*, ed. Neil J. Roy and Janet E. Rutherford (Dublin: Four Courts Press, 2010), 156–80, here at 178.

[23] Jones and Armstrong, *Resurrecting Excellence*, 135.

[24] For further reflections on the topic of this paragraph, see William H. Johnston, "Pope Benedict XVI on the Postconciliar Liturgical Reform: An Essay in Interpretation," *Antiphon* 17, no. 2 (2013): 118–38, esp. 129–32.

[25] Ibid., 136–37, and n. 26; Seamus Heaney, *The Redress of Poetry* (New York: Farrar, Straus and Giroux, 1996); Simone Weil, *Gravity and Grace* (New York: G.P. Putnam's Sons, 1952—we will cite this New York edition, though Jones and Armstrong reference London: Routledge, 2002).

that in any group or institution there will be countervailing forces, in the form of divergent factions of persons with differing and even conflicting values and priorities. Such differences can become divisive and create "winners" and "losers" in the community. In the midst of this dynamic, "the activity of counterweighting involves trying to avoid any sense of permanent 'losers.'"[26] Cardinal Ratzinger saw the preconciliar liturgy and those Catholics still attached to it threatened with this very condition. The preconciliar liturgy was, in this frame of reference, relegated to the status of "permanent loser" by being proscribed by Paul VI upon promulgation of the reformed liturgy. Its adherents moreover could be or were, Ratzinger believed, looked upon in the years after the council with disdain; an advocate for some continuing allowance for the old liturgy could be, he said, "treated like a leper."[27] By restoring the legal status of the 1962 Missal, even if only as the extraordinary form of the *lex orandi* of the Roman Rite, he repositioned it in the constellation of the church's liturgical life, recalling it from being permanently lost, and insisting it "must be given due honor for its venerable and ancient usage" (SP, art. 1). If, further, the honor shown the ritual were in some sense to redound to its adherents as well, then SP would contribute to their liberation from that demeaning and divisive stigma of loser. Clearly, for his part, Ratzinger did not view them this way; he recognized, rather, that they could be "individuals totally rooted in the faith of the church," individuals whose deep pain at "arbitrary deformations" in the celebration of the reformed liturgy was grounded not simply in recalcitrance or nostalgia but in legitimate concern for a real and threatened good, namely, the dignity and beauty of the church's worship (CGF 4).[28]

We should also note the way counterweighting may move a discerning pastoral leader at one time one way, at another time another, depending on circumstances (a characteristic of mindfulness). "At times," for example, "counterweighting calls us to attend more to preserving tradition, because too much change can result in chaos.

[26] Jones and Armstrong, *Resurrecting Excellence*, 137.

[27] Joseph Ratzinger, *God and the World: Believing and Living in Our Time, A Conversation with Peter Seewald* (San Francisco: Ignatius Press, 2002), 416.

[28] Compare the similar remarks of Peter Jeffery, *Translating Tradition*, 105–6.

At other times, it calls us to take greater risks, because too much focus on tradition can become stifling."[29] This description of pastoral flexibility and even back-and-forthing seems nicely to describe, and provides a hermeneutic to aid in interpreting, the varying approaches Joseph Ratzinger took regarding the liturgy and its reform over the last half century. He saw the latter context (tradition as stifling) to pertain at the time of the council; that assessment guided his understanding of the situation and of appropriate courses of action to take. Accordingly, he was then fully in support of and ready to defend conciliar liturgical reforms even or indeed precisely in so far as they represented "a basic reversal" from the post-Tridentine liturgy, which had become "a rigid, fixed and firmly encrusted system" with its "prescribed forms."[30] The former context (turning to tradition as a remedy amid chaos) in Ratzinger's view arose and became more salient after the time of the council—indeed, elements of it were visible to him in 1966[31]—and this assessment guided his understanding of the situation and of appropriate courses of action

[29] Jones and Armstrong, *Resurrecting Excellence*, 137.

[30] See Ratzinger, *Theological Highlights of Vatican II* (New York: Paulist Press Deus Books, 1966), 84–88; "basic reversal" (88); "encrusted system" and "prescribed forms" (86). See also Joseph Ratzinger, "Catholicism after the Council," *The Furrow* 18 (1967): 3–23, especially at 6–10. In this article (originally "a lecture delivered to the Katholikentag of 1966 in Bamburg," an editorial footnote informs us), he identified then-current objections to the liturgical reform (regarding use of the vernacular and an emphasis on the community dimension of worship) as "superficial and unjustified" (6), and spoke of the reforms as being "not only justified but even necessary" (10).

[31] See Ratzinger, "Catholicism after the Council," 10–13. This section of cautionary and critical remarks began with this sentence: "While the Council's liturgical reform therefore may be seen to be not only justified but even necessary, the same cannot be said of all the ways in which it has been realized in practice" (10). He made reference here, for example, to the denigration of medieval developments he thought could be rightly considered positive, the use of jazz music in the liturgy, the emphasis given to revision of liturgical forms (to the apparent relative neglect of the realization "that divine worship is first and foremost something which is done for God" [11]), a certain degree of "self-consciousness" in worship, Mass always and only *versus populum*, and so on. "We can no longer deny," he said, "that exaggerations and aberrations have crept in which are both annoying and unbecoming" (11). Some of the themes sounded here echo with some frequency in his later liturgical writings.

to take in the new circumstances; this explains the critical and negative element of his writings and addresses on the liturgy, evident in *Das Fest des Glaubens* in 1981 (published in English in 1986 as *The Feast of Faith*) and consistently thereafter.

Such shifting of assessments does not, it seems to me, constitute a "flip-flopping" inconsistency but can be seen as the mindful, rational calculations of a pastoral leader who has discerned a change in circumstances and responded with counterweighting. This may become clearer if we read the description of counterweighting given in the excerpt from Simone Weil cited by Heaney: "If we can know in what way society is unbalanced, we must do what we can to add weight to the lighter scale . . . we must have formed a conception of equilibrium and be ever ready to change sides like justice, 'that fugitive from the camp of conquerors.'"[32] Ratzinger changed sides or at least changed his emphasis so as to "add weight to the lighter scale," for the sake of a liturgical "equilibrium." At the time of the council he positioned himself over against "tradition" when it weighed too heavily and restrictively on the liturgical life of the church; in the years after the council he came to take his stand with tradition against liturgical excesses as they emerged and spread. He thus showed himself, as Weil desired, "ever ready to change sides" for the sake of maintaining balance, and of sustaining in the church's liturgical life the equilibrium that he saw articulated in the council's liturgy constitution.[33]

[32] Heaney, *The Redress of Poetry*, 3, citing Weil, *Gravity and Grace*, 224.

[33] See Ratzinger, "40 Jahre Konstitution," where he spoke of "the balance of the conciliar texts" (*die Balance des Konzilstextes*), and of the "right" or "proper inner balance" (*die rechte inner Gleichgewicht*), which the liturgy constitution sought to establish (210). Others interpret this feature of the conciliar texts under the rubric of "juxtaposition" (see Henk Witte, "Reform with the Help of Juxtapositions: A Challenge to the Interpretation of the Documents of Vatican II," *The Jurist* 71, no. 1 [2011]: 20–34), or "compromise," or "contradictory pluralism," or even the "compromise of reciprocal dishonesty" (see Peter Hünermann, "The Ignored 'Text': On the Interpretation of the Second Vatican Council," in *Vatican II: A Forgotten Future*, Concilium 2005/4, ed. Alberto Melloni and Christoph Theobald, 118–36 (London: SCM Press, 2005), at 128, and 135, n. 39, referencing Otto Hermann Pesch, *Das II. Vatikanische Konzil 1962–1965* (Würzburg: Echter, 1993), 151. Ratzinger, rather, would speak of "a difficult balance" (*eine schwierige Balance*), such as the liturgy constitution

Counterweighting, then, is one key skill of the pastoral leader as reconciler. Another skill of reconcilers, as described by Jones and Armstrong, is "overaccepting," a term from the world of improvisational theater.[34] In that context, when one person by word or gesture invites a certain gambit in the acting, this is an "offer." The other person has two obvious options: either to "accept" the offer and proceed according to that premise, improvising in accord with that gambit, or else to "block" the offer, to "undermine or negate it," at which point the action stops moving forward in that direction.[35] A third way to respond to an offer, however, is by overaccepting, which is to accept the offer but "with a view to a larger story, moving it forward by reconceiving it in a new and redemptive way."[36]

---

maintains regarding different kinds of church music—the balance between preserving "the treasury of sacred music" (*Thesaurus Musicae sacrae*, SC 114) and fostering "religious singing by the people" (*Cantus popularis religiosus*, SC 118); see Ratzinger, "Zur theologischen Grundlegung der Kirchenmusik," in his *Theologie der Liturgie*, 503.

It is interesting to see Ratzinger himself use the image of counterweighting, in reference to his theological schooling, to describe the value he saw in studying Augustine: "But then from the beginning, Augustine interested me very much—precisely also insofar as he was, so to speak, a counterweight to Thomas Aquinas" (idem, *Salt of the Earth*, 60; cited in Rowland, *Ratzinger's Faith*, 4).

[34] Jones and Armstrong, *Resurrecting Excellence*, 137–38. Jones and Armstrong's use here of the world of improvisational theater draws on the work of Samuel Wells in his book, *Improvisation: The Drama of Christian Ethics* (Grand Rapids, MI: Brazos Press, 2004).

[35] Jones and Armstrong, *Resurrecting Excellence*, 138.

[36] Ibid. See also Wells, *Improvisation*, 133: "Overaccepting fits the remarks of the previous actor into a context enormously larger than his or her counterpart could have supposed." To explain the concept Wells recounts a story in which a young child plays random notes on a piano and a master pianist responds with an improvised simultaneous accompaniment of surrounding notes and chords that incorporate the child's notes into a larger and beautiful harmonic framework (131–32). Wells finds the concept of overaccepting widely applicable, suggesting, for example, that we "can see the whole sweep of the scriptural narrative as a long story of overaccepting" (134); he then interprets numerous features of the gospel accounts of Jesus' life in accord with this rubric (135–40).

If the history of the liturgical renewal of the church in the roughly forty years preceding SP was a story not only of good intentions, well-meant efforts, and positive results but also of serious shortcomings even to the point of "fragmentation," "deformations," "anarchy" and the like,[37] then the offer this complex historical situation made to Joseph Ratzinger upon his becoming Pope Benedict XVI in 2005 and thus the chief liturgist of the church was not one he would wish simply to accept (since there were serious shortcomings) or to block (since the reform also yielded genuine good). The needed response in this situation would be overaccepting, which Benedict accomplished in one way with his postsynodal apostolic exhortation *Sacramentum Caritatis*, and in another with SP and its provisions together with CGF and its explanations. In this latter initiative, the larger story he had in mind was one that neither rejected outright the traditional, preconciliar liturgy nor simply revived it as the reestablished norm but rather accepted anew its enduring value and gave it a designated place and role in the church by which it could, as an integral yet subsidiary part of the Roman Rite, both enrich and be enriched by the church's living liturgical life and practice (the ordinary form). By such an improvisational move, Pope Benedict sought to bend the long, richly diverse, sometimes surprising, and continuing story of the church's liturgy in a new direction, moving out of the impasse in which it has found itself since the 1960s.[38]

It seems to me the categories Jones and Armstrong use to describe the role of a pastoral leader can be applied to Pope Benedict and help us understand his intentions in *Summorum Pontificum*—not to dismantle the reformed liturgy but to foster and promote its continuing development, acting as an interpreter, a visionary, and a reconciler. In so doing he sought to exercise the care for the church

[37] For "fragmentation," see *Looking Again*, 148; "deformations," CGF 4; "anarchy," "Response to Father Gy," 99.

[38] An interesting extension of this line of thought might be to look at a further element of improvisation that Wells describes, namely, "reincorporating the lost." This refers, in improvisational theater, to previously shelved elements of the story that the improviser brings back—perhaps as the Missal of 1962 has been brought back through SP by Benedict the improviser. See Wells, *Improvisation*, chap. 10, "Reincorporating the Lost," 143–53.

and its (reformed) liturgy that he understood to be his responsibility as pope.

BUT THIS FORM OF MASS JUST SHOULD NOT ANY LONGER EXIST

These words express one sentiment regarding *Summorum Pontificum*. According to this view, through SP the 1962 Missal has been given a place in the contemporary church that it simply should not have, and this for at least four reasons: because (1) Pope Paul VI of set purpose forbade its use, (2) the ecumenical council found it wanting and of set purpose mandated its reform, (3) its theology is at least problematic if not erroneous, given conciliar developments in church teaching and its articulation, and (4) celebrating two distinctive liturgical systems (e.g., calendars) together in the same place is at least confusing and potentially divisive. Each of these objections can be proposed as sufficient reason to oppose the provisions and legitimacy of SP. Let us review each in turn, seeking to do so mindfully.

1. *Forbidden by Pope Paul VI*

Pope Paul VI did indeed forbid use of the 1962 Missal. As he once wrote, "[W]e have sanctioned the [postconciliar liturgical] reform with our own authority and directed its obligatory use by all who call themselves Catholic," rendering "unlawful" the "practice of celebrating the 'Mass of St. Pius V.'"[39] Even the exceptions made and indults granted in that era were not for use of the Missal in its 1962 form, but only as incorporating the intermediate reforms of 1965 and 1967. Pope Paul's intentions were clear, and Pope Benedict's actions clearly diverged from them.

For perspective we might turn to the consideration offered by liturgist J. D. Crichton at the time the liturgical reforms were being introduced, arguing in support of Pope Paul's revision of the Missal of Pius V: "What Pius could do, Paul can undo. If the primacy

[39] Paul VI, Epistle *Cum te* to Archbishop Marcel Lefebvre (October 11, 1976); in International Commission on English in the Liturgy, *Documents on the Liturgy 1963–1979: Conciliar, Papal, and Curial Texts* (Collegeville, MN: Liturgical Press, 1982), document no. 61, at paragraph no. 569. Hereafter, references from this text will appear as follows: DOL 61 at no. 569.

of the Pope does not mean that, it means nothing."[40] Apply this not only to legislative matters but to administrative and pastoral priorities and procedures as well. While Pius XII silenced theologians, for example, John XXIII preferred "the medicine of mercy." Different popes adopt different styles than their predecessors, take different steps, and make different prudential judgments on matters large and small. Pius XII's prudential judgment regarding a centuries-old practice of celebrating the Easter Vigil on Holy Saturday morning was to change that practice, returning the celebration to Holy Saturday evening, first as an experiment, then as a legislated, mandated reform. In reference to Pope Benedict's prudential judgment regarding the liturgy, as enacted in the publication of SP, a helpful perspective is proposed by Alcuin Reid, who commented that, "yes, it does change the rules excluding the older rites enacted by Pope Paul VI. It is perhaps best understood as a recognition that we are at a new point in the history of the Church and of the liturgy—that we are no longer in the 1970s. Today, at the beginning of the third Christian millennium . . . a more inclusive liturgical policy has been judged desirable."[41]

A changed and more inclusive polity, in other words, for changed times and circumstances, for a different context. Dramatic speeches and political maneuverings at the Second Vatican Council in the 1960s manifested then a hitherto unsuspected degree of divergence and even divisiveness in the church of that era, publicized and perhaps abetted by such publications as Xavier Rynne's (Redemptorist Father Francis X. Murphy's) influential series in *The New Yorker*,

[40] J. D. Crichton, *Christian Celebration: The Mass* (London: Geoffrey Chapman/Macmillan, 1971), 49.

[41] Alcuin Reid, "The Genius of the Roman Rite, Part 6—After *Summorum Pontificum*: A New Era for the Roman Rite," *Music and Liturgy* 36, no. 4, issue 340 (February 2011): 6–10, here at 9. Compare Catherine Bell's remark to the same effect, that the liturgical situation has changed: "Oddly enough, although liturgical authority, conformity, and dignity had been seen as obstacles thirty years ago, we are here [in 1993] formulating the problem of their absence"; Bell, "The Authority of Ritual Experts," in *Foundations in Ritual Studies: A Reader for Students of Christian Worship*, ed. Paul Bradshaw and John Melloh (Grand Rapids, MI: Baker Academic, 2007), 176–98, at 193—originally published in *Studia Liturgica* 23 (1993): 98–120. We should note that Bell prescribes no answers and speaks against "any return to easy authoritarianism" (198).

"Letter from Vatican City." Pope Paul VI, in his effort to promote church unity under these newly emergent conditions, favored the method of "assimilation"—a term of social psychology describing the merging of subgroup identities into a common identity within a larger society or "superordinate" group. Such an approach as applied to the liturgical renewal during the 1960s and 1970s meant, for Pope Paul, that all Roman Rite Catholics (left, right, and center) were to be one in adopting the 1970 Missal. Most notably, he denied permission for Archbishop Lefebvre and his followers to use the 1962 Missal, in part because he understood (rightly) their demand for such use to be an expression of a much wider and deeper opposition to the council. Thirty-five years later, also seeking unity, and partly in view of the significant ecclesial "separation" created by Archbishop Lefebvre's schismatical act in 1988, Pope Benedict chose to try an alternate method: "integration." Here, subgroup identities are not merged into but are maintained within a superordinate group, creating a context in which subgroups and the superordinate group are both valued. To apply this method in the changed ecclesial liturgical context of 2007 meant, for Pope Benedict, the creation of two legitimate uses within the one Roman Rite.[42]

Dominant cultures as a rule favor assimilation (all subgroups adopting the same culture, typically that of the dominant culture), while minority cultures favor integration (acceptance of minority cultures within a superordinate group).[43] Paul VI acted from the position of a dominant culture that he saw himself responsible to safeguard and preserve—the one and united Roman Catholic Church, implementing the reforms of the Second Vatican Ecumenical Council—vis-à-vis the minority position of Archbishop

[42] On the social psychological categories of assimilation, integration, separation, and marginalization, see for example John F. Dovidio, Samuel L. Gaertner, and Tamar Saguy, "Another View of 'We': Majority and Minority Group Perspectives on a Common Ingroup Identity," *European Review of Social Psychology* 18 (2007): 296–330, at 306; see also, by the same authors, "Commonality and the Complexity of 'We': Social Attitudes and Social Change," *Personality and Social Psychology Review* 13 (2009): 3–20, at 9–10.

[43] See, for example, Dovidio, Gaertner, and Saguy, "Commonality and the Complexity of 'We,'" 10.

Lefebvre and his movement, which sought to preserve the church in its preconciliar forms. Pope Benedict—seeing a postconciliar liturgical disharmony and disunity that grew and persisted for decades (the ongoing "liturgy wars"), and seeing as well that formal ecclesial separation had occurred and still continued (the SSPX), all under the policy of assimilation—judged it time, before it became too late, to try something new to bring about the same desired result of unity. Keeping in mind "minority cultures" such as the SSPX and others attracted to the *usus antiquior*, Benedict hoped the alternate method of integration might serve to foster their reconciliation and unity within the larger church—the former (SSPX) regaining unity, the latter remaining in unity (see CGF 8).

Anyone is certainly free to agree or disagree with Pope Benedict's prudential judgment to allow, under new conditions and to a limited extent, what Pope Paul forbade under the conditions of his time. What this study aims to do is understand Pope Benedict's judgment, as much as possible from his perspective, and see what positive potential for good his plan, if given a chance, could hold forth for the church. The social psychological categories just cited can help us understand his intentions—not to deconstruct the reformed liturgy or indulge liturgical nostalgia but, among other ends, to serve the reestablishment and strengthening of church unity. As to his legislative authority to do what he did, this is not in doubt.

2. *Mandated for Reform by the Ecumenical Council*

But—here is the next objection—the Second Vatican Council judged the 1962 Missal in need of reform; it took the matter in hand as its first major order of business and gave directions for that reform in its constitution on the sacred liturgy; that reform was then authoritatively carried out under the watchful eye of the reigning pontiff, who promulgated both that constitution in 1963 and the resulting reformed Missal in 1970. Yet it is this very 1962 Missal, unreformed, that Pope Benedict more widely reauthorized and relegitimated. Is it not clear this act in itself constitutes an undermining of the council and a rejection of its mandate?

Let us first place this objection in perspective. If Pope Benedict had abrogated all liturgical directives and ritual books issued after 1963 and declared only the 1962 ritual valid for Catholic worship today, *that* would have undermined the council and rejected its mandate. (Whoever holds that such an outcome was Benedict's ultimate aim simply and significantly misunderstands his thinking.) Instead, after SP just as before, the Vatican II reformed liturgy is still the church's ordinary liturgy and the one most commonly, indeed almost universally, celebrated. The 1962 Missal is allowed, but with some limitations; it is mandated for no one, but made more available for Catholics who choose it; it is given new status, but remains non-normative ("extraordinary") and optional; it is part of the church's liturgy, but only as subject to change (i.e., reform), including change under the influence of the postconciliar reformed liturgy—just as that reformed liturgy is subject to change from the influence of the extraordinary form, through the process of mutual enrichment.

This arrangement can actually be seen not as inimical to Vatican II and a reversal of its liturgical reform but as supportive of the effort to examine again its liturgy constitution and implement its provisions with new attentiveness and even renewed fidelity—including attentiveness and fidelity to the conciliar mandate "that any new forms adopted should in some way grow organically from forms already existing" (SC 23). It can be debated to what extent this happened after the council; different scholars hold different views on the matter. If one thinks "organic growth" does not describe the way the reformed Missal came to be, Pope Benedict's call for the mutual enrichment of the two forms (ordinary and extraordinary) going forward can in a sense and to a certain extent bring it about retroactively. If one thinks the reformed Missal does represent organic development from its predecessor, mutual enrichment can make that living connection of the two forms more visible and perhaps stronger. In either case, mutual enrichment knits a closer, more organic connection between the extraordinary and ordinary forms (that is, between the church's liturgy in its preconciliar and postconciliar forms), in fulfillment of the text and spirit of SC 23. In this way the FE will be subject to the liturgical principles of *Sacrosanctum Concilium* and enriched by the riches of the reformed liturgy, while the ordinary form will be enriched by the riches the FE has to offer, and may come to embody certain of the liturgy constitution's principles or provisions more closely than some current celebrations of the FO typically do. Again, should this eventuate, through a balanced and generous implementation of SP, that document will turn out not to undermine the council but to serve and fulfill its intentions more fully.

One further observation. The view maintained here is that the postconciliar reformed liturgy remains still dominant as the ordinary form, with the FE still secondary as the extraordinary form, though with new legitimacy and higher status than before. Some, viewing this situation, may oppose *Summorum Pontificum* and the creation of the extraordinary form for a double reason—a judgment that, in this new situation, the council's mandate has been reversed and its authority impugned, and a sense that the opponents of the reform have become newly and unfairly privileged. This would, I believe, represent a misunderstanding and an overreaction, but perhaps of a recognized and understandable kind. Social psychologists give the term "relative deprivation" to the sense among members of a dominant culture that injustice has been done when, though they remain dominant, a minority culture has been newly privileged in some way at their (the dominant culture's) expense.[44] It would be worth investigating to what extent this recognized social psychological phenomenon may be in play and may help to explain a certain sense among some FO adherents that the extraordinary form and its adherents have "gained too much" while the authorized liturgical reform has been unduly disrespected, denigrated, or undermined—all while the reformed liturgy has been reaffirmed as the church's *ordinary* form and the preconciliar liturgy legally established only as a supplementary, *extraordinary* (outside the ordinary) form.

3. Theologically Problematic

According to the third objection, the former Missal and liturgy (as a *lex orandi*) are now theologically problematic because they do not convey as well as the reformed liturgy the council's devel-

[44] On relative deprivation, see Marilyn Brewer, *Intergroup Relations* (Buckingham and Philadelphia: Open University Press, 2003), 14–16; for example, "relative deprivation may be experienced even by those who are objectively advantaged but feel they are losing by comparison to previous expectations" (15). See also Rupert Brown, "Relative Deprivation (RD)," in Manstead and Hewstone, eds., *The Blackwell Encyclopedia of Social Psychology*, 475–77.

opments in Catholic thought and teaching (its *lex credendi*)—or indeed, that they convey in some ways teaching that is now fundamentally flawed. This is a substantive concern, for there have been significant developments in the church's thinking and articulation of its teaching—on how to understand the church's relation with non-Catholic Christians and non-Christian religions, on the laity and their participation in the mission and liturgy of the church, on the theology of grace, on the understanding of the church's relationship with the modern world, and so on. Many such aspects of the church's *lex credendi* are expressed in her *lex orandi*, with varying degrees of divergence between the two Missals.

Archbishop Lefebvre, from his perspective, found the divergence too real and great to be endured, preferring to remain faithful to preconciliar forms and formulations and rejecting conciliar and postconciliar developments. Pope John Paul II condemned Lefebvre's schismatical act of ordaining four bishops in 1988 and reaffirmed the legitimate conciliar development of tradition at Vatican II. But John Paul also recognized the difficulty some Catholics had in seeing the coherence-in-development of the church's pre- and postconciliar *lex credendi*. And so he urged theologians to work harder at understanding and explaining that coherence—what he called "the Council's continuity with Tradition," and what Pope Benedict called "innovation in continuity"[45]—to make that continuity more evident and visible.

The same need exists also for those who, from another angle, see such discontinuity between pre- and postconciliar teaching that they can only judge the 1962 Missal unacceptable and illegitimate on the grounds that, *as* preconciliar, it diverges too significantly from the postconciliar reformed *lex credendi*. Here, interestingly, the same theological task exists—that is, to demonstrate more clearly that conciliar reform and development (theological development in general, and liturgical development in particular) has been a "combination of continuity and discontinuity at different levels," yielding "innovation" that is, nonetheless, fundamentally "in

[45] John Paul II, *Ecclesia Dei* 5.b (*Concilii perpetuitas una cum Traditione*); Benedict XVI, "Expergiscere," Address of His Holiness Benedict XVI to the Roman Curia Offering Them His Christmas Greetings, *Acta Apostolicae Sedis* 98, no. 1 (2006): 40–53, at 49 (*novità nella continuità*).

continuity" with Catholic tradition rather than a break from it.[46] This would open the way to recognizing in the extraordinary form something not irreconcilably at odds with that tradition as developed by and inclusive of Vatican II, and thus in principle as one valid expression of the church's *lex orandi*. At the same time, the task would still remain of building the bridge in the other direction as well, so to speak, and enriching the *usus antiquior* with the *lex credendi* of the council—a task Pope Benedict's process of mutual enrichment can foster, and is in fact designed to foster.

4. Conflicting Liturgical Systems

Finally, there is the confusion and perhaps conflict generated by putting into practice in the same place (e.g., parish community, religious house) two liturgical systems that differ as do the ordinary and extraordinary forms. Again, the point has merit, as the Vatican's worship office once argued.[47] It is not simply a question of differing styles of worship, or *artes celebrandi*, but of differing lectionaries and calendars governing the church's liturgy, in both the temporal and sanctoral cycles. Different members of the same community will celebrate the liturgy with different readings and prayers at Mass throughout the year, with different saints commemorated on the same day, with some observing Ordinary Time while others are already observing the pre-Lenten Sundays of Septuagesima, Sexagesima, and Quinquagesima, and so on.

[46] Benedict XVI, "Expergiscere," 49 ("*insieme di continuità e discontinuità a livelli diversi . . . novità nella continuità*"). With its respect for the voice of the past and its continuing relevance, there is a resemblance here to the often-quoted remark of G. K. Chesterton, that tradition "means giving votes to the most obscure of all classes, our ancestors. It is the democracy of the dead. Tradition refuses to submit," said Chesterton in his colorful language, "to the small and arrogant oligarchy of those who merely happen to be walking about." *Orthodoxy* (Garden City, NY: Image / Doubleday, 1959), 49. Ratzinger quotes words of Cardinal Joachim Meisner to much the same effect in Ratzinger, *Called to Communion: Understanding the Church Today* (San Francisco: Ignatius Press, 1996), 154, n. 9.

[47] Congregation for Divine Worship and the Discipline of the Sacraments, "Responsa Officialia" (Prot. n. 1411/99), *Notitiae* 396–97, vol. 35, nos. 7–8 (1999): 307–9, here at 308.

Objectively, this concern is significant. The liturgy is the source of Christian life. Given the formative power of the word of God, liturgical prayer, and the observance of seasons and feasts, to form members of the same community into the Christian life through the differing liturgical pathways of divergent lectionaries, missals, and calendars seems questionable at least and, conceivably worse, even an impediment to ecclesial unity. Subjectively, though, the impact may vary from person to person. How often do Catholics in their parishes or among themselves, for example, communicate and relate in such a way that having had the same Sunday (or weekday or saint's feast day) readings and prayers is of critical importance? Awareness of the difference may often simply not arise. Moreover, when it does, whether it is perceived as divisive disunity or diversity within unity may depend much on the attitudes of the persons involved or the spirit cultivated in the community—that is, it is an open question, which can be resolved irenically if so decided.

Perhaps also an observation in Ellen Langer's book on mindful learning may be instructive here—if not so much regarding differences of lectionary and calendar (though perhaps there as well), at least regarding differences in the liturgical *ars celebrandi*. She reports that various expert piano players "recommended organ practice" to improve one's piano skills, and that "Yehudi Menuhin said he thought his violin playing improved after he took up the viola."[48] It seems, in other words, that learning "two similar but different instruments" helps prevent taking one's way of playing either instrument for granted and instead "encourages an alert and mindful state" in one's musical practice.[49] Might something similar occur in one's liturgical practice, by worshiping in both usages of the Roman Rite? Might participating in the ordinary form in a more alert and mindful (that is, a more full, conscious, and active) way conceivably be fostered, for those open to it, by learning to participate also in the "similar but different" liturgy of the extraordinary form? Such may be the positive potential that can follow from an appreciative reading and implementation of SP.

[48] Ellen J. Langer, *The Power of Mindful Learning* (Reading, MA: Addison-Wesley, 1997), 27.

[49] Ibid., 28.

WHY NOT BE AS ACCOMMODATING TOWARD PROGRESSIVE LITURGICAL DEVELOPMENT?

It was sometimes raised as an objection that Ratzinger showed openness and concern toward those resistant to the liturgical reform (those customarily termed the *right*), such as his willingness to make accommodations for the separatist SSPX so as to make room for them in the church, while for those on the other side (customarily termed the *left*) promoting ongoing reform—as through further local inculturation—who remained within the church, he had harsh words of critique and even condemnation. Why, the question was asked, is he not more evenhanded and balanced? It can be difficult for someone on the left to adopt the spirit of openness toward the right that SP/CGF invites, when seeing little evidence of a reciprocal openness going the other way. For perspective on this we might consider first Joseph Ratzinger's role as prefect of the Congregation for the Doctrine of the Faith, and then his writings and recommendations regarding the liturgy.

As prefect of the Vatican's doctrinal congregation, Cardinal Ratzinger took note of those ordinary Catholics disturbed in their faith by the work of theologians whose speculations could find their way quite quickly (before due sifting within the theological community) into the popular press, catechetical materials and processes, or liturgical practice—speculations that could, to cite an observation of Pope Paul VI in 1968, "give rise, as is unfortunately seen in these days, to disturbance and perplexity in many faithful souls."[50] This concern goes part way to explain CDF cautions and admonitions in Cardinal Ratzinger's day toward the speculative left: they were interventions to make clear the boundaries of the faith, ultimately for the sake of the ordinary faithful troubled by such speculations and unable to weigh their merits.[51] As for cautions toward the right, Archbishop Lefebvre experienced, first,

[50] Paul VI, *Credo of the People of God*, 4.

[51] See the document of the Congregation for the Doctrine of the Faith, *Donum Veritatis* (Instruction on the Ecclesial Vocation of the Theologian), signed by Cardinal Ratzinger; it expresses the conviction that the church's magisterium "must protect God's People from the danger of deviations and confusion" (no. 14)—as might arise, for example, by the communication in pastoral contexts of theological speculation of the kind just mentioned.

suspension for his anticonciliar actions and then in 1988 excommunication for his ordination of four bishops, penalties more severe than such critiques addressed to those on the liturgical left as John Paul II's remarks in *Vicesimus Quintus Annus* (at no. 13), or the instruction *Redemptionis Sacramentum*.[52]

In the realm of liturgy, Cardinal Ratzinger would say he saw the left flourish and the right be deprived or suppressed. That is, he saw the freely creative and experimental be permitted and continue in pastoral practice, in some communities becoming normal and expected, while "all tolerance ends" for those who appreciate the prior Missal (as reauthorized for use in 1984 with the indult *Quattuor Abhinc Annos*).[53] SP can be understood as Pope Benedict's effort to level the playing field, legislating in a new way what his predecessor's combination of legislation and exhortation proved insufficient to bring about: a measure of pastoral tolerance for the *usus antiquior*—without making it normative for the church at large or minimizing the ordinary form in any substantive way.

The sense that Ratzinger, as theologian, prefect, and pope, has been soft on the right and hard on the left might not be so strong had he voiced more often and clearly the appreciative judgment he expressed in his preface to a book published shortly before he became pope: that "the [reformed] eucharistic Liturgy, and likewise the Liturgy of the Word, is often celebrated reverently, and 'beautifully,' in the best sense, on the basis of people's faith."[54] It is interesting that in this same essay, having offered this affirmation, he

[52] See also Joseph Ratzinger with Vittorio Messori, *The Ratzinger Report* (San Francisco: Ignatius Press, 1985), 31–32, noting that these remarks were made three years before the 1988 excommunications.

[53] Ratzinger, *God and the World*, 416. On creative and experimental, see, for example, Ratzinger, *Salt of the Earth: The Church at the End of the Millennium, An Interview with Peter Seewald* (San Francisco: Ignatius Press, 1997), 177: "Unfortunately, in Germany tolerance for bizarre tinkering is almost unlimited, whereas tolerance for the old liturgy is practically nonexistent." See also idem, *God and the World*, 414–15; idem, *Called to Communion*, 137–38.

[54] Joseph Ratzinger, preface to Alcuin Reid's, *The Organic Development of the Liturgy: The Principles of Liturgical Reform and Their Relation to the Twentieth-Century Liturgical Movement Prior to the Second Vatican Council*, 2nd ed. (San Francisco: Ignatius Press, 2005), 12. For an essay maintaining that Joseph Ratzinger's fundamental assessment of the postconciliar liturgy was not simply

can also lament, without contradiction, that those well instructed by the preconciliar liturgical movement to an informed appreciation of the liturgy as it existed "on the eve of the Second Vatican Council can only stand, deeply sorrowing, before the ruins of the very things" they were taught to understand and love.[55] As for his words of critique for postconciliar liturgy, they have always been aimed not at that liturgy wholesale but at what he perceived as its shortcomings and excesses, at what in CGF (no. 4) he called "deformations" and two years earlier, in that same preface, described as "the dangers, which unfortunately in the last few decades have by no means remained just the imaginings of those traditionalists opposed to reform."[56]

Here it should be noted that he ranged himself against such traditionalists as well—not Catholics who continue to appreciate the traditional liturgy while also accepting the council, but those who are "the embittered critics of liturgical reform—critical not only of its application in practice, but equally of its basis in the Council," and who can "see salvation only in total rejection of the reform."[57] Joseph Ratzinger, whether as cardinal or pope, was never among their number. Rather, Pope Benedict sought to serve the dual goal of both maintaining and amending the reform, by appreciating and preserving what is best in both forms; this is what SP was intended to promote.[58]

---

negative but fundamentally positive, see Johnston, "Pope Benedict XVI on the Postconciliar Liturgical Reform."

[55] Ratzinger, preface, *Organic Development of the Liturgy*, 11.

[56] Ibid., 13.

[57] Ibid., 9.

[58] Other commentators point out the same. Alban McCoy speculates that liturgical changes resulting from implementation of SP could lead to "a convergence of the two forms," ordinary and extraordinary, and their "[coalescing] into a form better than both currently in use"—in other words, into "a single reformed rite in which we regain what was lost and retain what was gained" in the postconciliar liturgical reforms; see McCoy, "Rites and Reality," *The Tablet* 263, no. 8782 (March 7, 2009): 12–13, at 12. Similarly, Peter Jeffery affirms that each form of Mass has something to offer—namely, "a different, but not false, way to encounter the infinite God, who is beyond all categories"—and thus "the task now is somehow to recover what was left behind without losing what has been gained, like the householder who brings forth both the new and

Nonetheless, that said, it remains a fair question to ask why the ongoing development of the Roman Rite and specifically of the ordinary form after SP would not remain open to new steps that emerge from both centers of gravity: not only, that is, from the influence of the extraordinary form (through mutual enrichment) but also through continuing discovery of new "legitimate variations and adaptations to different groups, regions and peoples, especially in mission lands" (SC 38), as the council fathers said—and not only there but, as we would recognize today, also in the local culture of every place the ordinary form is celebrated and calls home. Organic development of the ordinary form can occur both along the pathway of "sound tradition," newly understood and affirmed in light of *Summorum Pontificum*, and the pathway of "legitimate progress" still being rightly discovered and pursued in light of *Sacrosanctum Concilium* (SC 23).

MAXIMIZING INTERPRETATIONS OF *SUMMORUM PONTIFICUM*

Among the diverse interpretations of SP, some err by reading more into it than it contains or intends. Consider the maximizing interpretation reportedly expressed by Cardinal Castrillón Hoyos, who is said to have proposed making the traditional Mass available even when there is no request for it.[59] The cardinal duly noted that

---

old (Matthew 13:52)"; see Jeffery, "Widening Our Hearts," *Commonweal* 134, no. 14 (August 17, 2007): 10–13, at 12–13.

[59] As reported in Christophe Geffroy, *Benoît XVI et "la paix liturgique"* (Paris: Les Éditions du Cerf, 2008), 225–26. See also the introduction to *Sursum Corda: Documents and Readings on the Traditional Latin Mass from the Council of Trent to Benedict XVI's Motu Proprio* (USA: David Pietrusza, 2008), by David Pietrusza, where Cardinal Castrillón Hoyos is quoted in an address to the Latin Mass Society of England and Wales in June 2008: "Let me say this plainly: . . . the Holy Father wants the ancient use of the Mass to become a normal occurrence in the liturgical life of the Church so that all of Christ's faithful—young and old—can become familiar with the older rites and draw from their tangible beauty and transcendence" (3). This may be so, or may be exaggerated. Pope Benedict may indeed have hoped celebrations of the FE would reach a sufficient "critical mass" to make a difference. But under the provisions he specifically put in place in SP, the eventual extent (geographic and demographic) of the *actual use* of the extraordinary form in the church's public worship (it is

this exceeds the requirements and provisions of SP, article 5, section 1, but stood by the proposal nonetheless. Another Vatican official has been quoted as maintaining that the church's liturgy will in due time make a complete return to the preconciliar forms. "The old rite is our past, and it will be our future. . . . The new Mass is a passing phase. In 50 years, that will be entirely clear."[60] Further, Michael Kunzler refers to "the hope often manifested by many supporters of the old rite," the hope that the permission given to use the extraordinary form will prove widely successful, that Catholics will flock to it, and that the reformed liturgy thus "perishes without a trace."[61]

In one sense, such maximizing may be seen as an understandable reaction to a prior situation of disestablishment—just as the sometimes excessive liturgical creativity of the immediately postconciliar era was an almost expectable reaction to the prior era of rubrically strict uniformity. And if ordinary form proponents may experience a sense of relative deprivation—in judging that the FO, as repositioned by the newly established legitimacy of the extraordinary form, has been deprived more than it actually has—perhaps it is not surprising if some extraordinary form proponents are experiencing a sense of what we might call "relative entitlement" or "relative ascendancy" in judging that the FE, as newly repositioned, has been made more central or raised higher than it actually has. In any case, there are indeed those who want the new liturgy gone and the old liturgy fully restored.

---

another matter for Masses *sine populo*) was in fact more in the hands of the laity and their decisions and requests than the clergy (including popes) and their decisions or preferences.

[60] This is the view of "at least one Vatican official," as reported in Robert Moynihan, "The Return of the Latin Mass," *Inside the Vatican* 18, no. 5 (May 2010): 30–33, 35, at 32. Moynihan also reports speaking with another official who thinks differently, that "the future of the Church's liturgical life will be a type of fusion between the old Mass and the new Mass of Paul VI"—a belief more in harmony with SP; Moynihan then described this as "the view of many" (32).

[61] Michael Kunzler, *Die 'Tridentinische' Messe: Aufbruch oder Rückschritt?* (Paderborn: Bonifatius, 2008), 119 ("die von manchen Anhängern des alten Ritus offen bekundete Hoffnung . . . sang- und klanglos untergeht").

Persons holding and voicing such views undermine *Summorum Pontificum*. Their claims not only misinterpret and misrepresent the document and, I believe, the pope who promulgated it but further discredit it and him in the eyes of those already doubtful and suspicious, (falsely) confirming the worst fears of SP opponents and strengthening the resistance they maintain for what they can now believe, on the basis of supposed evidence (the maximizing interpretations), to be good reason. In this way maximizers make it more unlikely that opponents will take an open-minded look at what SP might actually mean, to see what good it might possibly bring about. They thus hinder rather than foster "sincere dialogue" and the internal reconciliation in the church that Pope Benedict sought. The way forward is for all parties to try to gauge the new situation created by SP as accurately as possible; the present book is offered as one effort in this cause.

I hope these reflections offer helpful perspectives on various objections that may stand in the way of an appreciative reading of *Summorum Pontificum* and reduce misconceptions about Pope Benedict and the liturgical aims he had in view. A consideration of those aims, which are multiple, is the topic of the next chapter.

Chapter 3

The Multiple Purposes of *Summorum Pontificum*

Let us try to clarify what *Summorum Pontificum* does and does not intend to accomplish.

It would be a misunderstanding, for example, to think SP a papal mandate imposing wider celebration of the preconciliar Mass on the postconciliar church. SP does grant an increased though still limited permission for such celebrations, for those who wish it; but for others in the church, it imposes nothing. After SP, just as before, the standard, ordinary liturgy of the Roman Rite is the liturgy as reformed after Vatican II, the Missal of Paul VI. Pope Benedict did nothing to change this; on the contrary, he took care to reaffirm it by designating this form of liturgy the "ordinary form" of the Roman Rite. After SP, just as before, Catholics who desire the old Mass need to take steps to seek it out; those who do nothing to seek it out will most likely not encounter it, unless it becomes, as has not yet happened, widely celebrated; and those who want no part of it need never celebrate it.

Granted, an exception to this is the clergy. Those ordained to the service of the church have a responsibility, in Pope Benedict's view, to serve the whole flock, including those friends of the old Mass whose desire for that form of worship is neither intentionally divisive nor a protest against the council. Pope Benedict, just as Pope John Paul II before him, believed the church—with pastoral charity, and without damage to unity but rather in service to it—had room enough to find some space for the existence of the *usus antiquior*, and for its celebration by those who desire it. This is what SP aims to provide.

It would also be a misunderstanding to infer that SP indicates Pope Benedict had the intention to return the old Mass to prominence in the church, perhaps to the point of marginalizing the reformed liturgy or even the council itself.[1] Rather, he foresaw a more limited role for the extraordinary form, if only because "use of the ancient Missal presupposes a certain degree of liturgical formation and a basic facility in the Latin language; [and] neither the one nor the other is found very often" (CGF 6). A year after making this remark he repeated the point, during a pastoral visit to France, referring to those adherent to the old Mass as "a small group."[2] And, as already noted, his designation of the 1962 Missal as the "extraordinary form" gave it legal sanction, yet in a subsidiary, supplementing position vis-à-vis the reformed Missal; it was intended to have an established place but not equal prominence, let alone favored status.

Further, it would overshoot the mark even to infer that SP manifests Pope Benedict's judgment that the preconciliar liturgy was superior or preferable to its postconciliar form. In fact he neither argued nor proposed that the extraordinary form was better than the ordinary—ritually superior, pastorally preferable, theologically more sound. There are FE adherents who will make these claims, but Pope Benedict was not, I think, one of them. He thought the *usus antiquior* should be better honored than it has been in recent decades for its venerable usage and not be considered positively harmful and fit only to be banned from the church's life. He did not consider it theologically suspect or illegitimate, even after the reforms of the Second Vatican Council, but a witness to Catholic faith and tradition through the centuries. He also recognized certain worthy features of FE celebrations that he found less typical

[1] See, for example, Massimo Faggioli's comment that "legitimizing the coexistence of two different ritual forms (ordinary and extraordinary; see *Summorum Pontificum* of 2007) is not far from renouncing Vatican II as such, stopping every pastoral effort aimed at receiving the liturgical reform and Vatican II through the liturgy"; see Faggioli, *True Reform: Liturgy and Ecclesiology in* Sacrosanctum Concilium (Collegeville, MN: Liturgical Press, 2012), 144.

[2] Those who desire the prior liturgy "form a small group, because this presupposes a schooling in Latin, a training in a certain culture"; from "Interview of the Holy Father Benedict XVI during the Flight to France" (September 12, 2008). Again in his 2010 interview with Peter Seewald he referred to "the small circle of people who use the old missal"; Benedict XVI, *Light of the World: The Pope, the Church, and the Signs of the Times. A Conversation with Peter Seewald* (San Francisco: Ignatius Press, 2010), 106.

or prominent in the FO, features he hoped would in time enrich the FO. But there was actually no stated or even implied claim the FE is the superior ritual form or pastoral practice.

Indeed, there is nothing in SP to discount the general judgment that the reformed Missal is the superior ritual form, a fundamental improvement along the lines laid out in the council's liturgy constitution. This seems to correspond with Cardinal Ratzinger's assessment, as indicated in the 1980s when he wrote that "as far as its content is concerned (apart from a few criticisms), I am very grateful for the new Missal," and when he stated in his memoirs that "there is no doubt that this new missal [of Paul VI] in many respects brought with it a real improvement and enrichment"[3]—in comparison, obviously, with the Missal it replaced: the 1962 Missal of Blessed John XXIII. And while he strongly and consistently critiqued certain aspects of the way the new Missal was implemented, he continued to recognize and commend its many riches, as he clearly did in his papal apostolic exhortation on the Eucharist, *Sacramentum Caritatis*.[4] Indeed, for these reasons I can even envision Pope Emeritus Benedict giving a sympathetic reading to Patrick Regan's comparison of the liturgical seasons in the ordinary and extraordinary forms—to much of Regan's detailed research and

[3] Joseph Ratzinger, *The Feast of Faith: Approaches to a Theology of the Liturgy* (San Francisco: Ignatius Press, 1985), 87 ("content"); idem, *Milestones: Memoirs 1927–1977* (San Francisco: Ignatius Press, n.d. [1998]), 148 ("no doubt").

[4] In *Sacramentum Caritatis* 3, for example, he reported, making his own, the positive assessment of the bishops at the 2005 synod on the Eucharist regarding the postconciliar liturgical renewal; they "acknowledged and reaffirmed [its] beneficial influence on the Church's life," offered "many expressions of appreciation," and judged its "benefits" and "validity" to "overshadow" the "difficulties and even the occasional abuses" that the synod did not ignore but took into account. In ibid., 40, Pope Benedict referred to the "great riches" to be found in the GIRM and reformed lectionary (which are among the "riches . . . yet to be fully explored" mentioned in no. 3). In ibid., 48, he spoke of the "inexhaustible theological and spiritual richness" to be found in the different eucharistic prayers, with specific reference to the eight basic elements that structure the new eucharistic prayers developed after the council; see also ibid., 13, on "the richness of the anaphora." Ibid., 38, spoke of "the liturgical norms in all their richness," meaning the norms and rubrics governing the ordinary form.

analysis, his praise of the theological richness of the reformed Missal and Lectionary, and even his summative judgment as to "the excellence and superiority of the reformed liturgy over the previous one."[5] At the same time, however, Pope Benedict thought and wanted the church to recognize that the extraordinary form is not deleterious but rather (granted its need for reform, as the council fathers affirmed nearly unanimously) that it was and remains a treasure that still has a beneficial work to do in the church today.

This, I suggest, is the best way to understand *Summorum Pontificum*. In Pope Benedict's vision and pastoral strategy, the church's traditional liturgy has a work to do in the church today, and SP was crafted to position it to do that work. In a real sense the *motu proprio* is not chiefly about the old Mass in itself; it is about a diverse agenda that includes clarifying ecclesiology, fostering reconciliation in the church, healing schism, promoting the church's fundamental mission, providing pastoral care, amending shortcomings in the celebration of the new liturgy, and guiding and redirecting the ongoing process of liturgical development. This single liturgical initiative of Pope Benedict, set forth in SP with some commentary in CGF, addresses this diversity of concerns. Let us review each in turn, seeing perhaps the first four representing his care for the church and the next three his care for the liturgy, and giving greater attention to the initial item in each list (thus, the first and fifth) as matters of particular significance for Pope Benedict.

1. AFFIRM THE UNITY AND CONTINUITY OF THE CHURCH—BOTH BEFORE AND AFTER VATICAN II

The Second Vatican Council was the most important event for the Catholic Church in the twentieth century, and its reforms led to significant changes in numerous aspects of Catholic thought and life. Those changes have at times been experienced and interpreted as so fundamental as to mark a definitive break between before and after, such that the postconciliar church is best understood in terms of its distinctiveness or even separation from its preconciliar forms. Pope Benedict saw in this perspective a widespread and influential

[5] Patrick Regan, *Advent to Pentecost: Comparing the Seasons in the Ordinary and Extraordinary Forms of the Roman Rite* (Collegeville, MN: Liturgical Press, 2012), x[illegible]; see also 305.

ecclesiological view, which he thought overstated a difference that was nonetheless real, insufficiently recognized a continuity that is also real, and was thus a one-sided understanding in need of revision.

One occasion when he gave voice to these concerns and to the role he envisioned for the liturgy in addressing them was the 2001 liturgical conference at Fontgombault. During his concluding address at the conference Cardinal Ratzinger said: "Personally, I was from the beginning in favour of the freedom to continue using the old Missal, for a very simple reason: people were already beginning to talk about making a break with the pre-conciliar Church, and of developing various models of Church—a preconciliar and obsolete type of Church, and a new and conciliar type of Church."[6] He was concerned, then, about ways of viewing and understanding the church, about operative interpretive models of church, in which postconciliar is to preconciliar, not as current is to prior but as updated is to obsolete or even good is to bad. It is the rejection of the

[6] Joseph Ratzinger, "Assessment and Future Prospects," in *Looking Again at the Question of the Liturgy with Cardinal Ratzinger*, Proceedings of the July 2001 Fontgombault Liturgical Conference, ed. Alcuin Reid, 145–53 (Farnborough, UK: Saint Michael's Abbey Press, 2003), 148. He already identified and spoke against this way of thinking in 1985, saying then, "there is no 'pre-' or 'post-' conciliar Church: there is but one, unique Church that walks the path toward the Lord. . . . There are no leaps in this history, there are no fractures, and there is no break in continuity"; Joseph Ratzinger with Vittorio Messori, *The Ratzinger Report: An Exclusive Interview on the State of the Church* (San Francisco: Ignatius Press, 1985), 35 (also 113). See also his remarks to the bishops of Chile on July 13, 1988, just two weeks after Archbishop Lefebvre ordained the four bishops. Available at http://www.catholicculture.org/culture/library/view.cfm?id=3032&repos=1&subrepos=&searchid=292734.

Walter Kasper expressed similar views in his 1989 book, *Theology and Church* (New York: Crossroad, 1989). In a chapter titled "The Continuing Challenge of the Second Vatican Council: The Hermeneutics of the Conciliar Statements," he wrote of the need to interpret the council "in the light of the wider tradition of the church. It is therefore absurd to distinguish between the pre-conciliar and the post-conciliar church in such a way to suggest that the post-conciliar church is a new church; or as if, after a long, dark age in church history, the last council had at long last rediscovered the original gospel. On the contrary, Vatican II itself belongs within the tradition of all previous councils, and it is this tradition which it wished to renew" (172).

church in its recent (in this case, its immediately preconciliar) form implied by "obsolete" that he found problematic; he preferred an ecclesiological perspective that sees, not this kind of "discontinuity and rupture," but rather ecclesial reform that recognizes a "combination of continuity and discontinuity at different levels."[7]

Often his critique is thought of as aimed at what is customarily termed the *left*, and so it is, when that perspective emphasizes discontinuity. But Ratzinger's critique of sharp distinctions between pre- and postconciliar was meant as much for the "right" as well, including "the Lefebvrists" who insist "that there are two Churches, and for them the great rupture becomes visible in the existence of two Missals, which are said to be irreconcilable with each other."[8]

In contrast, Ratzinger believed "the very essence of the Church" requires recognition of an "unbroken continuity throughout the history of faith, expressed [liturgically] in an ever-present unity of prayer," and he faulted both sides for failing to maintain this sense of continuity. In liturgical terms, he faulted both "those who 'opt' for a book [the Missal of Pius V] supposed to have been produced four hundred years ago," thus critiquing those on the right, and also "those who would like to be forever drawing up new liturgies," with mild hyperbole critiquing the left.[9] That at least some proponents on each side would decline or refuse to celebrate Mass with the other, even under conditions legitimating both forms of celebration (in one way since *Quattuor Abhinc Annos* in 1984, in another since SP in 2007), constitutes a de facto mutual excommunication, a kind of internal schism. This exemplifies the depth of the

[7] Benedict XVI, "Expergiscere" ("Address of His Holiness Benedict XVI to the Roman Curia Offering Them His Christmas Greetings," December 22, 2005), *Acta Apostolicae Sedis* 98, no. 1 (2006): 40–53, at 46 ("discontinuity" and "reform") and 49 ("combination").

[8] Ratzinger, "Assessment and Future Prospects," 148–49. See also R. W. Franklin, "Chronicle: The Liturgical Schism," *Worship* 62 (1988): 448–51; he described "Lefebvrism" as "a counter-church, founded in revolt against Vatican II and dedicated to the virulent condemnation and the uprooting of the work of the Council everywhere. . . . Above all, Lefebvrism has stood for the rejection of the liturgical reforms of Vatican II" (448–49).

[9] Ratzinger, *The Feast of Faith*, 87.

problem, not just liturgical but ecclesial, whose solution requires an "internal reconciliation in the heart of the church."[10] Ratzinger the theologian considered it necessary to address this problem in a way that could reknit a fracturing unity, recognizing and reaffirming ecclesial continuity and identity through time; Benedict's sense of responsibility as pope to serve as visible source and foundation of the church's unity (LG 23) moved him to take action, as in SP, to maintain and make clear that synchronic and diachronic unity, identity, and continuity of the church.

Cardinal Ratzinger described, in that 2001 address, how the Missals of John XXIII and Paul VI can serve this ecclesiological end: "It seems to me essential, the basic step, to recognize that both Missals are Missals of the Church, and belong to the Church which remains the same as ever,"[11] in and through changes from age to age. If the church can recognize some measure of worth and validity in both Missals, the liturgical gap, and the ecclesial rupture that gap symbolizes and sustains, can be at least incipiently overcome.

How to bring about such recognition and overcome this gap? Cardinal Ratzinger thought it could work this way: "to emphasize that there is no essential break, that there is continuity in the Church, which retains its identity, it seems to me indispensable to continue to offer the opportunity to celebrate according to the old Missal, as a sign of the enduring identity of the Church."[12] There is his point: to reauthorize use of the old Missal, (1) not by way of exception, through an indult, but (to use the language he would later develop for SP) as the authorized "extraordinary form" of the Roman Rite, and (2) not as an unchanging ritual artifact but as a living liturgy subject to ongoing development—to do this, as he saw it, would constitute an administrative act accomplishing a theological end. This is what Pope Benedict intended SP to do: to instantiate legally and liturgically, and in this way to demonstrate *ipso facto*, the essential ecclesiological truth and reality he thought had been obscured and needed to be clarified—namely, the "enduring identity of the Church" through history, Christ's same church

[10] CGF 8. See also Ratzinger with Messori, *The Ratzinger Report*, 32.
[11] Ratzinger, "Assessment and Future Prospects," 149.
[12] Ibid.

through all its changes, reforms, and developments, including those occasioned by the Second Vatican Council.

One wonders if he learned this strategy from the council itself—learned, that is, how historical facts such as legislative acts with the ecclesial structures and dynamics they create have theological impact. In an address delivered in January 1963 reflecting on the first session of the council, Father Ratzinger commented on actions taken during that session regarding the liturgy, including a decision to allow regional bishops' conferences not simply to deliberate but actually "to legislate in liturgical matters for their own countries," and thus act not "as mere delegates of Rome, but in the exercise of a power which belongs to themselves."[13] He judged this act "a radical innovation for the Latin Church" carrying "immense ecclesiological significance," of such weight and impact as conceivably to influence the theology of the church and the episcopacy more significantly than would the words of the eventual conciliar document on the church, then in development.[14] "For here," he said, "a fact has been established and the weight of the factual, as history teaches, in a matter of this kind is greater than mere exposition."[15]

With SP, a liturgical fact was established.[16] To show the identity and continuity of the church before and after the council, Pope Benedict gave the preconciliar liturgical forms new status, with legal legitimacy and wider scope in the postconciliar church. In

[13] Joseph Ratzinger, "The Second Vatican Council: The First Session," *The Furrow* 14 (1963): 267–88, here at 276.

[14] Ibid.

[15] Ibid., 277. On a different scale but the same point, compare Pope Benedict's remark on Pope John Paul II's long illness: "You could see that the lesson of the suffering Pope was a magisterium that was even more eloquent than the magisterium of the speaking Pope." Benedict XVI, *Light of the World*, 80.

[16] Because it can be misunderstood, we should recall again what that liturgical fact is: not the replacement of the reformed liturgy by the preconciliar, or preferencing the latter over the former, or positioning both as equivalent liturgical practices; rather, the affirmation and continuation of the postconciliar reformed liturgy as the church's liturgical standard, its ordinary practice, but coupled now with the preconciliar Mass as a fully legitimate option to which both priests in their Masses *sine populo* and stable groups of the faithful desiring it have a right, to which others are fully welcome if they wish, while it is required of none, and with each form subject to mutual enrichment by the other.

his view, that the church can thus still validly worship today in the forms it used then incontrovertibly establishes and confirms the fact of continuity in ecclesial identity. It makes it visible that what the council brought about was, in the words of his address to the curia in 2005, "renewal in the continuity of the one-subject church which the Lord has given us. It is a subject that grows in time and develops, yet remaining always the same, the one subject of the People of God on journey."[17]

In several general audience speeches in the months following this address to the curia, Pope Benedict spoke further about "the mystery of the relationship between Christ and the Church," seeking "to understand Jesus' original plan and thereby grasp the essential of the Church that lives on through the changing times."[18] In one speech, for example, he spoke of the church as "that ecclesial communion . . . inspired and sustained by the Holy Spirit and preserved and promoted by the apostolic ministry," a single communion embracing in this way (through the Holy Spirit and the apostolic ministry) believers of every place and time.[19] "Thus, we have a two-fold universality: a synchronic universality—we are united with believers in every part of the world—and also a so-called diachronic universality, that is: all the epochs belong to us, and all the believers of the past and of the future form with us a single great communion."[20] In a later speech devoted to reflection on Saint Paul, Pope Benedict recalled another factor marking the church's enduring identity—that Christ "identified himself with the Church" when he revealed himself to Paul on the road to Damascus.[21]

[17] Benedict XVI, "Expergiscere," 46 ("rinnovamento nella continuità dell'unico soggetto-Chiesa, che il Signore ci ha donato; è un soggetto che cresce nel tempo e si sviluppa, rimanendo però sempre lo stesso, unico soggetto del Popolo di Dio in cammino").

[18] Benedict XVI, *Jesus, the Apostles, and the Early Church: General Audiences 15 March 2006–14 February 2007* (San Francisco: Ignatius Press, 2007), 7 ("the mystery") and 20 ("to understand").

[19] Ibid., 24.

[20] Ibid.

[21] Ibid., 124–25.

In Benedict's vision, the church is constituted by such realities—Christ, the Spirit, the apostolic ministry. The church is the ecclesial communion of all those incorporated into Christ by the Spirit and served in some way by the apostolic ministry—all one people of God through history and its changes, including those of the Second Vatican Council. To affirm and demonstrate this ecclesial reality, this fundamental identity of the church in all ages, was one of the principal purposes of SP, intended by Pope Benedict as an exercise of his care for the church.

2. CONTRIBUTE TO HEALING THE INCIPIENT SCHISM WITH THE SOCIETY OF SAINT PIUS X (SSPX)

Pope Benedict enacted SP, in part, to further the cause of overcoming and healing the separation between the Society of Saint Pius X and the Catholic Church of and after Vatican II. As early as 2001, the Society insisted on seeing two concrete acts by the Vatican before, as they saw it, sufficient conditions would exist to warrant entering upon substantive theological discussion on matters of division, with a view to incorporating the Society in the full communion of the Catholic Church. They asked that the 1962 Missal be freed for unrestricted use in the church, and that the excommunications of the SSPX bishops be lifted.[22] Pope Benedict fulfilled both conditions—if not fully, at least sufficiently to have accomplished the objective of enabling the substantive theological discussion between the Vatican and the SSPX to commence, as it did on October 26, 2009.

This reaching out to the SSPX, anathema to some both in itself and because interpreted as an indicator of Pope Benedict's true leanings, is better interpreted as evidence of his sense of history and of pastoral responsibility, charity, and even creativity. Actions have consequences, and actions taken in mutual antipathy can spawn consequences lasting generations, centuries, or millennia. The bitterness at "the parting of the ways" between Christians and

[22] See, for example, "Statement of Bishop Fellay to SSPX Members and Friends" (January 22, 2001), available at http://www.sspx.org/sspx_and_rome/statement_of_bishop_fellay_jan22_01.htm; for after SP, see "Superior General's Letter to Friends and Benefactors #73" (October 23, 2008), available at http://www.sspx.org/superior_generals_news/sup_gen_ltr_73.pdf.

Jews early in the common era led the way to the long-standing teaching of contempt toward Jews; that teaching lasted until the mid-twentieth century and the promulgation of *Nostra Aetate* and is still in process of working its way out of the Catholic system. A break between the Christian East and West, conventionally dated to 1054 CE, has lasted nearly a millennium; rapprochement is under way, but full communion is yet to be achieved. The harshness of Protestant and Catholic views toward each other in sixteenth-century Europe created a rift that is approaching five hundred years and counting; changes for the better developed in the last century, but the rift still continues.

Pope Benedict's assertion that in the past not enough was done in situations such as these to maintain unity as separations and schisms were beginning (CGF 8) represented a way of reading past events and their ongoing relevance for us today—a reading that bids us weigh with great care the potential long-term consequences of inaction today (such as disinclination or refusal to dialogue), however principled such inaction might appear to those at the time. Schism is so serious a matter, so directly contrary to the will of Christ (John 17:20-21), that despite internal misunderstanding and opposition from Catholics who already view the SSPX as anathema, Benedict chose to reach out to that society, even going the extra mile. His actions viewed appreciatively can be seen as taking the long view and doing his utmost to heal this still-young separation before it becomes permanent, attempting in this way to serve the unity of the Body of Christ, something he as pope was uniquely responsible for and uniquely positioned to do something about.[23] It is another example of his care for the church.

[23] As Benedict also said, among other things in explanation and defense of his action, "Was it, and is it, truly wrong in this case to meet half-way the brother who 'has something against you' (cf. *Mt* 5:23ff.) and to seek reconciliation?" Benedict XVI, "Letter of His Holiness Pope Benedict XVI to the Bishops of the Catholic Church concerning the Remission of the Excommunication of the Four Bishops Consecrated by Archbishop Lefebvre" (March 10, 2009). The letter *in toto* is highly instructive—necessary reading to understand his views regarding the SSPX, and even regarding his own sense of priorities as pope in this present age.

3. PROMOTE THE CHURCH'S FUNDAMENTAL MISSION

SP can serve the church's mission of evangelization in two ways. First, a wider availability of the *usus antiquior* in the church's life today may draw more actively into that life Catholics previously distanced from it—either attitudinally distanced, disaffected by postconciliar liturgical "deformations," or institutionally distanced, as are members of the SSPX. Pope Benedict recognized that such Catholics, despite disaffection or distancing from the church, may nonetheless have a strong faith and a living relationship with Christ and be commendably inclined to share that faith with others. SP seeks to draw these *Christifideles* into the service of the church's evangelizing mission that so prominently concerned him as pope: as he once said, "leading men and women to God . . . is the supreme and fundamental priority of the Church and of the Successor of Peter at the present time."[24]

Moreover, since there are places where "the faith is in danger of dying out like a flame which no longer has fuel, the overriding priority is to make God present in this world and to show men and women the way to God."[25] This can happen in many ways. For some, it can come through an experience of the sacred, of "sacrality," of the transcendent God as approached and encountered in the ritual forms of the traditional liturgy—elements of which, it could be noted, bear a certain resemblance to the liturgies of Taizé which attract so many, especially young adults, who are also among those attracted to the *usus antiquior*.[26] For persons who experience God

[24] Ibid. Looking beyond common stereotypes of the SSPX, Pope Benedict asked his readers to consider whether, for example, the commitment of their priests might manifest "a love for Christ and a desire to proclaim him and, with him, the living God." He also wrote, recalling his personal experience with members of the SSPX and others in the late 1980s and 1990s, "I saw how returning to the bigger and broader Church enabled them to move beyond one-sided positions and broke down rigidity so that positive energies could emerge for the whole." His hope was that SP could encourage this phenomenon more widely.

[25] Ibid.

[26] For comments on the worship practiced at Taizé, see, e.g., Brother John of Taizé, "A Spiritual Crossroads of Europe: The Taizé Community's Adventure with the Young," in *Passing on the Faith: Transforming Traditions for the Next Generation of Jews, Christians, and Muslims*, ed. James L. Heft (New York: Fordham

in such ways, whether they be relatively few or many, Pope Benedict made that ritual form more available again, adding it to the church's "toolkit" of pastoral resources for fulfilling its mission.[27] If any who are seeking can be brought to an experience of God by the experience of the traditional Mass, this, as Benedict saw it, justified the pastoral presence and use of that form of Mass.

4. SHOW PASTORAL CARE FOR THOSE CATHOLICS DRAWN TO USE OF THE PRIOR LITURGICAL FORMS

In 1988, responding to the illegitimate ordination by Archbishop Lefebvre of four bishops for the SSPX, John Paul II, after the excommunication of the archbishop and the four bishops, referred also to the "rightful aspirations" (*observantiam . . . appetitionum*) of Catholics who remained "attached to some previous liturgical and disciplinary forms of the Latin tradition," chiefly the 1962 Missal of

---

University Press, 2006), 147–61, esp. at 152–55. One interesting remark is that the young speak of Taizé prayer as "free" even though, as Brother John says, it follows an order of service that "does not change" and in which "there is little improvisation" (154). After describing features of the services, he then reflects that, "paradoxically, perhaps, the set organization of the prayer favors the creation of an open space where body, mind, and heart are liberated; we discover that structure and freedom need not be mutually opposed, but that, correctly understood, the former can make the latter possible" (ibid.)—an affirmation presumably applicable to the extraordinary form with its "structure" as well. John XXIII similarly commended such an "open space" for prayer in the invariant order of service to which he was accustomed. In an address in 1961 to the choir boys of Pueri Cantores he described good worship as including, among other things, "active participation, through dialogue and chant, yet with that discretion which leaves room for personal, silent prayer," something possible during and even characteristic of the preconciliar Mass; quoted in Robert F. Hayburn, *Papal Legislation on Sacred Music 95 A.D. to 1977 A.D.* (Collegeville, MN: Liturgical Press, 1979), 538 (acknowledging citation from *The Pope Speaks* 6 [1961]: 60–63).

[27] On the concept of pastoral toolkit, see Jackson W. Carroll, *God's Potters: Pastoral Leadership and the Shaping of Congregations* (Grand Rapids, MI: Eerdmans Publishing, 2006), adopting the toolkit imagery from Wendy Griswold, *Cultures and Societies in a Changing World* (Thousand Oaks, CA: Pine Forge Press, 1994); Griswold's book is presently in its third edition, published in 2008.

John XXIII.[28] He further called everyone, in words meant especially for the world's Catholic bishops, to show "respect . . . for the feelings" of such Catholics by granting "a wide and generous application" of the provisions of the 1984 indult, *Quattuor Abhinc Annos*, allowing bishops to permit celebration of that form of Mass in their dioceses.[29]

Also in 1984 and shortly after the indult was issued, an international group of bishops and liturgists gathered in Rome to assess the liturgical renewal after twenty years of implementation.[30] Many of those present expressed "grave concern, regret and dismay" at the decision to allow renewed use of the 1962 Missal, for such reasons as the apparent retreat from the ecclesiology of Vatican II, the support shown those who opposed the liturgical reform, and ignoring the voice of the world's bishops who a few years earlier had almost unanimously expressed opposition to the idea of such a permission.[31] When the pro-prefect of the Vatican congregation issuing the document indicated that the dual "considerations of compassion and pluralism" contributed to the decision, "most participants," reportedly, "did not find this very convincing."[32] It was not explained why pastoral compassion and liturgical pluralism were judged unconvincing or inadequate considerations; perhaps it was implied: inadequate in comparison with the reasons just mentioned. Compassion in the service of liturgical reconciliation and church unity, however, was precisely one of the reasons Cardinal Ratzinger supported John Paul II's actions in the 1980s, and why in 2007 Pope Benedict issued SP—describing it as "merely an act of tolerance, with a pastoral aim," something he considered "a normal requirement of the faith and pastoral concern of any Bishop in our Church."[33] For him, even Catholics who prefer the traditional liturgy deserve pastoral

[28] John Paul II, *Ecclesia Dei*, 5.c, (July 2, 1988).

[29] Ibid., 6.c.

[30] See the report in "Chronicle: A Minisynod on Liturgical Reform," *Worship* 59 (1985): 72–81.

[31] Ibid., 77.

[32] Ibid.

[33] Benedict XVI, "Interview of the Holy Father Benedict XVI during the Flight to France" (September 12, 2008).

compassion, manifested in a degree of legal sanction and limited tolerance for that form of worship.

5. LESSEN OR ELIMINATE POSTCONCILIAR "DEFORMATIONS" (CGF 4) OF THE LITURGY, AND FOSTER A GREATER SPIRIT OF REVERENCE OR "SACRALITY" (CGF 7)

Bishop Marc Aillet begins the concluding chapter of his book on *Summorum Pontificum* by affirming rightly that the document is not really about the old liturgy itself. "But it is trying," as he says, "to invite pastors and faithful to take another look at the way they celebrate the liturgy according to the ordinary form of the Roman rite."[34] If and insofar as the 1970 Missal was introduced in an era characterized by an "experimental" and even "de-sacralizing" spirit and practice, and may still to a certain extent be celebrated by some priests and in some communities in that spirit and with those practices, SP hopes that something of the "'great reverence'" typically associated with the *usus antiquior* can come to enrich the Missal of Paul VI, especially "in the art of [its] celebration"—"this," Aillet affirms, "is what is really at stake."[35]

In his memoirs Cardinal Ratzinger referred to the 1960s as "a period of experimentation that had often deformed the liturgy."[36] Some may find the term deformation too strong, even offensive; others may find it too weak. It refers to liturgical practices and ways of celebration that have been described variously over the years, with comments and warnings about excessive and unauthorized experimentation damaging to the cause of liturgical reform, in communications from the Consilium, the Congregation of Rites, and Pope Paul VI in the 1960s and 1970s, and from a variety of liturgists both in that era and subsequently.[37] Statements and appeals

[34] Mark Aillet, *The Old Mass and the New: Explaining the Motu Proprio* Summorum Pontificum *of Pope Benedict XVI* (San Francisco: Ignatius Press, 2010), 91.

[35] Ibid.

[36] Joseph Ratzinger, *Milestones*, 146.

[37] See DOL 31 at nos. 411–12, DOL 35 at no. 433, DOL 36 at no. 441, DOL 41 at nos. 480–81, DOL 47 at no. 495, DOL 52 at no. 512. Many of these sources offer positive commendations for the developing liturgical reform along with warnings and appeals for cessation of harmful and ongoing experimentation.

for such practices to cease continued through the end of John Paul II's pontificate with the 2004 instruction *Redemptionis Sacramentum*. Seeing that such methods employed for forty years did not yet, at least in some circles, achieve their aim (liturgical practice regularly observant of liturgical norms[38]), Pope Benedict attempted to address the same concern and reach the same outcome by trying a different approach, a more grassroots method he hoped would amend such practices through a "mutually enriching" process by which the experience of celebrations in the extraordinary form would influence those in the ordinary form in such a way as to heal the continuing deformations.

Louis-Marie Chauvet offers a helpful analysis of the nature of those postconciliar ritual shortcomings. He explains that "a ritual always involves a symbolic rupture with the everyday, the ephemeral, the ordinary"[39]—spaces are set apart for sacred use (church, temple, etc.), as are times (Sunday, seasons), material objects (chalice, vestments), agents (priest), language (Latin, an elevated liturgical vernacular), and so on. This is termed "hetero-topy"—such phenomena are given in ritual an "other-place," set apart from the ordinary. The issue for a community then becomes to "find the right distance. In what concerns our Christian liturgies, the problem is to measure the symbolic distance between the two extremes

---

Ratzinger was aware of both lights and shadows over this period as well, but his characteristic concern was to focus on what hindered good liturgy and how to remove those hindrances that lead to "deformations." For a sampling of twenty-first century descriptions of deformations from some broadly representative voices, see Cesare Giraudo, "La costituzione 'Sacrosanctum Concilium': il primo grande dono del Vaticano II," *La Civiltà Cattolica* 154, no. 3684 (December 20, 2003): 531–32; Michael Kunzler, *Die 'Tridentinische' Messe: Aufbruch oder Rückschritt?* (Paderborn: Bonifatius, 2008), 119–20; Nicola Bux, *Benedict XVI's Reform: The Liturgy between Innovation and Tradition* (San Francisco: Ignatius Press, 2012), 141–42.

[38] Michael Kunzler, for example, could still refer in 2008 to "the wide-spread bad habit" of deliberately contravening liturgical regulations ("die weit verbreitete Unsitte . . . gegen liturgische Vorschriften bewusst zu verstoßen"); Kunzler, *Die "Tridentinische" Messe*, 112.

[39] Louis-Marie Chauvet, *Symbol and Sacrament: A Sacramental Reinterpretation of Christian Existence* (Collegeville, MN: Liturgical Press, 1995), 330.

of the 'too much' and the 'not enough'"[40]—that is, too much or not enough separation from the ordinary, the extremes of maximal and minimal hetero-topy.

Too much distance is termed "hieratism," when ritual and its sacred space, time, objects, and so forth, become so set apart as to be experienced as distant and "foreign"—the state of the liturgy for many on the eve of the council.[41] In recent years the church experienced an overreaction ("perhaps . . . historically inevitable," under the circumstances, but an overreaction all the same[42]) to this excessive ritual distance and formalism. Postconciliar changes moved in the direction of a minimal hetero-topy, a development whose characteristic shortcomings Chauvet details. "Trivialized under the excuse of being 'relevant'; employing only everyday language, gestures, and objects; often drowned in a verbiage of explanation and moralistic sermonizing, rites become no more than pretexts for doing something else. People's ideologies are given free rein and often become in their turn more rigid than the constraint of the ritual programming [that is, the hieratism] they wish to combat."[43] Such efforts, intended to make the liturgy accessible, fail to maintain "a minimum of *symbolic distance*" from the everyday, and thus violate "the anthropological and sociological laws for the functioning of rituals, beginning with the law of the symbolic rupture."[44] Without that distance from the everyday, Christian liturgical celebrations can easily come to "function in fact (and doubtless in all good faith) as an excuse for smug self-celebration."[45] The rite be-

[40] Ibid., 331.

[41] Ibid., 332–35. Chauvet's treatment is more extensive, including psychological speculation on the dynamics of hieratism as well.

[42] Ibid., 336.

[43] Ibid., 335.

[44] Ibid., 336 ("a minimum," emphasis in the original) and 337 ("the anthropological").

[45] Ibid., 338. Others echo the perception of "self-celebration." Besides Ratzinger, see John F. Baldovin, "*Sacrosanctum Concilium* and the Reform of the Liturgy: Forty-Five Years Later," *Studia Liturgica* 39 (2009): 145–57, with "self-congratulation" at 156. Chauvet later says, of ritual "deprogramming" intended to counteract hieratism, that it "carries the risk of a *new intolerance* perhaps more redoubtable than the old" (343), for whereas one could be present at a more hieratic ritual in multiple ways (of one's own choosing, such

comes a means of expression of the community's values, "a self-justifying expression of 'correct thinking' within the group," leading to a perhaps unperceived anthropocentrism: "Under cover of Jesus Christ and the Spirit, it is the group itself which continues to speak itself in the liturgical prayer. The indirect addressee (the group) displaces the direct addressee (God), who serves as an alibi"[46]—a critique to be found in the writings of Ratzinger as well.[47]

It is "deformations" of this insufficiently hetero-topic kind that Pope Benedict sought to amend by making salient in the liturgical life of the church that more highly hetero-topic ritual, the *usus antiquior*, so that the two tendencies or forms (ordinary and extraordinary) can, by mutually influencing or "enriching," draw each other toward a middle ground that will be newly "negotiated pastorally, avoiding both the 'too much' and the 'not enough'" by embodying characteristics of both forms.[48]

In place of "deformations," Pope Benedict sought greater "sacrality" or perhaps what others, more generally, describe as

---

as rosary, devotional prayer, personal meditation, using a hand missal, etc.), "everyone must now submit to the often preachy ideology which has been imposed on rite. . . . There ensues, in spite of good intentions, a de facto elitism which practically excludes those who are not able to fit the new ideological mold . . ." (344). Among those so excluded one would count persons who remained or became attached to the *usus antiquior*.

[46] Chauvet, *Symbol and Sacrament*, 344.

[47] See, for example, *Milestones*, 149: "Then the community is celebrating only itself" (149); also Joseph Ratzinger, *A New Song for the Lord: Faith in Christ and Liturgy Today* (New York: Crossroad, 1996), 39, 91; or *The Feast of Faith*, 148–49.

[48] Chauvet, *Symbol and Sacrament*, 342. Marc Aillet affirms much the same when he writes that "Benedict XVI is hoping to lessen the distance that currently exists between the two forms of usage of the Roman rite, particularly in the art of celebration"; Aillet, *The Old Mass and the New*, 91.

I have drawn here on Chauvet's critique of the "trivializing" response to hieratism, as most relevant for our efforts to understand Pope Benedict's concerns. Chauvet offers as well a corresponding critique of hieratism, and it should be noted that he does not put the two excesses on the same plane. For our own times (he was writing in the 1980s), he considers hieratism the more problematic tendency to avoid, and deprogramming (or at least greater flexibility in ritual programming) the more necessary agenda to pursue; see *Symbol and Sacrament*, 345, and especially 353–55.

"worthy" celebrations.[49] Michael Kunzler concludes his book on SP on the same note, by affirming that the permission the document gives for use of the traditional liturgy can be a starting point for something new rather than a step backward "if it is understood as a complement and a healing for what the reformed liturgy yet lacks here and there"[50] in the way it is celebrated. Thinking perhaps especially of those drawn to the traditional liturgy, he writes that "if the reformed liturgy makes encounter with the living God possible through the beauty and holiness of its celebration, then will it also be loved and accepted by the faithful, as is today already the case wherever the reformed liturgy is celebrated worthily."[51] He goes on to say that if such beneficial "healing" of and "complement" to the reformed liturgy should prove to be the fruit of SP, "then we can only be grateful to the pope for his decision and welcome the

[49] E.g., Albert Gerhards, "'Die Sorge der Päpste': Das Motu Proprio Benedikts XVI. zur Wiederzulassung der alten Liturgie," *Herder Korrespondenz* 61, no. 8 (2007): 398–403, at 400 ("die Sorge [of Pope Benedict] um einen würdigen Vollzug"); from the 1990s, J. D. Crichton, "Worshipping with Awe and Reverence," *Priests and People* 9, no. 12 (1995): 451–55, at 455; see also Keith Pecklers, "Importance and Dignity of the Eucharistic Celebration," in *A Commentary on the General Instruction of the Roman Missal*, ed. Edward Foley, Nathan D. Mitchell, and Joanne M. Pierce (Collegeville, MN: Liturgical Press, 2007), 99–112, at 111, where he speaks of a bishop's responsibility "to lead the people of his diocese to a deeper appreciation of the liturgy's riches through beautiful, prayerful, and dignified celebrations."

[50] Kunzler, *Die "Tridentinische" Messe*, 123 ("Die allgemeine Wiederzulassung des 'alten' Ritus kann auf diese Weise sogar ein Aufbruch sein, wenn sie als Ergänzung und Heilung dessen begriffen wird, was der erneuerten Liturgie hier und dort noch fehlt").

[51] Ibid. ("Wenn die erneuerte Liturgie die Begegnung mit dem lebendigen Gott ermöglicht durch die Schönheit und Heiligkeit ihrer Feier, dann wird sie auch von den Gläubigen geliebt und angenommen werden, wie es heute schon der Fall ist, wo immer der erneuerte Gottesdienst würdig gefeiert wird"); also ibid., 117. Cf. Joseph Ratzinger, "Dix ans après" 12: "When this liturgy truly moves the faithful with its beauty and profundity, then it will be loved, and then it will not be in irreconcilable opposition to the new Liturgy—provided that these criteria [SC 34–36] are truly applied as the Council wished"; Ratzinger, "The Church Has Never Abolished Orthodox Liturgies," *Inside the Vatican*, 6, no. 10 (December 1998): 58–59, at 59.

motu proprio without reserve."[52] Approaching the same point from the other direction, we have suggested that welcoming the *motu proprio* (not necessarily "without reserve," but) in a fundamentally appreciative way will create the conditions that allow it to do what good it can for the liturgy—that is, for the ordinary form—and for the church.

The point to see here is that the "deformations" are not principally in the postconciliar liturgy as set forth in its liturgical books, but rather as celebrated in pastoral practice—in what is commonly called the *ars celebrandi* (and what we can also call the *ars praesidendi* of presiders[53]). "The problems arose," Cardinal Ratzinger said, "where a wild creativity caused the disappearance of the sacred mystery," clarifying that this took place "only in a sporadic way"[54]—that is, the problems should not be exaggerated, for they exist here and there, not everywhere. But to address the problems where they exist, as well as to strengthen the liturgy where the problems are negligible, the challenge is the same: attend to the *ars celebrandi* (*ars praesidendi*).

Patrick Regan affirms the same. At the conclusion of his major study comparing the ordinary and extraordinary forms (specifically, the liturgical seasons in each form), he identifies the Missal and Lectionary of the ordinary form as "treasures of inestimable value," in themselves. But he also acknowledges that these treasures are not fully or sufficiently enriching the church because of the way the liturgy is still celebrated in actual practice. He concludes his book by stating: "One of the most urgent pastoral challenges facing the church today is to raise the *ars celebrandi* of the ordinary form to the same level of excellence as these books."[55]

With this, Regan repeats a recommendation he made forty years earlier. At that time he analyzed implementation of the liturgical

[52] Ibid. ("dann kann man dem Papst zu seiner Entscheidung nur gratulieren und das Motuproprio rückhaltlos begrüßen").

[53] See chap. 7, p. 232 for a discussion of these terms.

[54] Ratzinger, "Dix ans après," 11, at "The Church Has Never Abolished Orthodox Liturgies," 59 ("Les problèmes se sont posés seulement de façon sporadique là où une créativité sauvage a fait disparaître le mystère sacré").

[55] Patrick Regan, *Advent to Pentecost*, 305.

reform and proposed that providing the church with "liturgical celebrations which are authentic both as liturgy and as celebration seems to be one of the most important tasks facing the American church as it marks the tenth anniversary of the Constitution on the Liturgy."[56] To meet that task would require two things: "considerable evolution in the theology of liturgy as well as in the art of celebration," or, as he later put it more bluntly, in "a vastly improved art of celebration."[57] It is sobering to consider that the riches of the reformed liturgy remain insufficiently present in the life of the church today for the same reason they were insufficiently present forty years ago: deficiencies in the way we celebrate the liturgy.

One way to view SP is as a new attempt, fifty years out, to find a means to realize an end desired and sought with insufficient success (not everywhere or not fully enough) during the intervening decades: actual worship celebrations worthy of the church's reformed liturgy as set forth in its ritual books. Such a statement raises more questions than it answers, but for our purposes it highlights that the deformations Pope Benedict sought to amend are less in the reformed books and more in the *ars celebrandi*, that he tried a new approach because for half a century other approaches had not yet succeeded, and that the problems are not everywhere but sporadic.

6. REDUCE OR ELIMINATE THE CAUSE OF SUCH DEFORMATIONS—THE PRINCIPLE AND HABITS OF CREATIVITY OR INVENTIVENESS, AND OF EXCEEDING, DISREGARDING, OR ALTERING LITURGICAL NORMS

Cardinal Ratzinger wrote about creativity in the liturgy and about liturgical presiders or local planning committees feeling free or even expected to be inventive, devising innovative ways to conduct the church's liturgical celebrations, including ways outside or contrary to the provisions of the church's ritual books (which themselves already include optional elements), and with or even without reference to the needs or sensibilities of the worshiping community. This "creative" habit of thought could be understood

[56] Patrick Regan, "Liturgy and the Experience of Celebration," *Worship* 47 (1973): 592–600, at 593.

[57] Ibid., 593 ("considerable evolution") and 600 ("vastly improved").

as a kind of principled (justified on pastoral grounds) and systematic replacement of *Sacrosanctum Concilium* 22, on regulation of the liturgy. It arose in the immediately postconciliar era—most would say in reaction (or understandable overreaction) to several centuries of rubrical rigidity, and under some influence of the anti-institutional, antiauthoritarian currents of thought and sentiment in the 1960s. Michael Kunzler maintains it is evident that "many a priest" let these "'ideals' of '1968'" encountered in his student days influence, then and since, his way of celebrating liturgy, "quite possibly unconsciously, and without any pangs of conscience at having embraced" what Kunzler calls "a false ideology."[58]

Cardinal Ratzinger found this spirit of creativity and innovation a mistaken principle and an unhelpful liturgical practice, able and even liable to generate liturgical excesses, the "deformations" mentioned in CGF 4.[59] If the practice began with conscious efforts in the experimental 1960s and 1970s to find new and creative ways to celebrate the reformed liturgy ("What shall we do for the Easter Vigil this year?"), his concern was especially for those contexts where this attitude, even if somewhat attenuated, has nonetheless continued and become habitual, perhaps (to allude to Kunzler) unconsciously and without qualms.[60] What he thought needed was "a new liturgical consciousness, to be rid of this spirit of arbitrary fabrication," and to realize anew that the liturgy "is not to be manipulated" but received.[61]

[58] Michael Kunzler, *Liturgie sein. Entwurf einer Ars celebrandi* (Paderborn: Bonifatius, 2007), 25 ("manch ein Priester . . . 'Idealen' der '68er' . . . möglicherweise auch ziemlich unbewusst und völlig ohne Gewissensbisse, einer falschen Ideologie gehuldigt zu haben"). Keith Pecklers spoke of "an era of experimentation" in the 1960s and even more so in the 1970s, and of "a certain anti-establishment bias [that] found its way into Church worship"; see his *Worship: A Primer in Christian Ritual* (Collegeville, MN: Liturgical Press, 2003, 2005), 112–13. See also J. D. Crichton's paragraphs on the "Swinging sixties" in his "Worshipping with Awe and Reverence," 453.

[59] See Ratzinger, *The Spirit of the Liturgy*, 166–69; *God and the World*, 414–17.

[60] Bishop Tena also remarks on the problem of liturgical practices that emerged in the early phase of reform having become habitual, and of it being considered "conservative" to observe the existing norms; see Pere Tena, "Celebrar la liturgia después de una reforma," *Phase* 309 (2012): 227–43, at 241–42.

[61] Ratzinger, *God and the World*, 415.

The church's liturgical norms can serve this purpose in several ways, and thus he, as his predecessors John Paul II and Paul VI, affirms the benefit and necessity of such norms. They keep each local worshiping community in visible communion with the wider church, with all who observe the norms. They protect the liturgy and individual worshiping communities from the results of misguided creativity at the local level.[62] And they can serve Pope Benedict's desire for internal reconciliation in the church, a reconciliation embracing both those on the left who assert the right and responsibility of local pastoral leaders to adapt official norms to local circumstances according to their best judgment even if beyond the options allowed in the norms, as well as those on the right who demand access to and use of preconciliar liturgical forms unchanged as the only reliable bulwark against such "arbitrary creativity." The church's given liturgical norms in the reformed liturgical books lay out a reasonable and legitimate common ground in the middle, where those from all sides can, if they are willing, come to stand together, thus more reconciled in liturgical and ecclesial communion. SP serves this end at least potentially, if a more careful observance of prescribed ritual norms, as characterizes celebration of the 1962 Missal, carries over (under the rubric of "mutual enrichment") into celebrations of the ordinary form as well.[63]

[62] See, for example, Joseph Ratzinger, "On the Structure of the Liturgical Celebration," in *The Feast of Faith*, 61–75, and the chapter on "Rite" in idem, *The Spirit of the Liturgy* (San Francisco: Ignatius Press, 2000), 159–70. John Paul II was of the same mind; see his encyclical *Ecclesia de Eucharistia*, 51–52, where he emphasized the importance and profoundly theological reasons for liturgical norms, mentioning also the existence of "*abuses* which have been a source of suffering for many" due to "a misguided sense of creativity and adaptation" (52, emphasis in original).

[63] Albert Gerhards described Pope Benedict's hope regarding the outcome of fruitful contact between the extraordinary form with its strict rubrics and the ordinary form—his hope, as it were, that the *ars celebrandi* of reverence that is in a sense rubrically inbuilt the extraordinary form might, by the process of mutual enrichment, draw the manner of celebrating the ordinary form more in that direction and away from the shortcomings or "deformations" that can sometimes characterize its celebration; see Gerhards, "Die Sorge der Päpste," 400. Andreas Heinz says this can occur even where there is little actual use of the extraordinary form. He reported in 2008 that SP had not occasioned much

7. FOSTER A DIFFERENT PROCESS OF LITURGICAL DEVELOPMENT—AND IN THIS WAY SUPPORT AND DIRECT A NEW LITURGICAL MOVEMENT

A new liturgical movement is underway. SP resources this movement and gives it direction by the place and function it accords the extraordinary form in the Roman Rite. It does so in a way corresponding in several respects with elements of "The Oxford Declaration on Liturgy" (hereafter ODL) of 1996, with which Cardinal Ratzinger was familiar, and which calls for "a *revival of the liturgical movement* and the initiation of a new cycle of reflection and reform."[64]

The declaration, for example, seeks a "resacralization of Catholic liturgical practice" (ODL 3), which Benedict thought the attractive "sacrality" of the extraordinary form can foster (CGF 7). The Declaration envisions a "greater *pluralism* of Catholic rites and uses" (ODL 5), which SP creates, designating two usages of the Roman Rite. The declaration calls for "ris[ing] above differences of opinion and taste to that unity which is the Holy Spirit's gift to the Body of Christ" (ODL 5), an inclusive unity for which Benedict appealed when he called the people of the church to "generously open our heart and make space for all that the faith itself allows" (CGF 8).

The declaration also voices the hope "that any future liturgical reform would not be imposed on the faithful but would proceed, with the utmost caution and sensitivity to the *sensus fidelium* [sense of the faithful], from a thorough understanding of the organic nature of the liturgical traditions of the Church" (no. 6, with a reference to SC 23). SP adheres closely to this prescription. It imposes

---

demand for the extraordinary form in Germany, but it "nonetheless had given rise to a happy side effect, in prompting a look at the quality of existing celebrations and in questioning taken-for-granted habits" ("a cependant provoqué un heureux effet latéral en stimulant la recherche de qualité des célébrations existantes et en questionnent les habitudes acquises"). Andreas Heinz, "Les recherches liturgiques dans le monde germanique," *La Maison-Dieu* 253 (March 2008): 121–28, here at 126.

[64] "The Oxford Declaration on Liturgy," 3; emphasis in the original, in this and all following citations. Text in Stratford Caldecott, ed., *Beyond the Prosaic: Renewing the Liturgical Movement* (Edinburgh: T&T Clark, 1998), 163–65, at 164; also available at http://www.secondspring.co.uk/spirituality/declaration.htm. Cardinal Ratzinger referred to the Declaration in "Dix ans après," 11.

nothing on the faithful but only makes celebrations of the 1962 Missal more available for those who desire them. In doing this, SP seeks to show respect for the sensitivity of the faithful who prefer either usage, more freely allowing celebrations of the extraordinary form while affirming the church's reformed liturgy as its ordinary form. And "organic" seems to describe well the understanding of liturgical evolution expressed by Pope Benedict when he spoke of the Roman Mass undergoing development: it "grew," he said, "and over succeeding centuries gradually took on forms which have a great similarity with the one in force in more recent generations" (SP 5). That is, it grew (as a living, organic process) and over succeeding centuries (the process is slow and continuous over time), gradually (since organisms typically grow step by step, stage following stage), took on forms which have a great similarity (not an exact identity, because the forms grow and change, but a similarity, because the change is not discontinuous) with the one in force (still living, growing, bearing fruit) in more recent generations.

We see a great concern here on the one hand for continuity, as instructed by Vatican II in the passage referenced by the declaration (SC 23), and on the other hand for the "legitimate development" affirmed in that same conciliar passage. SP fosters a form of continuity with the long liturgical tradition in making provision for Roman Rite Catholics more freely to participate in celebrations of the Latin Mass that, with changes over time, had been in use for much of the church's history; SP also fosters what we might call a continuity with the present, with no "rupture" from or in our very recent past (the church's history since promulgation of the liturgy constitution on December 4, 1963), for the new liturgy remains the norm. At the same time, Pope Benedict's liturgical initiative brought further development, with his call for three simple yet symbolic changes to be made in the traditional liturgy: the possibility of vernacular readings (SP, art. 6) and the introduction of recently canonized saints into the calendar and new prefaces into the 1962 Missal (CGF 7). That there are any changes at all is of great significance, for it brings the old Missal into new prominence not as the restoration of the *status quo ante* or of a museum piece to be preserved unchanged, but as a recovery-with-development, making the traditional rite a living liturgy again in process of organic growth. That these three symbolic changes are made under the influence of the reformed liturgy exemplifies the hoped for "mutually enriching" interaction of the two forms (CGF 7).

Where will this development via mutual enrichment take place? Certainly in parishes where both forms are celebrated. But also in religious communities, which can, with permission, use the prior liturgical forms "often or habitually or permanently" (SP, art. 3); in this way, even if the traditional Mass remains relatively rare in parish life, it may take root in nonparochial settings. In this, the new liturgical movement may resemble the old, where change gestated in monasteries and religious houses. If so, there would be an intriguing historical resonance, if the very places that once, while celebrating the old liturgy (the living liturgy of its day), patiently worked for the new, now came to house the return of what they once strove to reform, precisely to nurture its contribution to the ongoing development and renewal of the church's living liturgy of our day. But wherever and however the process of mutual enrichment unfolds,[65] it puts in place the conditions for a future development of the Roman Rite arguably more organic than that which occurred through multiple papal initiatives in the middle years of the twentieth century—more precisely, in the quarter century between circa 1950 and the mid-1970s.

Finally, the declaration makes this interesting and important challenge: "Those who love the Catholic tradition in its fullness should strive to *work together in charity*, bearing each other's burdens in the light of the Holy Spirit, and persevering in prayer with Mary the Mother of Jesus" (ODL 5). Who is meant by, or who would lay claim to be, "those who love the Catholic tradition in its fullness"? Those who stand by the *usus antiquior* maintain that it preserves a richness of Catholic tradition lost or abandoned by the 1970 Missal of Paul VI, with reference to those components of the old liturgy that were not preserved but eliminated in the new. Those who hold to the *usus recentior* maintain that it recovers a fullness of Catholic liturgical tradition lost or attenuated over the centuries and then enshrined in that attenuated form in the 1570 Missal of Pius V and embodied in its customary manner of celebration in the centuries following. So the declaration, with this

[65] For more on the process of mutual enrichment, see chap. 7.

appeal, invites a kind of reconciliation of opposites. It calls both groups to "work together" in this new phase of liturgical reflection and reform, not in a spirit of antagonism but "in charity," and so, "bearing each other's burdens" (see Galatians 6:2). What burdens? Perhaps the burden of rising above differences, of staying charitable while encountering and accommodating each other's divergent and even conflicting convictions, opinions, and preferences; perhaps the burden of the sense of loss that may come with granting some legitimacy to and space for the liturgical theology and practice of the other, which one thinks mistaken and even harmful; and perhaps the burdens of patience, and of openness to change, required of all.

❐ ❐ ❐

Part 1 was written to prepare the ground for a fruitful reading of *Summorum Pontificum*, because how the document is read and received will determine the effect it has in the life of the church. Readers can, of course, freely decide how they will choose to receive and interpret it. This may well be affected by their understanding of and response to the *usus antiquior* itself, the Mass as celebrated according to the 1962 Missal of Blessed John XXIII. The complicating factor is that for many, and especially those who see themselves as decidedly on one or the other side of divisions in the Catholic Church, that Mass is not simply a particular ritual form of worship but has come to function as a powerful symbol—as Wilfrid Haunerland has said, a "symbol for the refusal to recognize and accept the council's reform impulse at all."[66]

As long as this remains the case, a dispassionate, fair-minded, and even historically tenable understanding by all concerned of that ritual form of eucharistic celebration and its place in the life of the church both before and after the Second Vatican Council can be difficult to achieve. This difficulty will, in turn, impede a fair-

[66] Winfried Haunerland, "Ein Ritus in zwei Ausdrucksformen? Hintergründe und Perspektiven zur Liturgiefeier nach dem Motu proprio 'Summorum Pontificum,'" *Liturgisches Jahrbuch* 58 (2008): 179–203, at 192 ("Symbol für die Weigerung, die Reformimpulse des Konzils insgesamt anzuerkennen und aufzunehmen").

minded reading and reception of *Summorum Pontificum*. It can, for example, tend to lead each side to think SP privileges the 1962 liturgy differently (more highly) than it does, thus intensifying either their adherence or resistance to that document, thereby intensifying further the underlying liturgical and ecclesial divisions the document was intended to alleviate. This dynamic works contrary to and undermines the effective fulfillment of Pope Benedict's hopes for "an internal reconciliation in the heart of the church" (CGF 8).

But with a different kind of reception—with, as this book proposes, a fundamentally appreciative reception—something different is possible. SP can become a pivotal text, a turning-point intervention, calling and helping the church to leave behind an era marked by divisive tensions where one particular form of Mass, the 1962 Missal, has become or been used as the chief symbol of opposition, and to open onto an era where SP itself with its liturgical provision for two forms of the one Roman Rite becomes, as Haunerland says, "a symbol for the overcoming of division in the church,"[67] and an agent of reconciliation and peace. This becomes possible when cultivation of one or the other form, ordinary or extraordinary, is no longer either intended or interpreted as a symbolic gesture standing for "a different church," for one way of being Catholic over against another; such intentions are best set aside, "for true liturgy is free of utilitarian ends and is not to be exploited."[68]

The analysis of SP and CGF that follows in part 2 attempts a fundamentally appreciative, if also critical and constructive, reading and interpretation of the texts.

[67] Ibid., 199 ("zum Symbol für die Überwindung der Spaltung in der Kirche wird").

[68] Ibid. "Church" ("eine . . . andere Kirche"), "true liturgy" ("Denn wahre Liturgie ist zweckfreies Handeln und darf nicht instrumentalisiert werden").

Part 2

Chapter 4

Summorum Pontificum

Translation and Commentary

SP 1

> *It has always been the care of the Supreme Pontiffs up to our own day that the church of Christ offer worthy worship to the divine majesty, "for the praise and glory of his name" and "for the good of all his holy church."*[1]

The two quotations in this opening sentence are taken from the order of Mass, from the response to the *Orate, fratres* prayer at the conclusion of the preparation of the gifts. With these phrases Pope Benedict XVI opened his apostolic letter, *Summorum Pontificum*, using words common to both the Missal of Saint Pius V (reissued by Blessed John XXIII in 1962) and the 1970 Missal of the Servant of God Paul VI. The phrases moreover echo the twofold fundamental purpose of worship, and indeed of the church, as the Second Vatican Council set it forth when stating that "the sanctification of men in Christ and the glorification of God, to which all other activities of the Church are directed as towards their end, is achieved in the most efficacious possible way" in the liturgy (SC 10).[2]

[1] [This and all subsequent SP quotes are my translation of *Summorum Pontificum*. The Latin original was published in *Acta Apostolicae Sedis* 99, no. 9 (2007): 777–81.—Trans.]

[2] From *Constitution on the Sacred Liturgy* (Collegeville, MN: Liturgical Press, n.d. [1963]). Pius XII identified this same twofold purpose as the end of Christ's whole redeeming work from incarnation to paschal mystery (*Mediator Dei* 17), and Pius X declared these two aims (adding "edification" to the sanctification of the faithful) to be the general purpose of the liturgy and thus of sacred music (*Tra le Sollecitudini*).

That popes have taken most seriously their *cura* (a word meaning care, solicitude, responsibility, or even anxious concern) regarding the liturgy is evident. Papal as well as episcopal *cura* for the liturgy was noted by Pope Paul VI in the opening sentence of his *motu proprio* of January 25, 1964, *Sacram Liturgiam*—the first document he issued in implementation of the Second Vatican Council's constitution on the liturgy, *Sacrosanctum Concilium*, promulgated December 4, 1963.[3]

At the same time, the way in which this papal care has been exercised and the understanding of what responsibility and authority the Roman pontiff possesses regarding the liturgy have varied across the centuries. A high view of this authority is articulated in the Constitution on the Sacred Liturgy of the Second Vatican Council: "Regulation of the sacred liturgy depends solely on the authority of the Church, that is, on the Apostolic See, and, as laws may determine, on the bishop" (SC 22.1).[4] That the pope has such authority with regard to the liturgy is recognized by Catholics today, but it is well to recall that this represents a development that emerged over time. One early step in the spread of Roman influence on liturgical practice elsewhere in the church came through the mission of Augustine of Canterbury (d. ca. 604) and the introduction of a Roman-oriented Christianity into England, with the Synod of Whitby in 664 a key turning point.[5] Significant and

[3] See also Pius XI in his apostolic constitution *Divini Cultus Sanctitatem* (1928); *Acta Apostolicae Sedis* 21 (1929): 33–41, at 34. The same idea is expressed in the opening words of Pius X's *motu proprio Tra le Sollecitudini* (1903) on sacred music, a document that played such a significant role in the twentieth-century liturgical movement.

[4] Even higher is Pius XII, *Mediator Dei* 58: "the Sovereign Pontiff alone enjoys the right to recognize and establish any practice touching the worship of God, to introduce and approve new rites, as also to modify those he judges to require modification. Bishops, for their part, have the right and duty carefully to watch over the exact observance of the prescriptions of the sacred canons respecting divine worship."

[5] Bede, *A History of the English Church and People*, trans. Leo Sherley-Price, rev. R. E. Latham (Baltimore: Penguin, 1968), passim; on the Synod of Whitby, see 185–92. Also Michael Driscoll, "The Conversion of the Nations," in *The Oxford History of Christian Worship*, ed. Geoffrey Wainwright and Karen B. Westerfield Tucker (Oxford: Oxford University Press, 2006), 175–215, at 177.

influential were the actions of the Frankish rulers, Pepin III (d. 768) and Charlemagne (d. 814), who sought liturgical books from Rome to use as models in their realm.[6] Additional measures were taken by Gregory VII (1073–85), though only in some regions; nonetheless his actions laid the groundwork for "the Roman church's legal right to insist on liturgical uniformity."[7] Another factor contributing to a commonality of worship was the role of itinerant Franciscan preachers, beginning in the thirteenth century, who spread abroad by their presence and liturgical practice the usage they had

[6] See Cyrille Vogel, *Medieval Liturgy: An Introduction to Its Sources*, trans. and rev. William G. Storey and Niels Krogh Rasmussen, with the assistance of John K. Brooks-Leonard (Washington, DC: Pastoral Press, 1986), 147–50; Michael Driscoll, "The Conversion of the Nations," in *The Oxford History of Christian Worship*, 177, 186, 188–89; Timothy Thibodeau, "Western Christendom," in *The Oxford History of Christian Worship*, 227; Marcel Metzger, *History of the Liturgy: The Major Stages* (Collegeville, MN: Liturgical Press, 1997), 114–19; Robert Cabié, *The Eucharist* (Collegeville, MN: Liturgical Press, 1986), 128–29; Joseph A. Jungmann, *The Mass of the Roman Rite: Its Origins and Development*, vol. 1 (New York: Benziger Brothers, 1951), 74ff. Yitzhak Hen, on the other hand, argues for the continuing liturgical diversity of the Carolingian era and against the notion of an attempted wholesale Carolingian imposition of Roman liturgical practices (except regarding Roman chant); see Hen, *The Royal Patronage of Liturgy in Frankish Gaul to the Death of Charles the Bald* (877) (London: Henry Bradshaw Society / Boydell Press, 2001), for example, at 81–89 or 148–54. See also Alcuin Reid's use of Hen in Reid, *The Organic Development of the Liturgy: The Principles of Liturgical Reform and Their Relation to the Twentieth-Century Liturgical Movement Prior to the Second Vatican Council*, 2nd ed. (San Francisco: Ignatius Press, 2005), 22–23 (the passage to which I owe, gratefully, my awareness of this source).

[7] Nathan D. Mitchell and John F. Baldovin, "*Institutio Generalis Missalis Romani* and the Class of Liturgical Documents to Which It Belongs," in *A Commentary on the General Instruction of the Roman Missal*, ed. Edward Foley, Nathan D. Mitchell, and Joanne M. Pierce (Collegeville, MN: Liturgical Press, 2007), 1–27, at 17 (see also 11–17); they make use of H. E. J. Cowdrey, "Pope Gregory VII (1073–1085) and the Liturgy," *Journal of Theological Studies* 58, no. 1 (2004): 55–83. See also Driscoll, "The Conversion of the Nations," 197–202; Thibodeau, "Western Liturgy," 225–26, 228; Cabié, *The Eucharist*, 129; Stephen J. P. Van Dijk and J. Hazelden Walker, *The Origins of the Modern Roman Liturgy: The Liturgy of the Papal Court and the Franciscan Order in the Thirteenth Century* (Westminster, MD: Newman Press, 1960), 70–74.

adopted, that of the Roman Curia.[8] This in turn, to some extent, helped pave the way of readiness for the sixteenth century development following the Council of Trent, when a revised version of that form of Mass (according to the custom of the Roman Curia) became the 1570 Missal of Pius V.

As part of its work for church reform, Trent dealt with the liturgy, issuing authoritative doctrinal statements on the Eucharist and other sacraments and addressing various points regarding the administration of the sacraments.[9] A particularly significant impetus by which the pope came to exercise throughout the church a genuine overarching authority over liturgical practice arose from a clause in the decrees of Trent's twenty-fifth and final session. As things were drawing to a close—in "the pell-mell rush of the council's final two days"[10]—it made disposition for various matters it had intended and begun to address but not brought to a conclusion. At the end of a paragraph devoted chiefly to the work done by some of the council fathers on developing censures for books deemed dangerous in that theologically turbulent time, we find these words: "[T]he council orders that all they have prepared

[8] For brief summaries, see Anscar J. Chupungco, "History of the Roman Liturgy until the Fifteenth Century," in *Introduction to the Liturgy*, Handbook for Liturgical Studies, vol. 1, ed. Anscar J. Chupungco (Collegeville, MN; Liturgical Press, 1997), 131–51, at 149; Thibodeau, "Western Christendom," 229–30; Cassian Folsom, "Roman Rite or Roman Rites?" in *Looking Again at the Question of the Liturgy with Cardinal Ratzinger*, ed. Alcuin Reid (Farnborough: Saint Michael's Abbey Press, 2003), 72–74; Jungmann, *The Mass of the Roman Rite*, I.101–02; D. M. Hope, rev. G. Woolfenden, "The Medieval Western Rites," in *The Study of Liturgy*, rev. ed., ed. Cheslyn Jones et al. (London: SPCK and New York: Oxford University Press, 1992), 279; Keith Pecklers, *The Genius of the Roman Rite: On the Reception and Implementation of the New* Missal (Collegeville, MN: Liturgical Press, 2009), 16–18. A standard work on the subject is Van Dijk and Walker, *The Origins of the Modern Roman Liturgy*.

[9] Decrees and canons on the Eucharist were issued in the thirteenth, twenty-first, and twenty-second sessions, and on the other sacraments in the seventh, fourteenth, twenty-third, and twenty-fourth sessions. Some minor ritual matters were addressed in the twenty-second session. Details are summarized in Jungmann, *The Mass of the Roman Rite*, I.134–35.

[10] James F. White, *Roman Catholic Worship: Trent to Today*, 2nd ed. (Collegeville, MN: Liturgical Press, 2003), 6.

should be presented to the pope and so by his wisdom and authority be completed and published. It gives similar orders in the matter of the catechism prepared by those commissioned, and of the missal and breviary."[11]

With that final phrase, in an almost off-hand fashion, the future of the liturgy was fundamentally altered. Those earlier phases in the wider spread of the Roman liturgy, described above, were intermittent or happenstance, and diversity remained a widespread fact, a fundamental feature of life in the Latin church throughout the middle ages and up to the time of Trent.[12] While there was recognition of a certain measure of papal authority regarding the

[11] Council of Trent, Session 25, in Tanner, *Decrees of the Ecumenical Councils*, vol. 2 (Washington, DC: Georgetown University Press, 1990), 797.

[12] Thibodeau, "Western Christendom": "it is impossible to speak of the 'absolute unity' of the Roman liturgy in the seventh and eighth centuries in any canonical or juridical sense" (226), and "a tremendous amount of liturgical diversity persisted in the monasteries, cathedrals, and parishes of Europe to the end of the Middle Ages" (230). Hope and Woolfenden, "The Medieval Western Rites": "There was a good deal of variation permitted, not only at regional level, but also at local" (278). Jungmann, *The Mass of the Roman Rite*: "Thus we find throughout the later Middle Ages a great variation in all those parts of the Mass-liturgy which were not fixed as a heritage of the ancient Roman sacramentaries, variation not only from country to country but from church to church, in fact, from Mass book to Mass book" (I.97). Clifford Howell, "From Trent to Vatican II" in Jones et al., *The Study of Liturgy*: "Every country, every diocese, almost every Church throughout the West had its own way of celebrating Mass, for there was no close control from any central authority" (286). Folsom speaks not so much of diversity as of "liturgical anarchy" prevalent *circa* 1500; Cassian Folsom, "Gestures Accompanying the Words of Consecration in the History of the *Ordo Missae*," in *The Veneration and Administration of the Eucharist*, trans. and ed. by members of CIEL UK (Southampton: The Saint Austin Press, 1997): 75–94, at 78. Also Klaus Gamber, *The Reform of the Roman Liturgy: Its Problems and Background* (San Juan Capistrano, CA: Una Voce Press, 1993), 25. Yet cf. Driscoll, "The Conversion of the Nations": "While much liturgical diversity existed at the time of Gregory I, by the time of Gregory VII there was much uniformity" (*The Oxford History of Christian Worship*, 209). Adolph Adam, *Foundations of Liturgy: An Introduction to Its History and Practice* (Collegeville, MN: Liturgical Press, 1992) also speaks of "a phase of consolidation" under and after Gregory VII (29).

liturgy,[13] it was simply not expected that the pope would intervene in individual dioceses to govern their liturgy, forbidding certain rites, establishing or imposing others. These were matters for individual bishops, regional councils, metropolitan bishops[14]—until, that is, this clause from the last session of the Council of Trent remanded the revision of the missal and breviary to the pope. With this development, "Rome was accorded unprecedented liturgical control."[15] The initial result was the 1568 Breviary and 1570 Missal of St. Pius V. The establishment of the Congregation of Sacred Rites in 1588 further solidified and became the means of implementing papal authority over particular churches in this matter, with the congregation's charge to regulate the liturgy, maintain uniformity, and assure fidelity to the Roman books—at least in those dioceses that were obliged or had chosen to adopt the Roman books, as became universal only in the nineteenth century.[16]

[13] For example, "by the end of the tenth century, there was growing sentiment to have popes, in virtue of their supreme authority," validate canonizations made at the local level by bishops, though the practice grew only gradually and the papacy did not take over the process fully until seven centuries later; see Kenneth L. Woodward, *Making Saints: How the Catholic Church Determines Who Becomes a Saint, Who Doesn't, and Why* (New York: Simon & Schuster, 1996), 65–66. And when there was a movement toward establishing Corpus Christi as a feast for the whole Church, it was understood that only the pope could bring this about.

[14] Jungmann, *The Mass of the Roman Rite*, I.97–98; White, *Roman Catholic Worship*, 6; Gamber, *The Reform of the Roman Liturgy*, 25. Chupungco writes of this period, "Liturgical usages varied from diocese to diocese because the bishops had control of the shape of worship in their respective local churches"; Anscar J. Chupungco, "History of the Roman Liturgy until the Fifteenth Century," 142.

[15] White, *Roman Catholic Worship*, 6. See also Sven Conrad, "Renewal of the Liturgy in the Spirit of Tradition: Perspectives with a View towards the Liturgical Development of the West," *Antiphon* 14, no. 1 (2010): 95–136: "With Trent, liturgical law ultimately became a matter of papal right" (101). Conrad also notes that "the origin of this pontifical right was indeed conciliar, because the bishops themselves handed over their right to the Pope" (101, n. 39).

[16] Clifford Howell voices the consensus view: "Trent ushered in four centuries of rigidity and fixation; it was an era of rubricism" which was "unprecedented in liturgical history"; Clifford Howell, "From Trent to Vatican II," in *The Study of Liturgy*, rev. ed., 285 (see also Jungmann, *The Mass of the Roman Rite*, I.139–41). James F. White adds that "the liturgical agenda of the period was

During this era, popes continued to attend to the church's liturgy in various ways: revised editions of the Missal published by Clement VIII in 1604, Urban VIII in 1634, Pius X in 1914, and Benedict XV in 1920; Benedict XIV's call in 1742 for more frequent communion of the faithful, from the sacrament consecrated at that Mass; Pius X's numerous liturgical initiatives, including his seminal 1903 *motu proprio* on the liturgy, *Tra le Sollecitudini*, and his call for more frequent Communion in *Sacra Tridentina Synodus* (Congregation of the Council, 1905); Pius XII's 1947 encyclical, *Mediator Dei*, and his several significant liturgical reforms during the 1950s, including the revisions of Holy Saturday and then Holy Week; and John XXIII's 1960 rubrical revisions for the Mass, as well as his addition of the name of St. Joseph to the Roman Canon in 1962 while the council was in session (see also SP 6).[17]

In other words, Pope Benedict was right to speak of abiding papal care and concern for the liturgy, and his own manifestation of such concern was fully fitting. What, then, were his views on the way this care should or may be exercised? What indication do his earlier writings give of the way he, as Pope Benedict XVI, would carry out this concern? To answer in a word, he saw the pope less (as Pius XII seemed to) as master and more as *servant* of the liturgy. He did not absolutize papal power: "the Pope can not do everything," he said just a few years before becoming pope, but is instead "to be the guarantor of obedience" to the church's liturgical

---

the Romanization of the liturgy"; White, *Roman Catholic Worship*, 10. This is so, though it should be noted the process was gradual. In both France and Germany, for example, diocesan liturgical books were still in use in the nineteenth century; see Reid, *Organic Development*, 49; Conrad, "Renewal of the Liturgy," 108; and J. D. Crichton, *Lights in Darkness: Forerunners of the Liturgical Movement* (Collegeville, MN: Liturgical Press, 1996), chap. 6, "The 'Neo-Gallican Books,'" 44–51. In view of this history, Conrad considers "simply false" (117) Bugnini's assertion that "for centuries the Church willed that all worship in the Roman Rite should everywhere show perfect uniformity"; Annibale Bugnini, *The Reform of the Liturgy 1948–1975* (Collegeville, MN: Liturgical Press, 1990), 42.

[17] One handy resource containing roughly six-hundred pages of papal statements pertaining to worship, including popes from Benedict XIV (1740–58) to John XXIII (1958–63), is *Papal Teachings: The Liturgy*, selected and arranged by the Benedictine monks of Solesmes, trans. by the Daughters of St. Paul (Boston: St. Paul Editions, 1962).

tradition, for "the Church cannot simply do as she likes."[18] With regard to the liturgy in particular and to correct a misunderstanding often attributed to the First Vatican Council's teachings on the papacy, he wrote that "the pope's authority is bound to the Tradition of faith, and that also applies to the liturgy. . . . Even the pope can only be a humble servant of its lawful development and abiding integrity and identity."[19]

Ratzinger offered the image of "humble servant" to indicate an attitude and manner appropriate for exercising what nonetheless remained (1) papal responsibility and authority, (2) to oversee the necessary and legitimate development of the liturgy, (3) doing so in a way that assured that new developments would maintain clear connections and continue the identity with what went before. These were the views of Joseph Ratzinger as cardinal and theologian, and they help us understand the way in which Joseph Ratzinger as Pope Benedict XVI recognized (1) papal authority and responsibility for the liturgy. This was the teaching of the Second Vatican Council; he accepted it, and took it as one of his duties to act accordingly. He recognized also that (2) the liturgy develops, quite legitimately and inevitably, as all living, growing things do. This conviction, with its implications, put him in tension with those who resist changes in the traditional Mass. He also recognized (3) his responsibility to see that new developments not create a break with the past but remain in clear continuity. The implications he drew from this conviction put him in tension with those who resist renewed contact with or a continuing presence and influence of the traditional liturgy in the church's liturgical life today.

With SP, Benedict enacted all three elements of the papal role. He created new liturgical legislation by papal authority, *motu proprio*, doing so in an innovative way, establishing two expressions or uses of the one Roman Rite. He reaffirmed the legitimacy of the liturgical development that is the Missal of Paul VI; he maintained it as the church's basic liturgical form, as the ordinary expression of the church's *lex orandi*, and put in place provisions for its further

[18] Ratzinger, "Assessment and Future Prospects," in *Looking Again*, 153 ("the Pope"); Ratzinger, *God and the World: A Conversation with Peter Seewald* (San Francisco: Ignatius Press, 2002), 377 ("guarantor" and "Church").

[19] Ratzinger, *The Spirit of the Liturgy* (San Francisco: Ignatius Press, 2000), 166.

development. That process of further development also touched the traditional liturgy, which was not only given new life and legal standing but also made subject to change by the provisions of SP—as we shall see later.

SP 2

> *As from time immemorial, so also into the future, let the principle be observed "according to which each particular Church must be in accord with the universal Church not only regarding the doctrine of the faith and sacramental signs, but also as to the usages universally received from apostolic and unbroken tradition. These are to be kept not only so that errors may be avoided, but also so that the faith may be handed on in its integrity, since the Church's rule of prayer* (lex orandi) *corresponds to her rule of faith* (lex credendi)*."*[20]

This citation from the *General Instruction of the Roman Missal* gives expression to two of Pope Benedict's deepest concerns: the unity of the church (diachronic and synchronic) and the integrity of the faith. Both, he believed, are manifested and maintained through the liturgy well celebrated; both are put at risk when the liturgy is mistreated and "deformed" in certain ways he believed were evident and enduring in the years since Vatican II. SP is not about mere decorum at Mass or nostalgia for a bygone ritual or way of Catholic life; it is about several more fundamental concerns, including the faith and unity of the church, today and into the future.

Benedict held, as the GIRM states, that there are ritual usages "received from apostolic and unbroken tradition" (no. 397)—that is, that come to us from the apostles and even before. In *Sacramentum Caritatis* he wrote, "with his word and with the elements of bread and wine, the Lord himself has given us the essentials of this new worship" (no. 12). More than twenty years earlier Cardinal Ratzinger had affirmed that the Catholic liturgy "reaches right back to Christ and the apostles and has come down to us from that time in

[20] *General Instruction of the Roman Missal*, 3rd ed. (2002), no. 397. [Note in original. Translation from *The Roman Missal, Third Edition* (Washington, DC: United States Conference of Catholic Bishops, 2011), 86.—Trans.]

a single, constant process"[21]—what the GIRM describes as "apostolic and unbroken tradition." Benedict was not simplistic or unhistorical in his understanding of how this process takes place. He understood that the eucharistic mystery is celebrated "in the liturgical forms which the Church, guided by the Holy Spirit, develops in time and space."[22] He also compared the process with the development of Scripture, affirming that "because of the historical character of God's action, the 'Divine Liturgy' (as they call it in the East) has been fashioned, in a way similar to Scripture, by human beings and their capacities."[23]

The analogy is illuminating and invites comparison with one of the council documents on which Father Joseph Ratzinger worked most closely, the Dogmatic Constitution on Divine Revelation, *Dei Verbum*. That document taught that the books of Sacred Scripture have "God as their author," *and* that in the composition of the biblical books God chose persons who "made full use of their powers and faculties so that, though he acted in them and by them, it was as true authors that they consigned to writing whatever he wanted written, and no more" (DV 11). It seems Cardinal Ratzinger held an analogous view regarding the composition of liturgical rites, seeing them as coming from God and as shaped by fully human, cultural, developmental historical processes.[24] His understanding of the dynamics at work here resonates with that of Edward J. Kilmartin,

[21] Ratzinger, *The Feast of Faith: Approaches to a Theology of the Liturgy* (San Francisco: Ignatius Press, 1986), 86. See also idem, *The Spirit of the Liturgy*, 221 (sacraments as "given to us in their substance by the Lord himself"); idem, *God and the World*, 447 (the liturgy "comes from the beginning"); idem, *God Is Near Us: The Eucharist, the Heart of Life*, ed. Stephan Otto Horn and Vinzenz Pfnür (San Francisco: Ignatius Press, 2003), 49 (the Roman Canon "developed directly from" the Jewish prayers of Jesus at the Last Supper).

[22] Benedict XVI, *Sacramentum Caritatis* 12.

[23] Ratzinger, *The Spirit of the Liturgy*, 167; see ibid., 169: "Christians know that God has spoken through man and that the human and historical factor is, therefore, part of the way God acts"; also Ratzinger, *God and the World*, 451–52, on justification, involving genuine human "cooperation" with God, as "genuine partners" and "real conscious agents" in the process.

[24] Compare the statement in the council's liturgy constitution: "For the liturgy is made up of immutable elements divinely instituted, and of elements subject to change" (SC 21).

who held that a study of "the elements of the sacramental celebrations shows that they consist in human language and corporeal expression, constructed by the human activity of the Church under the inspiration of the Holy Spirit."[25]

The point is that Pope Benedict had at once a high view of the divine origins of the church's liturgy and a clear understanding of the divinely guided yet fully human and historical character of the development of the liturgy. When he also affirmed that the liturgy, thus developed and still developing, comes to us "in a single, constant process," we see an expression of his concern for continuity in handing on the liturgy from one generation to the next. This concern explains the dismay he felt, upon publication of the Missal of Paul VI, that the prior missal was prohibited. As he understood it, this prohibition "introduced a breach into the history of the liturgy whose consequences could only be tragic."[26]

Ratzinger saw in this breach the breaking of a tradition going back to the apostles. One of the reasons for the publication of SP was Pope Benedict's desire to heal this breach and reestablish a kind of continuity by reintroducing the *usus antiquior* into the living liturgical practice of the church, not as its ordinary liturgy but as its extraordinary form, as which it participates once again in the ongoing process of liturgical development—now through the process of its mutual enrichment of and by the *usus recentior*.

SP 3

> *Among the Pontiffs who have exercised such requisite concern, the name of Saint Gregory the Great stands out. He took care to transmit to the new peoples of Europe both the Catholic faith and the riches of worship and culture accumulated by the Romans during the preceding centuries. He made provision that the form of the sacred liturgy as celebrated in*

[25] Edward J. Kilmartin, "Theology of the Sacraments: Toward a New Understanding of the Chief Rites of the Church of Jesus Christ," in *Alternative Futures for Worship*, vol. 1, *General Introduction*, ed. Regis A. Duffy (Collegeville, MN: Liturgical Press, 1987), 123–75, at 172. See also Kilmartin, *Christian Liturgy: Theology and Practice, I. Systematic Theology of Liturgy* (Kansas City, MO: Sheed & Ward, 1988), 192–93.

[26] Ratzinger, *Milestones: Memoirs 1927–1977* (San Francisco: Ignatius Press, n.d. [1998]), 148; see 146–48.

the city of Rome, both the sacrifice of the Mass and the Divine Office, be established and preserved. He greatly encouraged monks as well as nuns who, soldiering under the Rule of Saint Benedict, everywhere illustrated by their life, along with the preaching of the Gospel, that most salutary saying of the Rule, that "nothing is to be preferred to the work of God" (chap. 43). In this way the sacred liturgy according to the Roman custom made fruitful not only the faith and devotion but also the culture of many peoples. Indeed, it is known that the Latin liturgy of the church in its various forms, in all the centuries of the Christian era, spurred on many saints in the spiritual life, and strengthened so many peoples in the virtue of religion and made their devotion fruitful.

Such a passage, with its vision of the cultural fruitfulness of the church operating through liturgy and monastery on a newly emerging Europe, puts one in mind of Christopher Dawson. In his *Religion and the Rise of Western Culture*, for example, in the chapter on "The Religious Origins of Western Culture: The Church and the Barbarians" (that is, those whom Pope Benedict, eschewing hegemony, called instead "the new peoples of Europe"), Dawson wrote: "In the West, after the fall of the Empire, the Church possessed in the liturgy a rich tradition of Christian culture as an order of worship, a structure of thought and a principle of life," which bore fruit and took varying shape in the various regional liturgical families of Western Europe. Through these diverse liturgical traditions "the vitality and continuity of the inner life of Christendom which was the seed of the new order were preserved." This could take place, Dawson said, because of a new religious institution, "which became the guardian of the liturgical tradition and the social organ of a new Christian culture"—namely, monasticism. From this religious and social location the energy for cultural transformation was generated; "it was in the monasteries rather than in the cities that the tradition of Latin culture and the patterns of Christian life were preserved. The monks," wrote Dawson, with their liturgy and work (*ora et labora*) and entire way of life, "were the apostles of the West and the founders of medieval culture."[27]

[27] All citations from Christopher Dawson, *Religion and the Rise of Western Culture* (Garden City, New York: Image/Doubleday, 1958), 43. Interestingly, Glenn W. Olsen observes that in the pope's Regensburg lecture, "Benedict pre

Historian of religion Mark Noll shares the same vision, affirming that the spread and influence of Christianity in Europe in the latter half of the first millennium "was unthinkable apart from the activity of monks."[28] He ascribes their impact and effectiveness to the full range of their cultural activity—to their study and prayer, yet also to the witness provided "by their life" (SP 3), through "draining swamps, clearing forests, breeding cattle and sheep, and raising grains," and passing along the skills involved to others, for the benefit of all.[29] This, he says, is why the saying arose "that the monks civilized Europe *cruce, libro, et atro*—with cross, book, and plane."[30] Whatever the proportion among these three factors, the liturgy was without doubt central and formative in the lives of the monks and nuns whose work had, as the pope and the scholar note, both evangelizing and civilizing effects.[31]

Ratzinger often expressed high regard for the contributions of monasticism, whether by recalling that Benedict of Nursia and early Benedictine monks preserved and renewed ancient Roman culture even as they transcended it in creating or contributing to a truly new, European culture, or by pointing out that Benedictine monasteries were the birthplace and heartbeat of the modern liturgical movement.[32] It is with this perspective, or perhaps we should

---

sented Europe in a very Dawsonian way"; see Olsen, "Why We Need Christopher Dawson," *Communio* 35, no. 1 (2008): 115–44, at 124.

[28] Mark A. Noll, *Turning Points: Decisive Moments in the History of Christianity* (Grand Rapids, MI: Baker Books, 1997), 99.

[29] Ibid., 102.

[30] Ibid., 100.

[31] Compare the vision evoked by Pius XI: "From the earliest times the simple chants which graced the sacred prayers and the liturgy gave a wonderful impulse to the piety of the people. History tells us how in the ancient basilicas, where bishop, clergy and people alternately sang the divine praises, the liturgical chant played no small part in converting many barbarians to Christianity and civilization." Pius XI, *Divini Cultus Sanctitatem* (1928); translation from *Papal Teachings: The Liturgy*, 245 (no. 374).

[32] For references to the culture-transforming impact of Benedict of Nursia and early Benedictine monasticism, see Ratzinger, *God and the World*, 389–93; idem, *Salt of the Earth: The Church at the End of the Millennium. An Interview with Peter Seewald* (San Francisco: Ignatius Press, 1997), 127–28 and 270; idem, "Europe's Crisis of Culture," in *The Essential Pope Benedict XVI: His Central Writings*

say this precedent, in view that we should read SP, article 3, on the role of religious communities in the implementation of SP, and their permission (in addition, of course, to using only the FO) to use only the FE or a combination of both. As for the civilizing potential of monastic communities today, Pope Benedict saw them as one form of the "creative minorities" he thought could become a source for Christian witness and cultural renewal.[33] And he certainly saw their potential today, as in the past, to be centers of liturgical vitality and renewal, as "oases that many people look to and from which they receive enrichment and renewal."[34]

Finally let us note Pope Benedict's use of the verb *fecundare* in this passage, twice, to give expression to the life-giving energy and force of the liturgy that can "fecundate" or "make fruitful" people's faith, devotion, and culture. A passage in the *Catechism of the Catholic Church* further specifies what I take to be his basic meaning here when it says, "The Church is catholic, capable of integrating into her unity, while purifying them, all the authentic riches of culture."[35] This affirmation supports the idea that the church's

and Speeches, ed. John F. Thornton and Susan B. Varenne (New York: HarperCollins, 2007), 325–36, at 336. See also Pope Benedict's Wednesday audience address (April 9, 2008) on his namesake, St. Benedict. Pope Benedict made monasticism central in his address to representatives of the world of culture, in Paris on September 12, 2008. On monasticism and the liturgical movement, see Ratzinger, "Assessment and Future Prospects," in *Looking Again*, 145–46.

[33] For example, Ratzinger, *A New Song for the Lord: Faith in Christ and Liturgy Today* (New York: Crossroad, 1996), 159: "In the crisis of culture we are experiencing, it is only from islands of spiritual concentration that a new cultural purification and unification can break out at all. Wherever faith reawakens in lively communities we also see how Christian culture develops anew." David L. Schindler, "Truth, Freedom, and Relativism in Western Democracies: Pope Benedict XVI's Contributions to *Without Roots*," *Communio* 32 (2005): 667–81, makes reference to the important role of "creative minorities" in Benedict's vision of the Church's mission in civil society; see especially 673–74, 676, and 680–81.

[34] Ratzinger, *God and the World*, 389. See also *Salt of the Earth*, 177: "Centers in which the liturgy is celebrated reverently and nobly without nonsense attract, even if one doesn't understand every word." It is in either form, FE or FO, that the liturgy can be celebrated "reverently and nobly without nonsense," as Ratzinger would readily have affirmed.

[35] *Catechism of the Catholic Church*, no. 1202.

liturgy, in accommodating cultural (and ritual) diversity, integrates that diversity in the unity of the church and purifies it in the light of the Gospel (the teaching of Christ and the apostles, the witness and standard of the cross, etc.), thereby respecting, fulfilling, and releasing the life-giving dynamic of each culture.[36] Ratzinger also recognized that the influence can move in both directions: "The Church embraces the many languages, that is, the many cultures, that in faith understand and fecundate one another."[37] One thinks, for example, of the influence of Gallican and Germanic forms of liturgy on the Roman rite during the eighth to eleventh centuries.[38]

SP 4–6

SP 4

> *Moreover, so that the sacred liturgy might fulfill this role more efficaciously, many other Roman Pontiffs across the centuries manifested particular solicitude, among whom Saint Pius V stands out. With great pastoral zeal, and urged on by the Council of Trent, he renewed the whole worship of the church, saw to the publication of liturgical books corrected and "restored according to the norm of the Fathers," and provided them for the use of the Latin church.*

[36] Compare ibid., no. 1204: "In order that the mystery of Christ be 'made known to all the nations . . . to bring about the obedience of faith,' it must be proclaimed, celebrated, and lived in all cultures in such a way that they themselves are not abolished by it, but redeemed and fulfilled" (internal citation from Romans 16:26). The *Catechism* puts these ideas particularly strongly when it maintains that "the liturgy itself generates cultures and shapes them" (no. 1207).

[37] Ratzinger, *Called to Communion: Understanding the Church Today* (San Francisco: Ignatius Press, 1996), 43–44.

[38] See Cyrille Vogel, *Medieval Liturgy*, 61, and passim; Jungmann, *The Mass of the Roman Rite*, vol. 1, chaps. 9–12 (74–141); Driscoll, "The Conversion of the Nations," in *The Oxford History of Christian Worship*, 175–215; Thibodeau, "Western Christendom," in *The Oxford History of Christian Worship*, 216–253; Marcel Metzger, *History of the Liturgy*, chap. 5 (113–21); Johannes H. Emminghaus, *The Eucharist: Essence, Form, Celebration*, rev. and ed. Theodor Maas-Edwerd (Collegeville, MN: Liturgical Press, 1997), 64–70.

SP 5

> *Among liturgical books of the Roman Rite, clearly the Roman Missal is preeminent. It grew in the city of Rome and over succeeding centuries gradually took on forms which have a great similarity with the one in force in more recent generations.*

SP 6

> *"It was toward this same goal that succeeding Roman Pontiffs directed their energies during the subsequent centuries in order to ensure that the rite and liturgical books were brought up to date and when necessary clarified. From the beginning of this century they undertook a more general reform."*[39] *This, indeed, is what our predecessors carried out—Clement VIII, Urban VIII, Saint Pius X,*[40] *Benedict XV, Pius XII, and Blessed John XXIII.*

These three paragraphs briefly trace papal involvement in the history of the liturgy from the sixteenth into the twentieth century, from Trent to the eve of Vatican II.[41] Pius V is duly highlighted for his 1570 Missal, which, in its 1962 revision by John XXIII, is being reestablished as the extraordinary form of the Roman Rite (SP, art. 1). SP 4 describes Pius V's work as that of renewing the church's liturgy (*cultum innovavit*) through correcting and reforming liturgical books, specifically the Breviary in 1568 and Missal in 1570.[42] SP 5

[39] John Paul II, Apostolic Letter *Vicesimus Quintus Annus* (December 4, 1988) 3: *Acta Apostolicae Sedis* 81 (1989), 899. [Note in original.—Trans.]

[40] Ibid. [Note in original.—Trans.]

[41] See White, *Roman Catholic Worship*; Alcuin Reid, *The Organic Development of the Liturgy*; Clifford Howell, "From Trent to Vatican II," in *The Study of Liturgy*, 285–94; Robert Cabié, chap. 3, "The Celebration of the Eucharist in the West from the Council of Trent to Vatican Council II," in *The Eucharist*, 173–85; Keith Pecklers, "History of the Roman Liturgy from the Sixteenth until the Twentieth Centuries," in Chupungco, *Handbook for Liturgical Studies*, vol. 1, *Introduction to the Liturgy*, 153–78.

[42] It seems exaggerated to say of Pius V that he "renewed the whole worship of the church" (*totum Ecclesiae cultum innovavit*, SP 4). The Council of Trent's decree handed on to him the task of preparing new editions of the Missal and Breviary only. Further elements of the liturgy were reformed by his successors; see James F. White, *Roman Catholic Worship*, 7–9. Moreover, Ratzinger himself spoke of the 1570 Missal as differing "only in tiny details" from the 1474 edi-

highlights the preeminence of the Roman Missal and its gradual, ongoing development through history. SP 6, with a citation from John Paul II, affirms again papal responsibility and authority regarding the ongoing updating of liturgical books, even to the point of authorizing a "general reform." In *God and the World*, Cardinal Ratzinger described it as Rome's historic task to keep watch over liturgical developments and cut back any overgrowth, or to "see where it is necessary and possible to supplement or to prune back in a way that is meaningful."[43] Pruning is certainly a form of amending and seems to describe well what Pius V (or the commission that handled the work) did, cutting back on such elements as feast days, sequences, octaves, and votive masses.[44]

What is not brought out here is that the organic form of liturgical development that Ratzinger saw as the natural and proper method (which he contrasted with liturgical change fabricated by "experts"—his description of what happened after Vatican II) began to come to an end in the post-Tridentine era, in particular with the institution of the Congregation of Rites by Pope Sixtus V in 1588. The guiding principles for the congregation's work vis-à-vis the new liturgical books produced after Trent were uniformity and invariability: everyone everywhere using basically the same unchanging liturgical books—that is, everyone everywhere who came, by mandate or choice, under the provisions of Pius V's *Quo Primum*, using books that did not change except periodically at the mandate of the reigning pope.[45] By implementing these principles, and being

tion, the first printed edition of the Roman Missal; Ratzinger, *The Feast of Faith*, 85.

43 Ratzinger, *God and the World*, 413, 414–15

44 Theodor Klauser, *A Short History of the Western Liturgy: An Account and Some Reflections* (London: Oxford University Press, 1969), 124–29. One of the guiding principles of the reform, according to Klauser, "was that the early centuries were the golden age of liturgical development, and that all that came afterwards was a rank undergrowth which could and should be cut down" (128)—that is to say, pruned back. See also Jungmann, *The Mass of the Roman Rite*, I.135–37; Cabié, *The Eucharist*, 175–76.

45 Michael Kunzler, *Die 'Tridentinishce' Messe: Aufbruch oder Rückschritt?* (Paderborn: Bonifatius, 2008), 110, names the two principles as "Einheitlichkeit" (uniformity) and "Unveränderlichkeit" (invariability). Keith F. Pecklers stated the Congregation's "primary function" was to foster "liturgical unification"

unable to authorize changes in the liturgy, the Congregation, as Jungmann said, "was not to be an organ for liturgical evolution."[46] Indeed, to the contrary, it was the administrative mechanism that in effect ended, or at least seriously circumscribed, the natural processes of organic growth that had characterized the church's liturgical life up to that point.[47] Organic development takes place (even when "outside" influences are involved) from the ground up—in ecclesiastical language, that is to say, in particular churches, local dioceses and parishes, and monasteries. Before the sixteenth century this was how liturgical development occurred; but from that point on, liturgy was increasingly and over time more widely regulated by the Congregation of Sacred Rites, whose goal was, again, uniformity and invariability. There were occasional subsequent revisions to the Missal, instances of which are mentioned by Benedict in SP 6, but these revisions came by papal mandate. In chapter 7 we will consider further the implications of this important develop-

---

throughout the West and see that the Roman rubrics were "faithfully observed"; Pecklers, "History of the Roman Liturgy from the Sixteenth until the Twentieth Centuries," 160. Due to these factors, in Jungmann's view, the natural forces by which the liturgy would have grown and developed organically were now diverted and instead "channeled into the narrow bed of a very inadequate devotional life"; idem, *The Mass of the Roman Rite*, I.141. The same basic point, though without the negative assessment, is made by Edmund Bishop in his famous essay, "Genius of the Roman Rite"; see idem, *Liturgia Historica: Papers on the Liturgy and Religious Life of the Western Church* (Oxford: Oxford University Press, 1918), 18.

[46] Jungmann, *The Mass of the Roman Rite*, I.139.

[47] Organic development, however, needs to incorporate the phenomenon—also seen in nature—of sudden and significant growth and change in form. As Aidan Kavanagh well noted, "history proceeds by fits and starts: Long periods of quiescence and status quo are followed by short, intense, and often frenzied periods of evolutionary progress or regress"; see his "Reflections on the Study from the Viewpoint of Liturgical History," in *The Awakening Church: 25 Years of Liturgical Renewal*, ed. Lawrence J. Madden (Collegeville, MN: Liturgical Press, 1992), 84. Examples of relatively short or quick periods of notable change could include the introduction of Roman liturgical influence into Carolingian realms within a generation either side of Charlemagne, the introduction of Romano-Germanic liturgical books into Rome in the tenth and eleventh centuries, and of course the liturgical changes effected in the single decade following the liturgy constitution of Vatican II.

ment, which have a bearing on the process of mutual influence by which, as Pope Benedict has indicated, the FO and FE are jointly to be reshaped into the future form(s) of the Roman Rite.

Finally, the reference to "a more general reform" (*ampliorem . . . redintegrationem*, SP 6) is important. It points to a unique, historically unprecedented feature of liturgical reform in the twentieth century—namely, the notion of a general reform of the whole liturgy of the church, to be adopted throughout the church. No prior ecumenical council or pope undertook such a thing. Even Pius V's *Quo Primum*, however wide its reach, did not in principle extend or even seek to extend to everyone—although it did manifest a universalizing papal authority, in that Pius's reformed Missal was, by his determination, made mandatory for everyone everywhere except under circumstances of his determination (prior and continuous use of an approved form of liturgy for at least 200 years). Pius X at the beginning of the twentieth century thought in still broader, more expansive terms when he considered undertaking a wide-ranging reform of the Breviary with all the attendant implications (such as reform of the calendar)—a process he expected would take "considerable work and time."[48] The liturgical commission established by Pius XII in 1946 specifically addressed itself to the task of a general reform of the liturgy.[49] John XXIII made reference to

[48] Pius X, *Abhinc Duos Annos* (1913), in *Papal Teachings: The Liturgy*, 226–27. John Paul II makes the same observation regarding Pius X; see *Vicesimus Quintus Annus* 3. On the USCCB web site, the essay on "The Theological Vision of *Sacrosanctum Concilium* and the Roman Missal" recalled that "the twentieth century opened with the establishment of a special Commission for a general reform of the liturgy by Pope Saint Pius X. Among the areas to which special attention was to be given by this Pontifical Commission were liturgical music, the Calendar, the celebration of Sunday, the reform of the Roman Breviary and changes in Eucharistic discipline." Available at http://www.usccb.org/romanmissal/resources-reflections.shtml. See also Bishop Paul Joseph Schmitt (of Metz), "A Propos du Missel de Saint Pie V," *Notitiae* 16, no. 3, issue 164 (March 1980): 110–15, at 111.

[49] See Nicola Giampietro, *The Development of the Liturgical Reform: As Seen by Cardinal Ferdinando Antonelli from 1948 to 1970* (Fort Collins, CO: Roman Catholic Books, 2009; Italian original, 1998), chap. 3, "Preparatory Studies and Partial Attempts at a General Reform of the Liturgy under Pius XII" (15–33). Also, Alcuin Reid, *The Organic Development of the Liturgy*, chap. 3, "The

this, in his *motu proprio* updating the rubrics in 1960, as something decided upon and to be undertaken by the upcoming ecumenical council.[50] And Vatican II explicitly authorized and set forth both general principles and specific directives for "a general restoration of the liturgy itself" (SC 21).[51] When assessing the liturgical constitution of the council, the postconciliar development of a new library of liturgical books, and specifically the Missal of Paul VI, and comparing this work with prior instances of liturgical reform, it is critical to keep in mind this pivotal and unprecedented concept of a general renewal of the church's liturgy undertaken at the mandate of an ecumenical council and authorized by the reigning pope—a general renewal that explicitly embraced a reform of the rite of the Mass (SC 47–58).[52]

Liturgical Movement and Liturgical Reform from 1948 to the Second Vatican Council" (145–301; see esp. 150–64).

[50] John XXIII, *Rubricarum Instructum*, in *Papal Teachings: The Liturgy*, 565–58, at 565; also in *The Introductory Matters of the Roman Missal of 1962*, ed. Christopher R. J. Rudder (Columbus, OH, 2009), 10–12, at 10.

[51] *Ipsius Liturgiae generalem instaurationem*. In some passages the liturgy constitution spoke in ways clearly mandating change: for example, "These [that is, elements of the liturgy that are 'subject to change'] not only may be changed but ought to be changed [*variare possunt vel etiam debent*, 'can or even should change'] with the passage of time if they have suffered from the intrusion of anything out of harmony with the inner nature of the liturgy or have become unsuited to it" (SC 21). In other passages, the impulse for change is clearly given limits: for example, "Finally, there must be no innovations unless the good of the Church genuinely and certainly requires them" (SC 23). The question of how to honor and balance both principles continues to exercise the church's theological thinking, pastoral discernment, and magisterial teaching.

[52] On the extent of the reform as unprecedented, see Benedict XVI's reference to the Second Vatican Council as "an event which launched the most extensive renewal of the Roman Rite ever known"; "Video Message of His Holiness Pope Benedict XVI for the Closing of the Fiftieth International Eucharistic Congress in Dublin." On how far that renewal went there is disagreement. For example, P. Johannes Nebel says what was unprecedented at Vatican II was that, at the behest of church authority, not only were there ritual revisions, but "the basic shape of the Rite itself underwent a revision" (*die Grundordnung des Ritus selbst einer Revision unterzogen*); Nebel, "Die 'ordentliche' and die 'außerordentliche' Form des römischen Messritus: Versuch einer Orientierungshilfe zum tieferen Verstehen beider Formen," *Forum Katholische Theologie* 25, no. 3

This factor should also inform our reading of SP, reminding us, for example, of the nearly unanimous mind of the bishops at the council (the final vote approving the liturgy constitution was 2,147 in favor and only four opposed) and of the pope, that the church's liturgy, including the Mass, as it existed at the time of the council, was in need of reform. The 1962 edition of the Missal was not meant, even by John XXIII who authorized it, to remain as it was. So also Pope Benedict did not mean to bring back that 1962 Missal as is, or for its own sake. He brought it back to do a work and to be a living and thus a changing, developing part of the church's life. Among its multiple purposes, reviewed in chapter 3, one worth particular mention in this regard is its intended role of influencing and being influenced by the ordinary form through a process of mutual enrichment, and thereby contributing in what Benedict considered a helpful, needed, and organic way to the future development of the liturgy—and to what can been seen as a new liturgical movement.

SP 7–8

SP 7

> *In more recent times, however, the Second Vatican Council expressed the desire that due respect and reverence for divine worship be renewed again and adapted to the needs of our age. Moved by this desire, our predecessor the Supreme Pontiff Paul VI approved in the year 1970 for the Latin Church liturgical books reformed [or: restored] and partly made new. These books, translated into many vernacular languages throughout the world, were gladly received by the bishops, and by the priests and faithful. John Paul II gave recognition to the third typical edition of the Roman Missal. This is how the Roman Pontiffs have acted, so that "this liturgical edifice, so to speak . . ." should appear "again, resplendent with dignity and proportion."*[53]

(2009): 173–203, at 184. Michael Kunzler, however, says a close examination of the double "use" of the Roman Rite shows a difference not in its basic structure (*Grundstruktur*) but in the manner of its celebration (*in der Weise seiner Feier*); Kunzler, *Die 'Tridentinische' Messe*, 106.

[53] Pope St. Pius X, Apostolic Letter motu proprio datae *Abhinc Duos Annos* (October 23, 1913): *Acta Apostolicae Sedis* 5 (1913), 449–50; cf. John Paul II,

> *In certain regions, however, some of the faithful—by no means few—adhered and continue to adhere to the prior liturgical forms, which so profoundly imbued their culture and spirit; for this reason the Supreme Pontiff John Paul II, moved with pastoral concern for these faithful, granted the faculty in 1984, in a special indult prepared by the Congregation for Divine Worship, "Quattuor Abhinc Annos," to use the Roman Missal edited by Blessed John XXIII in the year 1962. Further, in the year 1988 John Paul II once again, in his apostolic letter "Ecclesia Dei" given* motu proprio, *urged the bishops to make a wide and generous use of this faculty in favor of all the faithful who sought it.*

In these two paragraphs Pope Benedict described, first, the authorization, development, implementation, and wide acceptance of the liturgical reforms of Vatican II, and then the continued adherence of some Catholics to the liturgy as celebrated before the council. Such Catholics, he noted, were "profoundly imbued" by that liturgy; this observation correlates with his comment in CGF 4, that some remained strongly attached to the prior liturgy, typically those from regions where the educational influence of the liturgical movement had been significant and had cultivated in them an appreciation for the liturgy as then celebrated. Care for these Catholics prompted John Paul II to make provision, fourteen years after the reformed liturgy was promulgated, for their renewed access to the prior liturgy—at the discretion of the local bishop, and under various restrictions. After Archbishop Lefebvre's unauthorized ordination of four bishops for the Society of St. Pius X in 1988, and his and their consequent excommunication, John Paul was faced with an incipient schism. Part of his response—to open the pathway for the return of members of the SSPX, to show a pastoral goodwill and respect for their religious sensibilities (while critiquing their theological objections to the teaching of the council), to prevent further defections to the SSPX, and to provide pastoral care for Catholics who simply still desired to worship God using the prior liturgical forms—was to urge Catholic bishops to be yet more

---

Apostolic Letter *Vicesimus Quintus Annus* (December 4, 1988) 3: *Acta Apostolicae Sedis* 81 (1989), 899. [Note in original.—Trans.]

generous in making use of the 1984 indult by granting permissions for groups seeking to celebrate the old Mass.

Cardinal Ratzinger later expressed himself unable to understand why his fellow bishops chose not to do what the pope asked, submitting instead to what he called "this rule of intolerance" toward Catholics drawn to the traditional Mass.[54] He saw the bishops' inaction, their continued choice not to make "wide and generous" use of the faculty given them to allow celebrations according to the prior Missal, as a kind of resistance or even opposition to fostering a much-needed reconciliation in the church. We can see SP as his response to such resistance, in one sense acting on the principle of subsidiarity. In this perspective, Benedict in SP provided from the papal level the "help" (*subsidium*) he deemed needed at the episcopal level so that the appropriate pastoral decision would be enacted, namely, permission for those desiring it to worship using the prior liturgical forms. This action certainly raises questions regarding the relationship between primacy and episcopacy and regarding how to balance, and who discerns what best constitutes, care for the universal church together with care for each particular church (diocese). However those questions of theology and governance may be answered, it remains a fact that Pope Benedict made the judgment that giving the *usus antiquior* a more prominent and legally established, though still clearly secondary, place in the life of the church would best serve the overall good of the church—and so he crafted SP accordingly.

SP 9

> *Having now for a long time pondered the pressing requests of those members of the faithful to our predecessor John Paul II, having listened also to the Father cardinals gathered by us in the consistory of March 23, 2006, having pondered all these matters fully, having invoked the Holy Spirit and relying on the help of God, with these apostolic letters* WE DECREE *the following.*

Pope Benedict tells us here he did all he could to make a sound decision. He listened to those making the requests and to the cardinals gathered in consistory. He gave the matter patient and serious

[54] Ratzinger, *God and the World*, 416.

thought, fully weighing all the relevant factors.[55] He called upon the Holy Spirit and relied on the help of God. This impressive description of his decision-making process can be read as his reassurance that he fulfilled his responsibility to the best of his ability, did his homework, exercised due diligence, and drew upon every possible resource, human and divine. It is also a strong invitation to his readers, an exercise in moral suasion, encouraging them to accept, support, and be at peace with this exercise of papal authority, it being thus well grounded.[56]

SP, ARTICLE 1

> *The Roman Missal promulgated by Paul V is the ordinary expression of the "lex orandi" of the Catholic Church of the Latin rite. The Roman Missal promulgated by Saint Pius V and reedited by Blessed John XXIII is to be regarded as the extraordinary expression of the same "lex orandi" of the church and is to enjoy due honor on account of its venerable and*

[55] The phrase used here (*omnibus mature perpensis*) is not uncommon in official documents rendering a decision; see its use, for example, by Paul VI, DOL 87 at no. 641, or by the Sacred Congregation for Divine Worship, DOL 248 at no. 1979, or by John XXIII in his 1960 apostolic letter *Rubricarum Instructum*; Pius V in *Quo Primum* expressed the same idea in different words (*mature adhibita consideratione*). All the same, we should have no hesitation in taking Benedict's words at face value, meaning just what they say.

[56] Pope Benedict's clear yet relatively gentle moral suasion can be contrasted with the style of Pope Pius X. Just two weeks after issuing his *motu proprio* on sacred music, *Tra le Sollecitudini* (November 22, 1903), Pius sent the vicar for spiritual affairs in the Diocese of Rome a letter detailing his expectations regarding implementation of the recent document. "All of you, We feel sure," he wrote, with reference to the clergy of Rome, "will second Us in the desired work of such restoration [of sacred music in the liturgy], not only with that blind submission which is always laudable, provided that it brings us to accept out of pure obedience orders that are painful and against our way of thinking, but also with that inner conviction that we should so act for reasons maturely considered, clear, evident and irrefutable." See "Letter *Il desiderio*, December 8, 1903, to Cardinal Respighi," in *Papal Teachings: The Liturgy*, 188 (at no. 249). Recognizing how significant and unpopular was the change he was mandating, Pius X later added, "As for you, my Lord Cardinal, do not be indulgent, do not grant delay. By postponing the matter, the difficulty will not lessen, but it will increase; as the cut must be made, let it be made immediately with firm resolution" (192, at no. 252).

ancient usage. These two expressions of the "lex orandi" of the church by no means introduce a division in the "lex credendi" of the church, for they are two uses of the one Roman rite.

Accordingly, it is permitted to celebrate the sacrifice of the Mass according to the typical edition promulgated by Blessed John XXIII in 1962 and never abrogated, as the extraordinary form of the liturgy of the church. The stipulations for use of this Missal established by the prior documents "Quattuor Abhinc Annos" and "Ecclesia Dei" are replaced as follows.

SP establishes "two uses of the one Roman rite" of the Catholic Church. It establishes the Roman Missal as promulgated by Paul VI and revised by John Paul II as "the ordinary expression of the 'lex orandi' of the Latin rite of the Catholic Church" (SP, art. 1). It establishes the Roman Missal in the form published by Blessed John XXIII in 1962, and under the conditions both permissive and restrictive set forth in articles 1 to 6 of SP, as once again a constitutive part of the liturgical life of the Catholic Church, as the "extraordinary expression" of the "'lex orandi' of the church," or the "extraordinary form of the church's liturgy" (SP, art. 1).

Regarding the word *extraordinary*, canonist Norbert Lüdecke judges that the pope's use of it in SP does not clearly match the usual canonical meanings of the term and concludes that "the *extraordinary character* of the celebration of Mass according to the old Missal is therefore *not* a *legal* one" entailing rarity, but is better interpreted as "a purely *factual* one and as such may be revised by increased usage."[57] Both Alcuin Reid and László Dobszay also think the pope's terminology is more statistical than canonical.[58] Canonist John Huels notes that in canon law the term extraordinary

[57] Norbert Lüdecke, "Canonical Remarks on the Motu Proprio *Summorum Pontificum*," *Antiphon* 13, no. 3 (2009): 193–227, at 219.

[58] Reid thinks the pope is designating the one form as "'ordinary' in the sense of being more frequently used and the other [as] 'extraordinary' in that its celebration is not so frequent"; Alcuin Reid, "The Liturgical Reform of Pope Benedict XVI," in *Benedict XVI and the Sacred Liturgy: Proceedings of the First Fota International Liturgy Conference, 2008*, ed. Neil J. Roy and Janet E. Rutherford (Dublin: Four Courts Press, 2010), 156–80, at 178. Dobszay thinks the term *extraordinary* reflects the fact that, in comparison with the *Novus Ordo*, the celebration of the traditional Mass is now and "will be, even after the general permission, so rare that it is nearly negligible"; László Dobszay, *The Restoration*

has different uses, identifies two he finds irrelevant to the interpretation of SP, then points to one he finds more pertinent. Canon 345 deals with synods of bishops and describes an extraordinary synod of bishops as, in Huels's words, "an additional form of synod subordinate to the ordinary form," just as the FE is "an additional usage of the Roman Rite . . . not on the same level as the ordinary form."[59] Huels's interpretation, in my judgment, illustrates more accurately than Lüdecke's the intentions of Pope Benedict in SP regarding the relationship of the two usages.

Pope Benedict explicitly addressed *both* the legal and factual dimensions of the reformed liturgy when he stated that "the new Missal [of Paul VI] will certainly remain the ordinary form of the Roman Rite, not only because of the juridical norms, but also because of the actual situation in which the communities of the faithful find themselves" (CGF 6). Lüdecke finds this statement "difficult to comprehend canonically with regard to the legal situation."[60] I hesitate to differ with a canonist on a matter of this nature but will venture an interpretation of the pope's statement.

It seems to me Pope Benedict affirms here the continuing validity of existing "juridical norms"—meaning by this the church's current liturgical legislation regarding the liturgy as revised after the Second Vatican Council. He voiced the same sentiment before becoming pope, at the 2001 conference in Fontgombault, when he said, "It seems clear to me that, in law, the Missal of Paul VI is the Missal in current use, and that using it is normal."[61] SP does noth-

---

and Organic Development of the Roman Rite (London: T&T Clark International, 2010), 61.

[59] John Huels, "Reconciling the Old with the New: Canonical Questions on *Summorum Pontificum*," *The Jurist* 68 (2008): 92–113, at 94. The judgment that the FE is "not on the same level" as the FO is disputed, for example by David G. Bonagura, Jr., who asserts that SP establishes "full parity" between the 1962 and 1970 Missals; see Bonagura, Jr., "The Future of the Roman Rite: Reading Benedict in the Light of Ratzinger," *Antiphon* 13, no. 3 (2009): 228–46, at 228. See also Lüdecke's contention, in "Canonical Remarks," that "there are no longer any limitations" (220) on the 1962 Missal.

[60] Lüdecke, "Canonical Remarks," 219.

[61] Ratzinger, "Assessment and Future Prospects," in *Looking Again*, 149. See also Benedict XVI's comments on his airline flight to France (September 12,

ing to change or lessen the juridical standing of the Missal of Paul VI as the normative Missal of the Roman Rite, to be used (as before, so now, and into the future) by Roman Rite Catholics as a matter of course, as the normal Roman Catholic ritual of the Mass; indeed, this is precisely what Pope Benedict means and intends to affirm, in explicitly designating the Missal of Paul VI the ordinary form of the Roman rite (SP, art. 1). What SP does beyond this is to enact additional new juridical provisions that establish and recognize the standing of the 1962 Missal promulgated by Blessed John XXIII as fully legal, though not the norm, but rather *extra* or outside the norm; it is permitted for use more widely than before SP, but not on a fully equal basis with the ordinary form, and still under certain conditions or within restrictions set forth in SP (noting also, however, that SP, art. 2, indicates those conditions under which there are no restrictions in use of the 1962 Missal).[62]

To understand the pope's statement about the "actual situation" of local communities one must take note of the immediately preceding sentence in CGF 6, which refers to the fact that the liturgical formation and the knowledge of Latin presupposed and prerequisite for celebrating the FE with conscious and active participation are not often present. Given that this is the "actual situation," the pope then drew the conclusion that, as a result, not many (in terms of the church's full membership of more than one billion) celebrate

2008), in response to a question regarding SP: "[I]t is clear that the renewed liturgy [and not the Missal of 1962] is the ordinary liturgy of our time."

[62] Sánchez-Gil draws the same conclusions, and speaks clearly of the Missal of Paul VI remaining "the ordinary—and, consequently, the prevailing—expression of the Roman Rite," while the Missal of Pius V/John XXIII is "the extraordinary—and, consequently, the subsidiary—expression of the same Roman Rite, which it is possible to use following the provisions set forth in the Motu Proprio." Antonio S. Sánchez-Gil, "Gli innovativi profili canonici del motu proprio *Summorum Pontificum* sull'uso della liturgia romana anteriore alla riforma del 1970," *Ius Ecclesiae* 19 (2007): 689–708, at 705 and 706, respectively ("l'espressione ordinaria—e, di conseguenza, prevalente—del Rito romano . . . l'espressione straordinaria—e, di conseguenza, sussidiaria—dello stesso Rito romano, che è possibile usare seguendo le condizioni stabilite nel Motu proprio").

or will celebrate using the old Mass.[63] On this score Lüdecke's comment seems apt: that this is the pope's "personal prognosis."[64]

Even if significant numbers began to participate in celebrations of the traditional Mass, however, it would remain the "extraordinary form." Its legal status—here I venture to differ with Lüdecke, and also Reid and Dobszay—is not dependent on or a reflection of statistics, as though, given time, if more people came to celebrate the FE customarily, it would no longer be the "extraordinary" form. On the contrary, the terminology of SP is not demographically descriptive, it is legislatively prescriptive. In this document Pope Benedict created legal categories that indicate with care and precision the relationship being established between the two usages—a relationship founded on principle and meant to endure, not merely reflective of circumstances and subject to change.

The FE, then, is given a new legal status, but not equal status with the FO, in the liturgical life of the church. SP allows a new measure of freedom in use of the 1962 Missal (as compared with the situation prior to SP) but does not establish the full parity of the two forms of the Roman Rite. This point will become clearer as we proceed and note restrictions upon use of the traditional liturgy. The previous restrictions, as set forth in QAA and continued in ED, were greater, but under the provisions of SP (which replace those in QAA and ED), restrictions, though lesser, continue.

In SP, article 1, Pope Benedict states that the 1962 Missal was "never abrogated," clarifying his meaning somewhat in CGF 4, saying there that it "was not ever juridically abrogated." These words have perplexed both canonists and liturgists. Lüdecke describes them as "canonically surprising," and Huels comments that "Pope Benedict must have something unique in mind" as he is not employing "the technical meaning of the term 'abrogated' in canon law"; this view is shared by Glendinning, who agrees that "it seems

[63] He made the same point during the interview on the airline flight to France in 2008 ("They form a small group"), and in Benedict XVI, *Light of the World: The Pope, the Church, and the Signs of the Times, A Conversation with Peter Seewald* (San Francisco: Ignatius Press, 2010), 106 ("the small group of people who use the old missal").

[64] Lüdecke, "Canonical Remarks," 219.

sensible to conclude that Benedict XVI is employing canonical terminology in a unique and non-technical fashion."[65] Rehak concludes his extensive review of the issue by saying, "In any case, a completely convincing canonical basis for the Pope's assertion regarding the lack of a legal abrogation [of the prior Missal] is not obvious."[66] Liturgists have voiced analogous questions and concerns from their perspectives.[67] Underlying these concerns is the

[65] Lüdecke, "Canonical Remarks," 201; Huels, "Reconciling the Old with the New," 95; Chad Glendinning, "Was the 1962 *Missale Romanum* Abrogated? A Canonical Analysis in Light of *Summorum Pontificum*," *Worship* 85, no. 1 (January 2011): 15–37, at 34–35. Winfried Haunerland, "Ein Ritus in zwei Ausdrucksformen?" *Liturgisch Jahrbuch* 58 (2008): 179–203, at 187, says Pope Benedict's affirmations cannot be explained by current rules of canonical interpretation.

[66] Martin Rehak, *Die außerordentliche Gebrauch der alten Form des römischen Ritus: kirchenrechtlichen Skizzen zum Motu Proprio* Summorum Pontificum *vom 07.07.2007* (St. Ottilien: EOS-Verlag, 2009), 55 ("Jedenfalls ist eine kanonistisch völlig überzeugende Begründung für die These des Papstes vom Fehlen einer rechtlichen Abrogation nicht ersichtlich"); see 36–55 for his treatment of the issue. Glendinning offers a careful summary of the situation, first by recalling "a general norm of law[,] which states that a later law abrogates or derogates from an earlier law if it states so expressly, is directly contrary to it, or completely reorders the entire matter of the earlier law (c. 20)." While some appeal to the first of these conditions and maintain that Paul VI's 1969 apostolic constitution *Missale Romanum* expressly abrogates the prior Missal, Glendinning here appeals more to the third condition: "With the promulgation of the revised *Ordo Missae* and *GIRM*, [thereupon] the *Rubricae Generales*, the *Ritus Servandus in Celebratione Missae*, and the *Defectibus in Celebratione Missae* of the 1962 *Missale Romanum* were explicitly abrogated." Chad J. Glendinning, "Adopting Pre-Conciliar Liturgical Practices in the Celebration of the Ordinary Form of the Mass," *Roman Replies and CLSA Advisory Opinions 2009*, ed. Sharon A. Ewart and Siobhan M. Verbeek (Washington, DC: Canon Law Society of America, 2009): 61–67, at 64.

[67] John F. Baldovin, "Reflections on *Summorum Pontificum*," *Worship* 83, no. 2 (March 2009): 98–112, at 105; Nathan D. Mitchell, "The Amen Corner: '*Summorum Pontificum*,'" *Worship* 81, no. 6 (November 2007): 549–65, at 557–58; Andrea Grillo, "Paolo VI, Pio V e la realtà virtuale: a proposito del Motu Proprio 'Summorum Pontificum,'" at www.statusecclesiae.net; Cesare Giraudo, "La Liturgia nel Solco della tradizione: Riflessioni in margine al *motu proprio* 'Summorum Pontificum,'" *Rivista Liturgica* 95, no. 2 (2008): 253–72, at 254, note 1. Others are cited in Antonio Finocchiaro, "Problematiche aperte nel *Web* sul

considerable body of documentation from the 1960s and later, from Pope Paul VI and various curial offices and officials, which clearly indicates that the reformed liturgical books replaced the prior books, which were then forbidden.[68]

Cardinal Ratzinger clearly knew this, and noted in his memoirs that he had been "dismayed by the prohibition of the old missal," on the grounds that it was unprecedented and that it "introduced

Motu Proprio *Summorum Pontificum*: Posizioni e valutazioni," *Rivista Liturgica* 94, no. 6 (2007): 947–75, at 956–60 (see also 961–63). Even Aidan Nichols, four years before SP, spoke as a matter of course of "the rite abrogated by Paul VI"; see his "Salutary Dissatisfaction: An English View of 'Reforming the Reform,'" in Thomas M. Kocik, *The Reform of the Reform? A Liturgical Debate: Reform or Return* (San Francisco: Ignatius Press, 2003), 195–210, at 210.

[68] See, for example, DOL 59 at no. 555, DOL 61 at no. 569, DOL 202, at no. 1366, DOL 209 at no. 1739, DOL 211 at no. 1758, DOL 216 at no. 1771, DOL 219 at no. 1784, and DOL 220 at no. 1786, a letter from Cardinal Villot, Vatican Secretary of State, to Bishop Coffy, president of the liturgical commission of France, in which Villot explicitly names *Quo Primum* as being no longer in force, after Pope Paul's *Missale Romanum* of 1969. See also Finocchiaro, "Problematiche," 961–63 and 966–69, and Rehak, *Der außerordentliche Gebrauch*, 40–41. At the same time one must always keep in mind the exceptions that were granted. In 1969 the SCDW Instruction *Constitutione Apostolica* gave a limited permission for continued use of the Missal in its 1967 form—that is, the 1962 Missal with the changes instituted in the Decrees of the Sacred Congregation of Rites, *Nuper Edita Instructione* of 1965 (DOL 196 at no. 1340), and *Per Instructionem Alteram* of 1967 (DOL 201 at no. 1356). The limited permission for continued use of the 1967 form of the Missal was specifically for "elderly priests who celebrate Mass without a congregation and who might encounter serious difficulty in taking up the new Order of Mass and the new texts of the Roman Missal and *Lectionary for Mass.*" Such priests "may, with the consent of their Ordinary, keep to the rites and texts now in use [in 1969]" (DOL 209 at no. 1751). In the case of priests who were "infirm, ill, or otherwise disabled," bishops could submit the matter to the SCDW (DOL 209 at no. 1752); see also the SCDW's 1971 *Instructione de Constitutione* (DOL 216 at no. 1772). There was also the indult for England and Wales, allowing occasional celebrations of Mass in its 1967 form for specific groups (see Bugnini, *The Reform of the Liturgy*, 297–98). None of the few exceptions given in this era granted permission to use the Missal in its 1962 form; that remained prohibited, without exception.

a breach into the history of the liturgy."[69] But we also know that at least as of 1986 he was of the considered opinion that the 1962 Missal had not been suppressed and was not abrogated. The "Commission of Cardinals" that met on December 12 of that year, of which Ratzinger was a member, is reported to have "come to the conclusion that this liturgy had never been abolished."[70] In an interview in 2008, the then-president of the Pontifical Commission *Ecclesia Dei*, Cardinal Castrillón Hoyos, presented portions of a report of the commission's recommendations to John Paul II for increasing the effectiveness of the 1984 indult *Quattuor Abhinc Annos*, which had permitted limited use of the 1962 Missal; the recommendations proposed a wider permission for use of that missal.[71] Though there is little in the report explaining the reasoning behind the commission's finding that the prior missal was not suppressed, there is one paragraph of interest in understanding why Pope Benedict could declare the 1962 Missal not juridically abrogated.

The paragraph begins: "Referring to the desires previously expressed, it is reaffirmed that it ought to be shown that there is a clear logical line of development between the documents of the Church and the free choice of the two Missals for the celebration of Holy Mass"—a position (the free choice of the two Missals) difficult to understand, in view of the documents and statements from that era, by pope and Vatican offices and officials, which speak consistently and unambiguously of the prior Missal being forbidden. But then comes this point: "and it is proposed that we show they [the Missals of 1962 and 1970] are not to be considered other than as a

[69] Ratzinger, *Milestones*, 146 ("prohibition") and 148 ("breach"); see also *Salt of the Earth*, 176 ("strictly forbidden").

[70] Gordon Read, "Motu Proprio Summorum Pontificum," *Newsletter: Canon Law Society of Great Britain and Ireland*, no. 151 (November 2007): 9–21, at 9. Veltri reports the decision was unanimous; see John Veltri, "Traditional Mass Never Forbidden," available at www.cfnews.org/tridmass.htm, reporting on an account given by Cardinal Alfons Stickler. See also Finocchiaro, "Problematiche," 954–55, and Nicola Bux, *Benedict XVI's Reform: The Liturgy between Innovation and Tradition* (San Francisco: Ignatius Press, 2012), 103.

[71] Various recommendations made by this meeting of eight cardinals can be found at http://www.newliturgicalmovement.org/2008/10/response-of-cardinal-president-of.html. For the Italian, see http://www.clerus.org/clerus/dati/2008-10/24-20/castrillon_rispost.html.

development of the one from the other, since liturgical norms, not being true or proper 'laws' cannot be abrogated, but 'surrogated': the earlier into the later."[72] This is a matter for canonical commentary, for which I am not technically trained; but regardless the commentary, this report informs us of a canonical view to which Cardinal Ratzinger along with the other cardinals apparently subscribed, and it is a view on the basis of which Pope Benedict could state that the preconciliar Missal "was not ever juridically abrogated" (CGF 4).[73]

Whatever may be the full significance of determining whether Paul VI in fact juridically abrogated the 1962 Missal, our immediate interest lies in exploring the consequences of Pope Benedict's affirmation that this missal was not abrogated. Let us consider two consequences. First, this affirmation by Pope Benedict in effect posited or at least suggested a certain measure of canonical legitimacy vis-à-vis the eucharistic celebrations conducted over the years within the Society of Saint Pius X; it was also a critical element in opening the way to substantive theological dialogue with the Society. Such dialogue is essential if there is to be any formal reconciliation between the pope and the Society, healing the schism. The Society was not willing to engage in this dialogue until the last pre–Vatican II edition of the Missal was declared (as they maintain) never to have been abrogated and also made more freely available in the church. On this point, one of Pope Benedict's purposes in issuing SP was fulfilled, for theological dialogue between the Vatican and the SSPX began in October 2009.

A second consequence of Pope Benedict's declaration that the 1962 Missal was never abrogated pertains to his judgment that Pope Paul VI's prohibition of the use of that Missal created a breach

[72] From "Response of the Cardinal President"; the paragraph comes at the end of the Castrillón Hoyos interview. See also Rehak, *Die außerordentliche Gebrauch*, 46, who cites the same passage. Consider here John Huels's comments on subrogation: "A new law adds something to an old law or norm such that the old law or norm is now incomplete and cannot stand on its own as the *ius vigens* on the matter; this is 'subrogation,' a derogation by the addition of new material." See *New Commentary on the Code of Canon Law*, ed. John P. Beal, James A. Coriden, and Thomas J. Green (New York: Paulist Press, 2000), 82.

[73] Rehak makes the same observation (*Die außerordentliche Gebrauch*, 54).

in the church's liturgical life—a gap in its otherwise unbroken tradition (SP 2). Pope Benedict in a way was asserting that what he saw as the recent (by Paul VI) *de facto* breach in liturgical history was at least not strictly speaking a *de iure* breach. He grounded this claim on the affirmation that the Missal, not being "juridically abrogated," was thus, "as a matter of principle . . . always permitted" (CGF 4). In this way he opened the door to affirming that the continuity of liturgical history remained unbroken, at least in a certain technical, juridical sense; it could also serve for him as grounds for his affirmation that there is "no rupture" in the history of the liturgy and "no contradiction between the one and the other edition of the *Roman Missal*" (CGF 9).

SP, ARTICLES 2 AND 4

SP, Article 2

> *In Masses celebrated without the people, each Catholic priest of the Latin Rite, whether secular or religious, can use either the Roman Missal edited by Blessed John XXIII in 1962, or the Roman Missal promulgated by the Supreme Pontiff Paul VI in 1970, and on any day except the sacred Triduum. For such celebration, according to one or the other Missal, a priest needs no permission, either from the Apostolic See or from his ordinary.*

SP, Article 4

> *The faithful, moreover, who seek it on their own initiative can be admitted to celebrations of holy Mass described above in Art. 2, all relevant laws being observed.*

Article 2 declares that Latin Rite priests are able to use either Missal (except during the Triduum) when they celebrate Mass without the people (*sine populo*).[74] Further, this article states that

[74] Huels identifies a Mass without the people as "a so-called 'private Mass,' one not announced or open to the public at large. Some faithful may participate in such a Mass, provided it does not lose its private character," that is, "it is not a public celebration of the liturgy that is publicized and open to all"; Huels, "Reconciling the Old with the New," 96. According to Lüdecke, "Canonical Remarks," a Mass without the people refers to one "in which, other than the celebrant, only the server or another member of the faithful (actually)

in such cases the priest "needs no permission" (*nulla eget licentia*), either papal or episcopal; neither of the persons, that is, who has pastoral and juridical authority over a priest (the priest's own ordinary, and the supreme pontiff, whose jurisdiction over all Catholics is immediate), have, according to Benedict, anything to say about which Missal a priest uses in such cases. It is entirely at his discretion.

This statement could conceivably be interpreted as affirming, by implication, that such has actually been the case all along. Nicola Bux has made the argument that the council intended and decreed its reform of the Mass to apply, *not* to a priest's celebrations *sine populo*, but rather and solely to celebrations with the people.[75] This point is based on his reading of the text of *Sacrosanctum Concilium* 49: "For this reason the sacred Council *having in mind those Masses which are celebrated with the faithful assisting*, especially on Sundays and holydays of obligation, has made the following decrees so that the sacrifice of the Mass, even in the ritual forms (of its celebration) may have full pastoral efficacy."[76]

At the time of its promulgation the text was not interpreted in the way Bux reads it. Frederick McManus, for example, a consultor to the Consilium, addressed the point directly in his 1967 commentary

participates," 206, altering slightly the *Antiphon* translation, which reads ". . . (virtually) participates"; the original is: " . . . *(faktisch) teilnimmt*," in N. Lüdecke, "Kanonistische Anmerkungen zum Motu Proprio *Summorum Pontificum*," *Liturgische Jahrbuch* 58 (2008): 3–34, at 14. See also the helpful discussion in footnote 1 of Mary Schaefer and Joanne M. Pierce, "Mass at Which Only One Minister Participates," chap. 4, sec. 3, in *A Commentary on the General Instruction of the Roman Missal*, 310–24, at 310–11. See the GIRM (1970), nos. 209–31 for "Mass Without a Congregation," and the GIRM (2003), nos. 252–72, for "Mass at Which Only One Minister Participates." In the rubrics in place for the 1962 Missal, no. 269 states that since the Mass "is an act of public worship . . . the expression 'private Mass' is to be avoided"; see *The Introductory Matters of the Roman Missal of 1962*, ed. Christopher R. J. Ruder (Columbus, OH, 2009), 38; this is a reference to the 1958 instruction, *De Musica Sacra et Sacra Liturgia* 2.

[75] Bux, *Benedict XVI's Reform*, 98. See also Nicola Bux and S. Vitiello, "Was the Old Rite Abrogated?" *Mass of Ages* (February 2008), as available on the web site of The Latin Mass Society of England and Wales at http://www.lms.org.uk/resources/articles-on-the-mass/was_the_old_rite_abrogated.

[76] Flannery translation; emphasis added.

on the liturgy constitution. Considering the possible interpretation that SC 49 meant the reform of the Mass was to apply only to congregational celebrations (Bux's interpretation), McManus explained: "Not at all. The reform of the rite of Mass is applicable, in different ways according to different circumstances, to every celebration. The whole point of Article 49 in this connection is that the community celebration, with the actual participation of substantial numbers of the faithful, must be attended to first"; then, subsequently, "the needs of the faithful having been considered, all the different forms of celebration may be suitably revised."[77]

To address the question of whether priests have been permitted all along to celebrate Mass using the 1962 Missal, an examination of the documentation from the 1960s and 1970s is warranted; such an examination shows clearly, I believe, that this was not the understanding at the time. Consider first the formula used in Pope Paul VI's 1969 apostolic constitution *Missale Romanum*, promulgating a new edition of the Roman Missal: "We decree that these laws and prescriptions be firm and effective now and in the future, notwithstanding, to the extent necessary, the apostolic constitutions [Pius V's *Quo Primum* of 1570 was an apostolic constitution] and ordinances issued by our predecessors and other prescriptions, even those deserving particular mention and amendment."[78]

[77] Frederick R. McManus, *Sacramental Liturgy* (New York: Herder and Herder, 1967), 68. Jungmann, also a consultor to the Consilium, made a similar point in his 1967 commentary, "Constitution on the Sacred Liturgy," in *Commentary on the Documents of Vatican II*, ed. Herbert Vorgrimler (New York: Herder and Herder, 1967), 35. Jungmann further pointed out that article 49 calls for focus on Mass with a congregation by way of contrast with the reform under Pius V, which treated instead the priest's private Mass as the norm (ibid.). This same point is also made by Peter Hünerman in his "Theologischer Kommentar zur Konstitution über die heilige Liturgie *Sacrosanctum Concilium*"; see *Herders Theologischer Kommentar zum Zweiten Vatikanischen Konzil*, ed. Peter Hünerman and Bernd Jochen Hilberath, Band 2 (Freiburg im Breisgau: Herder, 2004), 123.

[78] Paul VI, *Missale Romanum* (DOL 202 at no. 1366). "We decree" in DOL translates *volumus*. *The Roman Missal* (2011) also translates, "We decree" (15). In Leo F. Stelten, *Dictionary of Ecclesiastical Latin* (Peabody, MA: Hendrickson Publishers, 1995), see the entry on "**vólo**, vélle, vólui: irreg.; will, wish, desire; determine, propose" (288, emphasis in original). The translation "decree" is in

Though some interpret Pope Paul's words as authorizing legitimacy of the Missal of Paul VI along with rather than in replacement of prior forms of the Missal, this was not the understanding of Paul himself or his administrative staff in the curia. In 1971 the SCDW issued a notification making it clear that the revised Roman Missal, the *editio typica* of which was formally promulgated in 1970,[79] was already permitted to be used in Latin, and that "from the date on which the translated texts [of the Missal, Lectionary, and Liturgy of the Hours] become obligatory for celebrations in the vernacular"—a date that was to be determined for itself by each episcopal conference, with confirmation by the Apostolic See[80]—"*only the revised form* of the Mass and the liturgy of the hours will be allowed, even for those who continue to use Latin."[81] A letter from the secretary of the SCDW to Bishop Sustar (then secretary of the Council of European Episcopal Conferences) explained that the "Missal of Pius V" was abrogated by Pope Paul VI's apostolic constitution *Missale Romanum*, as its final paragraph made clear.[82] A SCDW notification in 1974 stated that "when a conference of bishops decrees that the translation of the Roman Missal, or any part of it, for example, the Order of Mass, is obligatory in a region, [then] Mass, whether in Latin or the vernacular, may be celebrated law-

---

line with Stelten's "determine." The English translation on the Vatican web site reads, "We wish that . . ."

[79] See SCDW, Decree *Celebrationes Eucharisticae* (March 20, 1970) (DOL 213 at no. 1765). This is why the (first edition of the) Missal of Paul VI is referred to as the Missal of 1970.

[80] See SCDW, Decree *Celebrationes Eucharisticae* (DOL 213 at no. 1765).

[81] SCDW, Notification *Instructione de Constitutione* (June 14, 1971) (DOL 216 at no. 1771; emphasis added).

[82] See Bugnini, *The Reform of the Liturgy*, 299: the first point the letter made was that "the 'Missal of Pius V' was definitively abrogated by the apostolic constitution *Missale Romanum*. One need only read the final paragraph." Bugnini describes why the letter, which expressed the understanding of the relevant Vatican officials, was informal and unofficial. As such, it had no legislative force. It is cited here not as an authoritative statement but as an indicator of the thinking of persons at the time who were in a position to know the existing state of affairs.

fully only according to the rite of the Roman Missal promulgated 3 April 1969 by authority of Pope Paul VI."[83]

In 1975 the Vatican Secretary of State, Cardinal Jean Villot, wrote to the president of the liturgical commission of France on these same matters, making clear the same points once again, this time with explicit reference to the apostolic constitution *Quo Primim* of Pius V in 1570, which was being used to defend continued use of the Missal of 1570, in its 1962 edition. In this context, Villot wrote: "Through the Constitution *Missale Romanum* Pope Paul, as you know, orders that the new Missal is to replace the former one, notwithstanding any constitutions or apostolic ordinances of his predecessors—including, therefore, all the determinations of the Constitution *Quo primum*. No one, in France or anywhere else, can therefore claim an indult granted by *Quo primum* and allowing use of the former Missal."[84]

Pope Paul made himself clear on these questions in his personal letter to Archbishop Marcel Lefebvre, founder of the Society of Saint Pius X, who dissented from certain teachings of the Second Vatican Council and insisted upon using the preconciliar form of the Mass. Pope Paul spoke of "the unlawful practice of celebrating the 'Mass of St. Pius V,'" and stated categorically: "We have sanctioned the reform with our own authority and directed its obligatory use by all who call themselves Catholic."[85] The unambiguous meaning of these words makes clear the mind of Paul VI and his intentions in his 1969 apostolic constitution *Missale Romanum*—always taking account, of course, of those exceptions duly granted.[86]

Finally, we can recall that after publication of the 1970 Missal indults were requested for permission to use an earlier form of the

[83] SCDW, Notification *Conferentiarum Episcopalium* (October 28, 1974) (DOL 219 at no. 1784). Bugnini reports that "the final text was approved by the Holy Father on October 28, 1974, with the words 'Suitable. P[aul],' and was published as a notification from the Congregation for Divine Worship" (Bugnini, *The Reform of the Liturgy*, 300).

[84] Secretariat of State, Letter of Cardinal J. Villot to Bishop R. Coffy (October 11, 1975) (DOL 220 at no. 1785).

[85] Paul VI, Epistle *Cum te* (October 11, 1976) (DOL 61 at no. 569).

[86] See infra, note 68.

Missal. Clearly the parties involved at the time considered indults needed, and that without them they had no permission to use the prior Missal.

The situation as we have just reviewed it was the status quo during the 1970s and up until the indult *Quattuor Abhinc Annos* of 1984, which was issued under the authority of John Paul II as his outreach to Catholics (members of the Society of Saint Pius X and others) disaffected by the liturgical reforms. This indult allowed bishops to grant permission in their diocese for celebrations using the 1962 Missal (without its subsequent emendations) in Masses with a congregation, under various restrictions. In his 1988 *motu proprio, Ecclesia Dei*, John Paul II encouraged bishops to be generous in granting such permissions to groups desiring it.

The situation Pope Benedict described (all Latin Rite priests able to use the 1962 Missal in Masses without a congregation, with no permission needed from anyone) is a new legal situation that did not exist before and was created by article 2 of SP. To read it otherwise, as though it described the situation that has existed all along since the 1960s, seems clearly contrary to the content of the ecclesiastical sources just reviewed and, if true, would have potentially and seriously deleterious consequences regarding the interpretation of ecclesiastical documents. Such an interpretation would understand Pope Benedict to be stating (in such a way as to correct the "received opinion" in the church over the last half century), not that he is *granting* priests full freedom at their discretion to use either Missal in Masses without the people, but that such permission (*licentia*) freely to use either Missal in that circumstance is not needed, from anyone (Apostolic See or ordinary), because that permission is and throughout this time period has been theirs already, in the nature of the case. But, as the texts we have just reviewed make clear, permission to use the 1962 Missal *was* taken away, with the granting of exceptions reserved to the supreme pontiff or, under conditions he stipulated (first in 1984, in QAA), to local ordinaries. The permission was taken away by Paul VI when he promulgated the reformed Missal. This act created the legal situation that continued afterward, during the pontificate of John Paul II, who clearly understood matters as did Paul VI; it took special authorization, under his (John Paul II's) authority, for legal permission to be granted for use of the 1962 Missal, as was done with the

1984 letter *Quattuor Abhinc Annos*—a legal oddity, or indeed an unnecessary, confusing, and misleading legal act, if it gave permission for what was already permitted.

The 2011 instruction of the Pontifical Commission *Ecclesia Dei*, *Universae Ecclesiae*, addresses precisely these matters and creates clarity. It states: "The faculty to celebrate *sine populo* (or with the participation of only one minister) in the *forma extraordinaria* of the Roman Rite is given by the Motu Proprio to all priests, whether secular or religious (cf. Motu Proprio *Summorum Pontificum*, art. 2). For such celebrations therefore, priests, by provision of the Motu Proprio *Summorum Pontificum*, do not require any special permission from their Ordinaries or superiors."[87] This text guides a proper interpretation of SP, article 2. It is not the case that Pope Benedict indicated that priests did not need and never needed explicit permission (*licentia*), whether from the Apostolic See or a priest's ordinary, to celebrate Masses without the people using the prior Missal, on the grounds that they already and always had such permission. It is rather the case that, in *and by* article 2 (*ad normam Litterarum Apostolicarum*), the pope *granted* the faculty (*Facultas . . . concessa est*) on the basis of which no (further) "special permission" (*speciali licentia*) is now needed by a priest from his ordinary (if he is a secular priest) or his superior (if he is religious). In this way the Instruction has helpfully clarified a possible ambiguity, forestalling any unintended consequences of a faulty interpretation of this passage.

SP, article 4, states that if there are members of the faithful who in some fashion learn of the celebration of extraordinary form Masses as authorized under article 2 and then request "on their own initiative" to participate in them, they "can be admitted" to such celebrations of Mass. This provision might seem to create a conundrum. SP, article 2, permits a priest to use the prior Missal "*in Missis sine populo*," in Masses without the people (that is, typically, with only a

[87] PCED, *Universae Ecclesiae* 23. ("Facultas celebrandi Missam sine populo seu uno tantum ministro participante, secundum *formam extraordinariam* Ritus Romani concessa est cuivis presbytero, tum saeculari, cum religioso [cf. Litterae Apostolicae *Summorum Pontificum*, art. 2]. Ergo, in huiusmodi celebrationibus, sacerdotes, ad normam Litterarum Apostolicarum, nulla speciali licentia Ordinariorum vel superiorum indigent").

server). SP, article 4, describes the conditions under which members of the faithful may be admitted to such Masses. If and when that happens, people are present and such a Mass is no longer a Mass *sine populo*; it becomes, in the language of the GIRM, a "Mass with the People," because "by Mass with the people is meant a Mass celebrated with the participation of the faithful" (GIRM [2011] 115). But in that case the conditions identified in SP, article 2, that permit a priest to celebrate Mass using the prior Missal are no longer present, and so, the priest would apparently no longer be authorized to use that Missal. Thus the seeming conundrum. But *Universae Ecclesiae* envisions the situation of "a priest . . . with some faithful" requesting to celebrate Mass in the extraordinary form as something "foreseen by articles 2 and 4" of SP (UE 16); in other words, UE sees no conceptual inconsistency in these two articles.[88]

In either case I think it reasonable, likely, and unobjectionable to hold that Pope Benedict did not mean to create a liturgical or canonical "Catch-22." Rather, he had in mind in these two articles various rights he wanted to honor. In article 2 he granted and recognized a right of priests to use the church's traditional form of Mass, contained in the 1962 edition of the Missal, specifying the conditions for the exercise of this right. Note that the conditions are such as to exclude regularly scheduled parish (or other forms of public) Masses, because such Masses should ordinarily be in the ordinary form, as the very terms indicate. One might say this preserves the right of the church to maintain in normal practice its given form of worship, the liturgy as reformed at the mandate of the ecumenical council.

[88] Alcuin Reid explains the situation similarly, though using the term "Private Mass," a term designating not how Mass is conducted (with or without people participating) but how it is scheduled or intended. He writes: "By a Private Mass is meant one which is not publicly scheduled. This often occurs when a priest travelling (either alone, or together with a group) offers Mass and, in practice, 'private' Mass is often celebrated in a church or chapel open to the public. *Summorum Pontificum* grants the faithful the right to attend such Masses should they so wish" (with a footnote reference to SP, art. 4); in Adrian Fortescue, J. B. O'Connell, and Alcuin Reid, *The Ceremonies of the Roman Rite Described*, 15th ed. (London: Burns & Oates, 2009), 242. Again, this interpretation eases or eliminates the conundrum and makes for a less difficult reading of SP.

But another underlying principle operative in the provisions and intent of SP is that every Catholic who desires to participate in the traditional Mass should be able to do so; this is a specific right Pope Benedict considered to have been neglected in the past, which he intended explicitly to honor here. Some of these Catholics are provided for in SP, article 5, section 1—namely, Catholics in a parish setting who constitute a "stable group" devoted to the prior liturgical forms and request of their pastor Mass according to the *usus antiquior*. Pastors are to provide for their request. If, however, there is no such stable group, yet there nonetheless exist members of the faithful who desire the traditional Mass, article 4 is a way to provide for them. It stipulates that if they of their own free initiative request to be admitted to such nonpublic celebrations of Mass as are permitted by article 2, this can be allowed (*admitti possunt*); this could occur in the parish setting, or in other settings, for example, during a spiritual retreat or when a group is on pilgrimage and a priest is available to celebrate using the 1962 Missal, or when a priest is traveling through and wishes to celebrate using that Missal and people wish to participate.[89] This, I think—and aside from the question of whether all the legalities line up perfectly[90]—is the kind of pastoral care Pope Benedict was trying to provide, by this linkage of articles 2 and 4 of SP.

SP, ARTICLE 3

> *If communities of institutes of consecrated life or societies of apostolic life, of either pontifical or diocesan right, desire to have the celebration of holy Mass according to the edition of the Roman Missal promulgated in 1962 in conventual or "communal" celebration in their own oratories, it is permitted them. If an individual community or an entire institute or society wishes to do such celebrations often or habitually or permanently,*

[89] PCED, *Universae Ecclesiae* 16 makes reference to this last scenario, when it speaks of a priest "who presents himself occasionally" ("occasionally" translates *obiter*, which can suggest the priest is en route, traveling through) and is "with some faithful" (an interpretive translation of *cum aliquibus personis*).

[90] For example, Lüdecke finds SP to be "odd in terms of legal terminology," referring as it does to "a *missa sine populo* even in the presence of several faithful" ("Canonical Remarks," 209).

the matter is to be decided by the major superiors according to the rule of law and their own particular laws and statutes.

Institutes of consecrated life or societies of apostolic life, in celebrating conventual or community Mass in their own oratories, may decide (and this may be done by an entire institute or society, or by its individual communities) to use the 1962 Missal either "often or habitually or permanently." Decisions on this matter are to be made "by the major superiors, in accord with the norm of law and according to particular laws and statutes" (SP, art. 3). "Often" (*saepe*) is a relative term. If understood in reference to "always," it could mean half the time or more, while compared to "never" (the frequency in religious houses of using the 1962 Missal from the 1960s up to SP) it could mean weekly or monthly;[91] perhaps something in between is applicable here. The word "habitually" (*habitualiter*) is in the official text in *Acta Apostolicae Sedis*. Earlier versions had *plerumque*, a word denoting that, empirically speaking, something happens as a rule, most of the time, in actual practice.[92] *Habitualiter* is stronger, indicating "that a situation continues uninterruptedly for an indefinite period"; most uses of the term in canon law can, according to Rehak, be translated *ständig*, "continuously."[93] *Permanenter* indicates an arrangement established on a permanent basis, with no time limit.

Pope Benedict was well aware of the decisive role played by monasteries in the nineteenth- and twentieth-century liturgical movement, as places of exemplary liturgical celebration and far-reaching liturgical education.[94] With this article he made it possible for such sites to play a significant role again in the new phase of the

[91] And so, to illustrate, a layperson not obliged to the Divine Office might say, "I pray portions of the Liturgy of the Hours often, three or four days a week," yet also "I need a retreat day often, so I go to a hermitage once a month or so."

[92] See Rehak, *Der außerordentliche Gebrauch*, 90–91.

[93] Rehak, *Der außerordentliche Gebrauch*, 91 (*dass eine Situation ununterbrochen auf unbestimmte Zeit andauert*) and (*ständig*). Rehak identifies ten uses of *habitualiter* in the Code of Canon Law, indicating eight of them can be translated *ständig*, "continuously," while two should be translated *auf Dauer* or *dauernd*, "perpetually," which seems more the equivalent of *permanenter*, as he also notes.

[94] See Ratzinger, "Assessment and Future Prospects," in *Looking Again*, 145–46.

liturgical movement that is now underway and which he fostered through SP. They can be, as he said only five years before becoming pope, "exemplary centers where the liturgy is celebrated in the right way, where people can experience what liturgy truly is," and be enriched and renewed thereby.[95]

Less than four years before becoming pope, at the July 2001 liturgical conference at Fontgombault, Cardinal Ratzinger mused on the "problem" of how to coordinate the use of both ritual forms in the practical life of the church, should the 1962 liturgy be made more widely available, as he thought it should.[96] The "very real problem" was how to avoid subdividing the church into self-chosen enclaves of the like-minded, on the basis of ritual preference. In Ratzinger's analysis, this "could genuinely damage the structure of the Church," which is built instead on the "objective criterion" of "local Churches" with an "episcopal structure" (and, derivatively, parochial).[97] He spoke in this regard of the possible role of "abbeys," which have a history of their own ritual practices (the Cistercians, the Dominicans, and so on), as being places where the old Missal could be used on a "nonsubjective" basis.[98] Religious communities deciding to use the prior Missal consistently but not exclusively also hold significant potential for mutual enrichment; communities of persons with some degree of willingness to celebrate both the ordinary and extraordinary forms, and doing so on a regular basis for an extended period of time, could become uniquely positioned to discover potential positive or negative forms of mutual influence, in a way that could be of service to the whole church.

SP, ARTICLE 5, SECTION 1

In parishes where a group of the faithful attached to the prior liturgical tradition exists stably, the pastor should willingly receive their requests

[95] Ratzinger, *God and the World*, 416; see also ibid., 388–89, and *A New Song for the Lord*, 159.

[96] See Ratzinger, "Assessment and Future Prospects," in *Looking Again*, 148–50.

[97] Ibid., 149 and 150.

[98] Ibid., 150.

to celebrate holy Mass according to the rite of the Roman Missal edited in 1962. Let him see to it that the good of these faithful harmoniously accords with the ordinary pastoral care of the parish, under the guidance of the bishop according to Canon 392, avoiding discord and fostering the unity of the whole church.

In parishes, celebrations of the 1962 Missal may and should take place when "a group of the faithful who adhere to the prior liturgical tradition exists stably" (*stabiliter exsistit*) and requests it.[99] Pastors are to receive such requests to celebrate the traditional Mass *libenter*, willingly, freely, and respond to them affirmatively.[100]

Article 5, section 1 of SP says this much, but also more. The pastor is to see to it that "the good of these faithful," those who adhere to and request the preconciliar Mass, "harmoniously accords with the ordinary pastoral care of the parish, under the guidance of the bishop according to Canon 392," which concerns a bishop's responsibility for church unity and discipline, including vigilance regarding worship and sacraments. SP also takes particular note of the risk of divisiveness when it adds that all this is to be done "avoiding discord and fostering the unity of the whole church"—one of Pope Benedict's overriding concerns, as we have seen. Several points just noted deserve some additional comment.

[99] One web site provides guidelines for making such requests—suggestions regarding tone, content, and procedure, along with a sample letter, for the three possible stages in the process: writing to one's pastor, to one's bishop, and to the Pontifical Commission *Ecclesia Dei*. See http://unavoce.org/s-p-resources/requesting-tlm-post-sp.

[100] Lüdecke sees this as a legal requirement: "The pastor is legally obligated willingly to accept this concern" ("Canonical Remarks," 211). According to Baldovin, "a pastor is encouraged (*libenter suscipiat*) to accede to the requests" (see "Reflections on *Summorum Pontificum*," 105). Falling in between is the interpretation of Rehak, who reads *suscipiat* as conveying expectation and duty more than strict compulsion—as a "Sollvorschrift" (a "should-decree") more than a "Mussvorschrift" (a "must-decree"); pastors will fulfill the request unless in individual circumstances this is not possible (*Der außerordentliche Gebrauch*, 114). As I read it, Baldovin's "encouraged" is too weak, Lüdecke's "legally obligated" is rather strong though perhaps not technically incorrect, and Rehak seems to capture it best.

In describing the group of the faithful who may request Mass according to the 1962 Missal, the text of SP as printed in the official Vatican publication, *Acta Apostolicae Sedis*, reads "stabiliter exsistit."[101] The word *stabiliter* suggests stability in the group whenever it was formed, whether before or after the promulgation of SP; it does not need to have existed prior to SP—an interpretation confirmed by UE 15. The word seems to exclude requests from a temporary or *ad hoc* gathering of people.[102] Huels tries to draw out implications of this provision and provide guidelines for determining when such a group exists; he proposes that a stable group "must be ongoing, committed to regular participation in the Mass, and genuinely attached to the former rites," ruling out requests based simply on curiosity or a desire for novelty.[103] Stability in this sense asks for a certain seriousness of purpose and spiritual motivation on the part of those who petition for the 1962 Mass. This seems to be a provision of SP that recognizes the potentially considerable demands it could place on the clergy and intends to free them from requests for the prior liturgy that do not arise from genuine pastoral need.

Article 5, section 1, requires pastors to respond favorably to requests for the FE from a stable group in the parish. It does not authorize pastors on their own authority or initiative to introduce Masses in the FE into the parish, and both Haunerland and Huels comment to that effect.[104] Subsequent to their commentary, however, an inquiry was made to the Pontifical Commission *Ecclesia Dei* by the Diocese of Rzeszów in Poland, and one of the questions was

[101] Benedict XVI, *Litterae Apostolicae 'Motu Proprio' Datae*, "De usu extraordinario antiquae formae Ritus Romani," *Acta Apostolicae Sedis* 99, no. 9 (September 7, 2007): 777–81, at 780. Earlier published versions of the text had the reading, *continenter exsistit*. See Haunerland, "Ein Ritus in Zwei Ausdruksformen?" 193, n. 54. Traces of this can also be seen in the presence of the word *continenter* in, for example, Lüdecke, "Canonical Remarks," 209, or Cesare Giraudo, "La Liturgia nel Solco della Traditione," 258.

[102] Lüdecke, "Canonical Remarks," 210.

[103] Huels, "Reconciling the Old with the New," 99.

[104] Winfried Haunerland, "Ein Ritus in zwei Ausdrucksformen?" 196; Huels, "Reconciling the Old with the New," 98.

on this very point.[105] The third question of this inquiry was: "May a pastor or another priest on his own accord publically celebrate the extraordinary form—beside the usual regular use of the new Form—'so that all the faithful—the young as well as the old—can make themselves familiar with the old rite and benefit from its notable beauty and transcendence?'"[106]

It is an important question that goes close to the heart of SP. Pope Benedict wanted the traditional Mass to have a genuine, realistic chance to be a positive, enriching influence on the new order of Mass, through the process of mutual enrichment (CGF 7). This is fundamentally a grassroots process involving the faithful in a way that depends on their having experience of both usages.[107] How are they to have that experience? The most straightforward and easily accessible way is in their own parish. But as I read SP, article 5, section 1, that can happen only if a stable group of the faithful requests it. This also presumes the presence of persons with a certain measure of knowledge of the old Mass (and of Latin—see CGF 6) as well as stability as a group adherent to the FE, who will take the initiative to request FE celebrations; this kind of group may not often be found, and the parishes where the request can be satis-

[105] For information, see the entry posted February 15, 2010, on the "New Liturgical Movement" blog: http://www.newliturgicalmovement.org.

[106] Text online at http://www.nowyruchliturgiczny.pl/2010/02/komisja-ecclesia-dei-odpowiada-na.html. ("Darf ein Pfarrer oder ein anderer Priester von sich aus öffentlich die außerordentliche Form—neben der üblichen regelmäßigen Verwendung der neuen Form—zelebrieren, 'damit alle Gläubigen—die jungen wie die alten—sich mit den alten Riten vertraut machen und von ihrer spürbaren Schönheit und Transzendenz profitieren können'?"). The web site contains both the text of the letter from the Diocese of Rzeszów, dated January 5, 2010, and the reply from the Pontifical Commission *Ecclesia Dei*, prot. n. 13/2007, dated January 20, 2010, and signed by the commission's secretary, Mons. Guido Pozzo.

[107] I see the process of mutual enrichment happening not simply through church authorities making changes in the ritual of one form based on elements in the other, but through the faithful, priests and laity, engaging in worship in both forms. The way they experience either usage can then form them in a way that affects the manner of their worship in the other usage. This grassroots process thus enriches, first of all, the faithful, and then, through them, eventually the rites. We explore this topic at greater length in chap. 7.

fied may be even fewer. What then? The FE may be available in other ways. A religious house that celebrates according to the *usus antiquior* may be nearby (SP, art. 3), or a designated FE parish (SP, art. 10), or a neighboring parish with celebrations of the traditional Mass begun there in accord with SP, article 5, section 1; on occasion the FE may be available under the provisions of articles 2 and 4. But again, all these options may be relatively rare. Even if they exist, it would require an unusual degree of initiative and commitment, on the part of regular Catholics with no particular connection with the old Mass, to seek out this unfamiliar thing in such ways. As a consequence, the pope's vision and plan for the future health and development of the liturgy, achieved through an interim process of mutual enrichment of the now existing two usages, FO and FE, could fail before it had a chance to succeed.

The Diocese of Rzeszów, perhaps with this scenario in mind, inquired about a step that would give the old rite more of a chance, making it more realistically possible for ordinary Catholics (those not already aware of and attached to it) to become acquainted with the 1962 Mass by allowing a priest to celebrate publically (not only in Masses *sine populo*) the traditional Mass even when this has not been requested by a stable group. The reply of the Pontifical Commission is interesting. Some blogs have said it gives the priest permission to start such Masses on his own;[108] this is not incorrect but is incomplete and thus a little misleading. The commission's reply reads: "To the 2nd and 3rd [questions]: we refer the question to the prudent judgment of the parish priest, while still insisting that the stable group of the faithful has the right to assist at celebrations of the Mass in the extraordinary form."[109] In other words, the answer is not simply: yes, priests can do this. The answer is: we trust and

[108] For example, Gregor Kollmorgen, "Important Clarifications from *Ecclesia Dei*," at http://www.newliturgicalmovement.org; or "LMS Chairman" (from the Latin Mass Society of England and Wales), at http://www.lmschairman.org/2010/02/pced-clarification-on-motu-proprio.html.

[109] "Ad 2 e ad 3: si rimetta la questione al prudente giudizio del parroco, fermo restando che il gruppo stabile di fedeli ha diritto di assistere alla celebrazione della Messa nella forma straordinaria." The second question asked whether a Mass in the FE could replace one of the regularly scheduled FO Masses in the Sunday schedule and not simply be added, at another and

count on you priests to be prudent. This reply should not send priests straight to revising the Mass schedule; it should send them first to their Aquinas, or Pieper, on the virtue of prudence,[110] and then to a careful, prayerful, prudent consideration of the pastoral needs and situation of their community and the church at large, and only then to a decision, one way or the other.

The second half of the reply is a reminder and reaffirmation that while it is in the priest's prudent discretion whether to inaugurate the FE Mass on his own initiative, it is not at his discretion whether to respond affirmatively to a request for that Mass from a stable group; in that case the group has a right, granted in SP, to the FE Mass, and he has a corresponding obligation to provide it.

The call for the pastor to integrate the care of persons seeking the prior liturgy into the overall pastoral ministry of the parish is not an extra requirement placed upon him but is better seen (1) as a measure meant to ease his burden, militating against what could tend toward a doubling of parish sacramental ministry for a small group functioning like a parish-within-a-parish, (2) as a word of encouragement or even expectation to the stable group attached to the *usus antiquior*, to enter willingly into the full pastoral life of the parish and not stand apart from it or be resistant to it, and thus (3) in general as another expression of Pope Benedict's overriding concern for reconciliation and unity in the church. Implementation of this provision will almost certainly call for adjustments, compromise, and goodwill on the part of all concerned—a spirit of patience and cooperation rather than either demand and expectation (on the part of the stable group) or avoidance and resistance (on the part of the parish staff).

The concern for reconciliation emerges even more clearly in the final phrase of article 5, section 1, on avoiding discord and fostering unity. These matters motivated and pervade SP and CGF throughout and could be taken here as simply one more expression of this characteristically Benedictine concern. But we can gain additional

typically more inconvenient time such as mid-afternoon. The same reply is given to both questions.

[110] Aquinas, *Summa Theologiae*, II–II, 47 and following. Josef Pieper, "Prudence," in his *The Four Cardinal Virtues* (Notre Dame, IN: University of Notre Dame Press, 1967), 3–40.

light on this subject by turning to Pope Benedict's other major liturgical document of 2007, *Sacramentum Caritatis*, his apostolic exhortation on the Eucharist following the 2005 Synod of Bishops on that topic. This document contains a section on eucharistic celebrations in small groups, and what is said there seems applicable quite directly to the situation of FE celebrations, insofar as they often are and in many cases will continue to be, *de facto*, small group celebrations.[111] The document indicates that small group celebrations often arise "in the interest of more conscious, active, and fruitful participation"—a topic quite relevant to FE celebrations, to which we will return later.[112] It acknowledges the formative benefit of such celebrations but immediately adds that they must "be consonant with" the pastoral life of the diocese and not be "in competition with, or parallel to, the life of the particular Church."[113]

The document then names several "necessary criteria" for such celebrations, criteria set forth at the synod. First, "small groups must serve to unify the community, not to fragment it"—a phrase directly parallel to that in SP. This poses an interesting challenge and perhaps fruitful line of thought for local pastoral leaders. The planning question it invites is not simply, "How can we hold FE celebrations in our parish (or diocese) while avoiding the fragmentation they might conceivably lead to or exacerbate?" but rather, "How can we do our FE celebrations in such a way as actively to foster unity in our community?" The latter question may help bring to the surface any hidden or ignored forms of fragmentation, opposition, or disunity that already exist, so that they can be addressed

[111] Benedict XVI, *Sacramentum Caritatis* 63. FE celebrations will be small group celebrations especially when a pastor of a regular (that is, FO) parish provides Mass according to the 1962 Missal for a stable but small group of parishioners. It may be less applicable in situations where a bishop establishes a personal parish dedicated to the celebration of the FE.

[112] See chap. 6. See also Huels's comments on the need for active participation in FE celebrations; "Reconciling the Old with the New," 99–100.

[113] *Sacramentum Caritatis* 63; all citations from the document in the following four paragraphs are from this section. Note that the concern for unity in this section of *Sacramentum Caritatis* (or the concern that small group celebrations not cause disunity) operates at the level of the diocese, the parish, and the family.

and healed, as well as forestall the rise of new divisions that could accompany the introduction of the FE. Also, by focusing on the positive rather than the negative (fostering unity rather than avoiding divisions), it draws the thinking and practice of pastoral leaders in a more life-giving, community-building direction.

The second criterion for small group celebrations is that "the beneficial results ought to be clearly evident." Here SP and *Sacramentum Caritatis* seem to be somewhat at odds. The latter speaks in terms of seeking "beneficial results" from small-group Masses; SP does not speak in terms of results for the community but of rights for the faithful, for members of those stable groups desiring the FE Mass (and for priests desiring to use the extraordinary form when they celebrate Mass *sine populo*). FE adherents might suggest there is no need to search for signs of beneficial results, seeing the celebration of the church's traditional liturgy in the parish as in itself a blessing for the community. Whatever the merits of this claim, I see no reason why a small "stable group" of FE adherents should be exempt either from the concern of *Sacramentum Caritatis* for the potential divisiveness of small group Masses in general, or from being assessed according to the criteria there articulated to moderate that negative potential. And so, inquiry as to the "beneficial results" of small group FE Masses is as valid and relevant as the same inquiry regarding small group FO Masses. The question then arises: what if, in a given instance, there are none? What if, instead of benefits, the introduction of such Masses gives evidence over time of fostering a spirit of fragmentation or competition in the community? *Sacramentum Caritatis* says nothing of how to proceed in such a case, nor does SP address it—a lacuna in the documents. What, then, should or could be done?

Pastoral prudence and common sense would suggest, first, a call and encouragement for renewed good-faith efforts on all sides, to recognize division and seek reconciliation and unity. If such efforts within the community could not be brought about, or were attempted for a reasonable period but without success, then parallel provisions in SP, articles 7 and 8, suggest recourse to the bishop. If his intervention and efforts also prove unfruitful, he can refer the matter to the Pontifical Commission *Ecclesia Dei*. This could be time-consuming (with the community all the while still experiencing competition or fragmentation) but seems in the spirit of SP and its desire to make the FE available where a stable group genuinely desires it. But the possibility remains that a community could suffer fragmentation from the effects of FE celebrations and that such results could persist, and require to be removed, by cessation of celebrations in the FE. While this course of action should not be taken simply because a pastor desires it, nor be chosen except as a last resort, it would seem it cannot be ruled out in principle even though there is no explicit provision for it in SP.[114]

The third criterion for small group celebrations expresses concern for the "fruitful participation" of all present, and for keeping families from becoming divided. This criterion applied to SP would caution against situations where some family members favor the FE and attend its celebrations while other family members remain with the regular FO liturgical life of the parish. This consideration could become an element of pastoral counseling, or a topic for discussion in parish catechetical efforts on SP or on family life, or even something to be touched upon in premarital catechesis, if it seemed relevant in a given community or for particular couples.

SP, ARTICLE 5, SECTION 2

> *Celebration according to the Missal of Blessed John XXIII can take place on weekdays; moreover on Sundays and feast days also one celebration of this kind can be held.*

Returning to our review of SP's permissions and restrictions regarding the FE: celebrations using the 1962 Missal may take place on weekdays; there is a restriction to only one such celebration on Sundays and holy days.[115] This is one of the clear indicators that the two

[114] Compare Lüdecke, "Canonical Remarks": "It is the aim of the regulations that the request of the faithful go unfulfilled only because of impossibility, not because of unwillingness" (218).

[115] Gribbin argues otherwise. The text, he notes, reads "*una etiam* not *una tantum*. It envisages one Mass on Sundays and holy days but does not strictly preclude more than one. The wording is concessionary rather than limiting in tone"; Anselm J. Gribbin, *Pope Benedict XVI and the Liturgy: Understanding Recent Liturgical Developments* (Leominster, UK: Gracewing, 2011), 149. As I read it, article 5, sec. 2 addresses how article 5, sec. 1 can be fulfilled. To meet the request of the stable group for celebrations using the 1962 Missal (as provided

forms have not been placed at full equality: the 1962 Missal is not to dominate the parish's Sunday Mass schedule but to be available once, only if requested. The Missal of Paul VI is to remain the normal form of Mass available for Catholics for their Sunday worship.

Does this limitation apply also in a personal parish established by the bishop to be an extraordinary form parish (SP, art. 10)? No explicit exception is made for such parishes, yet such an exception is needed if the intent of article 10 is to be fulfilled. It surely seems the intent of SP and permissible in a personal parish established in order to offer the extraordinary form, to provide Mass according to the 1962 Missal for the faithful seeking it, even when this requires more than one Mass on a Sunday. Perhaps this assumed permission will at some point be made explicit by the PCED.

SP, ARTICLE 5, SECTION 4

> *Priests using the Missal of Blessed John XXIII should be qualified and not impeded by law.*

Priests who celebrate using the 1962 Missal are to be *idonei*, qualified or fit or suitable. What this means is not spelled out in SP but is explicitly addressed in the instruction *Universae Ecclesiae*. There has been concern among FE adherents that bishops reluctant to implement SP in its full vigor in their dioceses might make use or have made use of article 5, section 4 to lessen or hinder FE celebrations in their dioceses. This would be contrary to the spirit of SP and even to its proper canonical interpretation since, as permissive rather than restrictive legislation, it should be given a generous reading. As though in response to such concerns, the instruction's first comment on *ideoneus* is to state that "every Catholic priest who is not impeded by Canon Law is to be considered *idoneus*

---

in art. 5, sec. 1), the first clause of article 5, sec. 2 allows such celebrations to be offered on weekdays, without specifying a number or limit; the second clause extends that permission also (*etiam*) to Sundays and feast days, this time limiting it to one such celebration (*una . . . celebratio huiusmodi*). This limitation is established, one presumes, in view of the priest's responsibility on those holy days of obligation to provide Mass(es) in the ordinary form for those under his care who celebrate in that form, in all likelihood the vast majority.

('qualified')" to celebrate in the extraordinary form (UE 20.a).[116] It then immediately names certain further requirements: that priests know enough Latin "to pronounce the words correctly and understand their meaning" (UE 20.b). Priests "who present themselves spontaneously to celebrate the *forma extraordinaria*" are presumed to be qualified if they "have celebrated it previously" (UE 20.c); this seems to presume a priest will first celebrate the FE under the provisions of SP, article 2, in Masses without the people—almost, as it were, for practice. The instruction elsewhere stipulates that those using the prior liturgical books "must know the pertinent rubrics and are obliged to follow them correctly" (UE 24). This too is a requirement for being *idoneus*—full knowledge and correct observance of the detailed rubrics of the FE.

Presumably one would also desire or expect at least the same "notable liturgical formation" and "profound, intimate familiarity" with the *usus antiquior* as possessed by the faithful who were well formed by the twentieth-century liturgical movement (CGF 4).[117] Further, a priest could be considered unqualified not only by shortcomings on technical grounds (insufficient knowledge of Latin or the rubrics) but also if his words or behavior fail (see SP, art. 5, sec. 1) to avoid discord or fail to foster unity.[118]

The question regarding a priest's qualifications to celebrate the FE, in particular with Masses with the people, is a question of importance for the implementation of SP. In the years before the council, complaints about the way priests celebrated the Mass were not uncommon. In 1964 the US Catholic bishops themselves cautioned against priests celebrating the liturgy, as they knew from (preconciliar) experience could be the case, "in a manner that is apparently hasty, matter-of-fact, and without attention to the meaning of the words," something that would be "irreverent and improper no matter what the language."[119] One thinks also of Dorothy Day

[116] There is an internal reference to canon 900, section 2, on what impedes a priest from celebrating the Eucharist licitly.

[117] See also Baldovin, "Reflections on *Summorum Pontificum*," 108.

[118] Lüdecke, "Canonical Remarks," 213.

[119] U.S. Catholic Bishops, "Use of Vernacular at Mass" (1964), no. 12; in *Pastoral Letters of the United States Catholic Bishops*, vol. 3, 1962–74, ed. Hugh J. Nolan (Washington, DC: United States Catholic Conference, 1983), 38.

recounting the advice that Father Pacifique Roy gave in the 1940s to a fellow priest discouraged at "the darkness of the times"; according to Day, Roy said to the priest "courageously (it is hard to correct a fellow priest in so personal a matter) that if only he would stop gargling the words of the Mass in his throat in a parody of oral prayer he would at least make a beginning."[120] In more recent years, Catholics looking back—even those of differing perspectives, from the left and the right—recall the same carelessness or incompetence.[121]

So while Pope Benedict has written of his positive memories of the traditional Mass, memories of a kind others certainly share and which convey a genuine dimension of the reality, beauty, and dignity of the extraordinary form, it must also be recognized that the old rite does not perform itself, can be done poorly (and often was) as well as beautifully—indeed, the former more easily than the latter, which requires assiduous care and considerable effort. Adequate knowledge of Latin, genuine skill in the ritual in all its intricate detail, *and* formation in a spirituality commensurate with its "venerable and ancient usage" and "sacrality" that would infuse the priest's *ars celebrandi* (or shall we say, *ars praesidendi*) would seem necessary for a priest to be truly *idoneus* today to celebrate using that Missal.[122]

[120] Dorothy Day, *Loaves and Fishes* (1963; repr. Maryknoll, NY: Orbis Books, 1997), 130. Virgil Michel lamented various clerical inadequacies in celebrating Mass; see "Why Do We Do It?" *Orate Fratres* 9, no. 2 (1934): 63–67.

[121] For example, Alice von Hildebrand said in an interview published in 2001 that priests, in offering Mass in the years before Vatican II, had "already lost the sense of the supernatural and the transcendent [a theme of earlier responses in her interview]. They rushed through the prayers, they mumbled and didn't enunciate them"; from "Present at the Demolition," in *The Latin Mass* (summer 2001), available at http://www.latinmassmagazine.com/articles/articles_2001_su_Hildebran.html. Peter Stravinskas recalls preconciliar "Masses which were sloppily and even sacrilegiously celebrated"; see "Why I Oppose a Tridentine Prelature," *The Catholic World Report* (February 1992), 38, as cited in Kocik, *The Reform of the Reform?* 77. Also Nathan Mitchell, "The Amen Corner: '*Summorum Pontificum*,'" 559; Aidan Kavanagh, "Reflections on the Study from the Viewpoint of Liturgical History," 91–92; Michael Kunzler, *Die 'Tridentinische' Messe*, 122.

[122] Consider here, especially regarding spirituality, comments by the Consilium in a 1968 editorial on gestures in the liturgy, spoken in reference to the

All three qualities (linguistic knowledge, ritual competence, spiritual depth) should be requisite, not as a limitation on the availability of the FE but as an aid and assurance toward providing what SP seeks to grant both FE adherents and the church at large.[123]

Yet, on the other hand, those strongly attached or drawn to the prior liturgical forms may reply that Mass poorly celebrated in the FE is for them preferable to Mass poorly celebrated in the FO and ask why they should be denied the former when they are offered the latter as their only alternative. FE and FO adherents may quibble over when or how often that would be the case, and over what constitutes a poorly celebrated "ordinary form" Mass, but the

---

reformed liturgy and its "noble simplicity," but equally relevant, I think, to the prior usage (and based on their experience of how that usage could be performed). The text cautions that correct observance of rubrics is necessary yet also insufficient in the celebration of the liturgy. There is a pointed critique of "gestures that have become mechanical from habit, sloppy from routine, half-hearted from apathy." These gestures, instead, "are meant to reveal Christ's presence," and will be able to do so "only to the degree that they are motivated directly by an inner vision, the contemplation of mystery" (DOL 42 at no. 487).

[123] If I may offer a personal observation: since 2007 I have participated in celebrations of the extraordinary form in several different parishes in three states. Only in one location, it seemed to me, did the priest say the words of the Latin text as though he were speaking an actual language, engaging in genuine communication—praying prayers to an actual Person, or inviting real people to genuine prayer in common (*Oremus*). In the other places, my impression was generally of priests manifesting an *ars praesidendi* (a manner of presiding) well described by the US Catholic Bishops in their 1964 statement: "hasty" and "matter-of-fact," almost workman-like. On this admittedly unscientific basis I think the Second Vatican Council's concern for priestly formation in the liturgy (SC 14–18) is fully as apt for priests newly celebrating the FE today as it was for those newly celebrating the FO just after the council—as when, for example, the council said that "it would be futile to entertain any hopes of realizing" the goals of liturgical reform (the council meant active participation of the faithful, Benedict would mean beauty in the *ars celebrandi* of the FE as well as the FO) "unless the pastors themselves, in the first place, become thoroughly imbued with the spirit and power of the liturgy, and undertake to give instruction about it" (SC 14). This kind of competence in the FE (in other words, becoming *idoneus*) cannot be taken for granted and requires intentional and serious formation—again, not to impede but precisely to enable the faithful implementation of SP and the worthy celebration of the extraordinary form.

question in itself seems fair and voices a concern with which Pope Benedict would have resonated. While he wanted priests celebrating the FE to be *idoneus*, he was also mindful and sympathetic regarding the deep pain that can be felt because of "arbitrary deformations of the [FO] liturgy" (CGF 4). It would seem that here, as so often is the case, good judgment and the willingness on both sides to go the extra mile for one's sister or brother is what is needed most.

SP, ARTICLE 5, SECTION 5

In churches which are neither parish nor conventual churches, it is for the rector of the church to grant permission concerning the foregoing.

This section provides for the administration of the provisions of SP in such settings as oratories or private chapels. It shows the legislator's concern that the extraordinary form be available wherever it is desired—that is, that it be available for the faithful wherever they worship.

SP, ARTICLE 6

In Masses according to the Missal of Blessed John XXIII celebrated with the people, the readings can be proclaimed also in the vernacular, using editions recognized by the Apostolic See.

Pope Benedict here legislated that lectionary readings in the vernacular can (not must) be proclaimed during extraordinary form celebrations. There was some question as to whether this referred to and thus authorized use of approved translations of the FO lectionary in celebrations of the FE Mass.[124] Huels, for example, speculated that it did, while Tattersall insisted it did not.[125] The January 2010 letter from the Polish diocese to the PCED asked about this matter:

[124] Haunerland, "Ein Ritus in zwei Ausdrucksformen?" 185.

[125] Huels, "Reconciling the Old with the New," 100–101; he thought "the proper readings from either liturgical book may be used" (101). Glen Tattersall, "*Summorum Pontificum*—A Commentary and Appreciation: 'And the Church Will Give Thanks for Benedict XVI,'" *The Priest* 11, no. 2 (November 2007): 22–23, 27, at 22–23; he speculated that the relevant translations were those approved for use during "the so-called 'interim rite' period, between 1964–1968" (23).

"Is it permissible for a holy Mass in the extraordinary form to use the calendar, the readings or the prefaces from the Roman Missal of 1970 instead of the corresponding texts of the Roman Missal of 1962?"[126] The commission's answer was: "negative." The answer makes sense. A major difference between the two usages is the lectionary, and with it the calendar. To interpose the new readings and calendar into celebrations of the old Mass at present (that is, before mutual enrichment has brought about changes, whatever they may turn out to be, by a slower, more organic process) would be too much too soon and out of keeping with the more patient spirit of SP.

The text states that readings may be done *etiam* in the vernacular, and the translation "also" is meant to convey that such vernacular readings supplement and do not replace the Latin.[127] This interpretation is sustained by the Instruction *Universae Ecclesiae*, with the exception, however, that in the case of Low Masses (*in Missis lectis*) the readings can be proclaimed "solely in the vernacular" (UE 26). Surely the purpose of this permission to use the vernacular is to allow lectionary readings to be proclaimed to the entire congregation in such a way that they can hear and understand them. This implies proclamation from the ambo, not the altar, and raises the question of the use of lectors.

SP, ARTICLE 5, SECTION 3

> *For the faithful or priests who request it, let the pastor permit celebrations in this extraordinary form even in other particular circumstances such as marriages, funerals, or occasional celebrations, for example, pilgrimages.*

SP, ARTICLE 9, SECTION 1

> *The pastor, having pondered all things well, can grant permission to use the prior ritual in administering the sacraments of baptism, matrimony, penance, and anointing of the sick, if the good of souls recommends it.*

[126] "Ist es zulässig, für eine hl. Messe in der außerordentlichen Form, den Kalender, die Lesungen oder Präfationen aus dem Missale Romanum von 1970 anstelle der entsprechenden Texte des Missale Romanum von 1962 zu verwenden?"

[127] For the same interpretation, see Gordon Read, "Motu Proprio Summorum Pontificum," *Newsletter: Canon Law Society of Great Britain and Ireland*, no. 151 (September 2007): 9–21, at 19.

One of the striking and potentially far-reaching provisions of SP is that it allows for use not only of the 1962 Missal but also, under varying conditions, of the 1962 form of most of the other sacraments. But this concession is addressed twice in the articles of SP, with some apparent difference between them. Article 5, section 3, calls upon the pastor to allow (*parochus . . . permittat*) use of the FE, when requested, in "occasional circumstances" (*in adiunctis peculiaribus*)—examples given are "marriages, funerals or occasional celebrations, for example, pilgrimages" (SP, art. 5, sec. 3). But what is the force of the pope's subjunctive here (*permittat*), translated "let the pastor permit . . ."? It is surely more than potential, merely suggesting compliance, but is it hortatory, only urging compliance, or jussive, actually commanding it? Perhaps it is meant to be hortatory for those inclined to comply and jussive for those inclined not to? In either case there is expressed a measure of expectation that it will happen—that the pastor will give permission for use of the extraordinary form in such cases.

Yet note the difference in SP, article 9, section 1, which states that the pastor can grant permission (*licentiam concedere potest*) for use of the preconciliar ritual in sacramental celebrations of baptism, matrimony, penance, and the anointing of the sick (as the text reads, not "Extreme Unction"). In this article, such permission is conditional upon his first having pondered all the factors well[128] and on that basis become persuaded it would serve "the good of souls"—and not, for example, simply satisfy his own desire or commitment to use the former ritual or meet the wishes of Catholics resistant to the council. This contrasts with requests from the stable group of the faithful for celebrations using the 1962 Missal. Those requests the pastor is to accept willingly and provide if at all possible (SP, art. 5, sec. 1); if he cannot, the bishop is to be contacted and he is

[128] The phrase is *omnibus bene perpensis* (SP, art. 9, sec. 1). Compare this with the phrase Pope Benedict used in describing his own actions before issuing SP: *omnibus mature perpensis*, "having pondered all these matters fully" (SP 9). The pope invites pastors making their decision (regarding the pastoral life of the church and the good of the faithful in their care) to be as careful and thorough as he was in choosing to promulgate SP. One might speculate that *bene* has replaced *mature* in view of the pastoral exigency of making such decisions in a good but also timely fashion.

"strongly entreated" to make such Masses available (SP, art. 7); if he has difficulty doing so, he is to contact the Pontifical Commission *Ecclesia Dei* for its guidance and help (SP, art. 8).

What we see here is that SP provides powerful support for the faithful who, as a stable group, seek the traditional Mass, giving them a genuine claim to it, including in circumstances such as those listed in article 5, section 3. It seems to be different when they seek the other four sacraments mentioned in article 9, section 1. In this case they have no such claim; rather, the pastor is to take great care in the matter and to grant the requests only when thorough investigation convinces him it would, in his judgment and all things considered, be for the good. All things considered might include the following: his assessment (and it should be pastorally generous and solicitous) of the spiritual needs and desires of the persons or families making the request; the impact of such celebrations on the overall life of the parish and diocese; the ability of himself, or other available clergy, and his staff to provide such celebrations and the attendant catechesis or pastoral ministry required, while continuing to serve well the needs of the entire pastoral community for which he is responsible; the bishop's assessment of the needs of the diocese; and so on. But it should also be noted that SP is a document of "favorable, permissive law," and as such the permissions it grants should be interpreted and applied as generously as possible.[129]

The pastor, thus, would seem to have a double responsibility to balance in regard to requests for these four sacraments: on the one hand, not to be automatic in granting permission for them, but to do so only after full and careful consideration of all factors, and if persuaded the good of souls calls for it; on the other hand, to lean in favor of those making the request, beginning one's consideration of relevant factors inclined or even determined to grant the request if possible.

[129] "As a favorable, permissive law, [SP] is subject to broad interpretation in keeping with the rule of law: 'Burdens are to be restricted, but favors are to be amplified.'" Huels, "Reconciling the Old with the New," 96.

SP, ARTICLE 7

> *Where some group of the lay faithful mentioned in Art. 5 sec. 1 has not obtained the permission sought from the pastor, let it make the diocesan bishop aware of the matter. The bishop is earnestly requested to answer their wish. If he is not willing to provide for this kind of celebration, let the matter be referred to the Pontifical Commission "Ecclesia Dei."*

SP, ARTICLE 8

> *A bishop who wishes to provide for such petitions of the lay Christian faithful but is impeded for various reasons can entrust the matter to the Pontifical Commission "Ecclesia Dei," which will give him advice and help.*

If a pastor has not provided the extraordinary form Mass when so requested by a stable group of the faithful (art. 5, sec. 1), that group is to make the fact known to the diocesan bishop, and the bishop is to see to it that the request is granted. No means are specified but are left to local circumstances. And so, for example, the bishop may (if the pastor is *idoneus*) persuade the pastor to preside at the extraordinary form Mass personally, or insist he do so, or have him secure the services of a priest willing and able to do so, or find a place in the diocese where the group may go for such Masses (compare UE 17, sec. 2), or send the pastor or other priests of the diocese for training in the extraordinary form (see UE 21), or invite into the diocese priests (for example, from the Priestly Fraternity of Saint Peter) qualified to celebrate in the extraordinary form or to teach others to do so (see UE 22)—or find some other way to provide for the request of the group.

Pope Benedict's charge to the bishop (*Episcopus enixe rogatur*) may be taken as a canonically polite form of insistence, stating what is intended functionally to be a requirement. Rehak considers it "by no means non-binding,"[130] and he references the canons in the Code that use the verb *rogare* to call for curial cardinals, diocesan bishops, and parish pastors to submit their resignations when they reach the age of seventy-five—something no bishop

[130] Rehak, *Der außerordentliche Gebrauch*, 152 (*keineswegs unverbindlich*).

takes to be optional or at his discretion but obligatory.[131] The implication could be drawn that SP wants bishops to provide for these requests with a similar sense of obligation. *Exaudiat* does not carry the meaning of hear but hear favorably, answer, comply with.[132] If the bishop is unwilling to see to the granting of the request,[133] the matter is to be referred to the Pontifical Commission *Ecclesia Dei*. The passive voice (*referatur*) leaves open the agency of the referral; this serves to protect the rights of the group. If the bishop is unwilling to provide for their request, he may also be slow or unwilling to communicate the fact to the PCED, and so SP makes provision, by means of the passive voice, for the group to have permission to contact the Commission. If the bishop *is* willing to provide for the group's request but finds he cannot fulfill it, he is the one who is to contact the PCED; Benedict put the matter in his hands in this case, considering it both proper to do so (since he is the bishop and it is his responsibility) and safe (since he has shown himself desirous of granting the group's request). Note that the entire process as found in article 5, section 1, with articles 7 and 8 enacts the principle of subsidiarity.[134]

SP, ARTICLE 9, SECTION 2

> *Moreover, the faculty is given to ordinaries to celebrate the sacrament of confirmation using the prior Roman Pontifical, if the good of souls recommends it.*

[131] Rehak, *Der außerordentliche Gebrauch*, 152, referring to canons 354, 401 sec. 1, and 538 sec. 3; the language is used in Vatican II, *Christus Dominus* 21. Canon 401, sec. 2, moreover, stipulates that a diocesan bishop who becomes less able to fulfill his responsibilities because of illness or another grave cause "is earnestly requested" to submit his resignation (*Enixe rogatur*), the very phrase used here.

[132] "Hear favorably," "answer": Stelten, *Dictionary of Ecclesiastical Latin*, 91; "comply with": *Oxford Latin Dictionary*, ed. P. G. W. Glare (Oxford: Oxford University Press, 1982), 632.

[133] An earlier version of the document spoke at this point of the bishop being unable to provide for the request (see also Rehak, *Der außerordentliche Gebrauch*, 153); the official version in AAS addresses the situation of the bishop who is unwilling (*non vult*). By doing so, articles 7 and 8 cover both scenarios—willing and unwilling bishops.

[134] See also Rehak, *Der außerordentliche Gebrauch*, 151–52.

Regarding the sacrament of confirmation, the bishop may use the former ritual if he is persuaded it would serve "the good of souls." Again, the emphasis is on the good of others rather than his own preferences (either for or against the FE)—a point fully consonant with Ratzinger's views of the pastoral office.[135]

SP, ARTICLE 9, SECTION 3

It is lawful for clerics constituted in sacred orders to use also the Roman Breviary promulgated by Blessed John XXIII in 1962.

Clerics may use the 1962 Breviary.

There is no specific indication this provision was added to SP because of a judgment as to the relative merits of the 1962 Breviary as compared with the 1970 Liturgy of the Hours.[136] On one level,

[135] See, for example, Ratzinger, *God and the World*, 456.

[136] How do the two compare? Judgments on their merits vary. László Dobszay finds that the 1970 reform departs so far from the Roman Office tradition (of which the Tridentine Breviary was only one form) in "structure, material and spirit" that "it cannot be called a new version of it, a new member of the same family," and that, accordingly, "it does not belong to the Roman Office as regards its content"; see *The Bugnini-Liturgy and the Reform of the Reform* (Front Royal, VA: Catholic Church Music Associates, 2003), 68. Robert F. Taft judges that "the basic skeleton of the Roman Office . . . has remained substantially the same from the sixth century until Vatican II"; see *The Liturgy of the Hours in East and West: The Origins of the Divine Office and Its Meaning for Today*, 2nd rev. ed. (Collegeville, MN: Liturgical Press, 1993), 307—though he also notes, in commenting on Pius X's reform of the breviary in 1911, that "for anyone with a sense of the history of the office, this was a shocking departure from almost universal Christian tradition" (312). And while Taft speaks of the reform of the Roman Office after Vatican II as "even more radical than that of Pius X," he also affirms that "the basic structure of the Roman hours was more or less respected," with a few exceptions—more Scripture, collects for each psalm, and hymns moved to the opening of each liturgical hour (313). Both Dobszay and Taft deem the 1970 reform flawed because it was designed to be private prayer for clergy and religious rather than public liturgy for the church as a whole (see Dobszay, 64, and Taft, 314–17). But Dobszay considers the 1970 changes to be serious deformations of the Roman Office which should be corrected by returning to its prior structures—indeed, predating not only the 1970 Office but also that of 1962, 1911, and 1568; see Dobszay, *The Bugnini-Liturgy and the Reform of the Reform*, chaps. 1 and 3, and also his *The Restoration and Organic*

Pope Benedict here was simply granting priests who might wish it permission to fulfill their obligation to daily prayer through use of the 1962 Breviary. But article 9, section 3 also serves one of Pope Benedict's general purposes in SP—to demonstrate, by reauthorizing elements of the prior liturgy for use in the church today, that there is no division or breach but rather "reform in continuity" between the so-called "preconciliar" and "postconciliar" church. This point is made by the simple fact of reauthorization, regardless whether anyone actually uses the old Breviary. And if in the first two sections of article 9 the pope stipulated criteria by which to make the decision regarding use of the sacraments in question, that was likely because the decision directly affected the faithful and he wanted to provide guidance in making the judgment; section three strictly speaking affects only those bound to pray the Divine Office and in all likelihood each cleric individually (insofar as private recitation of the Breviary largely remains customary), so the pope left it to each cleric's individual preference—just as with use of the 1962 Missal in Masses *sine populo*.

The instruction *Universae Ecclesiae* makes an interesting and challenging stipulation for clergy who wish to choose, under article 9, section 3 of SP, to use the 1962 Breviary. The stipulation is that the Breviary "is to be prayed entirely and in the Latin language" (*integre et Latino sermone*, UE 32). Baronius Press sells a 1962 Breviary that is English-Latin, surely a help to clerics interested in the FE who do not know Latin well; but according to UE they cannot *pray* that Breviary in English, only in Latin. The instruction thus seems to presume (and in effect requires) for use of the 1962 Breviary what it requires for use of the 1962 Missal: that clergy be *idoneus* to use it, possessing a sufficient knowledge of Latin to understand the words they pray. This provision is clear and a challenge for the many clergy ignorant of or weak in Latin. Also, there is some ambiguity in the word "entirely" (*integre*); does it apply only to each hour of the Office for which one chooses to use the old Breviary (for example, no switching during Matins between psalms in Latin

---

Development of the Roman Rite, chap. 15. Taft, on the other hand, thinks many of the structural changes in 1970 that Dobszay laments were in fact "admirable" (Taft, 313), and that various problematic features of the prior Breviary needing reform "were faced with imagination and resoluteness" (314).

and readings in English), or does it mean the choice to use the 1962 Breviary entails (on any given day?) using it alone, for all the canonical hours, without use of the reformed Liturgy of the Hours for any of the hours?

Does this provision authorize religious communities to return to their preconciliar celebration of the hours? The answer seems unclear. The fact that article 3 explicitly (under the conditions there mentioned) grants religious communities permission to use the prior Missal, and article 9, section 3, does not do the same for the Breviary, may suggest an answer in the negative. But the spirit of SP seems open to an answer in the affirmative, and if the document is by the rules of canon law to be given an expansive, permissive reading, then it seems acceptable and perhaps preferable to think an affirmative answer is to be presumed. This is another point on which the PCED could provide clarity.

SP, ARTICLE 10

> *It is lawful for the local ordinary, if he judges it opportune, to erect a personal parish, in accord with the norm of Canon 518, for celebration according to the prior form of the Roman rite, or appoint a rector or chaplain, all relevant laws being observed.*

Article 10 is noteworthy if only for the fact that Cardinal Ratzinger had expressed reservations about this option a few short years before enacting it into law as pope. At the 2001 conference in Fontgombault he said, "Perhaps the 'personal parish' might be a solution, but that is not without difficulty either."[137] The point he raised there was of real significance to him, touching upon what we could call lived ecclesiology. He was concerned lest Catholics think of parishes as "life-style enclaves" where one chooses with whom one will associate. For him this view represented, and reinforced, a fundamental misunderstanding of what it is to be part of the body of Christ. Properly understood, as part of that body one does not choose with whom to associate but accepts all as brothers and sisters.[138] Establishing a personal parish for the FE creates the condi-

[137] Ratzinger, "Assessment and Future Prospects," 150.
[138] Ibid., 149.

tions for a segregating of FE adherents with each other, into what might be called an "ecclesial-style enclave" or "ghetto"[139] and apart from the wider church.

While some FE and FO adherents may both find a certain appeal in the thought of not having to deal with each other, this provision hardly serves Benedict's larger purpose of bringing about "an interior reconciliation in the heart of the Church" (CGF 8) but rather works directly against it by fostering or at least risking, as social psychologists would point out, the divisive dynamics of ingroup favoritism (thinking too highly and uncritically of those in one's group) and outgroup derogation (thinking too critically and negatively of those in the other group). While the overall social psychological dynamics of the combined provisions of SP/CGF may tend to foster reconciliation rather than division, nonetheless the danger of division exists, and it is article 10 that makes the church most vulnerable to it. In addition, Rehak sees an inconsistency between, on the one hand, Pope Benedict's insistence that priests of communities adhering to the *usus antiquior* not "as a matter of principle, exclude celebration according to the new books" (CGF 9)—a principle Rehak holds would apply to the faithful as well as to priests, a view confirmed in UE 19—and on the other hand the permission given in SP, article 10, for the creation of parish communities that, of set purpose and by design, exclude celebration according to the reformed liturgical books. Indeed, for Rehak, creating ecclesial structures intentionally for exclusive use of the prior liturgy is "theologically problematic."[140]

The issues created by article 10, then, are not insignificant. So why did Pope Benedict include it in SP? Consider what the article does. It offers a bishop, if he needs it (as he well may, at least for a time) a relatively priest-effective way to fulfill his responsibilities under SP to make the FE available for those in his diocese who desire it. In many diocesan circumstances, with extensive demands already placed upon priests stretched thin by the responsibilities of pastoral care for many persons and perhaps multiple assignments,

[139] Christophe Geffroy, *Benoît XVI et "la paix liturgique"* (Paris: Les Éditions du Cerf, 2008), 281 ("ghetto").

[140] Rehak, *Der außerordentliche Gebrauch*, 173.

establishing a designated FE parish (with perhaps only one priest, its pastor) could be the only really practicable way to provide the FE generously or even adequately. In this light, article 10 can be read as an indicator of how much Benedict wanted to make the extraordinary form available for those who seek it or how highly he rated and wished to honor their right to have access to it (especially in contexts marked by a shortage of clergy)—so much that he was willing to risk the divisive potential of the separate FE parish.[141]

The alternative that might lessen this potential would be for bishops to try to make provision, with the cooperation of seminaries and clergy continuing education programs, for more priests to be well trained and willing to celebrate the 1962 liturgy, thereby allowing that liturgy to be present in a diocese in a more integrated way, within rather than apart from regular parish life. This latter situation would help to avoid one potential cause of divisiveness and also make distinctly more possible the liturgical "reconciliation" in the church, and the mutual enrichment of the two usages, that were among Pope Benedict's principal long-term goals.

SP, ARTICLE 11

> *The Pontifical Commission "Ecclesia Dei" erected by John Paul II in 1988*[142] *continues to carry out its function.*
>
> *This Commission is to have the form, duties, and procedural norms which the Roman Pontiff may wish to give it.*

After the publication of SP, through his *motu proprio* of 2009 *Ecclesiae Unitatem*, Pope Benedict supplemented the role of the PCED and joined it more closely with the Congregation for the Doctrine of the Faith, whose prefect now also serves as president of the Commission. Benedict took this step so that the Commission and Congregation could more directly and effectively address the doctrinal questions still at issue between the Catholic Church and

[141] Peter Stravinskas also opposes this kind of arrangement, seeing it as having "divisive repercussions, in effect, building a church within the Church"; in his "Why I Oppose a Tridentine Prelature," *The Catholic World Report* (February 1992): 38, as cited in Kocik, *The Reform of the Reform?* 93.

[142] Cf. John Paul II, Litterae Apostolicae motu proprio datae *Ecclesia Dei* (July 2, 1988), 6: *Acta Apostolicae Sedis* 80 (1988) 1498. [Note in original.—Trans.]

the SSPX. As he said, with this change "I have wished in particular to show fatherly solicitude to the 'Society of St. Pius X' in order that it rediscover full communion with the Church."[143] His driving concern throughout is for the unity of the church, as is clearly expressed in *Ecclesiae Unitatem* 1, as well as 3 and 4.

SP, ARTICLE 12

> *The same Commission, beyond the faculties it already enjoys, will exercise the authority of the Holy See in keeping watch regarding the observance and application of these dispositions.*
>
> *We order everything decreed by us in these apostolic letters given* Motu proprio *to be established and ratified, and to be observed from the fourteenth day of September of this year, on the Feast of the Triumph of the Holy Cross, anything to the contrary notwithstanding.*

This article grants the Pontifical Commission *Ecclesia Dei* "the authority of the Holy See" in implementing the provisions of SP. This is a challenging responsibility.

With those provisions Pope Benedict crafted with care and precision a way to offer but not impose the 1962 Missal—to make it available in the life of the church for those who seek it, while maintaining the reformed liturgy as the ordinary form of the Roman Rite of the Catholic Church. Such balance and discretion may be difficult to maintain. Administratively, it cannot be taken for granted that a staff, when carrying out a nuanced directive, over a period of time, will successfully avoid under- or overemphasizing one or another feature of it, whether intentionally or inadvertently. The concern expressed here echoes that voiced by John F. Baldovin in his comments on Cardinal Ratzinger's understanding of the concept of Christian sacrifice; while Baldovin found Ratzinger's theology on this point "very nuanced," he then added, "I do not find the same sophistication in his followers."[144]

[143] Benedict XVI, Apostolic Letter, *Ecclesiae Unitatem* (2009) 7. For more on the history and role of the PCED, see http://www.vatican.va/roman_curia/congregations/cfaith/ced_documents/rc_con_cfaith_20090930_ecclesia-dei_en.html.

[144] John F. Baldovin, "Idols and Icons: Reflections on the Current State of Liturgical Reform," *Worship* 84, no. 5 (September 2010): 386–402, at 394.

I have a similar concern regarding the interpretation and implementation of the nuanced provisions of SP by the papal staff and members of the PCED. This concern arises from no animus toward those who serve the pope but is based on specific comments reportedly made by some of them. Recall from chapter 2 the comments of Cardinal Castrillón Hoyos, proposing that the traditional Mass be made available even where it is not requested in accord with article 5, section 1 of SP, and of the Vatican official who asserted that the new Mass would pass and the old Mass return as the church's liturgy. These views represent, if not an ignorance of, then either a misunderstanding of or disregard for the mind of the legislator as expressed in SP and CGF, and the intentions for the church's liturgy expressed therein. If the unnamed Vatican official or others similarly minded have a role to play in the future of SP, one can only conclude their influence will hinder an implementation of that document that is fair and faithful to its stated provisions. It is on the basis of such comments by Vatican officials that concern is warranted for the manner in which SP may be administered. It is to be hoped instead that future decisions and developments in implementation of SP correspond with and do not vary from, fall short of, or exceed the document's actual provisions.

"This year" that SP, article 12 referred to was 2007. "Anything to the contrary notwithstanding" means the provisions of SP update or replace those of prior church documents (legislative, dogmatic, etc.) relative to the matters at hand; this would include John Paul II's *motu proprio Ecclesia Dei* (1988), the CDWDS's letter, *Quattuor Abhinc Annos* (1984), Pope Paul VI's apostolic constitution *Missale Romanum* (1969), the Second Vatican Council's constitution on the sacred liturgy, *Sacrosanctum Concilium* (1963), Pope Blessed John XXIII's *motu proprio Rubricarum Instructum* (1960), or Pope Saint Pius V's apostolic constitution *Quo Primum* (1570). Those provisions went into effect on Friday, September 14, 2007, the Feast of the Triumph of the Holy Cross in the calendar of both the ordinary and extraordinary forms.

Given at Rome, at Saint Peter's, on the seventh day of July in the year of our Lord 2007, the third of my pontificate.

Chapter 5

Con Grande Fiducia

Translation and Commentary

CGF 1

> *Dear brothers in the episcopacy, with great trust and hope I put in your hands as pastors the text of a new apostolic letter* "motu proprio data" *on the use of the Roman liturgy prior to the reform made effective in 1970. The document is the fruit of long reflection, many consultations, and prayer.*[1]

In his letter to the Catholic bishops of the world, accompanying and explaining *Summorum Pontificum*, Pope Benedict placed this liturgical initiative into their hands in their role "as pastors," in a spirit of "great trust and hope." To make salient their role as pastors was to highlight his and their responsibility to serve the needs and foster the good of those entrusted to their care, like the good shepherd of a flock, even when this calls on him to stretch beyond his own preferences to make room for something nonetheless legitimately Catholic.[2]

This raises the question of how a bishop is to discern when his ideas of what would be best are personal preferences that he should be willing to sacrifice for the good of others and when they

[1] [This and all subsequent CGF quotes are my translation of *Con Grande Fiducia*. Italian original published in *Acta Apostolicae Sedis* 99, no. 9 (2007): 795–99.—Trans.]

[2] This understanding of Pope Benedict found expression also in the instruction of the PCED, *Universae Ecclesiae,* which states that "Diocesan Bishops, according to Canon Law, are to monitor liturgical matters in order to guarantee the common good and to ensure that everything is proceeding in peace and serenity in their Dioceses, always in agreement with the *mens* of the Holy Father clearly expressed by the Motu Proprio *Summorum Pontificum*" (no. 13).

are sound judgments that he should hold to and carry out even if others disagree or oppose. It can at times be difficult to know when a bishop should allow or even positively foster manifestations of faith (such as those in the diverse movements in the church today) not to his liking. But the general perspective taken by Ratzinger was that Catholicism is a living reality that cannot ultimately be "institutionally and academically planned and managed, but [that] appears ever again as a gift, as a spiritual vitality" that manifests itself with great "diversity."[3] This "diversity of paths is something in accordance with the breadth of Catholicity," and "one ought not simply to reject it, even when it is something contrary to one's own taste."[4] If Ratzinger here expressed a mentality or spirituality applicable for all Catholics in their understanding of the church and their relations with one another, he applied it also (and we can say, *a fortiori*) to the bishop, whose office requires him not merely to allow but, as part of his *munus regendi*, "to guarantee the breadth" that is characteristic of Catholicism by creating and maintaining space in his diocese for diverse manifestations of spiritual vitality—again, even those he may not personally favor.[5] The biblical principle at work here would be, "Do not quench the Spirit" (1 Thess 5:19, cited in LG 12, and AA 2).

As for what to do regarding use of the traditional Mass, in this case the difficulty of discernment has been removed, for Pope Benedict made clear by the very provisions of SP what a bishop's judgment and actions in this matter are to be. If this were to entail, for any particular bishop, authorizing and facilitating pastoral activity in his diocese that fell outside his preferences and even his judgment, Pope Benedict expected him still to do so, as a good shep-

[3] Ratzinger, *God and the World: A Conversation with Peter Seewald*, trans. Henry Taylor (San Francisco: Ignatius Press, 2002), 455.

[4] Ibid., 456.

[5] Ibid. See also Ratzinger, "Church Movements and Their Place in Theology," in *Pilgrim Fellowship of Faith*, 176–208; for example: "The local Churches too, however, and even the bishops, have to be told that they should not indulge in any pursuit of uniformity in their pastoral arrangements or planning. They should not set up their own pastoral plans as a yardstick of what the Holy Spirit is allowed to do" (207). See also Ratzinger, *Called to Communion: Understanding the Church Today* (San Francisco: Ignatius Press, 1996), 100.

herd, for the sake of the greater good as identified with clarity by him (as pope) with whom and under whom (*cum Petro et sub Petro*) bishops share in the governance and care of the whole church (LG 22, 23). Benedict encouraged the bishops' trust in this judgment of his by assuring them here that it was the fruit of "long reflection, many consultations, and prayer"; he assured them also in SP that it was made only after "having invoked the Holy Spirit," and with reliance on "the help of God" (SP 9), phrases that can serve at once to reassure and persuade.

Pope Benedict put this initiative into the bishops' hands "with great trust," because theologically they are his episcopal brothers and collaborators and because administratively he must. Their positive reception of SP is essential to its implementation and critical to its success, and so in a spirit of collegiality and to win their support he wrote this letter (CGF), sharing with them the factors, thoughts, concerns, and purposes that moved him to take this step. He acted with "hope" because the matter at hand was so dear to his heart, fundamental to his understanding of the church, and, in his strategic vision, full of potential for contributing to the church's efforts to preach the Gospel today to cultures and persons increasingly shaped by the premise that God does not exist or does not matter—as if God were not part of the picture, *etsi Deus non daretur*.[6] For Pope Benedict, to overcome and heal liturgical divisions, a principal goal of SP (see CGF 8), would be to unify and build up the church as communion, which in turn would strengthen it for its evangelizing mission in and for the world.

As to whether the world, in fact, is increasingly irreligious, the data apparently point in two directions. David B. Barrett and colleagues comment, for example, after reporting a numerical growth but percentage decline during the twentieth century in the number of Christians in the world, that "it is not Christianity alone which

[6] The phrase of Grotius, *etsi Deus non daretur*, was common in the writings of John Paul II, and addressing the issues it raises was of concern to Ratzinger as well. See, for example, "Europe's Crisis of Culture," in *The Essential Pope Benedict XVI: His Central Writings and Speeches*, ed. John F. Thornton and Susan B. Varenne (New York: HarperCollins, 2007), 325–35, at 334–35; or the brief reference in a liturgical context in Joseph Ratzinger, *Milestones: Memoirs 1927–1977* (San Francisco: Ignatius Press, n.d. [1998]), 149.

is static or in decline; it is the entire phenomenon of religion. All the other major world religions have suffered similarly, some catastrophically."[7] On the other hand, "revivals of religion are taking place in widespread secularized areas. One must therefore be careful not to exaggerate the progress of secularization."[8] Even if the focus is strictly on Christianity, the evidence is not entirely negative. The percentage of the world's population that is Christian declined slightly in the twentieth century, from 34.8 to 33.2 percent, but this decline, largely in the global North, is being more than offset by gains in the global South, which should lead to an overall increase in the percentage of Christians.[9] Benedict may have religious decline in his sights by looking above all at Europe; while concern for evangelization is at the heart of his responsibilities as pope, the world situation seems to offer lights as well as shadows.

CGF 2

> *News reports and judgments made without sufficient information have created not a little confusion. There are very diverse reactions ranging from joyful acceptance to harsh opposition, concerning a project whose contents were in reality not known.*

Here, Pope Benedict made reference, with perhaps "une petite pique,"[10] to prejudgments regarding SP, of widely diverse types, with resulting confusion. Before its publication the document had

[7] "The World by Countries: Religionists, Churches, Ministries," in *World Christian Encyclopedia: A Comparative Survey of Churches and Religions in the Modern World*, ed. David B. Barrett, George T. Kurian, Todd M. Johnson, 2nd ed. (Oxford: Oxford University Press, 2001), 1:1.

[8] Ibid.

[9] See Todd M. Johnson, David B. Barrett, and Peter F. Crossing, "Christianity 2010: A View from the New *Atlas of Global Christianity*," *International Bulletin of Missionary Research* 34, no. 1 (2010): 29. The authors, from the Center for the Study of Global Christianity at Gordon-Conwell Theological Seminary, foresee Christianity expanding to 33.8 percent by 2025, and to 35 percent by 2050. The most rapid growth is in Pentecostal forms of Christianity. On this, see, for example, Allan Anderson, *An Introduction to Pentecostalism: Global Charismatic Christianity* (Cambridge: Cambridge University Press, 2004).

[10] Christophe Geffroy, *Benoît XVI et "la paix liturgique"* (Paris: Les Éditions du Cerf, 2008), 10.

been expected for some months, with eager anticipation from those who favored the prior liturgical forms and with opposition by some who opposed the use of those forms. To the extent CGF was written largely to explain the pope's motives to those opposed to the provisions of SP, we might take these words as intended primarily for them, but they apply to supporters as well. What he critiqued here were the prejudgments (*giudizi*, in the plural) whether from opponents who argued against "a project whose contents were in reality not known" or, we should also think, from supporters who expected (or demanded) too much. Both groups, by arousing false fears or hopes, contributed to a situation of tension, opposition, and confusion that only served to muddle and polarize the church community to which the pope wished to address himself with irenic and reconciling intent.

CGF 3

> *To this document two fears most directly opposed themselves, which I would like to confront a little more closely in this letter.*

This sentence speaks of two fears regarding SP and its consequences, which Pope Benedict then addressed in CGF 4–7.

The first fear is that implementation of the provisions of SP would function to cast doubt on the authority of the Second Vatican Council and its liturgical reform. The thinking goes something like this. The first document approved at the council was its 1963 constitution on the sacred liturgy, which set forth general norms and specific directives for the reform of the church's liturgy, including the Mass. The very point of the constitution was to bring about a "general reform" (or "restoration," *generalem instaurationem*, SC 21) of the Roman Rite as it existed in 1962 when the council began. But with this *motu proprio* Pope Benedict reestablished the 1962 Missal as a legitimate expression of the Roman Rite, as its extraordinary form, reauthorizing its use on a wider basis than was the case under the 1984 and 1988 norms put in place by John Paul II. Does not this action of Pope Benedict call into question the council's decision to mandate reform of that 1962 liturgy and give both legal and moral support to those who have opposed the liturgical reform, including those who have also opposed the council as a whole? At least could not those so inclined understandably interpret it this way and thus be reaffirmed and encouraged in their opposition? Such reflections begin to describe the first of the two fears, to which Pope Benedict responded in CGF 4–5.

The second fear is related: will not implementation of SP be divisive, separating Catholics along ritual lines, creating and sustaining a kind of extraordinary form church, a community *de facto* distinct from those who celebrate the ordinary form? Pastors and bishops are expected and arguably required by SP to provide celebrations of Mass according to the 1962 Missal for Catholics who exist or come to exist as a stable group—Catholics who may resist the council and its liturgical reform to a greater or lesser extent, and perhaps hold aloof from the life of ordinary postconciliar parishes. Might not this provision of an alternate worship service, enabling and sustaining their absence from the parish's normal FO Masses, make their separation from the ordinary life of parish and diocese deeper and even permanent? Might not their increased visibility (as the people who go to "that other Mass we have at the parish") potentially attract others, if at first simply to investigate the extraordinary form, perhaps ultimately to enter into a quasi-separatist community, allowing it to build and strengthen—all to the detriment of unity and peace in the church? Such are the kinds of questions and concerns of the second fear, to which Pope Benedict responded in CGF 6–7.

CGF 4

> *In the first place, there is the fear that here the authority of the Second Vatican Council could be harmed and that one of its essential decisions—the liturgical reform—could be cast into doubt. Such fear is unfounded. In this regard it must first of all be said that the Missal published in two editions by Paul VI and then republished a third time with the approval of John Paul II obviously is and remains the normal form—the* forma ordinaria*—of the Eucharistic liturgy. The last version of the* Roman Missal *before the council which was published with the authority of Pope John XXIII in 1962 and used during the council, will be able to be used, instead, as the* forma extraordinaria *of the liturgical celebration. It is not appropriate to speak of these two versions of the Roman Missal as if they were "two rites." We are dealing rather with a twofold use of one and the same rite.*
>
> *As for the use of the Missal of 1962 as the* forma extraordinaria *of the liturgy of the Mass, I would like to draw attention to the fact that this Missal was not ever juridically abrogated and, consequently, as a matter of principle remained always permitted. When the new Missal was intro-*

duced, it did not seem necessary to issue specific norms for the possible use of the prior Missal. Probably it was supposed it would be a matter of a few individual cases that would be resolved case by case on the local level.

After, however, it soon became clear that not a few remained strongly attached to that use of the Roman Rite which from childhood had become familiar to them. This happened first of all in countries in which the liturgical movement had given many people a remarkable liturgical formation and a profound, intimate familiarity with the prior form of the liturgical celebration.

We all know that in the movement led by Archbishop Lefebvre, fidelity to the old Mass became an external sign; the reasons for the split which began here, however, are found in deeper matters.

Many people who clearly accepted the binding character of the Second Vatican Council and were faithful to the pope and the bishops nonetheless also desired to find again the form of the sacred liturgy dear to them. This happened first of all because in many places there were celebrations unfaithful to the prescriptions of the new Missal; indeed it even came to be taken to authorize or even require creativity, which often led to deformations of the liturgy, to the limit of what could be endured. I speak from experience, for I myself also went through that period with all its expectations and confusions. And I have seen how profoundly wounded, by arbitrary deformations of the liturgy, were persons who were totally rooted in the faith of the church.

CGF 4 and 5 address the fear that the provisions of SP will undermine the authority of the Second Vatican Council in general and its liturgical reform in particular. CGF 4 offers first of all a clear affirmation that the reformed Missal, in the *editio typica tertia* of 2002, is and remains the given, standard, still fully normative, default liturgy of the Roman Rite—its *forma ordinaria*. This central point must always be borne in mind when discussing these matters. SP also adds a new dimension to the Roman Rite by allowing limited use of (and calling upon pastors to provide, if requested) the 1962 Missal as the *forma extraordinaria*, made available for Catholics wishing to worship according to this form. Pope Benedict then affirmed that this new situation does not create two rites but a twofold use (*un uso duplice*) of the one Roman Rite, or "two uses of the one Roman Rite" (SP, art. 1, *duo usus unici ritus Romani*). His aim was to create not division but diversity within unity.

After stating that the 1962 Missal was not abrogated and so was in principle still permitted (see chap. 4, pages 98–103 for commentary on this point), Benedict then pondered why no particular norms were issued pertaining to its use, speculating that it was anticipated there would be no need for them since few clergy would seek to use the prior Missal, and such situations could be handled ad hoc on the local level. But is it not rather the case that norms *were* issued on this matter, at the highest level, to make clear under what (very limited) circumstances the prior Missal could continue to be used, by way of exception to the law? This happened, in two ways: (1) by provisions written into the appropriate liturgical books and (2) by indults granting exemptions.

As for the new Missal itself, once issued, it was to be mandatory, to be used instead of the prior Missal; why else did the council want the Roman Missal reformed, except to be used as reformed? But (1) as the reformed Missal was in development, the situation of elderly and infirm priests was foreseen and taken into account in the composition of the liturgical legislation. Accordingly, the 1969 instruction *Constitutione Apostolica* set forth the conditions under which those priests would be exempted from the new universal law of the church and allowed instead to celebrate Mass using the prior Missal (yet, be it noted, the prior Missal not in its 1962 edition but in its 1967 revision).[11] Then, (2) after the reformed Missal was in force, and at the request of Cardinal Heenan of Westminster, Pope Paul authorized an indult allowing bishops in England and Wales to permit celebration of the Mass on special occasions—again, using the 1962 Missal as emended in 1965 and 1967.[12] This latter

[11] Sacred Congregation for Divine Worship, *Constitutione Apostolica* 19–20. The exemption was granted only for Masses without a congregation; further, it was not for use of the 1962 Missal as such, but for that Missal using "the rites and texts now in use" (DOL 209 at no. 1751), that is, as emended in 1965 and 1967. This instruction was issued on October 20, 1969, half a year after the promulgation of the new Missal by Paul VI (April 3, 1969) but before it had officially gone into effect.

[12] See Bugnini, *The Reform of the Liturgy 1948–1975* (Collegeville, MN: Liturgical Press, 1990), 297–98. This is the "Agatha Christie Indult," so called because the famous mystery writer was among the signatories to the request and her name was reportedly remarked upon by Paul VI, "an admiring reader"; see Geffroy, *Benoît XVI et «la paix liturgique»*, 132–34. Carol Zaleski thinks the tale "probably apocryphal"; see Zaleski, "Worshiping with Agatha Christie," *Christian Century* 124, no. 17 (August 21, 2007): 35.

example shows, on the part of Cardinal Heenan who conveyed the request to the pope, and on the part of the several dozen prominent English Catholics who signed the request, that it was clearly understood that the traditional Mass could no longer be celebrated, and that only the pope could exempt from that prohibition. Moreover, that the pope granted such permission by means of an indult shows that he also understood himself to be granting an exemption from a binding norm of law. And so, actually, specific norms for use of the prior Missal were enacted at the time the new Missal was introduced.

Pope Benedict then remarked that "it soon became clear" that "not a few" (*non pochi*) continued to remain "strongly attached" to the prior liturgical usage, which they had known from childhood and had come to appreciate deeply, thanks to the educational efforts of the liturgical movement. He had remarked elsewhere that it was precisely "in those places where the liturgical movement had created a certain love for the liturgy" that the loss of that liturgy was felt most keenly.[13] In saying "not a few," Benedict was urging the reasonableness of his permission for use of the traditional

[13] Joseph Ratzinger, "Dix ans après," no. 11. This address was given in 1998 at the conference in Rome marking the tenth anniversary of John Paul II's *motu proprio Ecclesia Dei*, addressing the situation created by Archbishop Lefebvre's illicit ordination of four bishops for the SSPX. The French original of Cardinal Ratzinger's address (whose first words are "Dix ans après") can be found online at http://lacriseintegriste.typepad.fr/weblog/1998/10/conf%C3%A9rence-du-cardinal-ratzinger-pour-les-10-ans-du-motu-proprio-ecclesia-dei.html. The English translation used here is from Joseph Ratzinger, "'The Church Has Never Abolished Orthodox Liturgies,'" *Inside the Vatican* 6, no. 10 (December 1998): 58–59. A different English translation can be found online at http://www.fssp.org/en/annivratz.htm. Paragraph numbers correspond to paragraph divisions as in the French online text.

His point (in the words cited from no. 11 of the address) is that when and where the educational efforts of the liturgical movement in the first half of the twentieth century were successful, people came thereby to a greater appreciation for the church's liturgy as it was celebrated then. The subsequent change of this liturgy was thus felt most keenly by those who had been taught and learned to understand and appreciate it most highly. Where such an informed appreciation for the preconciliar liturgy had not been developed, the change or loss was not felt so greatly.

liturgy as being an act of pastoral care toward a constituency whose numbers, if small, are not insignificant.

On the other hand, Benedict also appealed to the fact that those who desire the old liturgy and whom he had in mind in promulgating SP were relatively few. He later asserted that SP does not represent a stepping back from Vatican II, because SP "is merely an act of tolerance, with a pastoral aim, for those people who were brought up with this liturgy, who love it, are familiar with it and want to live with this liturgy," and who, moreover, are not many but only "form a small group."[14] It is worth keeping this observation in mind, as it will necessarily contextualize—one might even say contradict—possible claims on the part of FE adherents (or fears on the part of FO advocates) that the underlying intention of SP and Pope Benedict was that ultimately the traditional liturgy would replace the liturgy as reformed after the council and once again become the liturgical norm for all in the church. This was simply not Pope Benedict's vision or intent; whatever the future of the traditional liturgy, it was intended in part as pastoral care for a group that is "small"—not least because appreciation for (and ability to participate in) this liturgy "presupposes a schooling in Latin, a training in a certain culture."[15] This observation repeated what was written in CGF 6 and will be commented on later in this chapter. Finally, after remarking that bishops owe such persons the "love and tolerance to let them live with this liturgy," Benedict then affirmed that "there is no opposition between the liturgy renewed by the Second Vatican Council and this liturgy."[16] Here, *no opposition* does not mean no difference; rather, he meant the two forms are in fundamental continuity, the newer does not necessarily cancel or make reprobate the former, the former does not call in doubt or invalidate the newer, and both can coexist harmoniously in the

[14] Benedict XVI, "Interview of the Holy Father Benedict XVI during the Flight to France" (September 12, 2008). See also his reference to "the small circle of people who use the old missal"; Benedict XVI, *Light of the World: The Pope, the Church, and the Signs of the Times: A Conversation with Peter Seewald* (San Francisco: Ignatius Press, 2010), 106.

[15] Benedict XVI, "Interview of the Holy Father Benedict XVI during the Flight to France."

[16] Ibid.

one church without causing division—indeed, they can coexist to their mutual enrichment.[17]

A sentence follows regarding the Society of Saint Pius X, the first but not last reference to this community in the letter. This Society was very much on his mind later, in CGF 8, with the reflections there on incipient schisms. The SSPX was led by Archbishop Marcel Lefebvre, who participated in the Second Vatican Council, was among the minority who resisted the general direction of reform taken by the council, and later became outspoken in his opposition to postconciliar developments and to several features of the teaching of the council documents, including the liturgy, religious liberty, ecumenism, and the church's relation with non-Christian religions. The sentence here notes that for them the preconciliar form of the Mass became a chief symbol of their overall opposition to the council (the second fear to be addressed in CGF 6–7) and of their choice to adhere to preconciliar ways, but that the dividing issues were actually much more extensive.

The following sentence in the text contains an affirmation central to understanding Pope Benedict's perspectives and pivotal to his argument: namely, that there are Catholics who are at once attached to the old liturgy *and* accept the reforms of Vatican II. In his view, the common perception that a Catholic who "favors the old Mass" invariably also "opposes the council" is overly simplistic and misunderstands the actual state of affairs; rather, he would contend, there are "many people" (*molte persone*) who fall outside the stereotype. This was not a denial that the common perception has merit and is to some extent true; it was only a denial that that perception is so invariably true as to constitute the only sound basis for pastoral action. That, it seems, is the error Benedict thought bishops had made—or rather let us say, we have come here to a point on which they (the pope and the bishops) saw different realities and drew different conclusions.

What did the bishops see? We know what they saw in 1980 and what their pastoral judgment was at that time. A survey of

17 Ibid. "Thus, there are certainly different accents, but nevertheless [there remains] a fundamental identity that excludes a contradiction, an opposition between the renewed liturgy and the previous liturgy."

bishops throughout the church was conducted that year by the Sacred Congregation for the Sacraments and Divine Worship.[18] Survey responses indicated, first of all, little interest among Catholics in having the Mass in Latin, whether according to the new Missal or the old; rather, "there is a vast silent majority that is satisfied with the liturgical reform and faithful to the established norms."[19] Further, the bishops said that "the problem of the Tridentine Mass is not a problem for the entire Church, but only for a tiny—but very active—minority that makes itself heard with much noise."[20] The bishops also reported that at least some groups adherent to the FE "regard themselves as the bearers of truth and orthodoxy, in contrast with the Roman Church, which is supposed to have fallen into heresy."[21] With views of this nature held by this active minority, the situation was not conducive to dialogue or peace within dioceses. Accordingly, we read, "a significant number of bishops . . . declare themselves flatly opposed" to concessions for use of the former rite; it was their judgment that such a step "would not be a basis for peace but rather of serious division and discord in the Church and even of a real loss of authority on the part of the ecclesiastical hierarchy."[22]

And yet, despite such clear comments, Pope John Paul II took a different approach in the 1984 indult issued by the Congregation for Divine Worship, *Quattuor Abhinc Annos*. The indult did acknowledge that, according to the 1980 survey, "it appeared that the problem of priests and faithful holding to the so-called 'Tridentine' rite was almost completely solved." Yet the next sentence stated that "the same problem continues," and on that basis John Paul, "in a desire to meet the wishes of these groups," chose to make it possible, by means of indult, for bishops to allow celebrations according to the 1962 Missal, under clear restrictions specified in the indult. After

[18] For a summary and the congregation's reflections on the survey, see "Latin Mass Survey Report," *Bishops' Committee on the Liturgy Newsletter* 18 (January 1982), as printed in *Thirty-Five Years of the BCL Newsletter 1965–2000* (Washington, DC: USCCB, 2004), 797–800.

[19] Ibid., 797.

[20] Ibid., 799.

[21] Ibid.

[22] Ibid., 800.

Archbishop Lefebvre's ordination of four SSPX bishops in 1988, and with renewed concern to reach out to members of the Society, John Paul urged, in his apostolic letter *Ecclesia Dei*, respect for the feelings of those attached to the prior liturgy. Further, he made an appeal for "a wide and generous application" of the 1984 indult, clearly wanting bishops to be *more* generous than they previously had been in allowing celebrations of the 1962 Missal.[23] Cardinal Ratzinger subsequently formed the impression that bishops failed to do as the pope had urged, showing on the contrary a continuing (as he called it) "intolerance" toward FE adherents—though it is possible (with reference to the 1980 survey) the bishops might instead have called it pastoral prudence in face of liturgical and theological intransigence, or an attempt to uphold respect for legitimate church authority against those who contemned or resisted it.

Whether bishops were acting with prudence or intolerance, and whether they should continue or change course, became moot points. SP replaced QAA and ED and created a new legal framework. The bishops who, under QAA, chose not to allow use of the 1962 Missal in their dioceses evidently did so because their eyes were on those who sought that use in a spirit of opposition to the new liturgy and perhaps to the conciliar reforms as a whole; Pope Benedict allowed wider use of that Missal because his eyes were on, I believe he would say, an insufficiently recognized group—namely, those who sought that traditional liturgical use while also accepting the conciliar reforms, including the validity of the new liturgy. SP represents a different pastoral strategy than QAA, in part because it has in view an additional constituency and so takes account of a wider or at least a different region of the pastoral landscape.

There is yet another shift of perspective that we can find in the concluding sentences of this paragraph of CGF. Pope Benedict did not simply recognize that "many people" who appreciate and seek the old Mass also accept the council. In his view they are in fact not less but more faithful to the council than at least some who favor the new liturgy. Benedict spoke of the former as having been wounded by those who were (are?) in fact unfaithful to the council

[23] John Paul II, *Ecclesia Dei* 6.c.

by being unfaithful to the actual provisions of the liturgical books reformed by mandate of the council—for example by carrying the creativity allowed by the new books beyond what those books in fact allow, to the point of what he calls deformations. Recognition of this perspective, he may hope, can turn the tables, inviting self-reflection leading to a new perspective on the part of those who habitually think of themselves, in contrast to FE adherents, as faithful to the council.

Here, with the reference to "deformations of the liturgy, to the limit of what could be endured" (*deformazioni della Liturgia al limite del sopportabile*), the pope interjected a personal note: "I speak from experience, for I myself also went through that period with all its expectations and confusions." Others who lived through that immediately postconciliar period also describe it as a unique era. James F. White referred to it as "the period of liturgical euphoria . . . when pent-up energy for reform burst the bounds of legitimate change and erupted in unofficial experimentation. . . . Everyone tried banners and balloons. Many went further."[24] Edward Schillebeeckx said the sense of liberation opened up by the council "unleashed a fervor that led, in some instances, to an impetuous approach [to the liturgy] that was hardly justifiable, either liturgically or theologically—counter to the still modest intentions of Vatican II."[25] Keith Pecklers described how "liturgical experimentation reached great heights in the 1970s with home-grown Eucharistic Prayers prayed aloud at times by the entire assembly," and Sunday Mass beginning or concluding with "popular music such as Bob Dylan's 'Blowin' in the Wind' or John Lennon's 'Imagine.' . . . Such experimentation led to the joke about Roman Catholic worship in the Netherlands during those years: 'Everything changes except the bread and the wine!'"[26]

[24] James F. White, *Roman Catholic Worship: Trent to Today*, 2nd ed. (Collegeville, MN: Liturgical Press, 2003), 130.

[25] Edward Schillebeeckx, "Towards a Rediscovery of the Christian Sacraments: Ritualizing Religious Elements in Daily Life," in *Ordo: Bath, Word, Prayer, Table. A Liturgical Primer in Honor of Gordon W. Lathrop*, ed. Dirk G. Lange and Dwight W. Vogel (Akron, OH: OSL Publications, 2005), 6–34, at 7.

[26] Keith F. Pecklers, *Worship: A Primer in Christian Ritual* (Collegeville, MN: Liturgical Press, 2005, 2003), 113.

There were authors at that time who said as much. Writing in 1970, Ralph Keifer thought the negative reaction of "a considerable part of the Catholic population . . . to the current [liturgical] ferment" was "justified by the manner in which current reforms are being implemented in many parishes." In his judgment, "a large number of parochial celebrations are ritually unbalanced, ugly, and dishonest. They are, in a word, squalid."[27] At a conference in 1967, Godfrey Diekmann discussed "a very widespread and seemingly uncontrollable phenomenon on the liturgy scene today. I refer, of course, to the multiple kinds of unauthorized experimental masses, the so-called basement, clandestine, or—sometimes—bootleg masses that are taking place to a greater or lesser extent in many countries, and which Cardinal Lercaro, head of the liturgical Consilium [to which Diekmann was a consultor], has sharply condemned."[28]

In 1965 Cardinal Lercaro had written to presidents of conferences of bishops urging patience in the process of liturgical reform, and a recognition that the "sense of community" fostered by the reformed rites needed to be balanced by "the sense of hierarchy" and communion with the church universal; such an awareness, he said, would "not deprive pastoral experiments . . . of their freshness and effectiveness," but would help to "put a brake on uncontrolled arbitrariness and on pointless variety," which could even descend "into chaos"[29]—such was how it seemed already in mid-1965. Two years later he wrote again to deplore unofficial liturgical experiments "that are introduced arbitrarily and on private initiative," noting that "the situation today is considerably more alarming than two years ago, due to the widespread nature of these experiments."[30]

[27] Ralph A. Keifer, "Squalor on Sunday," *Worship* 44, no. 5 (May 1970): 292–96, here at 292.

[28] Godfrey Diekmann, "Worship," in *Theology of Renewal Proceedings of the Congress on the Theology of the Renewal of the Church: Centenary of Canada, 1867–1967*, vol. 2, *Renewal of Religious Structures*, ed. L. K. Shook (New York: Herder and Herder, 1968), 88–99, at 95.

[29] G. Lercaro, "Le renouveau liturgique" (June 30, 1965), Letter to presidents of the conferences of bishops (DOL 31 at no. 411).

[30] G. Lercaro, "Dans sa récente allocution" (June 21, 1967), Letter to presidents of the conferences of bishops (DOL 41 at no. 480).

These are only two of many official statements from this period to the same effect.

What these statements and judgments indicate is that, in the era of the council and immediately after, in the view of church authorities and some liturgists at that time, liturgical enthusiasm and pastoral experimentation "spiked" to a fever pitch. Since then the fever subsided but, in the view of Pope Benedict, had not entirely or sufficiently abated. Where it continued, he would diagnose its underlying, enduring cause as a mistaken and now habitual attitude of freedom and creativity that treats the norms of the liturgical books as recommended guidelines or even simply as options, a template to be followed unless local liturgical leaders think otherwise. Without the parameters of liturgical norms, Benedict envisioned local adaptations to the liturgy taking conceivably any shape suggested by the theological or pastoral vision or preferences of individual priests or liturgy planning committees. For him, such unlimited potential for alteration of the liturgy served not to foster but more to threaten the beauty of the liturgy, the rights of the faithful, and even the unity of the church. The cure he prescribed was, first, and simply, observance of the rite—mere fidelity to the liturgy as handed on in the church's living tradition and expressed in its liturgical books; then, in addition, the cultivation of beauty in the various dimensions of the ritual (space, music, objects, vesture, movement, words, etc.) so that the liturgy can manifest a spirit of sacrality—the better to become a proverbial *thin place* where worshipers can experience a particularly "close communication between God and themselves."[31]

But here is a key question for assessing SP. Pope Benedict associated his personal experience of liturgical "deformations" with "that period" of the postconciliar years (the mid- to late-1960s, extending into the 1970s). But if SP was meant as a cure for the "fever" of that era, the question arises: was Benedict's prescription no longer needed, the fever having largely subsided with the passage of

[31] Gerald O'Collins and Mario Farrugia, *Catholicism: The Story of Catholic Christianity* (Oxford: Oxford University Press, 2003), 66.

time? This, I think, would be a not uncommon view—that those liturgical excesses were a thing of the past.[32]

Benedict, however, believed the problem still persisted in a measure sufficient to impact negatively the church's liturgy today. He wrote in 2001 "of the liturgical chaos that has spread out to many places and to some extent is still on the increase."[33] Is this reading of the contemporary situation sound, or was he overly influenced by powerful memories of the past, perhaps confirmed by negative correspondence sent to the Vatican?

This interpretation of the situation was not his alone; it is shared by others such as Godfried Danneels, James Sweeney, and Michael Kunzler.[34] Italian liturgical scholar Cesare Giraudo offered

[32] For example, Archbishop Rembert G. Weakland wrote, "I can honestly and truthfully say that the aberrations that arose in the late 1960's from excessive zeal and exuberance had begun to run their course and to disappear by the early 1980's"; Weakland, "Liturgical Renewal: Two Latin Rites?" *America* 176, no. 20 (June 7–14, 1997): 12–15, at 14. Mark Searle said the same in his 1982 article, "Reflections on Liturgical Reform." As he recalled, gently poking fun at the era, "Our faith bubbled up in song, our love in tearful protestations of mutual acceptance, our hope in the cult of spontaneity." He then added, "Now that seems to have passed, by and large"; Searle, "Reflections on Liturgical Reform," in *Vision: The Scholarly Contributions of Mark Searle to Liturgical Renewal*, ed. Anne Y. Koester and Barbara Searle (Collegeville, MN: Liturgical Press, 2004), 97. Yet seven years later Searle still had words of critique regarding some characteristics of liturgy as then celebrated in the United States: "The air of informality, the use of humor, the casual posture, are unique to the American Church"; he also referred with some disparagement to "presiders who grin at you while they are supposed to be speaking to God." See Searle, "Culture," in *Liturgy: Active Participation in the Divine Life*, ed. James P. Moroney (Collegeville, MN: Liturgical Press, 1990), 27–51, here at 41 and 42.

[33] Ratzinger, "Um die Erneuerung der Liturgie. Antwort auf Reiner Kaczynski," *Stimmen der Zeit* 219 (2001): 837–42, at 842 ("dem liturgischen Chaos, das sich vielerorten ausgebreitet hat und zum Teil immer noch steigert?").

[34] Michael Kunzler wrote in 2008 (after saying there is no going back on the reformed liturgy) that it "would also be a backward-step not to scrutinize further our adherence to the misguided developments and misunderstandings which must also be linked with the renewal of the liturgy"; Kunzler, *Die 'Tridentinische' Messe: Aufbruch oder Rückschritt* (Paderborn: Bonifatius, 2008), 119–20 ("Ebenso rückschrittlich wäre aber auch das nicht weiter hinterfragte Festhalten an den Fehlentwicklungen und Missverständnissen, die mit der Erneuerung der

an extended and pointed reflection in this vein in his 2003 essay marking the fortieth anniversary of the council's liturgy constitution. After praising the liturgical reforms, he then also noted there were "'shadows' and even 'abuses'" in that reform; he spoke of them as "smudges which have obscured and [here is the point] unfortunately continue to obscure the liturgy."[35] He detailed a list of such problematic practices in three paragraphs, each beginning with the word *Spesso* (Often)—in other words, not always and everywhere, but still often enough to be worthy of note, forty years after the council. His list includes an "invasion" of new instruments while the organ gathers dust, applause that risks confusing the liturgy with a concert, and "those priests who, sometimes and in some places, arrogate to themselves the right to use wild Eucharistic prayers, or to make up the text or parts of it right there on the spot."[36] We have gone, he contends, from extreme to extreme, "from an excessively rigid framework to an excessively free framework. If before there was fixity, rigidity of forms, unnaturalness, that made the liturgy at that time a 'liturgy of iron,' today there is

---

Liturgie ebenfalls verbunden werden müssen"). Kunzler follows with a brief list of such misguided practices. See also Godfried Danneels, "Liturgy Forty Years after the Council: High Point or Recession?" *The Jurist* 69, no. 1 (2009): 190–207. Also James Sweeney, "How Should We Remember Vatican II," *New Blackfriars* 90, no. 1026 (2009): 251–60, who notes: "Many silly things were said and done [immediately] after the Council, for example at the wilder reaches of liturgical experimentation." He then continues: "And the threat of radical discontinuity might not be entirely past. The Dutch Dominican proposal last year, for example, for a Eucharistic presidency legitimated by the parish community and without the necessity of episcopal ordination seems to ditch any Catholic theology of Orders. Rome is not being simply alarmist" (258).

[35] Cesare Giraudo, "La costituzione 'Sacrosanctum Concilium': il primo grande dono del Vaticano II," *La Civilta Cattolica* (2003/4): 521–33, at 530 ("sbavature che hanno offuscato e purtroppo continuano a offuscare la liturgia").

[36] Giraudo, "La costituzione 'Sacrosanctum Concilium,'" 531–32 for the three paragraphs, 531 for the quotation ("quei sacerdoti che, talvolta e in taluni luoghi, si arrogano il diritto di utilizzare preghiere eucaristiche selvagge, o di comporne lì per lì il testo o parti di esso"). Regarding "wild Eucharistic prayers," compare the reference to "Wild Masses" (*Messe selvagge*) in a 2008 interview with Cardinal Castrillon Hoyos, "Risposte del Cardinale Presidente della Pontificia Commissione 'Ecclesia Dei' a certi quesiti," available at www.clerus.org/clerus/dati/2008-10/24-20/castrillon_rispost.html.

naturalness and spontaneity, undoubtedly sincere, but often misunderstood, mistaken, which makes—or at least risks making—the liturgy a 'liturgy of rubber,' slippery, sliding, soapy, which sometimes expresses itself in an ostentatious liberation from every rubrical set of norms."[37]

The responsibility for this state of affairs lies not in the reform itself, Giraudo says, but in our inadequate implementation of it, "that is, in our inability to understand it and actualize its true value."[38] We have reformed, he says, the liturgical texts (*testi*) but not our heads (*teste*). "This misunderstood spontaneity, which actually can be identified with improvisation, superficiality, carelessness, permissiveness, is the new 'model' that charms countless pastoral ministers, ordained and lay." And it is these characteristics of the reformed liturgy as they sometimes occur in local pastoral settings in the life of the church that can and do give rise to a negative response. "It is worship lending itself to this new idol [of "misunderstood spontaneity"] that stirs up today the reaction—unjustified to be sure, but to a certain extent understandable—of aversion toward the liturgical reform."[39]

In place of the opposition between these two extremes, imaged in the material metaphors "liturgy of iron" and "liturgy of rubber," Giraudo proposes a bodily metaphor, that of the spine or backbone, which allows for human life and action by being at once both firm

[37] Giraudo, "La costituzione 'Sacrosanctum Concilium,'" 532 (". . . siamo passati da un quadro eccessivamente rigido a un quadro eccessivamente libero. Se prima c'erano fissatà, sclerosi di forme, innaturalezza, che rendevano la liturgia di allora una 'liturgia di ferro,' oggi ci sono naturalezza e spontaneismo, indubbitamente sinceri, ma spesso fraintesi, malintesi, che fanno—o perlomeno rischiano di fare—della liturgia una 'liturgia di caucciù,' sgusciante, glissante, saponosa, che a volte si esprime in un ostentato affrancamento da ogni normativa rubricale").

[38] Ibid. (". . . cioè della nostra incapacità di comprenderla e di valorizzarla").

[39] Ibid. ("Questa spontaneità fraintesa, che si identifica di fatto con l'improvvisazione, la faciloneria, il pressapochismo, il permissivismo, è il nuovo 'criterio' che affascina innumerevoli operatori della pastorale, sacerdoti e laici. È il culto prestato a questo nuovo idolo che scatena oggi la reazione—ingiustificata certo, ma in parte comprensibile—degli avversari della riforma liturgica"). The same point is made by Denis Crouan, *The Liturgy Betrayed* (San Francisco: Ignatius Press, 2000), 64, see also 67.

and flexible. The liturgy, he says, should be the same, knowing how to faithfully harmonize fidelity to tradition and adaptability to the church's ever-changing present circumstances.[40]

So others as well as Pope Benedict see certain problematic post-conciliar liturgical developments as a still current concern. SP was devised and issued as a pastoral initiative on this assumption and in order to address and correct such views and practices. It put in place procedures that create a new situation on the ground, in the pastoral life of the church, intended to foster a natural, organic (from the ground up) amelioration of the situation—doing this instead of issuing further top-down directives, the *modus operandi* at work since the 1960s that Benedict innovatively decided, after forty-some years of its not resolving the issues, not to replace but to supplement with this new and different approach.

CGF 5

> *This is why Pope John Paul II saw himself obliged to provide, with his* motu proprio "Ecclesia Dei" *of July 2, 1988, a normative framework for the use of the Missal of 1962—a framework however which did not contain detailed provisions but made an appeal in a more general way to the generosity of bishops toward the "just aspirations" of those faithful who requested this use of the Roman Rite again. At that time the pope wanted in this way to help above all the Society of St. Pius X to return to full unity with the successor of Peter, seeking to heal a wound felt ever more painfully. Unfortunately this reconciliation has not yet come to pass; nevertheless, a succession of communities has with gratitude made use of the possibilities of that* motu proprio. *Difficult, on the other hand, has remained the question of the use of the Missal of 1962 outside these groups for whom there were no specific juridical norms, above all because often the bishops in these cases feared that the authority of the council would have been placed in doubt. Immediately after the Second Vatican Council one could have supposed that requests for use of the Missal of 1962 would be limited to the older generation that had grown up with it, but in the*

[40] Giraudo, "La costituzione 'Sacrosanctum Concilium,'" 533. Compare the sentiment of Denis Crouan: "It is necessary to learn to implement the Roman liturgy in the spirit of tradition: a spirit of stability and continuity that is opposed to a spirit of immobility and sclerosis as well as to a spirit of fluctuation and rupture"; Crouan, *The History and the Future of the Roman Liturgy* (San Francisco: Ignatius Press, 2005), 245.

meantime it has clearly emerged that young persons as well have discovered this liturgical form, feel themselves attracted by it, and have found there a form particularly appropriate for them to encounter the mystery of the most holy Eucharist. Thus a need has arisen for a clearer juridical regulation, which one could not have foreseen at the time of the motu proprio *of 1988. These norms intend also to free the bishops from the need always to evaluate anew how to respond to diverse situations.*

Pope Benedict here described the legal provisions John Paul II established in his *motu proprio Ecclesia Dei*, for use of the 1962 Missal as "not . . . detailed." John Paul appealed to the bishops to make a "generous response" to what he called the "legitimate aspirations"[41] of those requesting use of that Missal. The legal provisions were "not . . . detailed" because he presumed, or so Benedict implied, the bishops would freely and readily do as asked and urged. The appeal was made first of all with the SSPX in mind, and on that front, as noted here, the desired reconciliation did not come about, though some individual communities attached to the prior Missal did establish full communion with the pope while retaining use of the traditional Missal (for example, the traditional priests of the Diocese of Campos in Brazil).[42] But, outside these groups and because "there were no specific juridical norms," Benedict says the question regarding use of that Missal remains difficult—which seems to mean that a significant number of bishops were not generous in granting permission for its use.

Accordingly, for Benedict the need became apparent, as it was not in 1988, for "clearer juridical regulation" in this matter. SP is this regulation, through which Benedict took matters into his own hands. John Paul II, to make the prior Missal available for those who requested it, called for and relied on the generous response of bishops to such requests; Cardinal Ratzinger took note that the response of many of the bishops was not generous; therefore, to achieve the same end (generous permission for use of the 1962 Missal), Benedict established different means. Intending, as he said elsewhere, "to extend and to update" the more general norms of ED (and thus of QAA) "by means of more precise and detailed

[41] John Paul II, *Ecclesia Dei* 5.c.

[42] For other communities, see Michael Kunzler, *Die 'Tridentinische' Messe*, 94–95.

norms,"[43] he granted by papal decree *motu proprio* in SP some measure of the permission the bishops were slow to give.

The intention stated in the final sentence of CGF 5 affirms by implication a general judgment, applicable in all cases: namely, that requests for celebrations using the prior Missal as envisioned in SP are warranted and deserve an affirmative response, because such a response would serve the good of the church as a whole and, presumably, of any particular church in which the request was made. Were this judgment mistaken, however, deleterious effects could arise for the church, universal or particular, as a result of thus foreclosing consideration of individual circumstances and calling for, indeed mandating, the same affirmative response to requests whose merit for such a response might vary from case to case.

Benedict's judgment, however, was that denying the requests of those, both young and old, who desire use of the 1962 Missal and the encounter with the mystery of the Eucharist, which such celebrations accord them, would not serve but harm the good of the church. He would say it fails to provide them pastoral care in the spirit of *Quattuor Abhinc Annos*, *Ecclesia Dei*, and now *Summorum Pontificum*, by denying them something authentically Catholic and, by the grant conveyed in these documents, permitted. He would also say it harms the unity of the church both by discriminating against some of its members without due warrant in a matter which should admit of freedom and by keeping closed a door that might, if opened, offer a way of reconciliation for members of the SSPX or others who have turned from the church because of post-conciliar liturgical "deformations."

CGF 6

> *In the second place, in discussions on the anticipated* motu proprio, *the fear was expressed that a wider possibility for use of the 1962 Missal would lead to disturbances or even to divisions in parish communities. This fear, too, does not seem to me to be well founded. Use of the ancient Missal presupposes a certain degree of liturgical formation and a basic facility in the Latin language; neither the one nor the other is found very*

[43] Benedict XVI, *Ecclesiae Unitatem* 3. The words here are "extend" (*amplificare*) and "update" (*aptare*), to describe what SP does to the provisions of QAA and ED; in SP itself the word is "substitute" (SP, art. 1, *substituuntur*).

> *often. Already from these concrete presuppositions one sees clearly that the new Missal will certainly remain the ordinary form of the Roman Rite, not only because of the juridical norms but also because of the actual situation in which one finds communities of the faithful.*

In CGF 6 and 7, Pope Benedict addressed the second fear regarding SP—namely, that it would prove divisive. He offered two reasons why use of the prior Missal in a diocese would not or need not be divisive: that not many people will use it (because not many people have the requisite knowledge or formation to do so), and that the Missal of Paul VI is and will remain the liturgy Catholics normally use, the only one most will ever use both because that is its juridical status and because that is the church's practice. In other words, FE adherents will not constitute a sufficient critical mass to be a divisive factor.

This was said, despite bishops having made known to the Vatican the vocal, divisive, oppositional spirit that can be maintained by some FE adherents. The 1980 Vatican survey of the world's bishops made this clear. Another example comes from a Canadian bishop regarding a small number of people: "After long consideration and after speaking with several pastors, I find that we have in this diocese a fistful of individuals petitioning for the 'Tridentine' liturgy. If their only motive was a personal desire to celebrate according to this rite"—that is, if the persons were those identified by Pope Benedict as loyal Catholics who accept Vatican II while also valuing and desiring the traditional Mass—"I would have no difficulty. What I am deeply concerned about is the very real possibility that their motivation is based more on a very critical attitude towards the Holy Father and the Second Vatican Council"—thus, giving cause regarding the first fear, discussed in CGF 4–5. "They will not stop their demands for the old rituals until they have funeral, weddings, and Mass in Latin in all our parishes, disturbing the scheduled Masses we presently have—at a time when a shortage of priests and an increase in the numbers of the faithful in our diocese require more unity, not less"[44]—thus giving cause regarding the second fear, divisiveness.

[44] From "A. Eucharistic Celebrations. 1. *Permission to Celebrate according to the Roman Missal of 1962* (Ecclesia Dei)," in *Roman Replies and CLSA Advisory Opinions 1990*, ed. William A. Schumacher and Lynn Jarrell (Washington, DC:

Such problems clearly existed in some places. Nonetheless, Benedict affirmed consistently that the availability of both Missals need not be divisive but rather can manifest legitimate diversity and thus foster unity. Since it is the case that divisiveness has arisen in the past and can still arise in the present in local churches due to issues surrounding the 1962 Missal and what it can be meant and be taken to symbolize, the simple statement that its use is not divisive is incomplete; something further is needed, to complete the thought and make it true. That something else pertains to the attitudes and practices of the persons involved. If those requesting celebrations using the 1962 Missal do not think of themselves in divisive ways (e.g., as more faithful, "better" Catholics) or seek to separate themselves in this liturgical way from their communities, and if the pastoral leaders of those communities do not interpret such requests as divisive when they are not so intended, then use of the 1962 Missal need not be divisive but can be accommodated within a legitimate, honest, and mutually respectful diversity. Lacking such attitudes, divisiveness seems possible.

We encounter then the remark that "use of the old Missal" takes some liturgical formation and knowledge of Latin, and "neither of these is found very often."[45] The implication, as noted above, is that not many people will choose the old Mass because not many will be able to participate in it in the way called for by the nature of the liturgy, that is, fully, consciously, and actively (see SC 14). The comment is interesting. It is safe to say that many, a wide majority, of the baptized Catholics over the centuries who have attended and participated in the Mass of the Roman Rite neither knew Latin nor had much liturgical formation; circumstances were such that it could not have been (or at least was not) otherwise. What we see here is a

---

Canon Law Society of America, 1990), 1–5, at 4 (my thanks to Chad Glendinning for this reference). The letter, dated June 1, 1989, is from the diocesan bishop to the Cardinal President of the PCED. The diocese is described as "a remote Canadian See" (1), and named "True North."

[45] Here, thinking of who will celebrate using the FE, the pope sees the glass as half empty. Earlier, in CGF 4, he remarked that in the years after the council, "not a few" (*non pochi*, rendered perhaps too expansively in the official translation as "a good number of people") "remained strongly attached" to the prior usage; there, he saw the glass as half full.

comment by Pope Benedict that is intelligible only on the premise that this kind of general nonparticipation (due to inability to understand the language or theology of the liturgy being celebrated) is not what he intended to legislate into existence again. Under the provisions of SP only those who specifically choose the FE will encounter it,[46] and what the pope was assuming—it seems almost an implicit requirement—was that they would seek this Mass, *not* to be present in the all-too-typical and often decried fashion of the past, as "strangers or silent spectators," but rather to participate actively with that measure of understanding that only a certain knowledge of Latin and some liturgical formation make possible.

This seems clear especially in light of Pope Benedict's observation concerning persons who remained strongly attached to the old Mass after the new had been introduced—namely, that they were those who had acquired through the influence of the twentieth-century liturgical movement "a notable liturgical formation and a deep, personal familiarity" with the liturgy then current (CGF 4). This describes what he hoped and expected would characterize those who make use of the provisions of SP to celebrate the liturgy according to the FE. In other words, just as SP, article 5, section 4, requires that a priest who uses the 1962 Missal be *idoneus* or qualified, it is clearly in the spirit and nearly in the text of CGF that the same be true, in its own way, of the faithful who seek, request, and/or participate in such celebrations. This kind of full and active participation, after all, was the hope of the liturgical movement, which so clearly influenced Joseph Ratzinger first as a child growing up and then as a young priest and theologian, and it is the principle value enshrined in the council's liturgy constitution, which remains valid for the liturgical practice of the church today, whatever usage or form of ritual is celebrated.[47] This in turn would

[46] If, however, the answer of the PCED in reply to the questions posed by the diocese in Poland are extended to the whole church, then it is conceivable that a person attached to the FO would need to attend Mass in the extraordinary form, if the FE Mass was scheduled at the only time that person could attend Mass on a day of obligation.

[47] Christophe Geffroy affirms that for Pope Benedict, the council's liturgy constitution is to serve as the point of reference for celebrations of Mass whether in the ordinary or extraordinary form; see Geffroy, *Benoît XVI et "la*

seem to imply a positive responsibility on the part of pastors and their pastoral staffs to assist such persons to become qualified—by helping them through catechetical formation to acquire "a notable liturgical formation and a deep, personal familiarity" with the FE. We will return to this subject in chapter 6, on the pastoral implications of SP.

On the FO remaining the ordinary form of the church's liturgy (however it may be revised through mutual enrichment, as mentioned in CGF 7), see the commentary on SP, article 1.

CGF 7

> *It is true that there have not been lacking exaggerations and at some times social aspects unduly linked to the attitude of the faithful bound to the ancient Latin liturgical tradition. Your love and pastoral prudence will be a stimulus and guide toward improvement. Moreover, the two forms of the use of the Roman Rite can be mutually enriching: new saints and some of the new prefaces can and should be inserted in the ancient Missal. The Commission "Ecclesia Dei" in contact with diverse entities dedicated to the* usus antiquior *will study the practical possibilities. The celebration of the Mass according to the Missal of Paul VI will be able to manifest, in a stronger way than has often been the case up to now, that sacrality that attracts many to the ancient usage. The surest guarantee that the Missal of Paul VI can unite parish communities and come to be loved by them consists in celebrating it with great reverence in conformity with the prescribed norms. This will make visible the spiritual riches and theological depth of this Missal.*

As CGF was in a sense written primarily to FO adherents, seeking to explain SP and bring about on the part of those who had fears or objections (CGF 2–3) a different and more positive way of looking at the situation, Benedict here addressed himself to what he called certain exaggerations and an ascription of attitudes or

paix liturgique", 272. Laurence Paul Hemming affirms the same in his *Benedict XVI: Fellow Worker for the Truth. An Introduction to His Life and Thought* (London: Burns & Oates, 2005). Cardinal Ratzinger, he writes, has "noted that the Second Vatican Council did not itself reform the liturgy, but laid down conditions under which Mass should be celebrated. These conditions apply, Benedict has argued, irrespective of the rite used—they apply equally to the pre- and post-1970 rites" (124).

behaviors unduly attributed to FE adherents. The sentence is reminiscent of the comment in his interview in 2000 with Peter Seewald, that someone who advocates for or participates in the traditional liturgy can on that account be looked down on by liturgical or pastoral professionals and even "treated like a leper."[48] Knowing that such views—looking down on FE adherents, considering them potential sources of trouble—continued to exist in some measure among the bishops, it was with his rhetoric of corrective encouragement that Benedict told them here that the love and pastoral prudence which they have (meaning: which they as bishops should have) will be able to move things in the right direction, that is, toward dissipating such exaggerations and mistaken ascription of attitudes.[49] What is meant by exaggerations or mistaken attitudes could include, for example, the view that all those attached to the old Mass are close-minded, separatist, difficult to deal with, prone to condemn other Catholics for not being *truly* Catholic, more than a little self-righteous, and the like. These terms could also include the idea that their appreciation for the traditional Mass and correlative forms of Catholic belief and practice and their reluctance in adopting newer and authorized developments always indicate rejection of the council as a whole, or are simply symptoms of an underlying psychological immaturity.

I think what Benedict would have deemed exaggerated about such views is that they are ascribed generally, without distinction, as characterizing *all* those attached to the prior liturgical forms. His own views were more differentiated, for while he often spoke in

[48] Ratzinger, *God and the World*, 416.

[49] Compare his remarks to the bishops of France in 2008, a year after SP went into effect: "I am aware of your difficulties" in the implementation of the document, "but I do not doubt that, within a reasonable time, you can find solutions satisfactory for all"—again, the language of corrective encouragement. What he meant by "solutions" is the mutual acceptance of all, including those who desire the traditional liturgy: "Everyone has a place in the Church. Every person, without exception [even FE adherents], should be able to feel at home, and never rejected." "Address of His Holiness Benedict XVI: Meeting with French Episcopal Conference" (September 14, 2008). The encouragement surely applies across the board, to FE adherents accepting the reformed liturgy and church as much as to FO adherents accepting the place of the extraordinary form and its adherents.

defense of the rights of FE adherents he could also find fault with their hopes, attitudes, or behavior.[50] Here, in CGF he was writing mainly to address and counter the objections he knew were held against the intentions and provisions of SP, and so for the matter at hand—how to understand the desires and behavior of FE adherents—he spoke in their defense and counseled against views that err because they apply to all the excesses of some. But in his letter to Catholic bishops explaining the lifting of the excommunications of the four SSPX bishops, we see another dimension of his views and experiences. In that letter, along with acknowledgment of their faith in Christ, he spoke of finding "arrogance and presumptuousness, an obsession with one-sided positions, etc.," among FE adherents who belong to the SSPX—that is, he was quite aware of a measure of truth to the ascription of negative or disruptive attitudes. But he pointedly also noted that these attitudes were only in "*some* representatives of that community" (emphasis added), whereas in others he saw clear evidence of "openness of heart."[51] This kind of willingness and ability to see beyond stereotypes, to look for and recognize the real mixture of positive and negative in persons and groups, even those one considers opposed to oneself, was what Benedict encouraged the bishops and the church more widely to adopt, in place of the all-too-natural but still mistaken and harmful exaggerations of a one-sided and more simplistic perspective.[52]

The reference to the two usages being "mutually enriching" is, I believe, one of the most pivotal features of this entire liturgical initiative. It is the concrete way, the practical pastoral mechanism,

[50] Consider, for example, Ratzinger, *The Feast of Faith*, 86 and 87; Ratzinger, "Dix ans après," nos. 12–16 (esp. 14–15); Ratzinger, "Assessment and Future Prospects" (his concluding remarks at the 2001 conference in Fontgombault), in *Looking Again at the Question of the Liturgy with Cardinal Ratzinger*, ed. Alcuin Reid (Farnborough: Saint Michael's Abbey Press, 2003), 152–53; and—to be cited shortly—Benedict XVI's letter to bishops in 2009 in regard to lifting the excommunications from the four SSPX bishops.

[51] "Letter of His Holiness Pope Benedict XVI to the Bishops of the Catholic Church concerning the Remission of the Excommunication of the Four Bishops Consecrated by Archbishop Lefebvre" (March 10, 2009).

[52] In social psychological terms, what Pope Benedict is doing is counteracting the dynamic of outgroup derogation.

by which the ongoing renewal of the church's ordinary liturgy is to take place. If genuinely implemented, it restores to the life of the church in a distinctive way the process of organic development in the liturgy, a process that had been effectively diminished since the mid- to late-sixteenth century. This important topic will be explored in chapter 7.

Pope Benedict's hope was that through mutual enrichment the ordinary form would come to be celebrated in such a way as to unite those parish communities that may currently experience division to some extent, where most parishioners fully accept the reformed Mass as the church's liturgy while some prefer the *usus antiquior*. He thought unity, in such contexts, would be served when the ordinary form Mass came to be celebrated more regularly both with "great reverence," influenced (enriched) by "that sacrality that attracts many to the ancient usage," and also "in conformity with the prescribed norms." Such celebrations would be more likely to attract those drawn by the FE, thus more closely reuniting them in the parish's regular liturgy—not losing the already community-friendly ordinary form Mass but enriching it with a more conscious and prominent dimension of theocentric worship, yielding a celebration notably characterized by both *communio* and *adoratio*. I think Pope Benedict would have recognized his goal and agenda voiced in words Pope John Paul II addressed to some bishops of the USA in 1998: "The challenge now is to move beyond whatever misunderstandings there have been and to reach the proper point of balance, especially by entering more deeply into the contemplative dimension of worship, which includes the sense of awe, reverence and adoration which are fundamental attitudes in our relationship with God. This will happen only if we recognize that the liturgy has dimensions *both* local *and* universal, time-bound *and* eternal, horizontal *and* vertical, subjective *and* objective."[53]

Two final remarks on CGF 3–7. Looking back at Pope Benedict's treatment of the two fears SP raises for some, there is something rhetorically noteworthy about his responses. After naming each

[53] John Paul II, "Address of the Holy Father Pope John Paul II to the Bishops of the Episcopal Conference of the United States of America (Washington, Oregon, Idaho, Montana, and Alaska)," 2 (October 9, 1998).

fear he immediately, briefly, and unambiguously pronounced it unfounded, and then explained why at some length, acknowledging no legitimate basis for either fear. Did this unduly minimize the two concerns? Those concerns were and are, after all, held by persons of responsibility, knowledge, and competence—bishops, pastors and pastoral ministers, theologians, members of the faithful, living in Catholic communities and having their own firsthand experience of the matters in question. Did he insufficiently attend to their views and advice? Ratzinger was known as an attentive listener capable of hearing, understanding, and attending to diverse points of view.[54] But the case here may be more comparable to his view (famously debated between himself and Cardinal Kasper) regarding the ontological and temporal priority of the church as a whole versus the concrete realizations of the church in individual congregations.[55] He once wrote that he considered that ontological priority of the church as a whole "so obvious that I find it difficult to understand the objections raised against it."[56]

[54] See D. Vincent Twomey, *Pope Benedict XVI: The Conscience of Our Age. A Theological Portrait* (San Francisco: Ignatius Press, 2007), 24–25; and Francis Schüssler Fiorenza, "From Theologian to Pope: A Personal View Back, Past the Public Portrayals," *Harvard Divinity Bulletin* 33, no. 2 (Autumn 2005), available at http://www.hds.harvard.edu/news/bulletin_mag/articles/33-2_fiorenza.html.

[55] For a list of the exchanges between Ratzinger and Kasper, see Paul McPartlan, "The Local Church and the Universal Church: Zizioulas and the Ratzinger–Kasper Debate," *International Journal for the Study of the Christian Church* 4, no. 1 (March 2004): 21–33, at 22. For an earlier work foreshadowing his later writings on this topic, see "The Origins and Essence of the Church," in Ratzinger, *Called to Communion*, 13–45, especially at 43–45 with his reflections on Acts 2 and Pentecost.

[56] Ratzinger, "The Ecclesiology of the Constitution *Lumen Gentium*," in *Pilgrim Fellowship of Faith*, 135. We find the same sentiment in his lecture, "Conference of Cardinal Ratzinger at the Opening of the Pastoral Congress of the Diocese of Aversa (Italy)," in *L'Osservatore Romano*, English Edition (January 23, 2002), as excerpted in *The Ratzinger Reader*, ed. Lieven Boeve and Gerard Mannion (New York: T&T Clark International, 2010), 101–8, at 108, where he (Ratzinger) comments, "These objections look like theological ravings." Kilian McDonnell also takes note of Ratzinger's self-expressed "inability to understand the opposition to ontological priority" in McDonnell, "The Ratzinger/

Perhaps here as well he found it difficult to understand the two objections raised against this liturgical initiative because, in his mind, neither consequence (undermining the council, dividing the church) logically or necessarily followed from the premise of SP. That such consequences could follow, he must surely have been aware, and that some persons think they would follow (because in the past they have), he understood. But that in themselves such consequences will or must follow, he denied, for in his judgment they clearly do not. On the contrary, he saw a healing of existing liturgical, and thereby ecclesial, divisions made more possible if those with disdain for others' liturgical forms (FE adherents for the FO, and FO adherents for the FE) could recognize Catholic validity in those forms and extend charity to those attached to them, and if a willingness by some to worship in both forms could lead those persons to an enriched celebration of each form and eventually to the enrichment of the ritual forms themselves. He also believed the result of such a process would be a form of worship more fully and authentically in accord with the general principles and specific directives of *Sacrosanctum Concilium* than characterized either form at present (the FE obviously, but to some extent the FO as well)—and thus, he believed SP would lead not away from but toward a more faithful fulfillment of the liturgical vision of Vatican II.

But in any case, since the author of these documents has made clear he did not intend, and they do not entail, either turning away from Vatican II or divisiveness in parish communities, the proper hermeneutic for reading and the proper method for implementing the documents should correspond. SP and CGF should be interpreted by readers and implemented in the life of the church by pastoral practitioners in such a way that Vatican II is affirmed and church communities are united. When this does not happen, SP is being misunderstood and unsuccessfully implemented.

Finally, I think a sound reading of Pope Benedict's full replies to the two concerns must recognize that he had a message not only to or about the persons who have the two fears (namely, FO adherents) but also to those whom such persons are concerned

---

Kasper Debate: The Universal Church and Local Churches," *Theological Studies* 63 (2002): 227–50, at 235.

about (FE adherents). In other words, when Pope Benedict in CGF explained why SP does not undermine the authority of Vatican II, he was not only saying to persons who raised the objection, "your fear is unfounded," but was also saying to those who seek to worship according to the preconciliar liturgy, "do not impugn or oppose Vatican II," that is, do not speak or act in such a way as to give grounds for this fear. Similarly, in dismissing concerns that a wider use of the traditional Mass could lead to "disarray or even divisions within parish communities" (CGF 6), he was simultaneously issuing a charge to those who request and attend the traditional Mass that they take care and take steps not to contribute to disarray or to a divisive spirit in their communities but rather participate in and contribute to the life of those communities in a spirit of peace and goodwill.

This is the same message offered near the end of "Dix ans après," when Cardinal Ratzinger critiqued the opposition of FE adherents to the call for a "new liturgical movement." Those adherents feared that such a call masked "a stratagem or ruse to eliminate the old liturgy entirely."[57] To this Ratzinger said, "Such anxieties and fears must cease!" and be replaced by a more visible acceptance of both the traditional *and* the reformed liturgy.[58] Earlier in the same address he made the point that *all* eucharistic celebrations after the council, whether using the Missal of Blessed John XXIII or the Missal of Paul VI, need to be in accord with the general norms set forth in the council's liturgy constitution, *Sacrosanctum Concilium* 34–36.[59] His point was that such acceptance by FE adherents of certain basic principles of the conciliar reform and of the Missal resulting from that reform, rather than a spirit of disdain, mistrust, or opposition, is the very thing that would demonstrate to bishops that "the presence of the old liturgy does not trouble or harm the unity of their diocese."[60]

[57] Ratzinger, "Dix ans après," no. 14 ("un stratagème ou une ruse, pour pouvoir éliminer enfin complètement l'ancienne liturgie").

[58] Ibid., no. 15 ("Il faut que de telles anxiétés et peurs cessent enfin!"—with *enfin* expressing perhaps a touch of impatience).

[59] Ibid., no. 5.

[60] Ibid., no. 15 (to start the quotation somewhat before the words cited: "nous pourrons aussi persuader les évêques, que la présence de l'ancienne liturgie ne dérange et ne brise pas l'unité de leur diocèse").

Pope Benedict, then, offered in this section of his letter a real challenge, as much to one side as to the other, to live up to a vision of liturgical tolerance and peace in the church, and indeed of appreciation for the richness of liturgical diversity—appreciation for both the ordinary and the extraordinary forms, by all in the church—which in turn was meant to serve and foster ecclesial unity and charity (the topic of the next paragraph of the letter, CGF 8). It is these goods that Pope Benedict invited and sought to evoke among the pastors and the people of the church through the provisions of SP.

CGF 8

> *I arrive then at that positive reason which has motivated me to update, through this* motu proprio, *that of 1988. It is a matter of reaching an internal reconciliation in the heart of the church. In looking back over the past at divisions that in the course of the centuries have torn apart the body of Christ, one continually has the impression that in critical moments in which the division was just beginning, not enough had been done on the part of those responsible for the church to keep or to gain reconciliation and unity. One has the impression that omissions in the church have had their share of blame in the fact that these divisions were able to harden. This look at the past imposes an obligation on us today: to make every effort so that all those who truly have the desire for unity be enabled to remain in that unity or to regain it anew. I am mindful of a phrase in the Second Letter to the Corinthians, where Paul writes: "Our mouth has spoken to you in all frankness, Corinthians, and our heart itself is wide open to you. You are truly not restricted by us: it is rather in your own hearts that you are restricted . . . . As recompense in kind, you also, in your turn,*[61] *open your heart!" (2 Cor 6:11–13). Paul says this certainly in another context, but his invitation can and should touch us also, precisely on this theme. Let us generously open our heart and make space for all that the faith itself allows.*

Lumen Gentium states that the Roman Pontiff, as successor of Peter, has been established by Christ as "a lasting and visible source and foundation of the unity both of faith and of communion" (LG 18). The pope, accordingly, bears unique responsibility

[61] The phrases "as recompense in kind" and "you also, in your turn," are from Max Zerwick and Mary Grosvenor, *A Grammatical Analysis of the Greek New Testament*, unabridged, rev. ed. (Rome: Biblical Institute Press, 1981), 546. Note: the Scripture translations here in CGF 8 and later in CGF 13 are mine, from Pope Benedict's Italian, and not from the New Revised Standard Version.

for the church's unity. Being also uniquely possessed of "full, supreme and universal power over the whole Church, a power which he can always exercise unhindered" (LG 22), he is able, in the service of unity, and thus duty bound, to take the steps that no one else can take. It is clear Pope Benedict recognized the demands and the seriousness of this responsibility and did so from the beginning of his papacy, as his first papal homily made clear. He spoke then to the cardinals who elected him, saying, "[I]t is before [Christ], supreme Judge of all living things, that each of us must stand, in the awareness that one day we must explain to him what we did and what we did not do for the great good that is the full and visible unity of all his disciples."[62] This responsibility entails efforts to maintain unity when it is present, strengthen it when it is weak, safeguard it when threatened, and regain it when lost.

In this paragraph of CGF Benedict placed SP squarely in this context of concern for unity. The scope of this concern included the weakened unity of those Catholics who differ with each other, sometimes bitterly, over liturgical matters, and he wanted to bring about what he elsewhere called "the necessary inner reconciliations within the Church."[63] But the paragraph here addressed itself more directly to regaining the unity that has been lost—or, he would say, was in danger of being lost—with the members of the Society of Saint Pius X. His perspective on this situation was shaped by a reading of history that is far from deterministic. He looked at ecclesial divisions that arose at various times in the past and thought of them as having been avoidable, had those responsible at the time those separations began to arise acted differently; instead, their culpable inaction had the result that those divisions, which were then only incipient, hardened—eventually but not at all inevitably—into

[62] "First Homily of His Holiness Benedict XVI at the End of the Eucharistic Concelebration with the Cardinal Electors in the Sistine Chapel," in *The Essential Pope Benedict XVI*, 28.

[63] Ratzinger, *God and the World*, 416. See also his "Assessment and Future Prospects," in *Looking Again*, 145, referring positively to "that Catholic Ecumenism within which there can be a reconciliation within the Church, in the midst of these [liturgical] differences which are both deep and hurtful."

permanence.[64] His verb, *consolidare*, can have a positive connotation of "strengthen" or "solidify" but here it is otherwise, and the standard translation does well with "harden"[65]—as cement, unattended, will harden over time, so too may hatred and divisions. Given attention and effort, however, the hardening can be avoided, and this is what Benedict was attempting. Out of his own desire and sense of obligation to go the extra mile and make every effort to create conditions that would allow those seeking unity in the church to find it, he was stirring the mix with the SSPX—authorizing wider usage of the traditional Mass, lifting the excommunication of the four bishops, and opening a formal theological dialogue—to see whether, with such continued attention and effort, this still incipient division could find resolution.[66]

Pope Benedict concluded his call for reconciliation with a citation from 2 Corinthians, a passage written, obviously and as he pointed out, for another context but which he found relevant for his purpose here, which was to appeal to Catholics today to cultivate a generous

[64] See Ratzinger with Messori, *The Ratzinger Report*, 32, in which he voices precisely the same perspective as expressed here in CGF 8.

[65] Benedict XVI, "Letter Accompanying Motu Proprio on the Tridentine Mass," *Origins* 37, no. 9 (July 19, 2007): 132–34, at 134.

[66] Cardinal Ratzinger had the same sentiments and goals when similar efforts were made in 1988, in dialogues conducted between the Vatican (with Cardinal Ratzinger the lead agent) and Archbishop Lefebvre. See Ratzinger's reference to this matter in his address to the bishops of Chile in 1988, shortly after these events occurred. The address began describing those efforts as having been carried out "with the sincere intention of creating for his [Archbishop Lefebvre's] movement a space within the Church that would be sufficient for it to live." In the address he invited the bishops and the church to some soul-searching, with the recognition that "schisms can take place only when certain truths and certain values of the Christian faith are no longer lived and loved within the Church," leading to the "marginalized" truth drawing to itself persons who may coalesce into a movement that can then detach from the church. He concluded the address by saying, "[I]f once again we succeed in pointing out and living the fullness of the Catholic religion . . . we may hope that the schism of Lefebvre will not be of long duration"—a hope he held in 1988, and was working to fulfill through SP. Ratzinger, "Cardinal Ratzinger's Remarks regarding the Lefebvre Schism" (Saint Paul, MN: The Wanderer, 2011), available online at http://www.catholicculture.org/culture/library/view.cfm?recnum=3032.

spirit and (here is the biblical phrase he found most apt and compelling) to "open our heart" toward one another, and in this way "make space for all that the faith itself allows."

The word *francamente* in the Italian translation of 2 Corinthians 6:11 ("in all frankness," whereas the Vatican's English translation has "open to you") is relevant for the context, since Benedict here spoke frankly to all in the church who feel divided from or in any way antagonistic toward those with different liturgical or ecclesial principles or preferences. The concept of "recompense" (rendered perhaps weakly in the Vatican's English translation, as "in return") further nudged readers to recognize a measure of real obligation to do what Saint Paul and the pope urged—namely, to generously open their hearts toward one another. The ellipsis dots (oddly placed in CGF 8, given the text of 2 Corinthians 6:13—they should instead follow the phrase, *Rendeteci il contraccambio*, "As recompense in kind,") mark omission of Paul's phrase, "I speak as to children." It is an image a pope, as Holy Father, might have used; Pope Benedict chose not to, as he was calling his readers to act like adults[67]—though it is not hard to imagine him wishing the parties involved would grow out of quarrels with their brothers and sisters in Christ and be mature enough to make room for a breadth of Catholic life, willing to live with the liturgical choices others make.

CGF 9

> *There is no contradiction between the one and the other edition of the* Roman Missal. *In the history of the liturgy there is growth and progress, but no rupture. What was sacred for prior generations remains sacred and great for us as well and cannot be all of a sudden entirely prohibited or even considered harmful. It is good for all of us to preserve the riches that have grown in the faith and prayer of the church and give them their rightful place. Obviously, to enjoy full communion also the priests of the Community adhering to the old usage cannot, as a matter of principle, exclude celebration according to the new books. A total exclusion of the new rite would in fact not be consistent with recognition of its value and holiness.*

[67] See also Benedict XVI, *Sacramentum Caritatis* 64.c, where he observed that "the aim of all Christian education . . . is to train the believer in an adult faith" (*ad fidem maturam*).

This paragraph is full of balancing corrections—which is to say, assertions made in the teeth of opposition which could be anticipated from both FO and FE adherents. And so, point by point (with reference back to the sentences in the paragraph): To those on *both* sides who see a qualitative distinction, to the point of fundamental difference or even mutual inconsistency, between the preconciliar and postconciliar Missals, or who in general see clear breaks in the history of the liturgy, with points (such as, for example, Vatican II) that divide before and after into different eras separate from each other, Benedict said: not so. To FO adherents who hold the prior form of Mass in low regard or consider it simply forbidden and harmful to the church's liturgy (*lex orandi*) or faith (*lex credendi*), Benedict said: not so, do not think this way. To those on both sides who see little in the way of riches in the other ritual, and no reason to give that ritual any place in the church today (and wishing, indeed, to see it permanently banned), Benedict said: not so, do not think this way. To FE adherents and priests in particular who would resist or even rule out use of the reformed liturgy as a matter of principle, denying it any genuine religious value or sacredness (or even, perhaps, sacramental validity), Benedict said: not so, do not think this way. The paragraph, in short, is a fine example of the Ratzingerian-Benedictine rhetoric of corrective encouragement—regarding a disputed point, making as statements of fact affirmations he considered true, to those who considered them false, with the intention and hope that, moved by rational or moral suasion to reconsider, they would come to recognize them as true.

In this paragraph Pope Benedict was very much about the work of reconciliation. He invited adamant FO adherents to a quite fundamental reorientation: that is, to let go from their minds and hearts their unyielding anathema to the old Mass. He hoped they would move beyond wholesale opposition, beyond thinking the traditional Mass actively harmful—whether in itself, or as a symbol of things preconciliar. Instead, "we absolutely have to recognize that what was fundamental before 1969 remains fundamental afterward" and cannot be considered "the most unacceptable thing."[68] He also invited—as did John Paul II with *Quattuor Abhinc Annos* in

[68] Ratzinger, "Assessment and Future Prospects," in *Looking Again*, 149.

1984—adamant FE adherents to accept the postconciliar liturgy in principle and practice, for if they do not how can they be in communion with the Catholic Church? His affirmation that there was "no rupture" in the history of the liturgy was directed in part to "the Lefebvrists" to counter and correct their contention that "there are two Churches, and for [whom] the great rupture becomes visible in the existence of the two Missals, which are said to be irreconcilable with each other."[69] Instead, Benedict invited them and all FE adherents to recognize the reformed Mass as something of worth and truly sacred, just as is the FE.

CGF 10

> *In conclusion, dear Brothers, it is very important to me to emphasize that these new norms do not diminish in any way your authority and responsibility, either for the liturgy or for the pastoral care of your faithful. Each bishop, in fact, is moderator of the liturgy in his own diocese.*[70]

CGF 11

> *Nothing, then, is taken away from the authority of the bishop whose role in any case remains that of taking care that everything proceeds in peace and serenity. If some problem should arise that the parish priest is not able to resolve, the local ordinary can always intervene, in full harmony, however, with all that has been established by the new norms of the* motu proprio.

One could sympathize with a bishop who found these paragraphs difficult to understand. Let us consider them in light of their context: the history of the use of the preconciliar Roman Missal in the postconciliar life of the church.

Upon promulgation of the new Missal in 1970 by Paul VI, the Missal in force up until that time was no longer permitted to be

[69] Ibid. The same point is made in Ratzinger, "The Theology of the Liturgy," in *Looking Again*, 18–31, at 23–24.

[70] Cf. Second Vatican Council, Constitution on the Sacred Liturgy, *Sacrosanctum Concilium* 22: "Regulation of the sacred liturgy depends solely on the authority of the Church, that is, on the Apostolic See and, as laws may determine, on the bishop." [Note in original.—Trans.]

used (with only a few exceptions, regarding its 1967 version, previously noted[71]). In 1984, Pope John Paul II authorized the indult *Quattuor Abhinc Annos*, whereby use of the 1962 Missal, up until that time forbidden under any circumstances, could once again be permitted in any diocese, but only at the discretion of the diocesan bishop, and under significant restrictions set forth in the indult. In other words, QAA did not diminish but in a real sense expanded the local bishop's authority regarding the liturgy and pastoral care in his diocese, insofar as this indult granted him an authority he previously did not have—namely, to allow, at his discretion, something otherwise and hitherto forbidden. This authority was qualified by John Paul II's 1988 *motu proprio Ecclesia Dei*, which created the Pontifical Commission *Ecclesia Dei*, "to collaborate with the bishops" and others to make it possible for those drawn in some way to Archbishop Lefebvre's movement to stay in full communion with the pope, "while preserving their spiritual and liturgical traditions."[72] This act established another agent (besides and even apart from the local bishop) possessing, as it turned out, authority to grant persons desiring to use the 1962 Missal (e.g., individual priests of a diocese) the permission to do so.[73]

[71] As noted before, this refers to the permission already granted to bishops under the authority of Paul VI to allow elderly or infirm priests to use the Missal of John XXIII as emended in 1965 and 1967. That permission was granted in the instruction from the Sacred Congregation for Divine Worship, *Constitutione Apostolica* (1969), nos. 19–20 (DOL 209 at nos. 1751–52); affirmed again in the notification *Instructione de Constitutione* (1971), no. 3 (DOL 216 at no. 1772); and affirmed again in the notification *Conferentiarum Episcopalium* (1974), noting with emphasis that the bishops could grant this permission "*only* for celebration *without a congregation*. Ordinaries cannot grant this permission for the celebration of Mass with a congregation" (DOL 219 at no. 1784; emphasis in original). Bugnini notes that Paul VI personally approved the wording of the 1974 text; Bugnini, *The Reform of the Liturgy*, 300.

[72] John Paul II, *Ecclesia Dei* (1988), 6.a.

[73] For an example of how this collaboration could work, see the section on "A. Eucharistic Celebrations. 1. *Permission to Celebrate according to the Roman Missal of 1962 (Ecclesia Dei)*," in *Roman Replies and CLSA Advisory Opinions 1990*, 1–5. In the documents there printed we see that the PCED did seek to work in collaboration with local ordinaries (as in the letter on page 5), yet also that it had the authority to grant individual priests in a diocese permission to use the

As of 2007, under the new provisions of SP replacing those of QAA and *Ecclesia Dei*, the diocesan bishop no longer determines whether the 1962 Missal is used in his diocese. Any Latin rite Catholic priest, at his own choice, can freely use it in Masses *sine populo* (SP, art. 2); any of the faithful who seek on their own initiative to attend such Masses may be admitted (SP, art. 4); and a stable group of the faithful may request the traditional Mass, and the pastor (SP, art. 5, sec. 1) and bishop (SP, art. 7) are to see that it is provided.

There is thus a notable difference in the situation before and after SP. Before SP, (1) between 1970 and 1984, the 1962 Missal was by universal law prohibited; (2) between 1984 and 1988 the diocesan bishop made the determination regarding use of the 1962 Missal, at his discretion, and under the restrictions of the indult QAA; (3) between 1988 and 2007 the bishop made this determination, or the PCED in response to specific requests. In other words, before 2007, the bishop had much say in whether the 1962 Missal could be used in his diocese. After and because of SP, in several circumstances the bishop does not make this determination, as it is freely in the hands of each priest at *his* (the priest's, not the bishop's) discretion, or in the hands of the stable group requesting it. Given this difference, one can understand how the post-*motu-proprio* arrangement could appear to a bishop to represent a diminishment of his authority over liturgy and pastoral practice in his diocese, by virtue of SP's limited but real transfer of decision-making authority in this matter from the bishop to the priests and the faithful.

But Pope Benedict took special care to emphasize that SP "in no way" (*in nessun modo*) diminished the bishop's authority or responsibility regarding liturgy or pastoral care. Given the foregoing, what might this mean? Let me offer two considerations.

First, I think it was Pope Benedict's judgment that bishops never authentically had the right to prohibit celebration of the 1962 Missal in their dioceses. Cardinal Ratzinger was part of the 1986 commission of cardinals that, according to reports, addressed this question and made this very determination—the determination

---

1962 Missal, and to grant such permission without consulting but only informing the ordinary of the diocese (as in the letters on pages 1–2).

that Paul VI did not grant bishops the authority to forbid use of the traditional Mass.[74] On this assumption, SP does not diminish a bishop's authority because it only clarifies an authority he did not have in the first place.

Yet this certainly seems an odd way of putting it, difficult to understand, for two reasons. First, Paul VI had already prohibited use of the prior Missal upon introduction of the new one. From the early 1970s, this was not a matter left up to bishops to decide one way or the other, the matter having already been decided by higher (that is, papal) authority. Second, John Paul II in QAA gave bishops permission to *allow* the traditional Mass, but it remained, otherwise, as before—that is, prohibited by authority of Paul VI. Accordingly, even after 1984, there was still no question of a bishop having or not having a right to *deny* use of the prior Missal, for such use was already denied by universal church law; a bishop's right under QAA was a limited right, granted by the indult, to *allow* use of the prior Missal, though only within new and carefully circumscribed parameters. So, again, to make the assertion, as though it corrects a prior and common misunderstanding, that bishops have no right to deny use of the prior missal, is an odd way of putting it.[75]

[74] Antonio Finocchiaro, "Problematiche aperte nel *Web* sul Motu Proprio *Summorum Pontificum:* Posizioni e valutazioni," *Rivista Liturgica* 94, no. 6 (2007): 947–75, at 954–55.

[75] Finocchiaro reports the following as the findings of the 1986 commission of cardinals: "The commission was of the opinion that Paul VI had never granted bishops the authority to prohibit priests the celebration of Mass according to the ritual of Pius V, also that priests cannot be required to celebrate Mass according to the new Missal, and that bishops can neither prohibit nor place limitations on the celebration of Mass according to the ritual of Pius V, whether in public or private"; Antonio Finocchiaro, "Problematiche aperte nel *Web* sul Motu Proprio *Summorum Pontificum,*" 954 ("La commissione fu dell'avviso che Paolo VI non aveva mai concesso ai vescovi l'autorità di proibire ai preti la celebrazione della messa secondo il rito di Pio V, inoltre che i preti non possono essere obbligati a celebrare la messa secondo il nuovo Messale, e che i vescovi non possono proibire, né porre limitazioni, alla celebrazione della messa secondo il rito di Pio V, sia in pubblico sia in privato"). I confess myself unable to recognize the basis for such claims, in view of the sources previously reviewed, and would be grateful to see the rationale explained in a way that did not involve historical revisionism.

Second, what Pope Benedict aimed to do in SP/CGF was make it easier for bishops to fulfill their proper episcopal responsibility, not impose something alien to it. In this case, that episcopal role and responsibility is, as Cardinal Ratzinger once said, to "guarantee the breadth" and "open up what is closed, what could lead to sectarianism, and to integrate it into the whole."[76] The former phrase calls and encourages the bishop to recognize the rights of and make room for FE adherents; the latter phrase bids him draw those adherents from a relatively narrow perspective (if, for example, they desire to maintain the FE unchanged, or to oppose the FO, or keep themselves apart from it or from the ordinary life and ministry of parishes where it is celebrated) and back into the wider life and practice of the whole church. Since this is what bishops are to do anyway, in Benedict's view, then the provisions of SP did not impose anything alien to their role and responsibility but rather created mechanisms of help or subsidiarity (such as the PCED, in SP, art. 8) more easily to fulfill it, and thus served to free bishops "from the need always to evaluate anew how to respond to diverse situations" (CGF 5).

These reflections represent speculation on Pope Benedict's affirmation that SP "does not diminish in any way" a bishop's authority regarding liturgy and pastoral care in his diocese.

CGF 12

> *Furthermore, I ask you, dear brothers, to write to the Holy See an account of your experiences, three years after this* motu proprio *takes effect. If truly serious difficulties come to light, ways can be sought to find a remedy.*

What is the force of *invito* here? It is not a mandate or requirement that Benedict was imposing, but a form of request. I chose to translate it with *ask*, a stronger word than *invite*, thinking he had real interest in knowing the early effect of his initiative—what the bishops were experiencing, how the initial phase of implementation was proceeding, what was happening in regard to each of the articles, what difficulties were arising, what fruits became evident,

[76] Ratzinger, *God and the World*, 456.

what ambiguities needed clarifying, what recommendations they might offer, and so on. Knowing that some of the bishops were opposed to this initiative, he might also like to know what their own thoughts and feelings were, after three years, regarding the provisions and purposes of SP or regarding the thoughts and feelings he expressed in this letter (CGF).

In any case, three years is a short time in which to see results even begin to emerge in the areas in which SP can and is meant to have an impact. One effect of requesting a report could have been, simply, to have bishops and their staffs give some attention to SP, if they had not done so yet to any great extent. The feedback could help the pope and his staff form an initial sense of how the bishops received the document, so as to know what next steps might best facilitate the ongoing reception and fruitfulness of SP.

CGF 13

> *Dear brothers, with grateful and trusting thoughts I entrust to your hearts as pastors these pages and the norms of the* motu proprio. *Let us always be mindful of the words of the Apostle Paul to the presbyters of Ephesus: "Take heed to yourselves and to all the flock, in which the Holy Spirit has made you overseers, to care for the church of God which he obtained for himself with his own blood" (Acts 20:28).*

The operative word is *all*, as in, "Take heed . . . to *all* the flock," meaning the FE minority as well as the FO majority. And with this passage from Scripture to conclude the paragraph, Pope Benedict makes salient his fundamental, underlying concern in issuing SP: "care for the church."

CGF 14

> *I entrust to the powerful intercession of Mary, Mother of the Church, these new norms and with all my heart impart my apostolic blessing to you, dear brothers, to the parish priests in your dioceses, to all the priests, your coworkers, as also to all your faithful.*
>
> *Given at Saint Peter's, July 7, 2007*

Part 3

Chapter 6

Pastoral Implications

This chapter addresses pastoral implications of SP, focusing on three topics in particular: (1) "active participation"—understanding the concept and assessing SP in light of it; (2) implications for educational institutions and catechetical ministry, asking how extensively study of the extraordinary form should become an ordinary part of seminary studies, university degree programs, and diocesan and parish catechetical work; and (3) the diversity of liturgical ministries and their place in the ordinary and extraordinary forms.

ACTIVE PARTICIPATION

The Second Vatican Council's constitution on the liturgy clearly stated the pivotal importance the council placed on active participation by all the faithful in liturgical celebrations. This goal of active participation was articulated by Pius X in his *motu proprio* of 1903, *Tra le Sollecitudini*, echoed in subsequent church documents,[1] and promoted by the liturgical movement throughout the twentieth century. It found expression in the rich and often-quoted passage from *Sacrosanctum Concilium* 14:

> Mother Church earnestly desires that all the faithful should be led to that full, conscious, and active participation in liturgical

[1] For a concise review of twentieth-century papal teaching up through the time of the council, see Colman E. O'Neill, "The Theological Meaning of *Actuosa Participatio* in the Liturgy," in *Sacred Music and Liturgy Reform after Vatican II*, ed. Johannes Overath (Rome: Consociatio Internationalis Musicae Sacrae, 1969), 89–108, at 89–99; for more detail, see Paul De Clerck, "La participation active: Perspectives historico-liturgiques, de Pie X à Vatican II," in *The Active Participation Revisited: La Participation Active 100 Ans après Pie X et 40 Ans après Vatican II*, ed. Jozef Lamberts (Leuven: Peeters, 2004), 13–31; also see Chad J. Glendinning, "The Significance of the Liturgical Reforms prior to the Second Vatican Council in Light of *Summorum Pontificum*," *Studia Canonica* 44 (2012): 293–342.

celebrations which is demanded by the very nature of the liturgy. Such participation by the Christian people as "a chosen race, a royal priesthood, a holy nation, redeemed people" (1 Pet. 2:9; cf. 2:4-5), is their right and duty by reason of their baptism.

In the restoration and promotion of the sacred liturgy, this full and active participation by all the people is the aim to be considered before all else; for it is the primary and indispensable source from which the faithful are to derive the true Christian spirit.[2]

This theme is echoed throughout SC and brought to bear on numerous aspects of the church's liturgical life and practice.[3]

How should *Summorum Pontificum* be evaluated in light of this positive and primary value of active participation? Is such participation truly possible in celebrations of the old rite? After all, when the council embraced "full, conscious, and active participation in liturgical celebrations" as the primary aim of liturgical reform, and then set down in SC the general principles, specific directives, and administrative procedures by which to realize this aim in the years after the council, it was precisely the 1962 liturgy that was the object of this wide-ranging reform effort, a reform the liturgy was deemed to need so that the conciliar vision of active participation could be better realized in practice. So by widening the permission for use of this unreformed liturgical rite, does SP constitute a setback for active participation?

To answer the question, let us first get our bearings by exploring the meaning of the term *active participation*, discussing the value of both "internal and external" participation (SC 19), and then making use of a three-part schema outlined by Mark Searle on the meaning of participation in the liturgy; we can then assess both forms accordingly.

The goal of active participation that oriented the work of the liturgical movement throughout the twentieth century was embraced and affirmed by the Second Vatican Council in its 1963 constitution on the sacred liturgy, and it guided the reform of the liturgical books and their postconciliar implementation in pastoral

[2] Translation from *Constitution on the Sacred Liturgy* (Collegeville, MN: Liturgical Press, n.d. [1963]), which provides the Latin text with English translation.

[3] See SC 19, 21, 26, 27, 30, 48, 50, 55, 79, 113, 114, 121, 124.

practice. Especially in the early years after the council, this led to concerted efforts to provide the faithful with more ways to become active participants and agents in the performance of the ritual itself. Cardinal Ratzinger's assessment of this development was positive. In the 1980s he stated clearly that the council embraced the principle of active participation "with good reason,"[4] and affirmed as "no doubt correct"[5] the understanding that active participation means the faithful will engage in the "something done"[6] that is the liturgy, which consists in part in external actions. He sees profound theological truths grounding, justifying, and demanding this form of liturgical participation. He makes reference specifically to "the theology of creation and the theology of the Resurrection (which includes and ratifies Incarnation)."[7] He sees also a pneumatological dimension, contending that "only in this way [that is, through liturgical participation "expressed in a bodily form"] can man and the world be 'humanized,' which means that matter is brought to its spiritual capacity and that the Spirit is expressed in the wealth of creation."[8] Still further, this kind of active bodily participation is a requirement flowing from the "irreplaceable anthropological significance" of the makeup of the human person, and also from the communal nature of liturgical celebration.[9]

For all these reasons, theological, pneumatological, liturgical, and anthropological, Ratzinger had no hesitation in affirming that the faithful are to participate in a bodily-behavioral manner in the liturgical event, actively involved in that external way as members of a united and differentiated worshiping community, each contributing to "a 'drama,' in which we all play our part" and which includes an "interplay of words and acts between the participants."[10] As Ratzinger said, "This was the discovery made by the liturgical movement, and it gave a new immediacy to the old words and

[4] Ratzinger, *The Feast of Faith*, 123.
[5] Ratzinger with Messori, *The Ratzinger Report*, 127.
[6] Ibid.
[7] Ratzinger, *The Feast of Faith*, 71.
[8] Ibid.
[9] Ibid., 74 (anthropological); 69 and 88–89 (communal).
[10] Ibid., 88 and 89.

gestures."[11] He saw all this as "self-evident," and considered its effects in the liturgical reform as "most fruitful." He added, significantly, "If one were to remove the active involvement which exists in today's liturgy—and the Council facilitated this involvement—it would immediately be obvious how much growth there has been. No one would want to be without it."[12]

So it is clear beyond doubt that one feature of Ratzinger's liturgical thought was his recognition and affirmation of the essential place of the participation of the whole person in liturgical celebration, including bodily-external activity as well as the internal participation of mind and spirit.

With this clearly understood, and within this context, we can then note further his concern that the meaning of active participation in the years after the council was, not always and everywhere but sometimes and too often, subject to a "fatal narrowing of perspective," misunderstood as consisting "only" in "discernible external activity,"[13] as if the goal was simply that "as many people, as often as possible, should be visibly engaged in action."[14] This was a constant theme of his critique of the liturgical reform as implemented, voiced again in his message to the Fiftieth International Eucharistic Congress in Dublin in 2012, when he said that "not infrequently, the revision of liturgical forms has remained at an external level, and 'active participation' has been confused with external activity."[15] It is worth noting that in this critique he simply joins liturgists of repute who have raised the same issue throughout the postconciliar era—not only, it should be noted, as

[11] Ibid., 89; see also *The Spirit of the Liturgy*, 208.

[12] Ratzinger, *The Feast of Faith*, 89. See also his reflections on the celebration of Corpus Christi, including its element of procession: "Our relationship to God needs not only the inward aspect; it also needs to be expressed. And as well as speech, singing and silence, standing, sitting and kneeling, expression also calls for this celebratory walking along together in the community of the faithful, together with the God in whom we believe" (132).

[13] Ratzinger with Messori, *The Ratzinger Report*, 127. The key word in Ratzinger's sentence, which expresses the specific target of his critique and keeps the underlying theology balanced, is the word "only."

[14] Ratzinger, *The Spirit of the Liturgy*, 171; see also *The Feast of Faith*, 90, 123.

[15] "Video Message of His Holiness Pope Benedict XVI for the Closing of the Fiftieth International Eucharistic Congress in Dublin" (June 17, 2012).

something characterizing the years immediately after the council but also as a concern in the decades that followed as well, persisting into the twenty-first century and the time frame of SP.[16] Surely they and Ratzinger are right to critique this development. It is only by a significantly broadened interpretation of the term that one can understand it properly, and it is only on that basis that one can fairly assess whether the FE is capable of allowing or of fostering "active participation."

What, then, is a fuller, more accurate understanding of active participation, beyond external activity? A basic and indisputable first point is that it includes *both* internal and external participation, not only the actions of the body but the intentions and sentiments of mind, heart, and will. It is the latter that authenticate the former and make them genuinely human—make them, to use an old distinction, an *actus humanus* (a genuinely human act, engaging the full human capacities of the person) and not merely an *actus hominis* (an act of a human done without engaging will or intentionality, performed more by instinct or rote). Pius XII made the point in his

[16] See, for example, Aidan Kavanagh, "What Is Participation?—Or, Participation Revisited," *Doctrine and Life* 23, no. 7 (July 1973): 343–53, on the problem of understanding participation "most superficially. . . . In the liturgy this has been construed as little more than 'get in there and sing, or say the responses, or pray vocally, or celebrate'" (344); again, "it seems that the more people can be got to say at Mass, and the louder they can be got to say it, nothing more should be required. We keep insisting that this is what participation . . . means" (345). Louis-Marie Chauvet, remembering this same era, remarked on the tendency then to measure "the degree of participation by the yardstick of its exterior expression, especially by liturgical song"; as a result, he recalled, "we tended to put forward 'expressive' liturgies inclined to be noisy and wordy." See his "Are the Words of the Liturgy Worn Out? What Diagnosis? What Pastoral Approach?" in *Worship* 84 (2010): 25–37, at 30. Nearly twenty years after Kavanagh, in the 1990s, Patrick W. Collins wrote, in *Bodying Forth: Aesthetic Liturgy* (New York: Paulist Press, 1992): "Early on and even now in many instances, *active participation* seemed to mean getting more people busy doing more things" (28–29). Yet again nearly twenty years after Collins and three years after SP, Paul De Clerck found it timely and necessary to critique this shallowly "activitist" understanding of participation as a current problem still needing to be dealt with "today" (*aujourd'hui*), in 2010; see his "La réforme liturgique: ce qui reste à faire," *Questions Liturgiques: Studies in Liturgy* 91, nos. 1–2 (2010): 64–75, at 73–74.

encyclical on the liturgy, *Mediator Dei*, first, by noting the necessity and naturalness of external liturgical participation—on the grounds that humans are "a composite of body and soul" and need to express themselves physically and to act together socially—and then by stressing that "the chief element of divine worship must be interior," lest those external actions be reduced to "mere formalism, without meaning and without content."[17] Later in the document he spoke of the efforts of the liturgical movement to bring about among the faithful a more active participation in the external ritual itself, appreciatively describing such efforts as aiming "to arouse those internal sentiments and dispositions" which join the participants' hearts to Christ as High Priest.[18] External and internal together are necessary, with the external serving the internal in two ways: both by giving expression to internal dispositions of faith and love, and by fostering and intensifying such dispositions.[19]

[17] Pius XII, *Mediator Dei* 23 and 24, as in Jackson, *An Abundance of Graces*, 130.

[18] Pius XII, *Mediator Dei* 106, as in Jackson, *An Abundance of Graces*, 150.

[19] For these reasons I beg to differ here from Robert A. Skeris, and his comment on a passage from the 1967 instruction of the Sacred Congregation of Rites, *Musicam Sacram*, no. 15. It is sound to say, as the instruction does, that participation "must be in the first place interior" (*in primis interior sit oportet*), "but should also be exterior" (*attamen etiam exterior esse debet*); so also is the instruction's comment that the exterior manifests the interior. But Skeris concludes that "*Participatio interior* is therefore the cause, and not the effect of *participatio etiam exterior*"; see Robert A. Skeris, "Sarto, the 'Conservative Reformer'—100 Years of the *Motu Proprio* of Pope St. Pius X," *Sacred Music* 130, no. 4 (Winter 2003): 5–9, at 8. It is better to see interior participation as *both* cause and effect of exterior (and so, exterior as both effect and cause of interior), and to recognize and foster the necessary place of both in liturgical celebration. In corroboration, and to illustrate this double function of exterior expression in worship, consider Augustine's comments on the practices of Christians who mourn the faithful departed. "For those who pray do, with the members of their bodies, that which becomes suppliants, when they bend their knees, extend their hands or even prostrate themselves on the ground, and whatever else they do visibly, although their invisible will and the intention of their hearts be known to God, and He does not need these signs that the mind of man be opened to Him. But hereby man excites himself more to pray and to groan more humbly and fervently, and somehow, since these motions of the body can not be made except by a previous motion of the mind, so on the other hand, when these same motions are outwardly made in a visible man-

But this is only the beginning of a fuller understanding of participation as it pertains to liturgy. We can go further by making use of Mark Searle's helpful three-part schema, distinguishing participation (1) in ritual behavior, (2) in the work of Christ, and (3) in the life of God.[20]

Searle's first level is the most obvious. Liturgy is ritual, and to participate in the liturgy is to engage in ritual behavior. Searle highlights here four characteristics of ritual: that it is collective, formal, performance, and formative. Ritual is collective, involving all members of a gathered community, who will have diverse roles to play; that is, all will participate but "not everyone is required to do everything at the same time."[21] Ritual is also formal, tends to work best "when the formalities are observed," and in this way is "marked by a certain weight and gravity."[22] In view of this element of the nature of ritual, Searle then offers a caution regarding the *ars celebrandi* (specifically a priest's *ars praesidendi*) that is relevant here and will also be useful to recall when we discuss how the FO and FE can be mutually enriching. "Trivializing the liturgy," he writes, or dismissing the importance of its formality, "only undermines the confidence of the participants in the seriousness of the activity in

---

ner, that inward invisible one which caused them is increased, and thereby the heart's affection, which preceded in order that they might be made, increases because they are made." Augustine, *On the Care to Be Taken of the Dead*, V.7, in *De Cura pro Mortuis Gerenda Sancti Augustini: Text, Translation, Introduction and Commentary*, trans. Sister Catherine Teresa Rapp (Master of Arts Thesis, Department of Ancient Languages, University of Notre Dame, 1931), 63–64.

[20] The following paragraphs are based on chapter 2 of Searle's posthumous book, *Called to Participate: Theological, Ritual, and Social Perspectives*, ed. Anne Y. Koester and Barbara Searle (Collegeville, MN: Liturgical Press, 2005). The basic outline of Searle's thinking was already formulated and can be found in his essay "Culture," in *Liturgy: Active Participation in the Divine Life*, ed. James P. Moroney (Collegeville, MN: Liturgical Press, 1990), 27–51, at 43–47.

[21] Searle, *Called to Participate*, 20. SC affirms the same, when no. 26 emphasizes the public, communal nature of liturgy and no. 28 the distinction of roles.

[22] Searle, *Called to Participate*, 21 and 22. In a similar vein Aidan Kavanagh proposed as the experimental 1960s were drawing to a close that it might be time, having lost it for half a decade, to rediscover "the humane enterprise of ritual formality"; Kavanagh, "Liturgical Needs for Today and Tomorrow," *Worship* 43 (1969): 489–95, at 489.

which they are engaged. Attempts to lighten up the liturgy slowly erode faith by drawing attention to the signifier and distracting from the signified."[23] This sobering observation invites serious reflection by clergy on the possibility that efforts, however well meant, to make the liturgy more accessible, lively, and friendly by making it more informal or casual, or to "personalize" the liturgy by one's own comments (made when the rite allows the option of speaking "in these or similar words," or at other times as well), may unavoidably have an unintended consequence. Such efforts of presiders may instead rather draw the congregation's attention too much to themselves (in either sense of the phrase: that is, to the person of the presider, or to themselves as a congregation) and away from a more direct ritual engagement with and intentional turning of attention to the Lord whom the faithful have (Searle and Pope Benedict would emphasize) come to worship. At the least, the observation suggests a danger for presiders to be aware of and take care to avoid.[24]

Ritual is also, Searle says, performance. This is the basic point that ritual does not exist or take place in books but is a communal and formal event that happens and has effects on the persons participating. Moreover, "instead of simply expressing who they [the participants] are, the rites also and more importantly redefine what they are,"[25] by giving them a new identity to grow into and by sustaining them in that identity. Finally, ritual is formative—and is so, precisely by being formal, given, beyond manipulation. Speaking

[23] Searle, *Called to Participate*, 22.

[24] Compare John Baldovin's observation, that "often the comments made by presiders at the beginning of the liturgy serve not their good intention of bringing the community together but rather as a distraction from the business of worshiping"; John F. Baldovin, "*Sacrosanctum Concilium* and the Reform of the Liturgy: Forty-Five Years Later," *Studia Liturgica* 39 (2009): 145–57, at 154. Jonathon Robinson proposed "a determined effort on the part of the clergy to allow the liturgy to do its work without the constant intrusion of their own personality and concerns"; Jonathon Robinson, *The Mass and Modernity: Walking to Heaven Backward* (San Francisco: Ignatius Press, 2005), 330. Aidan Kavanagh said simply, "The liturgical minster will begin by affecting nothing that calls untoward attention to himself or herself"; Aidan Kavanagh, *Elements of Rite: A Handbook of Liturgical Style* (New York: Pueblo Publishing, 1982), 94.

[25] Searle, *Called to Participate*, 23.

directly to a certain perspective on liturgy and pastoral practice particularly operative in the late twentieth century, Searle affirmed that, "hard as it may be for us to grasp, we are not free to make liturgy up as we go along but are required to carry it out, enact it, and perform it, so that it may form us."[26] The more we form and shape the liturgy ourselves, the less likely it will be able to form us in its dimensions, for it will tend instead to reflect and reinforce who we already are, or even serve (to use a phrase of Aidan Kavanagh) to "confirm us in our illusions—that this liturgy belongs to us."[27] But the more we give ourselves over to the liturgy, celebrating it as given and received from the church at large, entering fully, consciously, and actively into that celebration of the wider church, the more likely we can then be formed by it into ways of prayer, faith, and Christian living that accord with and are enriched by that wider, deeper tradition, what Pope Benedict called "the living Tradition."[28] In all these four ways—where Searle seems remarkably sympathetic with Ratzinger's sensibilities—one participates in the liturgy as ritual.

From this, a second dimension of liturgical participation opens up: our sharing in Christ's obedience to the Father, his earthly and perpetual sacrifice and offering of himself. Offering our ritual prayer to God through, with, and in Christ as eternal high priest, those ritual acts we perform and engage in (the first level of participation) are "subsumed into this second level of participation in the liturgy of Christ, which, however, is no ordinary ritual celebration but the endless self-giving of Christ into the hands of God from whom he receives back his life."[29] Baptism initiates us into this role,

[26] Ibid., 25.

[27] Aidan Kavanagh, "Reflections on the Study," 94. Kavanagh is critiquing certain 1980s-era assumptions; the passage begins by affirming of the liturgy: "In no way must it confirm us in our illusions—that this liturgy belongs to us, or our social class, or our culture, or our world; that we are without sin; that our salvation is sure in spite of what we do . . . ," and so forth.

[28] Benedict XVI, *Sacramentum Caritatis* 37.

[29] Searle, *Called to Participate*, 28. Compare Kevin W. Irwin, *Context and Text: Method in Liturgical Theology* (Collegeville, MN: Liturgical Press, 1992), who agrees that "'active participation' means more than *doing something* in the liturgy. On a more fundamental level it means that *God does something among us*

this sharing in Christ's priesthood, and this is what is understood, thanks to Aquinas, by the sacramental "character" of baptism, the sacrament that changes our relationship with Christ, incorporating us into Christ and thereby into the church-as-Body-of-Christ which represents Christ in the world and is called and charged to carry on his redeeming work.[30] This corporate, ecclesial identity and mission, in which the baptized participate and for which they bear responsibility, is properly understood as a dimension of worship. For genuine worship "has to be the worship not of lips but of obedience: an offering of one's whole self, with and in Christ, to God," which entails for Christians what it entailed for Christ, a "participation in the paschal mystery of Christ's obedience unto death,"[31] a self-giving without reserve to and for the Father, and all whom the Father loves. The implications this has for the Christian way of life are outlined by Pope Benedict in the third part of *Sacramentum Caritatis*, where he explores the topic of "The Eucharist, a Mystery to Be Lived" through love in action, moral transformation, and Christian witness.

Searle then introduces a third level of participation by referencing the "two sets of effects resulting from the sacraments," using here the traditional categories of the *res et sacramentum* and the *res tantum*.[32] He describes the former, consisting for some sacraments in the sacramental "character," as a "socio-ecclesial effect" and identifies it with the second level of participation which also includes embracing and living the Christian way of life in common. This in turn leads to the further effect (the *res tantum*) that does not lead to anything further but is itself the final, ultimate aim of sacramental practice, Christian living, and human existence: namely, participation in the life of God, "what the Latins call 'sanctification' and the Greeks call 'divinization.'"[33] Full, conscious, and active par-

---

at liturgy, namely, to allow us to *take part in* and to become *partakers* and *sharers in* the priesthood of Christ" (145).

[30] Searle, *Called to Participate*, 29–31.

[31] Ibid., 28. See Ratzinger, *The Spirit of the Liturgy*, 34, at the conclusion of his chapter on sacrifice, "Liturgy—Cosmos—History."

[32] Searle, *Called to Participate*, 37.

[33] Ibid., 43.

ticipation in the liturgy inherently and ultimately leads to this, and consists in this: theosis.

Searle concludes his chapter with this summary of the dimensions of this key phenomenon of participation. It consists in the three levels of:

1. "participating in the *rite* as a whole according to one's assigned role and doing so in such a way that one is
2. "participating in the *priestly work of Christ* on behalf of the world before the throne of God and thus identifying with Christ dead and risen; and
3. "participating in the *trinitarian life of God* as human beings."[34]

When Searle then says that in these ways "we are also participating in God's work in human history," he identifies the necessary "social and political consequences" of liturgical participation[35]—the relationship of liturgy and life, and in particular its necessary connections with efforts in the promotion of human dignity, justice and peace, and respect for life, so well emphasized in contemporary theology and catechesis.

As is obvious from all this, active participation means much more than "doing things" in the liturgy. It means the interplay and operation of all three dimensions just described. As Searle contends, these dimensions truly "belong together, and together they constitute that 'full, conscious and active participation' in the liturgy that has always been integral to the Christian life and that the council sought to facilitate through its general reform of the liturgy" (that is, of the 1962 liturgy).[36]

So we come again to the question with which we began this section. By making the liturgy and in particular the Mass in its 1962 form more available, as an adjunct to the reformed liturgy, does SP constitute a setback for the cause of active participation? Or can active participation take place in and be fostered by celebrations of the traditional as well as the reformed liturgy? Let us think through the questions, keeping in mind Searle's admonition that "the sole

[34] Ibid., 44; organization and emphasis in original.

[35] Ibid.

[36] Ibid., 42.

criterion we must follow is this: Does everything done at level 1 lead to levels 2 and 3?"[37] That is, the real question is not how well each form (ordinary or extraordinary) fosters level 1 participation, but how well each form's level 1 ritual (including the kinds of participation it allows and calls for) fosters, among those worshiping in that form, their participation in levels 2 and 3.

The other perspective to keep in mind here is that, while we can compare the relative merits of each form of liturgy, the value or legitimacy of either does not stand or fall on its comparison with the other. Should the FE be deemed in some ways inferior to or less effective than the FO in fostering active participation and actual worship in some or all of these three dimensions, that would not thereby render the FE pastorally void of merit and reveal SP to be ill-advised or indefensible. For if the FE, well catechized and well celebrated, can foster genuine active participation in some ways for some members of the church, or through mutual enrichment can influence the FO in such a way as to enhance or broaden its ability more effectively to foster for at least some members of the church participation in any of the three dimensions, that would constitute sufficient warrant to value and support the liturgical and pastoral provisions of SP. And should the FO itself be deemed in some ways deficient or less effective in fostering active participation and actual worship in some or all three dimensions—again, that would not render it indefensible. For if the FO, well catechized and well celebrated, can lead some people to genuine worship and liturgical celebration, or through mutual enrichment can enrich the calendar, ritual, or way of celebrating and participating in the FE, this is a benefit. What SP envisions and invites is not a contest or decision between the two usages but a collaborative partnership in which each contributes its best to the ongoing development of the church's liturgy in a way that fosters reconciliation among those who are currently divided by their way of favoring one usage over or even in opposition to the other.

[37] Searle, "Culture," 46. Compare Kevin Irwin's affirmation that "the active participation of the faithful in the act of liturgy is not the goal; it is a means toward the deeper and always elusive goal: to take part in the mystery of God"; see Irwin, "Authentic Worship in Spirit and in Truth," *Pastoral Music* 33, no. 1 (October 2008): 51–60, at 58.

At the level of the ritual, level 1, both forms allow for external participation. Yet the FO is the FE reformed, in order to comply with numerous provisions in *Sacrosanctum Concilium* formulated precisely and intentionally to foster fuller participation. It does this first of all in that it unites the entire congregation, priest and people, in a single shared act of worship, where all present are participating in and offering the liturgical prayer of the church together. Various provisions of the liturgy constitution serve this aim—affirming that communal celebrations with active participation are to be preferred (SC 27), making greater allowance for use of the vernacular to render the service more understandable (SC 36 and 54), encouraging the people's external participation through "acclamations, responses, psalmody, antiphons, and songs, as well as by actions, gestures, and bodily attitudes," and also "a reverent silence" (SC 30), valuing the pedagogical potential of "the visible signs used by the liturgy" (SC 33), simplifying elements of the liturgy for the sake of comprehensibility (SC 34 and 50), and so on. Because of this concern for active participation that has guided the reform of the ritual, Aidan Kavanagh maintained that the reformed liturgy is "an incomparably more rich, vital, and traditional liturgical settlement in the truly Catholic sense than that of Trent"; I take the first two adjectives here, rich and vital, to pertain especially to its intention to promote and its capacity to foster the participation of all those who celebrate it.[38]

Aidan Nichols holds an alternate perspective, thinking "the absence in the postconciliar Liturgy of the atmosphere of intense silence and devotion once so striking to observers raises the question as to whether *actuosa participatio*, assessed in terms of Flanagan's criterion, is more advanced or less advanced than it was before the Council opened."[39] Mark Aillet suggests, further, that certain

[38] Aidan Kavanagh, "Reflections on the Study from the Viewpoint of Liturgical History," in *The Awakening Church: 25 Years of Liturgical Renewal*, ed. Lawrence J. Madden (Collegeville, MN: Liturgical Press, 1992), 83–97, at 91.

[39] Aidan Nichols, *Looking at the Liturgy: A Critical View of Its Contemporary Form* (San Francisco: Ignatius Press, 1996), 66. Nichols thinks the question legitimate, though he is aware of and cautions against "tricks of memory and nostalgia, as well as wishful thinking based on ecclesiastical partisanship, [that] may deceive us" (66). The Flanagan criterion mentioned is that "active,

features characteristic of the extraordinary form foster more than hinder active participation, such as celebrations *ad orientem*, in Latin, using Gregorian chant—features, interestingly, either permitted or recommended for the ordinary form as well.[40] Along these lines we can take note as well of a suggestion made more than once by Cardinal Ratzinger of a form of liturgical celebration and participation combining elements both postconciliar (single worshiping community, prayer in the vernacular) and preconciliar (mostly silent canon). The suggestion is that, after suitable liturgical education of the faithful on the theological meaning and the ritual structure and flow of the eucharistic prayer, that prayer might on occasion be prayed by the priest quietly except for the first few words of the various sections of the prayer; this practice would create a sacred silence allowing people to meditate on the meaning of the prayer as it is prayed.[41] Ratzinger described what can result—"a church united in the silent praying of the Canon"—as a powerful and communally participatory "Spirit-filled act of prayer."[42] Such a practice can, he argued, enhance the quality of people's actual participation, insofar as one's "internal appropriation of the words" and meaning may have the potential to attain a certain

outward participation is to be evaluated according to 'the degree to which it generates inner appropriation, interior assent'" (65)—a reference to Kieran Flanagan, *Sociology and Liturgy: Re-presentations of the Holy* (London: Macmillan, 1991).

[40] Marc Aillet, *The Old Mass and the New: Explaining the Motu Proprio* Summorum Pontificum *of Pope Benedict XVI* (San Francisco: Ignatius Press, 2010), 89–90. His rationale is based on a theological understanding of liturgy in which the *sensus fidei*—a "*supernatural sense of faith* [that] altogether precedes explicit assent to a clearly formulated faith and is in a certain sense far richer" (88)—is a more primary grounding for liturgical celebration and a depth of interior engagement than the *intellectus fidei*, the understanding or intelligence of faith. He draws a conclusion: "So we can understand why the liturgy . . . ought not to be intelligible in the first instance, but should, on the contrary, retain a certain opacity so as to facilitate that experience of the divine which one will then be better able to articulate as adequately as possible, but always in a way that falls short of the mystery, through the confession of faith and the practice of the Christian life" (89).

[41] Ratzinger, *The Feast of Faith*, 72–73; idem, *The Spirit of the Liturgy*, 214–16.

[42] Ratzinger, *The Spirit of the Liturgy*, 215.

interior depth not necessarily fostered by "an uninterrupted loud recitation."[43]

This proposal by Ratzinger, which has not won favor, was bound up with his general assessment of the reformed liturgy as overly verbal, and his general support for giving greater scope to silence, precisely as a way to allow those present to become more actively engaged in the liturgy and interiorly receptive to the Word.[44] He was not alone in this assessment. Brian Harrison critiqued "the constant patter of words" in the celebration.[45] John Baldovin remarked in 1988 that "there are simply too many words," and twenty years later referred again to "the over-verbalization of the rite (especially by means of commentary) on account of which people are not invited to enter into the liturgy on its own terms."[46] The latter is an interesting observation, suggesting that in some way an excess of words spoken by liturgical ministers can distract people's focus and impede their participation in the liturgy. Recommendations for amending the situation and enhancing liturgical participation by cutting back to some extent on the words spoken would seem, then, to be reasonable and should be welcomed. Harrison, Baldovin, and Ratzinger have all offered suggestions to this end.[47] The pros and cons of each could be compared, as well as other

[43] Ratzinger, *The Feast of Faith*, 73.

[44] See Ratzinger, *The Spirit of the Liturgy*, 209–16, and *The Feast of Faith*, 72–73. The relevant reference in the council's liturgy constitution is SC 30: "And at the proper times all should observe a reverent silence" (*sacrum . . . silentium*). In the most recent edition of the GIRM, see no. 45, as well as nos. 54, 55, 56, 66, 71, 84 (an underutilized element in the ritual referenced by Ratzinger in *The Feast of Faith*, 72), and 88.

[45] Brian Harrison, "Postconciliar Eucharistic Liturgy: Planning a 'Reform of the Reform,'" in Thomas Kocik, *Reform of the Reform? A Liturgical Debate: Reform or Return* (San Francisco: Ignatius Press, 2003), 151–93, at 190.

[46] John F. Baldovin, "Pastoral Liturgical Reflections on the Study," in Madden, *The Awakening Church*, 108 ("too many words"); Baldovin, *Reforming the Liturgy*, 97 ("over-verbalization").

[47] Harrison, "Postconciliar Eucharistic Liturgy," 170–86. Baldovin, "Pastoral Liturgical Reflections," 108, and *Reforming the Liturgy*, 152–53. Ratzinger, *The Feast of Faith*, 72–73; *The Spirit of the Liturgy*, 210–16 (suggestions regarding silence).

suggestions entertained. New perspectives might emerge in the process, resulting in unanticipated but potentially fruitful practices of external participation (perhaps including some currently thought deficient or counterproductive) that can foster genuine internal participation.

As for internal participation, that is of course quite possible under the FE, as every leader and proponent of the early twentieth-century liturgical movement from the time of Pius X to that of Pius XII and John XXIII took for granted, for they called for such participation in and through the liturgy of the day—what we now call the extraordinary form.[48] At the same time, that liturgy was subject to reform throughout the twentieth century precisely in order to foster more active participation, before and above all during the pontificate of Pius XII; these reform efforts, culminating in the Second Vatican Council's liturgy constitution, and the consequent development of the reformed liturgy, took place precisely to make possible and promote a *more* full, conscious, and active participation, internal and external.[49] Yet whether a given participant's internal participation (degree or intensity of faith, love, attentiveness, devotion) is on a given ritual occasion greater or lesser depends ultimately more on the person than on the ritual form. One might recall here Kavanagh's observation, made ten years after the promulgation of the council's liturgy constitution. He spoke of "the marked increase in the faithful's active participation in the liturgy" during those years. But then he added, "The quantity of participation, however, seems to have grown," even "as thoughtful reflection upon the reality of participation has declined."[50] The FO's greater capacity

[48] See, for example, Pius XII's 1947 encyclical, *Mediator Dei*, 24–27, 31–32, 86–93, 98–99, 103–104, 145, 197 (passages chosen from among others addressing internal participation, dispositions, intentions).

[49] See Chad J. Glendinning, "The Significance of the Liturgical Reforms prior to the Second Vatican Council in Light of *Summorum Pontificum*," *Studia Canonica* 44 (2012): 293–342.

[50] Kavanagh, "What Is Participation?" 344. It should be noted that Kavanagh, four years after John Paul II first authorized limited use of the 1962 Missal, declared himself "a creature of the Second Vatican Council" and an opponent of "the revival of the Tridentine Mass liturgy." He considered that endeavor, however "well meaning" it might be, a "vast mistake," because of

for fostering due external participation does not in itself guarantee or always foster the internal participation to which it is oriented.

Cardinal Ratzinger reminded us of the kind of rich internal participation possible under the old liturgy, at least where the faithful had the benefit of that greater understanding and appreciation of the liturgy fostered by the educational efforts of the liturgical movement pioneers—as was the case to some extent in his family growing up, a fact which should never be far from mind in interpreting his comments as cardinal or pope on the preconciliar liturgy.[51] And so he affirmed, with reference to his own experience as a child and youth, that, "compared with the merely external busy-ness which became the rule in many places [after the council], the quiet 'following' of Mass, as we knew it in former times, was far more realistic and dramatic: it was a sharing in the action at a deep level, and in it the community was silently and powerfully mobilized."[52]

Note in that final phrase the way certain principles that guided the liturgical reform were embedded in his affirmations regarding the prior usage: that what was happening was "a sharing in the action" of the liturgy itself (not divorced from it), that it took place "at a deep level" (not merely rubrically, externally, superficially), that it formed those present into a genuine community (and not merely disparate individuals or strangers praying their own prayers), even as it was also silent (not totally depending on the laity's performance of external actions, or fundamentally hindered by the limited opportunity to do so). Ratzinger's knowledge, based on experience, that this kind of active, engaged participation was possible in celebrations of the *usus antiquior* always informed his assessment of that liturgy *per se*. Yet the critique his comment made of the reformed liturgy (as characterized by "mere external busyness") must be seen in its properly limited context, for he immedi-

what he saw as the incomparable superiority of the reformed liturgy; Kavanagh, "Reflections on the Study," 91.

[51] See Ratzinger, *Milestones*, 18–20; also idem, *The Feast of Faith*, 127.

[52] Ratzinger, *The Feast of Faith*, 90. See also his reference to "relearn[ing] this silent, inner co-praying with each other and with the angels and saints, the living and the dead, and with Christ himself" (*A New Song for the Lord*, 181–82).

ately then added: "Of course, to say this is not to impugn 'active participation' as I have defined it [as consisting in 'inner processes' and not just external actions]; the criticism only applies where this participation has degenerated into mere externals."[53] His critique, then, was not of the reformed liturgy itself or even of its implementation as such; his objection was limited and targeted, pertaining only to those instances of liturgical reform that became concerned with mere externals—that focused, that is, only or disproportionately on externals, a critique we have seen shared by Kavanagh and others.

For this first level of participation, then, we can recognize that active internal participation is possible under either form, while affirming that the reformed liturgy aims to elicit and foster it in more explicit ways by providing for more kinds of external participation than did the liturgy as provisioned in 1962—itself the result of various earlier efforts to foster a more active participation of the faithful in the liturgy. More pointedly, we should take note of what may be considered a characteristic and even crowning achievement of the liturgical reform: the ritual sea change by which the reformed liturgy incorporates the entire gathered congregation into one and the same liturgical action as a single worshiping community, with priests, liturgical ministers, and people all praying the same worship event together as one body.[54] This point above all and alone constitutes the ordinary form as a qualitative advance over the extraordinary.

Is the second level of participation—in the priesthood of Christ, in his obedient self-offering to the Father and his paschal mystery, in the church's communal worship and its witness and service to the world—possible under either form? Surely so. To deny it of the extraordinary form would be in effect to say the church failed in its identity and mission in the years and centuries before Vatican II, when the FE was the church's liturgy; to deny it of the ordinary

[53] Ratzinger, *The Feast of Faith*, 90; the reference to "inner processes" is from 89.

[54] See David N. Power and Catherine Vincie, "Theological and Pastoral Reflections," in *A Commentary on the General Instruction of the Roman Missal*, ed. Edward Foley, Nathan D. Mitchell, and Joanne M. Pierce (Collegeville, MN: Liturgical Press, 2007), 46–72, at 50.

form would be to say the same of the church in the years after Vatican II. To make either claim is highly contentious, hypercritical, and clearly partisan.

And yet such is the state of affairs that these charges may appear to both sides warranted. Opponents of the ordinary form might build a case around the judgment once expressed in Cardinal Ratzinger's memoirs: "I am convinced that the crisis in the Church that we are experiencing today is to a large extent due to the disintegration of the liturgy."[55] If such a view has any merit, does it not show that postconciliar liturgy is not only unable to nurture Catholic faith and life but actually inimical to it? Opponents of the extraordinary form, for their part, might simply point to the stated aims of the Second Vatican Council itself. If the council felt so strongly the need "to impart an ever increasing vigor to the Christian life of the faithful" (SC 1), in part by "undertak[ing] with great care a general restoration of the liturgy itself" (SC 21), does this not indicate that preconciliar liturgy's fundamental failure and inability adequately to sustain the vigor of Catholic faith and practice?

The divide may be this deep, with each side's perspective invisible to the other. Yet we can find compelling witness to the contrary, affirming each form's life-giving potential—including positive witness on behalf of the *usus antiquior* from those most familiar with it, those who lived with it and celebrated it daily in the years before the council, and witness for the *usus recentior* from reliable voices among those familiar with its celebration after the council. These witnesses maintain of each form that it sustains Christian life and is rich in ethical impact, deepening the conversion of the faithful and nourishing them for the church's mission in society.

This dimension of the *usus antiquior* was expressed, for example, by Gerald Ellard in 1927 in discussing the effects Pius X envisioned through the faithful's "participation in the holy mysteries. It is ever the same: Christ-life in the individual, and the Christian ferment in the world."[56] After a study of the early issues of the liturgical journal *Orate Fratres* (subsequently *Worship*), founded in the 1920s,

[55] Ratzinger, *Milestones*, 148.

[56] Gerald Ellard, "Pius Tenth and the New Liturgy," *Orate Fratres* 1, no. 8 (1927): 241–46, at 245.

Timothy P. O'Malley saw firsthand evidence, in what those then celebrating the liturgy said, that "when participated in intelligently, with spiritual fervor," inspired by the liturgical movement, the Mass of that era "produced real fruits. . . . Simply, a form a liturgical participation that was genuine, authentic, spiritually fruitful existed before the Missal of Paul VI and vernacular translations."[57] And Virgil Michel affirmed in the 1930s that "where the liturgical spirit flourishes in the hearts of men, it will not be to remain hidden there, but will needs burst forth openly in the world into the most abundant fruits of human endeavor or into a true Christian culture for the glory of God and the greater sanctification of man."[58] Indeed, in great part because of Michel the social justice dimension of the liturgy was a constitutive theme of the American liturgical movement.[59]

Similar claims are made for the *usus recentior*. As the liturgical reforms were beginning, Paul VI said to the laity in a general audience address in 1965, "the activity that you devote to understanding and sharing in the liturgy fully becomes translated into an activity revitalizing society."[60] John Paul II regularly emphasized the charity and justice implications of the Eucharist.[61] Ratzinger explained that the true aim of liturgical education lies in leading participants "toward the essential *actio* that makes the liturgy what it is, toward the transforming power of God, who wants, through what happens in the liturgy, to transform us and the world."[62]

[57] See O'Malley, "Re-reading *Orate Fratres*: The American Liturgical Movement Is Born (1926–27)," in the blog *Oblation: Catechesis, Liturgy, and the New Evangelization*, at http://blogs.nd.edu/oblation/2012/09/20/re-reading-orate-fratres-the-american-liturgical-movement-is-born-1926-27.

[58] Virgil Michel, "Christian Culture," *Orate Fratres* 13, no. 7 (1939): 296–304, at 304. See also idem, "The Scope of the Liturgical Movement," *Orate Fratres* 10, nos. 11–12 (1936): 485–90; or idem, "The Liturgy the Basis of Social Regeneration," *Orate Fratres* 9, no. 12 (1935): 536–45.

[59] For a survey see Keith F. Pecklers, *The Unread Vision: The Liturgical Movement in the United States of America: 1926–1955* (Collegeville, MN: Liturgical Press, 1998), chap. 3, "The Liturgical Movement and Social Justice" (81–149).

[60] DOL 24 at no. 392. The address was given on January 13, 1965.

[61] John Paul II, *Dominicae Cenae* 6; *Ecclesia de Eucharistia* 20; *Mane Nobiscum Domine* 27–28; etc.

[62] Ratzinger, *The Spirit of the Liturgy*, 175.

Benedict XVI drew out the same implications of liturgical participation and celebration, as already noted, in the third section of *Sacramentum Caritatis*—as when affirming that "the union with Christ brought about by the Eucharist also brings about a newness to our social relations" (no. 89), and that "the eucharistic mystery thus gives rise to a service of charity toward neighbor" (no. 88).

This appears, then, to be an element of similarity between the two forms. Persons who celebrate either form affirm that that form intends to foster and is capable of fostering participation at Searle's second level, in the self-offering of the faithful in union with Christ's self-offering to the Father for the life of the world. I think the evidence sufficient to support the claims, even if today some adherents of each form may be unpersuaded by those who witness for the other.

Is the third level of participation, in the Trinitarian life of God, possible under either form? Clearly so. Thomas Aquinas taught, of the liturgy of his day, that "the proper effect of the Eucharist is the transformation of man into God."[63] Virgil Michel wrote that "the sublime function of the liturgy of the Church [is] to assimilate us unto Christ, to make us partakers of the Christ-life, of the eternal life of God."[64] In his 1947 encyclical on the liturgy, Pius XII referred to the church's "sacraments and sacrifice" as having "that 'objective' power to make us really and personally sharers in the divine life of Jesus Christ."[65] Of course the same is true of the church's liturgy after Vatican II. Cardinal Ratzinger said in 1977 that "in the Church's Eucharist . . . what is taking place is the mystery of God, communicated to us by Jesus Christ through his death and Resurrection."[66] Pope Benedict XVI affirmed in 2007 that "Jesus Christ . . . makes us, in the gift of the Eucharist, sharers in God's

[63] As translated in Gerard Austin, "*Theosis* and Eschatology," *Liturgical Ministry* 19 (Winter 2010): 1–8, at 3; Austin references Aquinas, *IV Sent.* d.12, q.2, art.1. See also Daria Lucas, "Active Participation in the Liturgy according to Thomas Aquinas," *Assembly* 34, no. 1 (January 2008): 6–16; Lucas writes, "Participation in the sacraments invites us to nothing less than deification" (6).

[64] Virgil Michel, *The Liturgy of the Church: According to the Roman Rite* (New York: Macmillan, 1937), 46.

[65] Pius XII, *Mediator Dei* 29.

[66] Ratzinger, *The Feast of Faith*, 94–95.

own life."[67] The Eucharist in any legitimate form offers the gift of union with God in Christ by the Spirit for those who participate with faith, proper dispositions, and full, conscious, active participation (SC 11, 14, 19). It seems right and best to say, then, that after SP, while the FO is normative and the FE is additional, both are legitimate and merit respect as forms of the liturgy of the Roman Rite, a liturgical tradition in which today, in either usage, "the Church celebrates . . . the Paschal mystery by which Christ accomplished the work of our salvation," and in which "the Holy Spirit's transforming power . . . causes us really to anticipate the fullness of communion with the Holy Trinity."[68]

To summarize: if we focus our attention on a broad and comprehensive understanding of liturgical participation, as we have tried to do here with the help of Searle, we reach the conclusion that active participation in the full and properly multidimensional sense can take place through both the ordinary and extraordinary forms. Even if one argues that the former is more apt for certain dimensions of active participation (in particular, at level 1) than the latter, a preference of this sort does not nullify the value of the latter, and a characteristically Catholic "both/and" or "*et . . . et*" mentality makes room for both forms, each with its distinctive charisms, as vehicles for worship that engages in differing ways the active participation of the faithful. If there are Catholics who today, along with others in the years since Vatican II, find themselves carried toward the second and third levels of active participation by means of the ordinary form of the Roman Rite, the reformed liturgy, this is cause to celebrate the worth and riches of that usage. If there are Catholics who, in these years after SP, and in continuity with those in the centuries before Vatican II, find themselves carried toward the second and third levels of active participation by means of the *usus antiquior*, the extraordinary form of the Roman Rite, this is reason to acknowledge and cause to celebrate the worth and riches of that usage.

[67] Benedict XVI, *Sacramentum Caritatis* 8 (published a few months before SP).

[68] *Catechism of the Catholic Church* 1067 (celebrates the Paschal mystery) and 1107 (Holy Spirit's transforming power).

Following this line of thinking regarding active participation, that concern so central to the liturgy constitution of Vatican II, it seems the members of the church should be able, or could seek to be able, to accept that the church has the capacity to make space for these two usages of the Roman Rite, as provided for in SP. Further, in this context each usage is now open and subject to development in the future through a process of mutual enrichment whereby the strengths of one can come to influence and be acquired by the other, to the benefit of both. The ordinary form, then, with its characteristics, has the potential in the realm of actual pastoral practice, through mutual enrichment, to exert whatever beneficial influence on the extraordinary form may seem best in the discernment of the faithful. So also the extraordinary form, with its characteristics, has the same potential through the same means to influence the ordinary form, again as seems best in the discernment of all the faithful.

Searle's categories, then, are able to help us appreciate the potential of both usages to foster active participation at its deepest levels. This perspective offers reason and encouragement, then, to heed Pope Benedict's call to give the extraordinary form its "due honor" (SP, art. 1)—and the ordinary form as well.

As a final consideration, let us take note that SP should be understood to have authorized use of the 1962 Missal, specifically as celebrated in the manner authorized and desired at the time, not simply in a manner at the discretion of a celebrating priest today. This means observing, for example, the provisions and intentions of the 1958 instruction of the Sacred Congregation of Rites, *De Musica Sacra et Sacra Liturgia*, which Pius XII personally reviewed and approved (in effect, *in forma specifica*), which gave much attention to forms of active participation and encouraged it, and which sparked considerable pastoral response and initiative in the following years (as a review of the pastoral update section of issues of *Worship* from that era illustrates).[69] While the instruction's detailed

[69] Sacred Congregation of Rites, *De Musica Sacra et Sacra Liturgia* (1958), available at http://www.adoremus.org/1958Intro-sac-mus.html. Bernard L. Mullahy called this document "epochal" and considered it "a kind of crowning achievement of his [Pius XII's] whole work" in the realm of liturgy; see Bernard L. Mullahy, "Pastor Angelicus: Pius XII," in *Participation in the Mass: 20th North American Liturgical Week* (Washington, DC: Liturgical Conference, 1960), 3.

categorizations of, for example, three degrees of participation in solemn Masses (no. 25) or four degrees of participation in low Mass (no. 31), may strike some as overly fussy, they are best seen as attempts within the context of then-existing theological categories and pastoral practices to spell out pedagogically useful and incrementally accessible steps for bringing about in congregational life the desired liturgical goal—a gradually fuller active participation by the faithful, internal and external, in the actual liturgy of the church. The document also shows a long-term systems-thinking perspective in its promotion of liturgical participation when it lays stress on the need for a coordinated educational effort stretching from the elementary school years through university education (nos. 104–108); indeed, it does this in a somewhat more articulated way than does *Sacrosanctum Concilium* (in nos. 14–19).

Promotion of the extraordinary form today in ways which do not call forth and work toward, let alone which do not allow, the preferred forms of congregational participation envisioned by such documents as *De Musica Sacra et Sacra Liturgia*, and which do not attend to the necessary complementary educational/catechetical efforts to foster understanding of the ritual as a basis for active participation in its celebration, do not yet fulfill the letter or spirit of SP.[70] Resuscitation, instead, of inadequate and deficient preconciliar practices of clerical presiding and congregational attendance widely recognized at the time as needing amendment—practices rendering the faithful present as "strangers or mute spectators" (*De Musica Sacra* 28, *Sacrosanctum Concilium* 48)—does not advance but hinders fruitful implementation of *Summorum Pontificum* and the further liturgical renewal to which it has the potential to lead.[71] And implementation efforts that neglect a coordinated catechetical

[70] An excellent treatment of this topic is Glendinning, "The Significance of the Liturgical Reforms."

[71] Kurt Poterak laments having "too many times encountered the practice of the low Mass with a silent—or virtually silent—congregation among Tridentine communities—at least in North America. . . . I have heard some current day traditionalists even try to justify intellectually a silent congregation as the ideal norm!"; Poterak, "Gnostic Traditionalists and Liturgical Singing," *Sacred Music* 136, no. 3 (Fall 2009): 72–73, at 73; see also idem, "Whither *Summorum Pontificum*?" *Sacred Music* 135, no. 1 (Spring 2008): 62–63, at 63.

initiative (proportional to the place of the FE in the church's liturgy—see the following section) will find it difficult to cultivate informed participants in extraordinary form celebrations, thus impeding the process of mutual enrichment. What SP needs is the extraordinary form celebrated at its present best, open to its future potential.

IMPLICATIONS FOR THE CHURCH'S EDUCATIONAL AND CATECHETICAL EFFORTS

How should *Summorum Pontificum* be incorporated in the church's education and formation of those preparing for ministry as ordained or lay ecclesial ministers—in seminaries, Catholic universities, deacon formation and diocesan ministry formation programs? What place should it have in the church's ministry of catechesis, both pre- and postbaptismal, whether in the setting of family, parish, school, or ecclesial movements? The proposal here is that it should have a normal and regular place in such educational and formational efforts, proportional to its place within the Roman Rite.

To resist this proposal—by adopting, for example, "the less said, the better" as the guiding principle, or by demeaning the *usus antiquior* in some fashion even as one teaches it—would require a prior judgment that SP is ill-advised and inevitably deleterious, and thus to be ignored or even opposed so as to minimize its potential effects. The argument of this book has been that such a judgment is unnecessarily negative and unwarranted, and that the church would be better served by giving SP and the extraordinary form a chance to have the reconciling effects its author intended and hoped they would have. On the other hand, to make *more* of SP in educational endeavors than proposed here—by treating the FE as equally normative in church law and pastoral practice as the FO, or by presenting it as the more honorable or preferred liturgical form—presumes an understanding that the document situates or favors the FE to that degree, or else the judgment that the document should have done so. The argument here is that such an understanding is mistaken and such a judgment ill-founded and biased, and that both do as much disservice to the reconciling purposes of SP and CGF as does the minimizing tendency. The key to effective implementation is equanimity or even magnanimity in attitude, authenticity to the documents, and proportion in the programs.

So what would a normal, regular, and proportional place for SP in the church's educational endeavors look like? Normal and regular means one encounters the extraordinary form educationally without having specifically to seek it out; treatment of it is not exceptional but built into the program. Proportional means it is always clear the ordinary form is ordinary, the default mode of Catholic worship, and the extraordinary form is not, but rather is complementary to it; it will be understood that, in the course of Catholic life, celebrations in the ordinary form are ordinary and typical, celebrations in the extraordinary form are available and optional; in the educational program more time, that is, most time, will be devoted to the ordinary form, while both will be presented with honor and respect.

What can be indicated by way of practical provisions? Let us first consider seminary formation. Implementing SP requires priests who are *idonei* and capable of celebrating the extraordinary as well as the ordinary form. This requires Latin in the curriculum so that seminarians acquire a knowledge of the language sufficient to pray the FE prayers and read its biblical readings and its rubrics with understanding (see UE 20.b); to this should be added adequate training in Gregorian chant.[72] Knowledge of the history, theology, and spirituality of the extraordinary form simply means that knowledge of the Roman Rite up to 1962 and, as such, should already be part of seminary education on the history of the liturgy.[73] Additional attention might now be given to the twentieth century: to explain the need for a liturgical movement and to follow its unfolding stages; to appreciate thereby the liturgical reform or restoration (*instauratio*) the council recognized as needed, intended to bring about, made provision for, and officially authorized; and

[72] Both these elements—acquiring a knowledge of Latin sufficient to celebrate Mass and ability in Gregorian chant—Benedict XVI desired to see as part of seminary formation for all future priests, not just in view of proficiency in the extraordinary form, but for proficiency in the Roman Rite; see *Sacramentum Caritatis* 62.

[73] The US Catholic Bishops' *Program of Priestly Formation*, 5th ed. (Washington, DC: USCCB, 2006), mentions that study of the liturgy should include its "historical" aspects (no. 213)—a point that should be more strongly emphasized.

to craft a study of the years from 1963 to 2007 that allows students to recognize both the "lights and shadows" of the postconciliar liturgical era and in that context to understand the logic of SP—that is, why Pope Benedict chose to position the *usus antiquior* in the church's *lex orandi* in the particular way he did, recognizing and maintaining the *usus recentior* as the church's ordinary form of liturgy and calling for both forms to be mutually enriching.

Should a practical course in the celebration of the FE (the Mass, the sacraments of baptism, penance, marriage, and anointing of the sick, and funerals) be a requirement or an elective in seminary formation? If bishops are to function as the prime movers in the implementation of SP, "elective" would make more sense, accommodating variation in practice from diocese to diocese. But while it was the case under the provisions of *Quattuor Abhinc Annos* and even *Ecclesia Dei* that bishops were the prime movers and local decision makers in the matters pertaining to the 1962 Missal, this seems less the case under SP. If the provisions of SP are to be well implemented, it could be argued that a basic practical course in the celebration of the FE should be required of all seminarians. The 2011 instruction *Universae Ecclesiae* does not explicitly do so—but may come close, as attention to its wording might suggest. Three key words or phrases in the text call for attention.

First, "ordinaries are asked to offer or provide their clergy the opportunity of acquiring" the *ars celebrandi*—what would be better called the *ars praesidendi*—in the extraordinary form.[74] The words "are asked" translate *enixe rogantur*. In our treatment of SP, article 7, in chapter 4, we saw that the verb *rogare* functions in the code of canon law to express an expectation that is to be met (pertaining to clerical retirement at the age of seventy-five); the word *enixe*, "earnestly," intensifies the already strong expectation further. If the same meaning is intended here in UE 21 (with the PCED exercising vicarious papal authority on these matters—see UE 9), then bishops must provide the appropriate opportunities; if the code's word usage is not strictly applicable here, it at least suggests by analogy that UE 21 makes a strong request.

[74] PCED, *Universae Ecclesiae* 21.

What about seminarians? On the Vatican web site we read: "This applies also to Seminaries," which are to provide future priests suitable formation; this includes learning Latin, "and, where pastoral need suggests it, the opportunity to learn the *forma extraordinaria* of the Roman Rite."[75] But here, too, the translation falls short. The word "also" inadequately renders what is, in fact, another intensifier: *potissimum*, "above all, chiefly, most powerfully." The instruction is concerned that *especially* in seminaries this kind of education be available. Yet specific reference to seminarians having opportunity to learn the FE is also qualified by the phrase, "where pastoral needs suggest it," *adiunctis id postulantibus*, which could also be rendered "where relevant circumstances require it." Determination of pastoral needs and circumstances would fall first of all to the bishop; this phrase thus accords him some discretion regarding the formation of his future clergy in the FE—to require it if he deems it necessary or beneficial, though not to prohibit it if a seminarian on his own initiative sought it.

This reading of UE 21 suggests that seminaries must provide formation in the extraordinary form, though not that seminarians must necessarily take part in it; it remains elective rather than required. Do other factors suggest such formation should be required rather than elective? Here are five considerations that may point in that direction. First, if it is to be considered preferable (or even normal) that the rights of a stable group of the faithful as articulated in SP, article 5 section 1 are to be respected within their own parish, then a pastor or another regularly available priest of the parish needs to be *idoneus* and know how to celebrate using the 1962 Missal; if future parish priests are, in general, to be so qualified, this is best achieved if they all acquire the requisite formation. Second, if a priest is to be able to exercise his own right to celebrate Mass *sine populo* in either form (SP, art. 2), he must know how to do so. Third, if the requests of the faithful call for it (see SP, art. 5 sec. 3) or the pastor's judgment regarding the "good of souls" suggests it (see art. 9 sec. 1), he or another priest needs to be able to celebrate other sacraments in the FE; again, this requires training. Fourth, the process of mutual enrichment will be enhanced the more priests have

[75] Ibid.

personal experience of both usages and can provide the same for the persons in their pastoral care. All these factors should be judged as to their relevance in determination of a seminary curriculum.

Finally, if the course is an elective, what may well follow? Quite possibly, that FE adherents will choose it and FO adherents will not, thus replicating and furthering in the seminary itself, with consequences that can carry over into the pastoral life of the dioceses and religious communities the seminarians will serve as priests, the kind of divisions and divisiveness Pope Benedict hoped to heal—regarding the liturgy but also, we can note, regarding seminary life itself. Benedict was aware that men come to the seminary today from widely different backgrounds and that, "as a result, candidates for the priesthood often live on very different spiritual continents."[76] He saw the seminary as a place where such differences should not divide but become the occasion for growth. In his hopeful and inclusive vision, "the seminary is a time when you learn with one another and from one another. In community life, which can at times be difficult, you should learn generosity and tolerance, not only bearing with, but also enriching one another, so that each of you will be able to contribute his own gifts to the whole, even as all serve the same Church, the same Lord. This school of tolerance, indeed, of mutual acceptance and mutual understanding in the unity of Christ's Body, is an important part of your years in the seminary."[77]

In this light, the seminary's practical course in the FE ritual could become the opportunity for FO and FE adherents (terms describing two of those "different spiritual continents") to discover and discuss the characteristic riches as well as inadequacies of the FE and its manner of celebration—just as they can both discover and learn together, in various courses and in the seminary's liturgical celebrations, the riches to be appreciated and cultivated and shortcomings to be avoided in the FO. This process could contribute, among a diverse body of seminarians, to greater mutual understanding of both of the respective rituals and of each other.[78] This healthy and

[76] Benedict XVI, "Letter to Seminarians," 7 (October 18, 2010).

[77] Ibid.

[78] It is conceivable that such a course could worsen rather than heal these divisions; much depends, then, on the course instructor and the spirit that

hopeful view of the seminary experience, with its potential for a significant salutary impact on the wider life of the church, will be difficult to realize unless those areas where differences and disagreements are most manifest and deep (such as the liturgy) are addressed openly, directly, and in a way consciously designed and effectively conducted so as to foster that desired tolerance and mutual understanding and acceptance among future priests.

These several reasons may be worth some consideration when determining the place of the FE in the curriculum and life of seminaries.

Regarding faculty, the council's liturgy constitution called for liturgy instructors in seminaries, religious houses, and theological faculties to be "properly trained for their work in institutes which specialize in this subject" (SC 15). This provision created a challenge of one kind in the mid-1960s—to find or train professors who could teach liturgy in the wholistic and comprehensive way the council intended (see SC 16) and in accord with the conciliar reform. It creates a new kind of challenge now when the liturgy to be taught is the FE—to find or train professors who can integrate a sound and well-balanced theological, spiritual, and ritual education in the extraordinary form into formation programs centered, properly, on the ordinary form.

Regarding liturgical practice in a seminary: it would seem that Mass in the extraordinary form should be part of the liturgical life of the seminary—perhaps (though judgment may well differ as to proper proportion) one day a week, or even two, alternating *Missa in cantu* and *Missa lecta*, with Mass the other days of the week celebrated in the ordinary form. The respective aspects of beauty, the similarities and differences, and the potential shortcomings or deficiencies of both forms can be personally experienced, along with the challenges of living an integrated liturgical life while following

---

he or she brings to the task. But in itself the context created by such a course holds positive potential. On this general suggestion, compare Geffroy's similar recommendation, that those in "diocesan" seminaries (where the FO is taught) learn to celebrate the extraordinary form, and that those studying to be priests in "traditional" institutes learn to celebrate the ordinary form as well; see Christophe Geffroy, *Benoît XVI et 'la paix liturgique'* (Paris: Les Éditions du Cerf, 2008), 285.

divergent liturgical calendars. If there were also occasion for theological-spiritual reflection on these experiences of both the FE and FO, conducted via guided face-to-face conversation, in small faith-sharing or prayer groups, this again could be an opportunity for all seminarians to learn with and from each other and their instructors about the positive features and spiritual riches of each usage, and their respective potential aspects of weakness, and to acquire or deepen in this way an appreciation of the full liturgy of the Roman Rite.[79] This would also foster the intention of the council, that seminarians "be given a liturgical formation in their spiritual life" and that the life of the seminary "be thoroughly influenced by the spirit of the liturgy" (SC 17)—a liturgy which in fact now consists, for all Roman Rite clergy, in both the ordinary and extraordinary forms.

Deacons have a role in Solemn Mass in the extraordinary form.[80] In the years before Vatican II it was not unusual for this function to be carried out by a priest, deacons being in short supply. Since the reintroduction of the permanent diaconate after the council, in some parts of the world (such as the United States) deacons are more common. While it may be difficult to manage, it would be appropriate for at least some deacons, permanent and transitional,[81] to learn their role in Mass according to the 1962 Missal. Again, such seems to be the logic of a full implementation of SP.

Subdeacons have a role in Solemn Mass, but the order of subdeacon was abolished by the 1972 *motu proprio* of Paul VI, *Ministeria Quaedam*; the functions of that order were assigned to the newly established ministries of reader and acolyte.[82] Here also, it seems appropriate for the implementation of SP that those now designated to

[79] The method for such reflection could well be based on the description of mystagogical catechesis in Benedict XVI, *Sacramentum Caritatis* 64.

[80] See Adrian Fortescue, J. B. O'Connell, and Alcuin Reid, *The Ceremonies of the Roman Rite Described*, 15th ed. (London: Burns & Oates, 2009), 135–42.

[81] "Both transitional and permanent deacons may function in the *usus antiquior*"; Adrian Fortesque, J. B. O'Connell, and Alcuin Reid, *The Ceremonies of the Roman Rite Described*, 56, n. 10; also, 135, n. 74.

[82] On the role of subdeacons in Solemn Mass, see Fortescue, O'Connell, and Reid, *The Ceremonies of the Roman Rite Described*, 127–35. There is no mention in this text of *Ministeria quaedam* or the suppression of the subdiaconate; it is noted that the PCED "has confirmed that the practice of an instituted acolyte

fulfill the functions of subdeacon be able to do so in the celebration of the 1962 Missal. The demand for such celebrations being relatively small, learning the requisite skills may reasonably be considered a kind of specialization, not required of all deacons, acolytes, or readers.

Catholic university degree programs in ministry and theology, and their courses in liturgy and sacraments, need to take some cognizance of SP. It makes sense that students be aware of the document, and of Pope Benedict's multiple intentions in issuing SP and reconfiguring the Roman Rite by the creation of the extraordinary form. They should understand and be able to explain those intentions so that others (such as those they will serve in ministry) can understand them and make it possible for them to contribute actively and intelligently to their realization—for example, in the process of mutual enrichment.

What about parish and other local catechetical efforts? How extensively should the extraordinary form be incorporated into regular catechetical programming, and should this be done proactively or reactively? We might think of the range of possible responses along a continuum running from *A* to *E*, as follows.

A. Ignore it; catechize as though SP did not exist, lest one promote the FE (the flawed ritual the council wanted reformed) among Catholics currently unaware of or uninterested in it.
B. Provide catechesis on the FE only as needed and only for those requesting it.
C. Incorporate the FE into regular catechetical efforts, when dealing with the liturgy, clearly distinguishing the two forms (one *as* the ordinary form, the other *as* extraordinary, devoting time to each accordingly); present information on the history (including the relevant teaching and legislation of Vatican II), theology, and spirituality of the FE, on how to participate actively in it, and on what the process of mutual enrichment invites.

---

acting as subdeacon may be tolerated" (ibid., 134, note 73)—though the subdeacon's functions include singing the epistle, which would seem a function not of the acolyte but of the reader. On the abolition of the subdiaconate and the assignment of its functions to the ministries of reader and acolyte, see Pau VI, *Ministeria Quaedam* (1972), IV–VI (DOL 340 at nos. 2929–2931).

D. Emphasize the FE because it is unfamiliar—largely forgotten by those who grew up with it (and may not have much understood or appreciated it), and new to most of those born after the council.
E. Teach the FE as the form to be preferred, the model liturgy of the Roman Rite and eventual successor to the FO.

Among these approaches, *A* is unduly restrictive and impedes the process of reconciliation sought by Pope Benedict, a process that depends upon some measure of awareness and, if people so choose, experience of both forms of the Roman Rite. This approach seeks to minimize that awareness and experience; in doing so, it preemptively, perhaps presumptuously, and effectively withholds from people the freedom, opportunity, and even the right the pope has given them to worship, to an extent of their choosing, in either the reformed or the traditional liturgy, prejudging for them that worship in the latter form is not to be chosen. Approach *B* is less deficient, providing as it does catechesis on the FE for those who seek it—hopefully doing so in a willing and positive spirit.

Approach *C* seems most consistent with the text and assumptions of SP and CGF and most likely to foster the aims they seek to fulfill. It recognizes that SP has made a real, significant, limited change in the Roman Rite, about which Catholics should be and have a right to be aware—understanding the perspectives and purposes behind the change, its potential short-term and long-term effects, and how to participate if they so desire in the process of mutual enrichment fully, consciously, and actively. Approach *C* also allows for a balanced implementation of SP, neither over- nor underrating the place and value of the newly established FE in the configuration of the Roman Rite. It seems to offer the best framework for bringing about a normal, regular, and proportional inclusion of the FE in the church's catechetical ministry.

Principles and structures of catechesis are one thing, though, and the people implementing them are another. Much depends in catechetical ministry on the person of the catechist, not only regarding knowledge of the subject matter and pedagogical skill, but also regarding her or his attitude toward the subject matter and the learner, as conveyed in the pedagogical process. Conveying a reluctant or otherwise negative attitude toward SP, the extraordinary form, or those who are receptively disposed toward it—for example, by treating SP as a papal act of dubious merit, emphasizing inadequacies of the FE to the neglect of its riches, or judging those attracted to it as, *tout court*, unhealthily nostalgic or liturgically regressive—would fall short in showing the FE "due honor on account of its venerable and ancient usage" (SP, art. 1), impede the reconciliation Pope Benedict aimed to promote, and sidetrack the process of mutual enrichment. Catechists holding a more positive attitude would appreciate and explain that SP affirms the normativity of the reformed liturgy (duly designated the ordinary form) while recognizing historical and liturgical value and pastoral benefits in the traditional liturgy, now newly situated in the overall structure of the Roman Rite as its extraordinary form. Doing this does not exclude consideration of shortcomings of the FE (needed to explain *Sacrosanctum Concilium* and the conciliar reforms), any more than a positive presentation of the FO excludes consideration of shortcomings it has or could give rise to. But in practical terms, if the positive potential of SP is to have a fair chance to be realized, a positive attitude among catechists in teaching the extraordinary form will be required.

Can approach *D* be favored on a temporary basis for pragmatic reasons? As long as the FE remains unknown and unfamiliar, some additional short-term catechetical focus may be reasonable, to convey basic information and satisfy curiosity during the early stages of implementation of SP (which may last many years) and until approach C has had time to bear fruit. In the larger catechetical scheme, however, the FE will always have a secondary place because, though fully legitimate, it is not the normative worship of the Roman Rite and should not detract from the principal liturgical concern of catechetical ministry—namely, to help bring the faithful to full, conscious, and active participation in the ordinary form.

Because approach *E* reads SP incorrectly regarding the status of the FE today and reads SP falsely regarding the future toward which it intends the church to move, it is a misleading and counterproductive catechetical agenda.

The need here is to activate a dynamic formational or catechetical process that can be conceptualized as having three component parts that synergistically overlap and build on each other: (1) catechesis (whether regular and ongoing, or occasional and immediate), which prepares persons for liturgical celebration, (2) the pedagogical nature and potential of liturgical celebrations themselves, and (3) mystagogical reflection upon these liturgical experiences. The third is the venerable practice of the early church, revived most notably in the *Rite of Christian Initiation of Adults* (Latin *editio typica* 1972) and recommended more generally by Benedict XVI (see *Sacramentum Caritatis* 64);[83] the second was recognized and legislated by the council (see SC 33–36), perhaps mindful of Congar's affirmation of "the liturgy's matchless value as an educative milieu";[84] and the first is the exercise of the church's fundamental catechetical ministry. Without going into details of content, regular catechesis on the FE would provide background information and a positive orientation to the *usus antiquior*, while immediate preparation for a given celebration could focus on its particular characteristics (low or high Mass, chant rehearsal as appropriate, background on the saint of the day or liturgical season, the Scripture readings, prayer texts, and the like). That kind of catechesis well-done will conduce to a more full, conscious, active, and spiritually enriching participation in the FE celebration itself. Mystagogical reflection after the fact can further draw forth the spiritual riches and social-ethical implications of the celebration—as well as note possible shortcomings (in one's own manner of participation, in the ritual as it was celebrated, or in its theological emphases if in tension with those of the council[85]). This process as a whole helps prepare those who engage in it for liturgical participation in future

[83] It is interesting to note the correspondence between the three-part process of mystagogical catechesis sketched by Pope Benedict in *Sacramentum Caritatis* (no. 64.a, 64.b, and 64.c), and the three elements of Louis-Marie Chauvet's "sacramental reinterpretation of Christian existence" (Scripture-sacrament-ethics) described in his *Symbol and Sacrament* (and also *The Sacraments* [Collegeville, MN: Liturgical Press, 2001]).

[84] Yves Congar, *Tradition and Traditions: An Historical and Theological Essay* (New York: Macmillan, 1963), 428. (At the same time, one should keep in mind Congar's caution on not "using" the liturgy to teach or proselytize; ibid., 356.) See also Benedict XVI, *Sacramentum Caritatis* 64: "By its nature, the liturgy can be pedagogically effective in helping the faithful to enter more deeply into the mystery being celebrated."

[85] See, for example, the concerns raised by Rita Ferrone, "Anti-Jewish Elements in the Extraordinary Form," *Worship* 84 (2010): 498–513.

celebrations of the FE—and of the FO as well, as a facet of the process of mutual enrichment.

LITURGICAL MINISTRIES

As Pope John Paul II wrote in 1988, in his reflections on the twenty-fifth anniversary of the liturgy constitution: "Since it is a celebration of the Church, the Liturgy requires the active, conscious and full participation of all, according to the diversity of Orders and of offices,"[86] adding that, in consequence, the church "encourages the formation of ministers, readers, cantors and commentators, who carry out a true liturgical ministry."[87]

In the years before the council, liturgical ministries were typically few, in the sense that Mass as often celebrated was low Mass with two servers or even one—though the number of servers could rise to as many as twenty-three for a bishop celebrating solemn

[86] John Paul II, *Vicesimus Quintus Annus* 10, with a reference here to SC 26. The final phrase is *pro ordinum munerumque varietate*. Translating *ordinum* as "of Orders" works; one might take it today in reference to the order of bishops, the order of presbyters, the order of deacons, the order of the faithful, and the order of catechumens. But "and of offices," while possible, may well be too "official" for *munerumque*. John M. Huels makes evident the distinction between *munus* and *officium* (despite unclarity and a range of meanings attaching to both terms), showing that *munus* is broader than *officium*; see Huels, "Towards Redefining the Notion of 'Office' in Canon Law," *The Jurist* 70 (2010): 396–433, at 399, 401, 408–9 (especially), 429, 430, 432, and 433. Huels indicates that "the most common meaning of *munus* in canon law is that of any kind of service or duty" (409), capable then of referring to the responsibilities and actions of those who perform any of the full range of liturgical ministries; yet *munus* is also used in canon law "in the generic sense of office itself," and is sometimes used "when *officium* could be employed" (409, see also 410). The Vatican's translation apparently takes it in the latter sense; I take the former as more likely or at least equally viable in SC 26, and thus in this citation from *Vicesimus Quintus Annus*. See also Huels, 409, where he uses the term *munera* for "all the extraordinary lay liturgical ministries and the other *munera* not conferred by canonical provision, such as lector and acolyte (conferred by liturgical institution)."

[87] John Paul II, *Vicesimus Quintus Annus* 10, with a reference here to SC 29; that conciliar text begins: "Servers, lectors, commentators, and members of the choir also exercise a genuine liturgical function," translating *ministerium* here as "function" (*vero ministerio liturgico funguntur*).

Mass.[88] Further, the liturgy was understood to be naturally and predominantly a clerical affair. In the council's decree on the laity, the church's "ministry of the word and of the sacraments" was described as being "committed in a special way to the clergy."[89] While the decree added that this "leaves room however for a highly important part for the laity," that part pertained more to the (non-liturgical) ministry of the word: "the part namely of 'helping on the cause of truth' (3 Jn 8)." In the area of liturgical ministry, even servers were expected or preferred to be clerics, at least in theory.[90]

But one of the notable characteristics of the liturgy in the post-conciliar era has been the variety of liturgical ministries and roles that have come to be fulfilled by the baptized laity, young persons and adults, male and female.[91] This development has taken place at times in accord with and at times ahead or outside of approved liturgical norms. In any case, the reality itself is now typically taken for granted by the faithful at large and seen by them as normal and entirely unobjectionable. It represents the result of the convergent effect of the emerging implications of several themes and currents in the texts and theology of conciliar documents. As already seen in the citation from John Paul II, the council's *Sacrosanctum Concilium* explicitly affirmed, as part of the hierarchical and communal nature of the liturgy (SC 26–32), that the church's liturgical actions "concern" or draw on each of the church's members "in different ways,

[88] Fortesque, O'Connell, and Reid, *The Ceremonies of the Roman Rite Described*, 54 and 201.

[89] *Apostolicam Actuositatem* 6.

[90] And so we read, for example, that "the rubrics suppose that the servers and even the members of the choir be (tonsured) clerics," though in practice, as it were out of necessity, "it is recognised that laymen may serve at Mass or at any function . . ."; Fortesque, O'Connell, and Reid, *The Ceremonies of the Roman Rite Described*, 56.

[91] Approval was given in 1994 by the Congregation for Divine Worship and the Discipline of the Sacraments for bishops to allow women and girls to be altar servers in their diocese. An article in *L'Osservatore Romano* (August 7, 2010) says this ended a form of inequality in the church. See Carol Glatz, "Allowing girl servers ended prejudice, inequality, says Vatican paper," available at http://www.catholicnews.com/data/stories/cns/1003218.htm.

according to their differing rank, office, and actual participation."[92] *Lumen Gentium* envisioned the church not as a clerical body with lay members but as a united and diverse people of God (LG, chap. 2) hierarchically ordered (LG, chaps. 3 and 4) in which each order has its part to play in the life and mission of the church.

Apostolicam Actuositatem spoke of the need for "zeal" on the part of laity (AA 1), emphasizing their role in society but affirming also "Church communities" as a legitimate field for their apostolic activity (AA 9, see also 10). And while the more typical reference in this decree to the church's liturgy has in mind the laity's active participation as members of the order of the faithful (see AA 4, 10, and 11, with SC 14 and 48 the proper background), there is also reference to certain functions or services or even offices (*munia quaedam*) which, though viewed as properly connected with the pastoral office (of the clergy), can also be entrusted to the laity; as an example, the text speaks of their service "in certain liturgical actions" (*in quibusdam actibus liturgicis*, AA 24). If one sought further warrant in this decree for the emergence of a wider range of ministerial roles or functions for the laity in the liturgy, one might argue such a development is implicit in references both to the laity's exercise of their apostolate "in the spiritual [order]" (*in ordine spirituali*; AA 5) as well as in the temporal, and also to their role in the church's "apostolate of evangelization and *sanctification*" (AA 6; emphasis added).[93] If one considers also the special circumstances of mission territories, the fulfillment of the church's pastoral responsibilities can depend on the involvement of laity who serve as "catechists" or "auxiliary catechists," roles in the exercise of which they, for example, preside at prayer services (*precibus praesunt*; *Ad Gentes* 17).

The result of the *de facto* working out in pastoral practice of the implications of such conciliar texts, themes, and trajectories can be seen in the average parish and college campus church or chapel, where as a matter of course laymen and laywomen function as

[92] SC 26 (*diverso modo, pro diversitate ordinum, munerum et actualis participationis attingunt*). Huels says the Canon Law Society of America's translation of the code consistently renders *munus* as "function" (Huels, "Towards Redefining the Notion of 'Office' in Canon Law," 410); that usage here would replace the translation "office" with "functions."

[93] See also nos. 2, 19, 20.a, 26, and 31.a.

ministers of hospitality (greeters/ushers), servers of various kinds (with cross, candles, and thurible, and at the altar), lectors, cantors, choir members, musicians, and ministers of the Eucharist (whether *ad hoc*, or extraordinary, or, for men, formally installed as acolytes). In places, they may bless throats on the Memorial of St. Blase, distribute ashes on Ash Wednesday, have their feet washed (or wash others' feet) on Holy Thursday, or serve as Master of Ceremonies at episcopal liturgies. In special circumstances, "the delegation of faculties is . . . appropriate for the extraordinary ministers of baptism (cc. 861, 2), the lay assistant at marriages (c. 1112), lay ministers of the word and sacramentals (cc. 230, sec. 3; 766; 1168), and those who lead Sunday celebrations in the absence of a priest or conduct funeral services (*Ecclesiae de Mysterio*, arts. 7, sec. 1; 12)."[94]

Besides these direct roles in liturgical ceremonies as such, another feature of the postconciliar liturgical books pertaining to the diversification of ministries is the closer and clearer linkage to be found between various liturgical, often sacramental, celebrations and the wider scope of ministry seen to be essentially connected with them. Perhaps the outstanding example is the *Rite of Christian Initiation of Adults*, which, replacing the custom of private and relatively brief catechetical instructions with the parish priest, explicitly identifies ministries and roles which laity can fulfill and which are required for the full and longer-term process of initiation in all its catechetical and liturgical dimensions. These ministries and roles are those of catechist, duly delegated by the bishop, presiding at such rituals as celebrations of the word, blessings, and minor exorcisms; sponsor and godparent, accompanying catechumens and elect on the journey of initiation and giving witness to their suitability for acceptance into the catechumenate (sponsor) or election to the sacraments of initiation (godparent); and, indeed, the role of the whole local community, charged to "help the candidates and the catechumens throughout the process of initiation," welcoming them

[94] Huels, "Towards Redefining the Notion of 'Office' in Canon Law," 428, n. 90; cited in Lynda Robitaille, "A Canonical Wish List for the Authorization of Lay Ecclesial Ministers," in *In the Name of the Church: Vocation and Authorization of Lay Ecclesial Ministry*, ed. William J. Cahoy (Collegeville, MN: Liturgical Press, 2011), 102–33, at 122, n. 57. My thanks to Robitaille for reference to the article by Huels.

during the precatechumenate, being present and taking part in ritual celebrations during the catechumenate, giving witness on the day of election, participating in the scrutinies and presentations during Lent, renewing their own baptismal promises at the Easter Vigil, and participating in the Masses for neophytes during the Easter season and helping them feel at home as members of the faithful.[95] Another noteworthy feature of the reformed liturgy is the attention given to the role of the faithful in ministry pertaining to the pastoral care of the sick and dying.[96] Laypersons, further, can give certain blessings; the *Book of Blessings* distinguishes between those reserved to bishops, priests, deacons, and laypersons.

This describes some of the new ministerial roles in the liturgical services of the church that more laypersons have come to exercise, as a result of the development of theological themes both explicit and implicit in various conciliar and postconciliar texts. Keith Pecklers has attributed this development to the "recovery of baptism as foundational for all liturgical ministry," which he judged "one of the greatest accomplishments at Vatican II."[97] But this development, of laity serving in these roles of liturgical ministry, largely disappears in the celebration of the extraordinary form. How should we assess this fact?

It seems to me one can embrace the essential theological distinction between the common and the ministerial priesthood, share concerns that the postconciliar church has overemphasized lay roles in church life and ministry while underemphasizing the laity's properly "secular" character and mission (LG 31), and be sympathetic to what might be called the "re-sacralizing" aspect of Pope Benedict's liturgical vision and agenda, and at the same time

[95] *Rite of Christian Initiation of Adults*, nos. 9 (for the faithful), 10 (sponsors), 11 (godparents), and 16 (catechists), using the paragraph numbering for the USA; nos. 41, 42, 43, and 48, respectively, in the numbering of the original *Editio Typica*, the *Ordo Initiationis Christianae Adultorum* of 1972.

[96] See *Pastoral Care of the Sick: Rites of Anointing and Viaticum*, nos. 32–37, the section on "Offices and Ministries for the Sick," and other portions of the ritual that mention the role of family, friends, health-care providers, and so on.

[97] Keith F. Pecklers, "Importance and Dignity of the Eucharistic Celebration," in Foley, Mitchell, and Pierce, *A Commentary on the General Instruction of the Roman Missal*, 99–112, at 101–2.

strongly affirm—on historical, conciliar, theological, and pastoral grounds—both legitimacy and great gain in the postconciliar development in the ordinary form of a wide range of lay liturgical ministries,[98] and great loss in their absence in the extraordinary form. This might be a realm in which the mutual enrichment of the two forms will have a positive effect.

OTHER PASTORAL MATTERS

Other pastoral matters could be addressed. One concerns the inculturation of the Roman Rite. The liturgy constitution makes provision, with certain conditions, for "legitimate variations and adaptations to different groups, regions, and peoples, especially in mission lands" (SC 38; see SC 37–40). We know from his apostolic exhortation, *Sacramentum Caritatis*, that Pope Benedict had no intention to pull back from the principle and practice of liturgical inculturation; on the contrary, he affirmed it, taking care to emphasize that even "the fact that certain abuses have occurred does not detract from this clear principle, which must be upheld."[99] What impact will the extraordinary form have in those settings where the reformed liturgy has been well and perhaps extensively inculturated? Will the church discover ways the sacrality, formality, or link with tradition characterizing the FE can enrich (or more fully enrich) various cultures and their styles of liturgical celebration? Or will the extraordinary form be experienced as alien, dated, and irrelevant, or even as a force positively inimical to the proper inculturation of the liturgy? How can such a negative outcome be prevented?

Then there is the phenomenal rise of pentecostal forms of Christianity, witnessing unparalleled growth over the twentieth century, with their free and enthusiastic styles of worship and prayer. It would be difficult to imagine a form of public worship more

[98] In an address on October 27, 1984, commemorating the council's liturgy constitution, John Paul II listed among the benefits of the liturgical reform as implemented thus far, "the increase of active participation by the laity in the liturgy, also in the exercise of ministerial tasks formerly reserved to 'clerics'" (no. 3) ("l'incremento della partecipazione attiva dei laici alla liturgia, anche nell'esercizio di compiti ministeriali, altra volta riservati ai 'chierici'").

[99] Benedict XVI, *Sacramentum Caritatis* 54.

different in style and temperament to this than the extraordinary form of the Roman Rite. Will reaffirming the FE be taken as proof the Catholic Church is out of touch with the movement of the Spirit in our times? Or as demonstrating a pastoral inclusiveness in its wide range of forms of worship accommodating the diversity of human temperaments and cultures in their response to the movement of God's Spirit?

These and other pastoral questions merit further study, but we will turn our attention now to that general process by which much of the effect of SP is to come about: mutual enrichment.

Chapter 7

Mutual Enrichment

Pope Benedict intended the two usages of the Roman Rite to be "mutually enriching" to each other (CGF 7). This is the pivotal mechanism for much of what he hoped to accomplish by means of SP, but how it is to take place was not spelled out. Let us speculate, then, as to how it might work and what it might yield.

A key feature of mutual enrichment, as a process of liturgical development, is the direct involvement of the people of the church. In this it differs, as Cardinal Ratzinger saw it, from the process by which the liturgical reforms came about after the council, when the revised liturgical books were developed during the 1960s predominantly by committee work, the work of the Consilium. He often critiqued this process for producing what he called a "fabricated liturgy" (*die gemachte Liturgie*),[1] and for making the liturgy "appear to be no longer a living development" occurring within and flowing naturally from the ongoing liturgical life of the church, but instead to be—referring again here to the work of the Consilium and Paul VI's liturgical legislative acts—"the product of erudite work and juridical authority."[2] I think a good explanation and defense

[1] Joseph Ratzinger, "Zum Gedenken an Klaus Gamber," in idem, *Theologie der Liturgie*, Gesammelte Schriften, Band 11 (Freiburg im Breisgau, Herder, 2008), 635. He put his critique concisely when he said, "Man himself cannot simply 'make' worship"; idem, *The Spirit of the Liturgy*, 21 (the original with its *gar nicht* (not at all) is even somewhat stronger: "Der Mensch kann den Kult gar nicht selber einfach 'machen'"; *Theologie der Liturgie*, 38). See also idem, *The Feast of Faith* (San Francisco: Ignatius Press, 1986), 66–68, 84–85, 149; or *Milestones: Memoirs 1927–1977* (San Francisco: Ignatius Press, n.d. [1998]), 148; or *The Spirit of the Liturgy* (San Francisco: Ignatius Press, 2000), 166, 168; etc.

[2] Ratzinger, *Milestones*, 148. See also Aidan Kavanagh's critique of committees as agents of liturgical change, in his "Liturgical Needs for Today and Tomorrow," *Worship* 43 (1969): 488–95, at 491–92; also idem, "How Rite Develops: Some Laws Intrinsic to Liturgical Evolution," *Worship* 41 (1967): 334–47, at 337.

can be made for both these features of the postconciliar reform process,[3] but the task at hand is to understand what Benedict had in mind as an alternate vision of liturgy and liturgical development in the life of the church.

An element of that vision appears in *The Feast of Faith* where we find Ratzinger's comment that "liturgy does not come about through regulation."[4] Elaborating on the point he suggested that "one of the shortcomings of the postconciliar liturgical reform is doubtless to be sought in the eagerness with which professors

---

This critique is grounded in the sense that "a liturgy's authors are not individuals but whole generations of Christians"; Aidan Kavanagh, *Elements of Rite: A Handbook of Liturgical Style* (New York: Pueblo Publishing, 1982), 90. For a different view, at once more complex, critical of Kavanagh's assumption (still commonly held) and affirming a greater role for individual liturgical experts, see Catherine Bell, "The Authority of Ritual Experts," in *Foundations in Ritual Studies: A Reader for Students of Christian Worship*, ed. Paul Bradshaw and John Melloh (Grand Rapids, MI: Baker Academic, 2007), 176–98. (Kavanagh addressed the role of liturgists in the process in "How Rite Develops," 346–47.)

[3] For example, given the centralization of authority and the policy of uniformity in matters liturgical operative in the church since the Council of Trent to now, significant liturgical reform (such as a general restoration or renewal of the liturgy) legislatively could emerge only from the central authority of the church—as it did, from the acts of Vatican II and subsequently of the pope who implemented the provisions of the council's liturgy constitution by means of an agency he established for that purpose, the Consilium. One also needs to take account of the experience of the liturgical movement—a half century of scholarly studies and pastoral initiatives preceding the council, with liturgical experimentation both official and unofficial, including implementation of supportive, even innovative papal liturgical legislation (especially that of Pius X and Pius XII), all of which informed the members and the work of the Consilium (as specifically instructed in SC 23). As a result, the reformed liturgical books were indeed "made," but not without reference to that prior period of liturgical research and pastoral experience. Finally, the useful and necessary role of scholars in the work of liturgical reform at many points throughout the church's history needs to be acknowledged as well—as it is, for example, in the GIRM (no. 8), in the fourth instruction on implementing the liturgy constitution *Varietates Legitimae* 30, by John Paul II in *Vicesimus Quintus Annus* 4, by Paul VI in his various addresses to the members of the Consilium (see DOL 81, 84, 86, 92, and 99)—and indeed also by Pius V in his 1570 apostolic constitution *Quo Primum*.

[4] Ratzinger, *The Feast of Faith*, 81.

devised at their desk," for inclusion in ritual books, "what would presuppose living growth" over a period of time; that is, he was suggesting liturgical changes need to emerge in and from the ongoing life of the community if such changes are to find an enduring place in pastoral practice, not in a sudden and disruptive, but rather in a natural, patient, and peaceable way.[5] Pope Benedict envisioned and intended mutual enrichment, I believe, to be just such a less disruptive, noncoercive, more involving, long-term, gradual, organic process for guiding the future development of the Roman Rite—or, better, for letting that development naturally unfold.

If mutual enrichment is not a process conducted chiefly by experts, then by whom? Again, it would seem to involve potentially anyone and everyone in the church: bishops, priests, deacons, and instituted acolytes and lectors who celebrate according to both usages; monks and religious who use both forms in their community liturgies; seminarians who participate in celebrations of both forms during their studies and prepare themselves to celebrate in both forms; lay Catholics who have some experience with both usages;

[5] Joseph Ratzinger, "Liturgie—wandelbar oder unwandelbar? Fragen an Joseph Ratzinger," in idem, *Theologie der Liturgie*, 615 ("einer der Mängel der nachkonziliaren Liturgiereform ist zweifellos in dem professoralen Eifer zu suchen, mit dem man vom Schreibtisch her konstruiert hat, was lebendiges Wachstum voraussetzen würde"). My working translation; for another version see Ratzinger, *The Feast of Faith*, 81. Again, "liturgy cannot be the result of church regulations, let alone professional erudition, but, to be true to itself, must be the fruit of the Church's life and vitality"; Ratzinger, *The Feast of Faith*, 87 (see also idem, *God and the World*, 414). Regarding the postconciliar liturgical reforms as sudden and disruptive—this may be less evident at a distance of half a century, but I have in mind the perspective voiced by many—for example, by Kavanagh in 1988, looking back twenty-five years with a historian's eye: "No ritual system in the history of world religions has ever undergone such substantial changes as those the council precipitated over the past quarter-century, or at so rapid a rate"; Kavanagh, "Reflections on the Study from the Viewpoint of Liturgical History," in *The Awakening Church: 25 Years of Liturgical Renewal*, ed. Lawrence J. Madden (Collegeville, MN: Liturgical Press, 1992), 83–97, at 84. Already by 1971 J. D. Crichton could say, "The style of liturgy has changed beyond recognition"; Crichton, *Christian Celebration: The Mass* (London: Geoffrey Chapman, 1971), 32. Sudden and disruptive was how it felt to many at the time, and not only those resistant to the change.

liturgical scholars as well as diocesan and parish liturgy staff and committee members who study and celebrate both expressions of the church's *lex orandi;* liturgy planners who work with both usages; liturgical musicians who prepare choirs and music groups for celebrations according to both forms; catechists who learn, appreciate, and then teach the faithful the history, theology, and spirituality of both usages as well as how to participate actively in the manner of each—and so on.

Identifying who is involved in mutual enrichment is a basic first step, for though Pope Benedict wrote of the two forms of the Roman Rite being "mutually enriching," it is of course not first of all the ritual *forms* that experience mutually enrichment, but the *people* who celebrate both forms. *They* can be enriched by that experience, and matters proceed from there. A preliminary requirement in the process would seem to be that persons bring to their study and experience of both forms an open-minded receptivity to the character or charism of each form, accepting each as a legitimate expression of the liturgy of the Roman Rite, as designated by Pope Benedict in SP. The process also wants their active participation in the liturgical celebrations, externally as fully as each form makes provision for at present, and internally as fully as each worshiper is able, through cultivating the "proper dispositions" for participation—as the council specified, lively faith, minds attuned to voices, cooperation with grace (SC 11, 59), to which we might add "the spirit of constant conversion" in one's life and "a missionary commitment to bring Christ's love into the life of society."[6]

What riches might be encountered in this process? This is the very point at which Pope Benedict became (I think intentionally) circumspect, specifying little. Were he instead to have detailed beforehand and then established by his legislative authority ritual changes he thought best, he would have repeated what he considered a misstep of the postconciliar liturgical reform, mandating "fabricated" liturgical change from the top down. The logic of his critique of that process required him to leave the outcome of mutual enrichment basically open-ended and receptive to what would arise from the ground up in the pastoral liturgical practice of the

[6] Benedict XVI, *Sacramentum Caritatis* 55.

church in implementation of SP—and that is what he did.[7] He offered only the briefest of suggestions regarding what that might or should entail, which we will note. And though his circumspection may be prudent, for our purposes we will speculate a little further as to other possible emergent attitudes and practices.

One critical question concerns the role of the liturgical norms set forth in the church's ritual books. The council clearly stated that no one, "even if he be a priest, may add, remove, or change anything in the liturgy on his own authority" (SC 22.3, see also canon 846 sec. 1)—one of the council's legislative provisions most frequently repeated and widely ignored in postconciliar years, at least early on and to some extent in the years since. But by this conciliar provision, no ritual changes or adaptations are to be made, beyond those already provided for in liturgical law or rubrics.[8] This rule obviously applies not only in the ordinary form but in the extraordinary as well, as the instruction *Universae Ecclesiae* makes explicit, stating that liturgical books in the extraordinary form "are to be used as they are," and those celebrating in the FE "must know the pertinent rubrics and in celebrations are obliged to follow them correctly."[9]

When observance of existing norms remains the rule, then mutual enrichment does not mean a modification or enrichment of the rubrics themselves but rather of choices made within the rubrics regarding the way a ritual is enacted by a community—choices by, variously, the one who presides, the different liturgical ministers, and all those participating.

[7] Haunerland calls this feature of Pope Benedict's project "unprecedented and therefore innovative" (*beispiellos und deshalb innovativ*); Winfried Haunerland, "Ein Ritus in zwei Ausdrucksformen? Hintergründe und Perspektiven zue Liturgiefeier nach dem Motu proprio 'Summorum Pontificum,'" *Liturgisches Jahrbuch* 58 (2008): 179–203, at 188.

[8] On liturgical adaptations and options as allowed in universal law, see John M. Huels, *Liturgy and Law: Liturgical Law in the System of Roman Catholic Canon Law* (Montréal: Wilson and Lafleur, 2006), 120–26.

[9] UE 24. "Are to be used" ("adhibeantur ut prostant") and "must know" ("tenentur rubricas relativas scire easque in celebrationibus recte exsequi"), with the translation here adding "in celebrations"—words missing in the Vatican translation.

Here we need a brief aside, to clarify terms. The phrase *ars celebrandi*—the art or manner of celebrating liturgy (or, as Dobszay says, "the rubrics referring to movement, gestures, signs and postures"[10])—is often used to name the priest's actions at Mass. But we will also give attention to aspects of liturgical celebration as experienced by all those present; for this meaning, *ars celebrandi* seems the best term, for it is in fact the entire gathered community that is said today to celebrate the liturgy—with, as is always understood, Christ the Head presiding.[11] Let us adopt this usage and employ the term *ars praesidendi* to designate the priest's way of presiding at Mass, with *ars participandi* naming the faithful's way of participating.[12]

THE EXTRAORDINARY FORM ENRICHING THE ORDINARY

If, then, in mutual enrichment the rubrics are observed, what kind of modifications might follow from an influence of the extraordinary form on the ordinary—that is, how might people's experience of celebrating the FE affect and shape their way of experiencing and celebrating the FO, priests influenced in their *ars praesidendi* and laity in their *ars participandi*? Pope Benedict's single

[10] László Dobszay, *The Restoration and Organic Development of the Roman Rite*, intro. and ed. Laurence Paul Hemming (London: T&T Clark International, 2010), 214.

[11] As the *General Instruction of the Roman Missal* phrases it, "the celebration of the Eucharist is the action of the whole Church," in which each one fulfills only and fully one's particular part (GIRM 5). The *Catechism of the Catholic Church*, in describing who celebrates the liturgy, also says "it is the whole *community*, the Body of Christ united with its Head, that celebrates" (CCC 1140, emphasis in original). It is legitimate and normative today, then, to say priests and people together *celebrate* the liturgy.

[12] The Roman Missal commonly uses the verb *praesidere* (to preside) for the priest's role in the Mass; see *Institutio Generalis Missalis Romani* (2002) 4, 27, 31, and elsewhere. The priest's role is also described with the verb *praeesse* (to be before, to preside over), as in IGMR 33, 93, 111, but our usage will be as indicated. Andreas Heinz also uses *ars praesidendi*, in "Ars Celebrandi: Überlegungen zur Kunst, die Liturgie der Kirche zu feiern," *Questiones Liturgiques—Studies in Liturgy* 83 (2002): 107–26, at 107. The lay faithful's role is described with the verb *participare* (to participate) in, for example, SC 11, 21, and 48, or GIRM 95, 112, and 311.

observation on influence in this direction was that FO celebrations "will be able to manifest, in a stronger way than has often been the case up to now, that sacrality that attracts many to the ancient usage" (CGF 7). So, more "sacrality" in celebrations of the reformed Mass, whether in the dispositions of those celebrating or in their manner of celebrating. (It is interesting to note Benedict named no specific ritual element of the FE as a feature to enrich the ordinary form ritual but only enrichment in its manner of celebration—in a spirit and manner manifesting "sacrality." More on this point later.)

This statement regarding sacrality should not be taken to indicate this quality is not, at least potentially, also a feature of the reformed liturgy; indeed, Pope Benedict's statement assumes it is.[13] Nonetheless, it is commonly said that the *usus antiquior* characteristically manifested a sense of the sacred, a spirit of transcendence and mystery.[14] People may experience this sense, effecting in them an interior attitude of reverence and adoration, through any of various

[13] Others also assert that one should not necessarily attribute a greater "sacrality" to the extraordinary form. See Pere Tena, "Celebrar la liturgia después de una reforma," *Phase* 309 (2012): 227–43, at 243; idem, "El motu proprio 'Summorum Pontificum': Análisis y reflexiones," *Phase* 280 (2007): 275–88, at 284; Michael Kunzler, *Die 'Tridentinische' Messe: Aufbruch oder Rückschritt?* (Paderborn: Bonifatius, 2008), 117.

[14] For example, Kevin Irwin spoke of the Tridentine Mass as conveying "an automatic sense of otherness and transcendence by the use of Latin, incense, and ritual silence"; Irwin, "Authentic Worship in Spirit and Truth," *Pastoral Music* 33, no. 1 (October 2008): 51–60, at 53. Roch A. Kereszty says, "The prayers whispered in a low voice, the carefully orchestrated gestures and movements, the dignity of the uniform Latin prayers did indeed foster a spirit of devotion and awe among the faithful"; Kereszty, *Wedding Feast of the Lamb: Eucharistic Theology from a Historical, Biblical and Systematic Perspective* (Chicago: Hillenbrand Books / Liturgy Training Publications, 2004), 157. According to Jonathon Robinson, "The perennial attraction of the Old Rite is that it provided a transcendental reference, and it did this even when it was misused in various ways"; Robinson, *The Mass and Modernity: Walking to Heaven Backward* (San Francisco: Ignatius Press, 2005), 307. Jean-Louis Bruguès remarked that even if, as is the case, the era of liturgical "happenings" has passed, we still have a long way to go to bring our celebrations into accord with "the grandeur of the mystery" we celebrate (in part because we have been influenced by a theological "horizontalism"); Bruguès, "L'eucharistie et l'urgence du mystère," *Nouvelle Revue Theologique* 130 (2008): 3–25, at 6–7.

external, observable features of the FE—Gregorian chant sung or heard, the use of the traditional Latin language, a prominence of silence, the more stylized gestures and theocentric focus of the ritual, forms of reverence regarding the eucharistic species, and the like.[15] Accordingly, priests in their *ars praesidendi* and people in their *ars participandi* might come to value more highly and observe more regularly the element of silence both before and during FO celebrations; this would be to cultivate a practice already encouraged by the GIRM yet not necessarily a prominent characteristic of many ordinary form celebrations.[16] Again, an ordinary form worshiping community's *ars celebrandi* might begin to incorporate Gregorian chant on a regular basis, perhaps at just one of the scheduled Sunday celebrations of Eucharist. This too is currently allowed in the FO and even called for. A genuinely Vatican II parish would consider chant "specially suited" to the reformed liturgy and give it "pride of place in liturgical services" (SC 116).[17] In the years after the council, however, chant largely disappeared; while practice may already be starting to change in this regard here and there, a more receptive climate for its incorporation in FO cele-

[15] Carol Zaleski expressed the hope that through the mutual enrichment of the two forms, "the postconciliar mass will gain in solemnity and fidelity to its Latin original, provoking, it may be hoped, a renewed sense of the mystery at the heart of Christian worship"; Zaleski, "Worshiping with Agatha Christie," *Christian Century* 124, no. 17 (August 21, 2007): 35.

[16] SC 30; GIRM 45, 56, 88, 127, 164, etc. See also Irwin, "Authentic Worship in Spirit and Truth," 55. Interestingly, this same concern for silence can prompt FO enrichment of the FE ritual; Dobszay, for example, thinks "the observance of some minutes for thanksgiving [after Communion] suggested in the *Novus Ordo* is a positive addition, and could also be inserted here in the classical Roman Mass"; see idem, *The Restoration and Organic Development of the Roman Rite*, 232.

[17] See also Benedict XVI, *Sacramentum Caritatis* 62. Use of chant is also commended in USCCB, *Sing to the Lord* (Washington, DC: United States Conference of Catholic Bishops, 2007), nos. 61–66 and especially 72–80, with no. 74 addressing what might be the most common situation, namely, "introducing Latin chant to worshipers who perhaps have not sung it before." The bishops make clear that, "while prudence, pastoral sensitivity, and reasonable time for progress are encouraged to achieve this end, every effort in this regard is laudable and highly encouraged."

brations could arise from the experience of chant well done in FE celebrations.[18]

Perhaps, as another example, the *ars praesidendi* of priests celebrating the FO might be enriched by the way the FE highlights the element of sacrifice—by no means absent in the ordinary form but prominent in the extraordinary in some distinctive ways.[19] Priests thus influenced might deepen their awareness that what they do at Mass is not only preside over or animate a gathering of the community; they might also realize more vividly that they do the priestly act of offering sacrifice—together with the priestly people who offer through and with them[20]—offering the very sacrifice of Christ on the cross (SC 47, GIRM 2). This double dimension of the priestly role (offer the eucharistic sacrifice, lead the liturgical community) is already clearly affirmed in the ordinary form; the GIRM states that priests "offer the Sacrifice in the person of Christ and . . . preside over the gathering of the holy people" (no. 4). But those clergy grown accustomed in FO celebrations (whether by habit or principle) to attending with greater conscious care to or finding satisfaction chiefly in the second dimension, the *communio* dimension, might, through celebrating the FE, come to think it a theological, spiritual, and pastoral enrichment for themselves and their congregations should they begin to cultivate in their FO celebrations a more balanced *ars*

[18] See also Chad J. Glendinning, "The Significance of the Liturgical Reforms prior to the Second Vatican Council in Light of *Summorum Pontificum*," *Studia Canonica* 44 (2010): 293–342, at 338. It should be added that chant poorly done creates disincentive to employ it in FO celebrations—and chant, especially of the propers, can be difficult to do well.

[19] On the Mass as a sacrifice, see John Paul II, *Dominicae Cenae* 9, and the commentary of Edward J. Kilmartin, in Kilmartin, *Church, Eucharist and Priesthood: A Theological Commentary on "The Mystery and Worship of the Most Holy Eucharist"* (New York: Paulist Press, 1981), at 81–83 and 39–43, respectively. John Paul II pointedly affirmed (with an eye, surely, on those who argued to the contrary): "Indeed, the liturgical renewal that has taken place since the Second Vatican Council has given, so to speak, greater visibility to the Eucharistic sacrifice" (*Dominicae Cenae* 9)—greater, that is, than in the preconciliar form of Mass.

[20] See SC 48, and GIRM 79.f and 95. See also Pius XII, *Mediator Dei* 92–93; that document discusses at length in what senses the faithful participate in offering the sacrifice of the Mass (*Mediator Dei* 80–111).

praesidendi by more consciously intending and attending to both dimensions and encouraging the same in the *ars participandi* of those gathered for worship.

Finally, the ordinary form *ars participandi* of Catholics who also attend FE celebrations may be influenced by their use in such celebrations of that preconciliar participation aid, the Latin-vernacular (or vernacular only) hand missal. As they do this, some may also find that in reading Mass texts such as the priest's prayers—the eucharistic prayer, but also the collect, prayer over the gifts ("Secret"), and prayer after Communion ("Postcommunion")—they pay renewed and closer attention to them, especially if catechists or preachers have encouraged them to do so. If so, that closer attention may carry over into their *ars participandi* in ordinary form eucharistic celebrations. In that setting, when they do not use a participation aid, such as a hand missal or missalette, but simply prayerfully listen as they hear those prayers proclaimed by the presider, they may now listen differently, perhaps more closely, and may notice, ponder, appreciate, and be formed by the theology of those prayers more deeply. Their participation in FO celebrations could in this way become more conscious—one of the council's principal goals—and the amen by which they affirm and make those prayers their own (GIRM 54, 77, 79.h, 89) would thus become enriched and more meaningful.

Beyond these examples, countless other possibilities can emerge for FE enrichment of ordinary form celebrations within the current rubrics and liturgical norms.

THE ORDINARY FORM ENRICHING THE EXTRAORDINARY

How, on the other hand, might people's experience of celebrating the FO affect their way of celebrating the extraordinary form—influencing, variously, priests in their *ars praesidendi*, laity in their *ars participandi*, and communities in their *ars celebrandi*? Here, interestingly, Pope Benedict spoke explicitly only of structural changes to the FE, recommending that "new saints and some of the new prefaces can and should be inserted in the ancient Missal" (CGF 7), and making provision that the readings can be proclaimed in the vernacular in FE celebrations with the people (SP, art. 6); he makes no mention of enrichments in the *manner* of celebrating the extraordinary form (*ars celebrandi*, *ars praesidendi*, or *ars participandi*). New saints means revision of the 1962 liturgical calendar, to introduce some of the recently canonized; the instruction *Universae Ecclesiae* indicates this "can and ought to be" done, "according to provisions which will be indicated subsequently" (UE 25)—an indicator or promise this official change in the 1962 ritual will be made, in due time.[21] The same likely applies to the introduction of some prefaces from the new Missal, given Pope Benedict's statements to that effect. Readings can already be proclaimed in the vernacular—in Low Masses it is permitted to proclaim the readings in the vernacular alone, or in Latin alone; in other Masses, a vernacular reading can follow the Latin (UE 26).

In their *ars participandi*, laity schooled to active participation in the ordinary form may find themselves initially confused or conflicted in FE celebrations. When the choir sings the introit while the priest is praying the prayers at the foot of the altar, what should one try to participate in—the sung introit, by listening to or joining in the chant, or the priest's actions, by reading and praying those prayers in one's hand missal? If one understands the prayers at the foot of the altar as essentially private prayers of the priest (with servers) and the introit as part of the liturgy, the question is answered by giving preference to the liturgy.[22] But the same issue arises at other times in the Mass such as the offertory, and especially the eucharistic prayer, which the priest can begin while the Sanctus is still being sung. Pastoral experience will need to bring to light some resolution of this dilemma, which represents, from the

[21] As Conrad indicates, adding some new saints to the 1962 calendar would call for removing some existing saints from it; Sven Conrad, "Renewal of the Liturgy in the Spirit of Tradition: Perspectives with a View towards the Liturgical Development of the West," *Antiphon* 14, no. 1 (2010): 95–136, at 131–32. This has happened periodically through history—and more than once during the twentieth century before Vatican II.

[22] Conrad, in "Renewal of the Liturgy," recommends "that the prayers at the foot of the altar remain a call/response prayer with the altar servers" (128; see 126–28 for context). He recommends the same for the responses after the readings, though this is not explained, is difficult to understand, and is surely unwise. As the GIRM well says, "by means of the reply [after the readings] the assembled people give honor to the Word of God that they have received in faith and with gratitude" (59).

perspective of the liturgical reform, a shortcoming of the extraordinary form—a ritual division where priest and people simultaneously engage in different actions, one (the priest's) liturgical and the other (the people's) not.[23] But, with this dilemma resolved, a person's good habits of FO participation could prompt efforts at a full, conscious, and active *ars participandi* in the ritual of the extraordinary form—presence and participation, that is, not as "strangers or silent spectators" (SC 48) but singing or saying the liturgical responses and the ordinary (and even proper) parts of the Mass, as fully as one can and as far as allowed, as means to express and deepen interior participation.[24]

Further, a community in its *ars celebrandi* might consider occasionally celebrating the extraordinary form using the *versus populum* orientation common in ordinary form celebrations—as was done at times before the council, with a view to fostering a more active or engaged participation of the faithful in the ritual action. This in turn might suggest reciprocal consideration of a community's occasional celebration of Mass *ad orientem* in the ordinary form, as is already allowed. It must be granted this double-proposal could easily generate strong reactions and heated dispute. Either step, if taken, would demand significant prior catechesis and dialogue within a community to explain and explore the liturgical, theological, historical, and canonical considerations. Such catechesis would want to surface the issues through a process of listening, acknowledging and addressing objections and concerns, defusing politicized interpretations, and highlighting the positive

[23] For a description of an approved liturgical experiment in the late 1950s (at the Abbey of Montserrat in Spain) attempting to address this problem, see "Liturgical Briefs," *Worship* 33, no. 2 (January 1959): 116–22, at 118–19. The key to the solution of the problem was described as honoring the "distribution of roles" among, for example, priest, choir, and congregation. The article averred that if this principle came into general acceptance, "the basic framework of active participation will have been re-established" (118). Within a few years this very principle would be enshrined in the liturgy constitution (SC 28).

[24] On degrees and stages of participation in the (preconciliar) Mass, from basic to more full, see the 1958 instruction *De Musica Sacra et Sacra Liturgia*, especially at nos. 22–34. For a contemporaneous commentary on the instruction, see Josef Loew, "The New Instruction," *Worship* 33, no. 1 (December 1958): 2–13; on active participation, see 6–9.

reasons underlying each approach, so that participants could enter into each practice as well-informed, consciously, receptively, and prayerfully as possible.[25]

How might a priest's *ars praesidendi* in the extraordinary form be influenced by his experience of the FO? The customarily welcoming, engaging way in which he conducts the various dialogues with the congregation in the FO ("The Lord be with you") could enrich the manner in which he understands and voices those same dialogues in the extraordinary form ("Dominus vobiscum"), doing so as an act of genuine human communication, in order genuinely and effectively to "foster and bring about communion between Priest and people" (GIRM 34).[26] Once again this presupposes prior catechetical ministry so the people in their *ars participandi* know the meaning and significance of the brief Latin phrases and can say or sing them with intelligence and intention. In this way the dialogues in the FE can truly constitute the profoundly ecclesial act they are (GIRM 34–35 and 50). Similarly, rather than say the prayers of the Mass in a rushed or mechanical manner (should he be doing so, as was not uncommon in preconciliar years), he would instead take care to speak the Latin with intelligence, decorum, and clarity, again as an act of genuine communication, addressed to God, who is listening. Even a congregation ignorant of Latin, as would be most common, would feel the difference in pace and spirituality in this manner of engagement with the liturgical texts; the priest's manifestly prayerful conduct of the liturgy by his *ars praesidendi* could, in turn, catechize and affect their *ars participandi* and contribute to the sacrality of the community's *ars celebrandi*.

It might further be sought how to manifest more fully in the FE the reality of the Mass not only as "the eucharistic sacrifice of [Christ's]

[25] For a one-page reflection on possible benefits in an occasional *ad orientem* celebration in the ordinary form, see Eamon Duffy, "Postscript: *Turning East*," in *Priests and People* 9, no. 11 (1995): 448; the essay concludes, "Maybe we should try it and see." See also Uwe Michael Lange, *Turning towards the Lord: Orientation in Liturgical Prayer* (San Francisco: Ignatius Press, 2004).

[26] Carol Zaleski speculates that through mutual enrichment, "the aspic will be melted off the Tridentine Mass, the fussiness will pass away, as it is celebrated in light of the communion ecclesiology and pastoral warmth of Vatican II"; idem, "Worshiping with Agatha Christie," 35.

body and blood" but also as "a paschal banquet in which Christ is eaten, the mind is filled with grace, and a pledge of future glory is given to us" (SC 47). If there is any truth to the perception that (and this may vary in liturgical celebration from community to community) the FE emphasizes the Mass as a sacrifice and the FO the Mass as a meal, mutual enrichment could lead in their respective *artes celebrandi* to highlighting more clearly the meal dimension of the FE and the sacrificial dimension of the FO—in both cases seeking a ritually and theologically balanced celebration of the reality of the Mass. Indeed, for too long "meal" and "sacrifice" have been too sharply differentiated, becoming politically charged theological epithets or banners of loyalty in the liturgy wars and used to distinguish and oppose the two ritual forms of celebration and those Catholics who favor one over the other. It is time to heed Klaus Gamber, Kevin Irwin, Roch Kereszty, and others in affirming, as a corrective to the false opposition of these two dimensions of the Eucharist, the historical, theological, and ritual legitimacy and necessity of both.[27]

MUTUAL ENRICHMENT: *PRAETER LEGEM* OR *CONTRA LEGEM*?

So far we have considered mutual enrichment conducted within the scope of existing liturgical norms and without change in the ritual forms themselves. But people influenced in the way they celebrate one form of the Roman Rite by the way they celebrate the other may be drawn in this way, in their celebration of either form, to do things they currently do not do, and not only things within but also things beyond or even contrary to existing liturgical norms—things *praeter legem* or *contra legem*, as the canonists say. This would require some new allowance, by pastoral leaders both at the local level and in Rome, for as yet unapproved practices to emerge. Current church law envisions two recognized ways in

[27] See Klaus Gamber, "The Sacrifice of the Mass—Since When?" in his *The Modern Rite: Collected Essays on the Reform of the Liturgy* (Farnborough: Saint Michael's Abbey Press, 2002), 15–24 and especially at 23 (e.g., "The meal and the sacrifice belong together"); Kevin Irwin, "Getting Past the Liturgy Wars: Reform at the Service of Renewal," *Church* 16, no. 3 (Fall 2000): 5–10, at 5–6; Roch A. Kereszty, *Wedding Feast of the Lamb* (Chicago: Hillenbrand Books/Liturgy Training Publications, 2004).

which this can take place, and these presumably are the points of reference relevant for a legitimate exercise of mutual enrichment.[28]

First, new practices can be introduced by a legislator. Currently, for liturgical practices, a conference of bishops can follow established procedures to request of the Apostolic See approval for adaptations within their conference. The origin of this process goes back to article 40 of the council's liturgy constitution, dealing with the "more radical adaptation of the liturgy" foreseen to be necessary or desirable to accommodate cultural diversity. The process outlined in SC 40 was further "elaborated and refined by the CDWDS [Congregation for Divine Worship and the Discipline of the Sacraments] in the 1994 Instruction on the Roman Liturgy and Inculturation, *Varietates legitimae* (*VL*), the major points of which are repeated in GIRM 395–399."[29] Following this procedure, the locus of initiative and direction for the mutual enrichment of the ordinary and extraordinary form rituals would lie with the conferences of bishops. Decentralization of authority in certain liturgical matters from pope to episcopal conference was desired by the council and makes sense for adaptation suitable for an entire cultural region.

But mutual enrichment does not happen first of all at the level of a bishop's conference; rather, it happens first of all in actual liturgical celebrations, to people and communities who have some experience celebrating both forms of the Roman Rite. Accordingly, the second legitimate means by which liturgical adaptation can take place comes into play: custom.

New practices can be introduced by way of custom arising in a community. As Huels grants, "the formation of a liturgical custom typically begins by an unauthorized liturgical adaptation,"[30] whether beyond existing law (when the law says nothing about it

[28] I rely in this section on Huels, *Liturgy and Law*, especially chap. 4, "Adaptation of the Liturgy by Law and Custom" (119–43). See also Huels's commentary on canons 5 and 23–28 in John P. Beal, James A. Coriden, and Thomas J. Green, eds., *New Commentary on the Code of Canon Law* (New York: Paulist, 2000), 53–54 and 86–94.

[29] Huels, *Liturgy and Law*, 127. Huels details the steps of the process on 129–30.

[30] Ibid., 132.

one way or the other) or contrary to it (by not doing what the law prescribes, or doing what it prohibits). An incipient custom, if well and widely accepted in a community, may continue as a living part of that community's life.[31] Practices that arise in this way can in time become binding practices: they can acquire the force of law, and they can eventually be approved by the legislator (a bishop or higher legislator). The Code of Canon Law specifies how these developments can take place, as well as how such practices can lose their legal standing. It seems clear that mutual enrichment of the ritual form—more specifically, of the rubrics of the ordinary and extraordinary forms—will most naturally take place and is meant to take place primarily by way of custom.

We can think of this process occurring in three phases. First, persons experience both forms of celebration and are influenced thereby. The positive features, the characteristic strengths or "riches" of one form come to influence the way people understand and celebrate the liturgy in either form. In this way new spiritual attitudes (a kind of liturgical piety) and ritual practices can arise.

Second, some of these attitudes or practices may not endure; though initially accepted, they are discerned over time within the community to be unhelpful or inappropriate for worship (i.e., to use more technical if harsh-sounding language, they are deemed *abuses*), and they fall out of use. Other practices may endure, becoming customary in a given community or locale. Some of these customs may remain local, while others may spread more widely and be adopted elsewhere. This phase can be ongoing for decades or generations.

Third, some form of official recognition and approval or even adoption into future liturgical books may be afforded selected atti-

[31] The terms "well" and "widely" are meant to capture aspects of Huels's description of the community that is capable of forming a custom—such as that the "greater or healthier part" of the community approves the custom (ibid., 137, n. 33) and wants it, with at least an interpretative intention, to be normative in their community. (An interpretative intention is an intention of which the community is not explicitly conscious; that a custom is accepted or approved by a community in this way comes to light when, for example, the custom is questioned or objected to, and the majority of the community affirms it wants the custom to continue. See Huels, 138.)

tudes (newly proposed in the *praenotanda*) and practices (newly described in the rubrics) that have become somewhat widespread and longstanding, bear fruit pastorally, and accord with the church's *lex credendi* and sound liturgical theology. This might take place, for example, for the whole church by mandate of an ecumenical council or a pope, or for a region by the procedure already noted whereby an episcopal conference petitions for a formal adaptation to the liturgy.

What might this mean in practice? What kind of customs arising in this fashion, whether beyond or contrary to existing norms, might emerge as instances of mutual enrichment?

As one example of a technically unauthorized rubric that some priests might think to adopt into their ordinary form *ars praesidendi* as a borrowing from the FE ritual, consider the priest's double genuflection at the consecration, not only after but also before showing the consecrated elements to the congregation. This gesture was removed from the Mass because the council called for simplifying the rites and omitting duplications (SC 34, 50). Might newly experiencing this practice again in the FE reveal it to be, not a useless repetition to be removed (SC 34), but a meaningful repetition, a gesture of adoration worth appreciating again and adopting as a still effective way to manifest "worship of the divine Majesty" (SC 33), to offer "instruction for the faithful" (ibid.) regarding the mystery of the Eucharist, and to cultivate the "dignity, spirit of reverence, and sacred character" which "the [postconciliar] rites must retain"?[32]

[32] The last two quoted phrases in this sentence ("dignity" and "rites must retain") are from the Sacred Congregation for Divine Worship's third instruction on implementing the liturgy constitution, *Liturgicae Instaurationes* (1970), article 1 (in DOL 52 at no. 512). This speculation regarding a double genuflection begs the question debated among theologians of when the "moment of consecration" should be understood to occur. Those who argue for the consecratory nature of the eucharistic prayer as a whole rather than at a specific "moment" during it would likely object to a reintroduction of this double genuflection, which supposes and is fitting only if Christ's presence "under the eucharistic species" (SC 7) occurs with and through the words of consecration and the action of the Spirit (that is, through the action of the Spirit at and through the words of consecration). On the other hand it might be proposed that the church's liturgical practice is better or at least more safely based on the theology of the reformed ritual books than on theological reflection that,

Experience of the ordinary form, on the other hand, might lead to currently unauthorized practices in the extraordinary form. A community's *ars celebrandi*, for example, might include female altar servers, or the extraordinary form celebrated as a Saturday evening vigil Mass, or reception of Holy Communion under both kinds.[33] People's *ars participandi* might extend beyond reciting the *Pater Noster* with the priest at Low Mass (see the instruction *De Musica Sacra et Sacra Liturgia* 32) to singing it with him during Solemn High Mass and High Mass. And a priest might modify his *ars praesidendi* in the FE by following that provision of the first instruction (in 1964) on implementing the liturgy constitution: "Parts belonging to the choir or to the people and sung or recited by them are not said privately by the celebrant."[34] When the choir or congregation sings the *Kyrie*, *Gloria*, and *Credo*, the priest would no longer recite those

---

however relevant and weighty, is still a proposal and not yet a wide and settled consensus. The theology of the GIRM on this matter is clear and carries the weight of tradition as well, stating that "the wondrous mystery of the real presence of the Lord under the Eucharistic species, confirmed by the Second Vatican Council and other teachings of the Church's Magisterium in the same sense and with the same doctrine as the Council of Trent proposed that it must be believed, is proclaimed in the celebration of the Mass, not only by the very words of consecration by which Christ is rendered present through transubstantiation, but also with a sense and a demonstration of the greatest reverence and adoration which strives for realization in the Eucharistic liturgy" (GIRM 3). Experiencing it in practice by celebrating the FE, and pondering it theologically in light of this postconciliar liturgical text and teaching, might turn some priests in their *ars praesidendi* not unreasonably or indefensibly toward adopting the custom, by way of mutual enrichment, of a double genuflection at the consecration of the bread and of the wine in their FO celebrations, precisely to give expression today as in the past to that great "reverence and adoration which strives for realization in the Eucharistic liturgy."

[33] For the first two practices, see Alban McCoy, "Rites and Reality," *The Tablet* 263, no. 8782 (March 7, 2009): 12–13, at 13. Another *ars celebrandi* development that has been suggested is celebration of the FE entirely in the vernacular—a proposal offered by Timothy Finigan, "'Mutual Enrichment' in Theory and Practice," *Usus Antiquior* 2, no. 1 (2011): 61–68, at 68. He reasons this would allow more priests to celebrate the FE and thus be influenced by its "reverence" and "sense of the sacred."

[34] Sacred Congregation of Rites, instruction, *Inter Oecumenici* 32 (DOL 23 at no. 324).

prayers privately and then wait or even be seated in silence while the community continued its sung prayer; rather, priest and community would jointly sing the prayers. This would be a basic step in reuniting priest and people in celebration of the liturgy of the Mass together. In such modest ways as these, as-yet-unauthorized extraordinary form practices may arise as enrichments from the ordinary form.[35]

Again, these are mere speculations.[36] Actual developments could be quite different and quite diverse. Some are surely already occurring, in this first phase of mutual enrichment. The next two phases can be described more summarily.

Some of these phase-one developments may prove popular—experienced in some way as spiritually and pastorally fruitful—and become local practices; those that endure over time become local customs. Some local practices may spread to other locations; over time, some may become customs there. This is the second phase of mutual enrichment. Practices and customs emerge and are tested by the *sensus fidelium* (sense of the faithful); they continue as long

[35] The foregoing examples have been of practices to consider adopting in a process of mutual enrichment. I have not attempted to list practices to avoid, or what might be called instances of mutual impoverishment—for example, bringing into the ordinary form the priest's practice, while choir and congregation sing the Gloria, of reciting it quickly at the altar himself and then sitting down on the side until the singing, in which he does not participate, concludes.

[36] The most extensive reflection on future possibilities in light of SP of which I am aware is Dobszay, *The Restoration and Organic Development of the Roman Rite*, a follow-up work to his earlier volume highly critical of the reformed liturgy, *The Bugnini-Liturgy and the Reform of the Reform* (Front Royal, VA: Catholic Church Music Associates, 2003). See also Christopher Smith, "Mutual Enrichment and the Reform of the Reform: A Game Plan?" *The Chant Café* (January 10, 2011), http://www.chantcafe.com/2011/01/mutual-enrichment-and-reform-of-reform_10.html. Also Conrad, "The Reform of the Liturgy," especially at 130–36. For similar speculations on the future of the liturgy written before the publication of SP, see Jonathon Robinson, *The Mass and Modernity: Walking to Heaven Backwards* (San Francisco: Ignatius Press, 2005), part 3, chap. 5, "'Know What You Are Doing,'" 314–44; and appendices III–VI in Thomas M. Kocik, *The Reform of the Reform? A Liturgical Debate: Reform or Return* (San Francisco: Ignatius Press, 2003).

as they serve the faithful (priests and people) in their liturgical worship and fall out of use when they do not. This takes time, and too hasty or too frequent preventive interventions by church authority in this phase would interrupt and forestall the process. While pastoral oversight remains necessary (just as good gardening requires intervention by the gardener), mutual enrichment is more typically characterized by pastoral patience. The gospel parable most instructive here is Matthew 13:24-30; upon hearing his field had weeds among the wheat, the householder said, "Let both of them grow together until the harvest" (13:30). In the same spirit, mutual enrichment works best if local practices have some freedom to grow, allowing discernment to take place initially within the life of worshiping communities themselves.[37]

The results of such discernment can come to the attention of pastoral authorities in various official and unofficial ways. The faithful can tell their pastors how they experience his "mutually enriched" *ars praesidendi* developments or describe to him their own enriched *ars participandi* practices. Pastors can request such feedback, receiving it informally (comments after Mass) or formally (surveys or scheduled listening sessions). Priests can inform the bishop of these matters, or parishioners can do so directly. The *sensus fidelium* can emerge during open dialogue at catechetical sessions studying both forms of the Roman Rite. Bishops can request feedback, perhaps making this a topic touched on in parish visitations, or having their worship office and commission give the matter attention. Bishops in their turn can pass along what they learn to Vatican authorities during *ad limina* reports and visits.

[37] Consider, in the USA, what the faithful have been doing with their hands during the Lord's Prayer, since the 1970s or so: some fold their hands in some fashion for prayer, some extend them in the *orans* posture, some hold hands with those beside them, perhaps only with family members or close friends, perhaps with strangers as well. The matter has been discussed by the US conference of bishops but no determination has been made to mandate, recommend, or prohibit any particular practice. Individuals and communities have preferences one way or another. Practices can differ from region to region, and over time within the same region, and even within the same congregation. Time will tell what has staying power.

The third phase of mutual enrichment comes when practices and customs in the celebration of the ordinary and extraordinary forms that emerge in phase one and prove themselves in phase two eventually receive formal approval or promulgation by church authority (on the model of the many liturgical initiatives of Pius XII, for example) or perhaps are included in future revisions of the liturgical books, in the *praenotanda* or as rubrics or approved options.[38] When this happens, those official liturgical revisions can be received by the church with equanimity, not as disruptive interventions or imposition by church authority but as a sanction of pastoral practices already proven and familiar in the life of the church.

Mutual enrichment, then, is a process in which people's experience counts, information circulates, listening is a priority, and mutual respect along with patience, humility, and a search for collective wisdom are needed. Perhaps what stands out most strongly and significantly is, to conclude this sketch where it began, that Pope Benedict put the future of the church's liturgy in the hands of the faithful who celebrate and pray that liturgy—all the faithful: people participating, priests presiding, experts studying, bishops overseeing, the pope moderating, guiding, and governing, through which he exercises the *moderatio* of which the council spoke (SC 22.1).[39]

MUTUAL ENRICHMENT AND THE ROLE OF CHURCH AUTHORITY: A BIAS TOWARD NONINTERVENTION

But just what manner of moderating, guiding, and governing by church authority does the process of mutual enrichment of the FO and FE ritual need? As already noted, I think that manner can best be described as biased toward nonintervention. Indeed to a great

[38] Paul A. McGavin suggests that "an incremental process of mutual enrichment employing the textual apparatus of brackets and footnotes," as is done in the printing of the Roman Canon to accommodate variations in the praying of that prayer, "would be more feasible" as a way to instantiate organic liturgical reform of the liturgy "than a restructuring of the rite." McGavin, "Brackets and Footnotes: A Way toward Mutual Enrichment," *Antiphon* 14, no. 3 (2010): 273–84, at 273–74.

[39] On this moderating function of church authority, see also Aidan Kavanagh, "How Rite Develops: Some Laws Intrinsic to Liturgical Evolution," *Worship* 41 (1967): 334–47, at 343, and see below, 253–57.

extent the process hinges on our finding how best to gauge the manner and extent of intervention by church authority.

What is at issue is a rethinking and modification of ways of governing the liturgy to which the church has grown accustomed over the past four-and-a-half centuries. The trend line over those centuries shows increasing papal responsibility, oversight, and control, culminating in the twentieth century—in the 1917 Code of Canon Law, the initiatives of Pius XII, and the papal promulgation of a reformed liturgy for the entire Roman Rite following the Second Vatican Council. The question is whether this exercise of authority will continue as is or be modified by the process of mutual enrichment. As an initial response it is natural to assume the former, and this is indeed explicitly affirmed regarding the FE in the instruction *Universae Ecclesiae*.[40]

But the logic of mutual enrichment seems, I wish to propose, to situate the primary, or at least the initial and generative, locus of liturgical development at the local level; this is where liturgical life and development through mutual enrichment and organic growth *happen*. Consequently, church authorities would exercise a largely noninterfering pastoral oversight that allows and is patient with local developments—even, as some of the foregoing examples suggest, those not currently provided for in the relevant ritual norms.

This should not be taken to extremes; cautionary or corrective interventions by church authority are by no means to be ruled out but rather can and would still occur. After all, one of Pope Benedict's chief objections to the postconciliar liturgical climate concerned the exercise of creativity to the point of creating "arbitrary deformations of the liturgy."[41] It is these he hoped to heal and amend; mutual enrichment was certainly not meant to be a rubric under which they continue and increase unchecked. Rather, church authority would still respond to developments arising through mutual enrichment, occasionally and prudently forestalling the con-

[40] In UE 24, as noted above. Gribbin says, "one must obviously work within current rubrics of the new missal"; Anselm J. Gribbin, *Pope Benedict XVI and the Liturgy: Understanding Recent Liturgical Developments* (Leominster, UK: Gracewing, 2011), 155.

[41] "Arbitrary deformations": CGF 4. See also Ratzinger, *The Spirit of the Liturgy*, 168, or *The Feast of Faith*, 66–68, 84–85.

tinuance or spread of a problematic emergent practice—perhaps something doctrinally questionable or pastorally eccentric or banal. For while, as Mary Collins once noted, "sometimes local worshipers [create] ritual forms of sufficient vitality that they warrant inclusion in the public repertoire of the Roman Catholic Church" (in our terms, the third stage of mutual enrichment), "at other times, the banality of the forms or their esoteric qualities invite conscious repudiation and even banishment from the ritual repertoire."[42] On occasion this repudiation or banishment may require the intervention of outside authority, which, though potentially experienced as overbearing authoritarianism, in fact represents an exercise of subsidiarity, when local creators of those forms prove unable to discern their banality or reluctant to self-initiate the banishment by giving up the practice. But in general, and granted the understandable need for occasional intervention, in the process of mutual enrichment the bias of church authority would ideally be toward not intervening but rather allowing room for the self-corrective give-and-take of organic development in ordinary church life and thus tolerating variations from universal norms—perhaps (to give the process form and order) within a framework of normative rite, defined uses, local customs, and permissible options.[43]

[42] Mary Collins, *Worship: Renewal to Practice* (Washington, DC: The Pastoral Press, 1987), 61–62.

[43] These terms and categories are drawn and adapted from the work of László Dobszay, *The Restoration and Organic Development of the Roman Rite*, chap. 12 (71–77). Dobszay proposes the fourfold structure of *ritus, usus, consuetudo*, and *optio* as a way to accommodate norms and variations. We could think of it this way. The broadest category is *ritus*, rite—in our case, the Roman Rite as a whole. Then *usus*, use or usage—such as the ordinary and extraordinary forms, celebrated anywhere; or geographically defined regional usages, as those specific to an individual bishops' conference; or the distinctive uses of religious orders. Then *consuetudo*, custom—local customs as might arise in a diocese, parish, religious community, or other locale (such as a university campus), perhaps handed on by local tradition, or developed in the context of the surrounding culture, or even dictated by the liturgical space. Finally *optio*, option—validly different ways of doing the same thing in a given place, at the discretion of the presider. Such categories offer a way to envision and ultimately to legislate how the church's liturgy, defined and well regulated by

Cardinal Ratzinger thought of liturgical development in a way that resonates with this approach: "You must look, with great respect for what is carrying the riches of the centuries within it, and see where it is necessary and possible to supplement or to prune back in a way that is meaningful"[44]—with small and occasional steps, judiciously taken. In this way, he said, regarding historical practice, "Rome kept watch" on liturgical developments in different regions in the past (during the Middle Ages) "and pruned back any overgrowth," but typically without undue intervention otherwise.[45] In a more general context but still relevant here, Ratzinger once spoke of "the art of *soprassedere*, of postponing," of not intervening too soon, thus allowing tensions to dissipate and the situation "to ripen and therefore to clarify itself."[46] This describes the way liturgical developments best take place, "without haste or aggressive intervention, like"—appealing to a biblical agricultural metaphor—"the grain that grows 'of itself' in the earth (cf. Mk 4:28)."[47]

Perhaps little more is needed for organic development and the process of mutual enrichment to succeed and be fruitful than for this *modus operandi* as described by Cardinal Ratzinger to be translated into Vatican policy and procedures, specifically those of the Pontifical Commission *Ecclesia Dei*, to which Pope Benedict entrusted jurisdiction over the implementation of SP. Little more, but nothing less. For without this, it seems to me, mutual enrichment is more or less stifled from the outset; with it, it can proceed and do its work.

It is worth noting again that such a development in the relation of the church's central authority and its local life would to us appear innovative, but in fact can be seen as traditional, as Ratzinger understood.[48] He knew that different ritual families were "not rigidly

---

norms, can also recognize and accommodate local variation without disrupting ecclesial order.

[44] Ratzinger, *God and the World*, 414–15.

[45] Ibid., 413.

[46] Ratzinger with Messori, *The Ratzinger Report*, 69. This is reminiscent of Blessed John XXIII's leadership philosophy, borrowed from St. Charles Borromeo: see everything, overlook much, correct a little.

[47] Ratzinger, *The Spirit of the Liturgy*, 169.

[48] See, e.g., in Ratzinger, *The Spirit of the Liturgy*, the section "Rite," especially pages 164–70.

fenced off from each other. There is exchange and cross-fertilization between them."[49] This is true not only for major Christian traditions (e.g., Rome and Byzantium) but within the Latin tradition itself, whose liturgical life and development during the Middle Ages was characterized by "mutual exchange and mutual stimulation," a process of cross-fertilization taking place in community practice or under the influence of individuals known and unknown, time and again yielding liturgical forms best described as hybrid.[50]

Already in the 1980s, Cardinal Ratzinger declared himself open to reviving features of this historical situation today, for the Roman Rite, in a way that promoted liturgical reconciliation.

> If it would foster devotion in many believers [both the "friends" of the *usus antiquior* and those who would be newly introduced to the "riches" of this liturgy] and encourage respect for the piety of particular Catholic groups [that is, ordinary form proponents showing respect for adherents of the extraordinary form] I would personally support a return to the ancient situation [before the era of increasing uniformity and standardization after Trent], i.e., to a certain liturgical pluralism [meaning a certain allowance of use of the traditional liturgy along with the reformed]. Provided, of course, that the legitimate character of the reformed rites was emphatically affirmed [that is, extraordinary form adherents acknowledging the legitimacy of the reformed liturgy] and that there was a clear delineation of the extent and nature of such an exception permitting the celebration of the pre-conciliar liturgy.[51]

[49] Ibid., 164.

[50] Joseph Jungmann, *The Mass of the Roman Rite*, I.91 ("mutual exchange"). Individuals known, such as Alcuin and William Durandus. Individuals unknown, such as an "anonymous author, a Frankish monk"; see Cyrille Vogel, *Medieval Liturgy: An Introduction to Its Sources* (Washington, DC: Pastoral Press, 1986), 153. For "hybrid," see Vogel, *Medieval Liturgy*, 150; Michael Driscoll, "The Conversion of the Nations," in *The Oxford History of Christian Worship*, ed. Geoffrey Wainwright and Karen B. Westerfield Tucker (Oxford: Oxford University Press, 2006), 175–215, at 186; John F. Romano, "The Fates of Liturgies: Towards a History of the First Roman *Ordo*," *Antiphon* 11, no. 2 (2007): 43–77, at 72; Adolph Adam, *Foundations of Liturgy: An Introduction to Its History and Practice* (Collegeville, MN: Liturgical Press, 1992), 34.

[51] Ratzinger with Messori, *The Ratzinger Report*, 124–25.

Pope Benedict made this delineation by designating the reformed liturgy "ordinary," and the *usus antiquior* "extraordinary," with limits on its celebration, doing this in order to make clear that the reformed liturgy is and is to remain the standard form of Roman Catholic worship. The provisions of *Summorum Pontificum* and its accompanying letter, *Con Grande Fiducia*, with its call for the mutual enrichment of the two forms, puts in place much of the vision sketched here.

We should also note, as relevant for the future development of the Roman Rite, that the process of mutual enrichment touches on the nature and exercise of the papal office. The gradual expansion of papal authority over the liturgy beginning in the sixteenth century was, as we have seen and as Ratzinger duly noted, a new development in the West. The more papal primacy came to the fore during this period, the more the question arose regarding its exercise in the realm of liturgical legislation, a question "which, of course, as such had never been considered."[52] Ratzinger saw the era after Vatican II as a high water mark in this process, when "the impression arose that the pope really could do anything in liturgical matters, especially if he were acting on the mandate of an ecumenical council."[53] With this view he found fault, affirming instead (with an appeal even to Vatican I, rightly understood) the limits of papal authority regarding both faith and liturgy. "The pope's authority is bound to the Tradition of faith, and that also applies to the liturgy. It is not 'manufactured' by the authorities. Even the pope can only be a humble servant of its lawful development and abiding integrity and identity."[54]

In light of these reflections by Cardinal Ratzinger, mutual enrichment begins to look like Pope Benedict's way of scaling back a historically contextualized but enlarged, even overreaching, understanding and practice of papal authority as regards the liturgy, reemphasizing instead the authority of the liturgy itself and its tradition. Given current legislation, he had to do this by papal fiat, his *motu proprio*; but having done it, a certain measure of authority, au-

[52] Ratzinger, *The Spirit of the Liturgy*, 165.

[53] Ibid.

[54] Ibid., 166.

tonomy, and initiative in this matter has been put back in the hands of the people of the church. In the church's process of discernment and determination regarding the course of future liturgical development, he made salient their decisions regarding and experience of the use of the ordinary and extraordinary forms and the mutual influence between them; the people, by their practice, have first say. Benedict structured the process this way to foster organic development of the liturgy; he preferred this to creating and legislatively promulgating liturgical enactments devised and favored by himself or his advisers, which would have been to fabricate yet another liturgical form. This seems to be another instance of a careful calibrating of legislative provisions to enact a distinctive theological and pastoral vision.

AIDAN KAVANAGH, THE DEVELOPMENT OF RITE, AND MUTUAL ENRICHMENT

Let us find a final perspective on the process of mutual enrichment, as well as on the past half century of Roman Catholic liturgical developments, with the help of a three-staged schema of ritual evolution outlined by Aidan Kavanagh in an address given in 1967 as the liturgical reforms were in process. On that occasion he discussed the role authority plays in religious bodies, helping them maintain identity and continuity through change, with ritual as a key means by which community members interiorize their tradition and identity. Periods of cultural shift call for ritual updating and community catechesis to negotiate the shift while maintaining identity. As a rule, Kavanagh said, "religious worship evolves authentically only from below,"[55] where Pope Benedict centered the process of mutual enrichment. Further, "this evolution is a process, and over it presides the community's authority structure . . . [which] *moderates* the process of liturgical evolution by relaxing, tightening, or modifying the conditions within which that evolution takes place"—just as Ratzinger described church authority keeping watch over liturgical developments, supplementing here, pruning back there.[56]

[55] Kavanagh, "How Rite Develops," *Worship* 41 (1967): 334–47, at 343.
[56] Ibid.; Ratzinger, *God and the World*, 413–15.

Kavanagh then sketched a three-stage process of liturgical evolution. In the first stage the religious community seeks to articulate "its consciousness that *it is* the living contemporary realization of its faith-tradition," and to do this "*in the idiom of the epoch.*"[57] This is an ongoing historical process that typically comes to consciousness only in periods of "drastic shift," such as our own. In this engagement with its contemporary era, especially in eras of cultural transition, the community's self-understanding and sense of identity also shift. The community then tends to think and act liturgically "in the symbolic constructs of its contemporary epoch—constructs that usually are not found in 'tradition'—inevitably lead[ing] to a thoroughly normal identity crisis in the community,"[58] a not inapt description of Roman Catholicism in the years since the council.

What happens next? "To preserve its identity, the community at large passes through a period of conservative reaction, of reemphasis on distinctive elements in its own peculiar faith-tradition."[59] While the Catholic community at large or on the whole has not (at least yet) undergone a strongly conservative reaction in the years since the council, conservative forces have remained and have arguably gained some momentum in recent years, with progressive forces continuing as well. John Paul II's limited reauthorization of the 1962 Missal in 1984 was meant as a pastoral outreach to the former; Pope Benedict's creation of the categories *ordinary form* and *extraordinary form* and his call for their mutual enrichment was a pastoral outreach to both groups, while his own style of celebrating Mass (music, vestments, communicants kneeling to receive Communion on the tongue, etc.) pedagogically reflected Kavanagh's "conservative reaction."[60]

[57] Kavanagh, "How Rite Develops," 343 and 344 (emphasis in original, in this and subsequent citations from Kavanagh's article).

[58] Ibid., 344.

[59] Ibid.

[60] What "pedagogically" means can be seen by Pope Benedict's remarks in *Light of the World*, 158–59, regarding the practice he adopted of giving Communion on the tongue to kneeling communicants. He had no opposition in principle to communion in the hand and standing but wanted with his new practice "to send a signal and to underscore the real presence [of Christ under the eucharistic species] with an exclamation point" (158). He had especially in view "a great danger of superficiality" that seemed to him liable to arise in very large eucharistic celebrations such as those at Saint Peter's in Rome (159).

Then, as the third stage in the process, Kavanagh said "*the community's authority structure enters in order to moderate the internal crisis.*"[61] It moderates in part by "interpreting the past and projecting the future."[62] This describes well what Pope Benedict was attempting to do. He invited the church to interpret its liturgical past (the extraordinary form) as neither so bad as it seems to some on the left (who find it theologically deficient and a positive detriment to healthy liturgical practice and church life) nor so sacrosanct as some on the right want it to be (revived unchanged and unchanging as a much-needed bulwark to preserve traditional Catholic worship and doctrine). The liturgical future Benedict projected is one enriched by the mutual appreciation and development of both ordinary and extraordinary forms.

The community's authority structure also moderates, says Kavanagh, by "edit[ing] the forms the liturgy has begun to assume," a process in which certain features are "weeded out," others are "encouraged," and "certain lines of future development may even be suggested."[63] Under Pope John Paul II, *Redemptionis Sacramentum* fulfilled this function in one way, "editing" various emergent ritual practices by identifying those to be "weeded out" (in its language, identifying "abuses" to be "reprobated"); this is the moderating function exercised by corrective intervention. Pope Benedict's way in SP was instead, quite notably, to return the locus of action, the initial editing function, back to the community itself, having first (herein consists his intervention) moderately reconfigured the forces at work on the ground by which such editing would be done—repositioning the *usus antiquior* into a more prominent though still intentionally secondary and subsidiary place in the church's liturgical life,

On such occasions the impression is easily formed, he said, "that everyone is just automatically supposed to receive communion—everyone else is going up, so I will too"; to this sentiment he "wanted to send a clear signal" that "something quite special is going on here! *He* is here, the One before whom we fall on our knees!" (159). The council taught that Christ is present in eucharistic celebrations in multiple ways, but "*especially* (*maxime*) under the eucharistic species" (SC 7, emphasis added); it is with concern to promote this conciliar teaching that Pope Benedict pedagogically adopted this ritual practice.

[61] Kavanagh, "How Rite Develops," 344 (emphasis in original).

[62] Ibid.

[63] Ibid.

calling for the ordinary and extraordinary forms to be "mutually enriching," and leaving the outcome in great part to the discernment of the people of the church, or, as Alcuin Reid put it, "to Divine Providence."[64] This was Pope Benedict's way of contributing to the process by which, as Kavanagh described it, "the evolutionary development of liturgical forms is not only controlled but spurred."[65]

There is another aspect to this dynamic that Kavanagh suggestively pointed out. Certain features of the "conservative reaction" in stage two can endure, he said, becoming again an established form within the community, and—this is the interesting part—these originally conservative reactions "may go on to fulfill real creative and prophetic functions in the community, calling it always to new and more adequate awareness of itself, and thus to greater vigor within its epoch."[66] Time will tell, but this was Pope Benedict's hope for the church through his liturgical initiative in SP: that the old liturgy, in its new subsidiary role, would become a living part of the church today as a legitimate ritual usage actually prayed by members of the church, a usage moreover that is subject, as is normal, to periodic ritual development; that this liturgy would play a creative and prophetic role by influencing the ongoing evolution of the Roman Rite, through the process of mutual enrichment with the ordinary form; that, as an enduring feature of community life, this new structuring of the Roman Rite with its two usages would call the church away from an ecclesial self-understanding defined by separation from its own recent past (the hermeneutic of rupture and discontinuity) and toward "a new and more adequate awareness of itself" characterized by ongoing ecclesial identity maintained and developed through a hermeneutic of reform, and specifically "reform in continuity." This, for Pope Benedict, marked the pathway of liturgical reform that SP can spur, a path intended to strengthen the church, more fully reconciled and united in itself, and thereby made capable of exercising "a greater vigor within its epoch" in various ways,

[64] Alcuin Reid, "The Liturgical Reform of Pope Benedict XVI," in *Benedict XVI and the Sacred Liturgy: Proceedings of the First Fota International Liturgy Conference, 2008*, ed. Neil J. Roy and Janet E. Rutherford, 156–80 (Dublin: Four Courts Press, 2010), at 178.

[65] Kavanagh, "How Rite Develops," 344.

[66] Ibid.

furthering the council's fundamental objective "to impart an ever-increasing vigor to the Christian life of the faithful" (SC 1).

CONCLUDING REFLECTIONS ON CHARISM AND ORDER

In view of the vision of mutual enrichment offered in this chapter, some questions may well arise. Will not this vision, and in particular the noninterventive bias of church authority, in actual practice simply open the door to abuse—or even open the floodgates to virtually endless liturgical variation, authorizing not merely diversity but unlimited idiosyncrasy to the point of chaos, thus worsening rather than ameliorating present conditions? More generally, how is there not within this vision of church practice a counsel of contradiction, suggesting at once that given norms be observed (SC 22, UE 24), and that emerging practices violating norms be tolerated (mutual enrichment via custom)?

Perhaps the beginnings of a response to these questions can be found in a comment of John Paul II on how to apply canon law—specifically, on how to strengthen communion in the church through good use of the "structures of participation" provided in canon law, such as priests' councils and pastoral councils. The passage is not specifically liturgical but canonical, in the context of a description of "the spirituality of communion"; yet see how its perspective on canon law can inform our reflections on liturgical law.

> While the wisdom of the law, by providing precise rules for participation, attests to the hierarchical structure of the Church and averts any temptation to arbitrariness or unjustified claims, the spirituality of communion, by prompting a trust and openness wholly in accord with the dignity and responsibility of every member of the People of God, supplies institutional reality with a soul.[67]

The sentence conveys a double affirmation: of "the wisdom of the law" and its function of beneficent government for the good of the community, and of "the spirituality of communion" as the mode of relating within the community that allows law, in itself abstract and capable of harsh application, to be humane, attributing to it, by analogy, a "soul." Only within such a community is the rule of law truly beneficent and life-giving; only with law, just in its provisions

[67] John Paul II, *Novo Millennio Ineunte* 45.

and humanely applied, can a community's life be conducted in good order and peace. It is the proper interrelation of both that is essential.

How this applies to the church's liturgical life and the process of mutual enrichment may be seen more clearly if we broaden our perspective and think of the underlying issue in terms of the relation of unity and diversity, or, even better, of order and charism. Can the liturgical life and practice of the church in general, and the process of mutual enrichment in particular, be conducted in a way characterized by order and charism in fruitful interaction? *Order*, here, would mean the willing observance (by all, including those who conduct or arrange liturgical practice in local pastoral settings) of norms serving as limits or parameters that would be flexible enough to accommodate a certain range of diversity locally yet clear and strong enough to maintain the necessary unity with the wider church. *Charism* would mean the willing allowance (by all, including those responsible for exercising pastoral authority in the wider community and preserving its good order) and even the conscious cultivation of organic growth that can blossom in diverse forms in diverse locations within the one ecosystem of the church.

When these two forces mistrust each other, they tend to exaggerate their respective claims—order makes norms more stringent, charism claims legitimate freedom from them, and the church suffers from a divisive and unfruitful tension. But when each proves trustworthy in the other's eyes, each recognizing and respecting the necessary role and legitimate concerns of the other, the tension can strengthen the life and unity of a social body. When charism says "I will abide," and willingly observes norms, order can make norms flexible, knowing the resulting diversity will not threaten unity; when order says "I will allow," and willingly respects and makes provision for diversity, charism can flourish, finding freedom for expression within norms that are capacious and adaptable.

This vision resonates, I think, with the teaching of the council. For it presumes at once what, on the one hand, might be called "charism exercised with good will"—charism seeking freedom but not the autonomy of free choice without accountability to the church as a whole; here, charism chooses to recognize that among the gifts given the church, "the primacy belongs to the grace of the apostles to whose authority the Spirit himself subjects even those who are endowed with charisms (cf. 1 Cor. 14)" (LG 7). The vision also presumes "order exercised with good will"—order seeking to preserve unity but without unduly restricting autonomy or imposing excessive uniformity; here, order takes care "not indeed to extinguish the Spirit, but to test all things and hold fast to what is good (cf. 1 Th. 5:12 and 19–21)" (LG 12), remaining open to good from whatever quarter it may emerge, mindful of the advice of Paulinus of Nola, "Let us listen to what all the faithful say, because in every one of them the Spirit of God breathes."[68]

This describes a delicate balance. If either side tips the balance, moved by fear or disrespect of the other or by an overreaching of its own role and claims, mutual enrichment will be hindered and its fruits diminished. But if order and charism are both of goodwill and operate in healthy interaction, this experiment of mutual enrichment can work.

I hope the reflections in this chapter on the process of mutual enrichment encourage further discussion of this key feature of the liturgical initiative launched by *Summorum Pontificum*. I have tried to think these matters through realistically, with an eye to what actually constitutes church life, law, and practice. This includes several things at once: a recognition of the role of liturgical norms, which are meant to be observed, which prescribe and proscribe certain things and not others, which change and develop, and which at times in pastoral practice are followed with a certain flexibility; the role of canon law, which aims for good order in the church through clear and reasonable regulations, yet can also recognize the legitimacy and regulate the practice of customs outside or even contrary to the law itself; and the role of pastoral practice, which seeks to encourage a fervor of faith and discipleship while accommodating the breadth of Christian sensibility and practice, a breadth wide enough and willing to "make space for all that the faith itself allows" (CGF 8).

[68] This quotation from St. Paulinus of Nola, *Epistula* 23, 36, to Sulpicius Severus, is cited by John Paul II in *Novo Millennio Ineunte* 45. The verb translated "listen" is not *audiamus* but *pendeamus* (from *pendo, -ere*), which suggests weighing carefully what is heard, perhaps with esteem; see *Oxford Latin Dictionary*, ed. P. G. W. Glare (Oxford: Oxford University Press, 1982), 1323 ("to consider or compare the importance of, weigh, estimate, evaluate"); or Leo F. Stelten, *Dictionary of Ecclesiastical Latin* (Peabody, MA: Hendrickson Publishers, 1995), 190 ("weigh, ponder, estimate, consider, esteem")—these are the characteristics of the careful listening incumbent upon order discerning charism.

Where these reflections are sound, I hope they promote the liturgical reconciliation *Summorum Pontificum* seeks; yet much here is speculative, and where it needs improvement or correction, I hope it is soon forthcoming. But mutual enrichment, as called for by Pope Benedict in his apostolic letter *Con Grande Fiducia*, and as illuminated by his own reflections over the years on the nature of the church and its liturgy, the history of liturgical development in the West, and the evolving role of the papacy—that process of mutual enrichment seems to me to assume and indeed require what this chapter describes, or something very like it.[69]

[69] Let me add, finally, a recommendation for a good pastoral article on mutual enrichment, cited previously—Fr. Alban McCoy, "Rites and Reality," *The Tablet* 263, no. 8782 (March 7, 2009): 12–13. "On the strength of personal experience," McCoy writes, "I can assure readers that it [the introduction of the FE alongside the FO in the practice of a single community] need not divide nor betoken a reactionary understanding of the liturgy and the Church" (12). He adopts and models a constructively appreciative posture toward SP and the post-SP shape of the Roman Rite, with its two uses, offering along the way both appreciation and critique for both sides. He foresees eventually "a single, reformed rite in which we regain what was lost and retain what was gained" (12) in the postconciliar reforms. In the meantime, if we proceed with open minds and hearts, McCoy believes, we can see the "peaceful and uncontroversial coexistence" of the two forms of the Roman Rite (13).

As to pastoral practice, the ritual developments he describes in his parish represent and suggest possible pathways forward; though some go beyond the given rubrics, they strike me as legitimate explorations in mutual enrichment. And he rightly reminds his readers that "both forms can be celebrated well or badly; both are open to abuse, albeit in different ways. But when celebrated with care, reverence and dignity and an acute awareness of the sacred Mystery at the heart of the Mass," describing here the kind of *ars celebrandi* and liturgical awareness Pope Benedict intended SP to foster in both forms, "the forms become secondary to the reality they celebrate" (13)—insofar, that is, as both forms, in different ways, celebrate the same ecclesial and sacramental reality, the same eucharistic *res*, "the unity of the faithful within the ecclesial communion" (Benedict XVI, *Sacramentum Caritatis* 15). This being so, McCoy is particularly critical of the factionalism stirred up surrounding SP, "where liturgical preferences are treated as sectarian badges" (12). All in all, this brief article is insightful and hopeful, and offers a model for what mutual enrichment can look like.

Chapter 8

Conclusion

> Finally, empathy . . . is a motivated behavior that more often than commonly believed is triggered voluntarily.
>
> —Jean Decety, "Perspective Taking as the Royal Avenue to Empathy" (2005)

> A spirituality of communion implies also the ability to see what is positive in others, to welcome it and prize it as a gift from God: not only as a gift for the brother or sister who has received it directly, but also as a "gift for me."
>
> —John Paul II, *Novo Millennio Ineunte* (2001)

> We can actively develop generous hearts about the tastes, practices and beliefs of those with whom we do not agree. There was a fair amount of alarm in 2007 when Benedict issued the *motu proprio* clarifying usage of the Latin Mass for those who had a deep affection for the Missal of Pius V. Some claimed it was a vindication for traditionalists. I happened to think this document suggested: "Let a thousand flowers bloom." I hope I am right.
>
> —Kathleen Hughes, "Hope and Harmony" (2010)[1]

[1] Jean Decety, "Perspective Taking as the Royal Avenue to Empathy," in *Other Minds: How Humans Bridge the Divide between Self and Others*, ed. Bertram F. Malle and Sara D. Hodges (New York: Guilford Press, 2005), 143–57, at 154; John Paul II, *Novo Millennio Ineunte* 43; Kathleen Hughes, "Hope and Harmony" (keynote address at the 2010 annual convention of the National

This book has offered commentary on the liturgical initiative that Pope Benedict XVI promulgated in his *motu proprio* of 2007, *Summorum Pontificum*. Part 2 provided commentary on the document itself and its accompanying letter, *Con Grande Fiducia*, approaching both texts in a fundamentally appreciative yet also critical and constructive spirit. Part 3 then addressed certain issues in the pastoral implementation of SP, considering in particular the process for the mutual enrichment of the two forms of the Roman Rite.

Part 1 sought to set the stage for reading the commentary on SP and CGF by offering rationale for an appreciative hermeneutic, addressing possible misconceptions that could stand in the way of a fruitful reading, and outlining the multiple purposes of the document. It was argued that Pope Benedict did not aim to impose the preconciliar liturgy on the postconciliar church, or claim a superiority of the preconciliar over the postconciliar reformed liturgy, or intend to marginalize that reformed liturgy or the Second Vatican Council, but rather that he relocated with some care and precision the place and use of the traditional liturgy and specifically its 1962 Missal, to put it in position to do a work in the church today. That work includes furthering church unity ("reconciliation in the heart of the church"), promoting a hermeneutic of reform-in-continuity regarding the Second Vatican Council, reestablishing what he considered a break in the liturgical continuity of the church, healing the incipient schism with the Society of Saint Pius X, strengthening the church's fundamental mission of evangelization, showing pastoral care for Catholics of all ages drawn to the *usus antiquior*, reducing "deformations" in the celebration of the reformed liturgy, fostering more worthy worship and increased fidelity to liturgical norms, and giving guidance and direction to the new liturgical movement and the ongoing development of the church's liturgy in the future.

A critic could easily imagine little good as the outcome of this multipurpose initiative, or even failure and reversal on all fronts—intrachurch tensions and divisions heightened rather than eased, evangelization hindered by the church looking more backward

---

Association of Pastoral Musicians; July 2010), at http://www.npm.org/Articles/Hope&Harmony.pdf, page 8.

than ever, and so on. But a deliberately appreciative reading and reception of SP will view the matter in a different light, looking for and helping to realize the good *Summorum Pontificum* can engender if its aims are supported. That positive potential could include the following:

- a sense of appreciation across the spectrum of theological and liturgical positions for the good there was in the church before the council and the good that came forth from the council, as well as recognition of the need for reform before the council and of the legitimate reforms brought forth by the council, best received as developments from, enrichments of, and in continuity with the church's tradition.
- a clearer realization that the church of any given age—the people of God of that age in their status as pilgrims or wayfarers journeying through time—becomes and is the church by being united with Christ and made one in his Spirit. It is in consequence of this identity, and in this sense, that that portion of the church thereby has a fundamental unity with the rest of the historically wayfaring people of God united with Christ and made one in his Spirit—that is, with the church of every age, including the church before Vatican II, even just before Vatican II. An implication is that every real and legitimate distinction drawn between the church and its forms of thought and practice in one era and the next, including just prior to and following Vatican II, is best understood within the context of the church's enduring identity and fundamental continuity both before and after that or any dynamic of change experienced over the course of its history.
- some increased measure of mutual understanding and tolerance between those who value either the ordinary or the extraordinary form of the Roman Rite, challenging both communities to cultivate among themselves the spiritual and theological renewal and maturity needed to make possible their reconciliation with each other for the good of the church.
- dialogue with the SSPX that moves toward reconciliation between that body and the Catholic Church united around the successor of Peter, or at least that keeps the door to such reconciliation open, for the sake of church unity.

- realization that persons of all ages can be drawn to an authentic experience of God and to genuine faith through the forms and celebration of the traditional liturgy, and thus recognition of the way that ritual form can contribute to serving the church's mission of evangelization.
- greater welcome into the mainstream of church life for Catholics who have felt to some degree on its margins because of their liturgical preferences—and a broadening of liturgical perspectives on both sides of that divide, with greater appreciation by each for the other.
- renewed openness toward forms of liturgy more overtly sacred and theocentric, and a deeper spiritual realization of the gift of God and encounter with God at the heart of Catholic worship.
- an increased and willing adherence to the given liturgical norms by individual presiders or planners who may for various reasons consider such adherence discretionary or unnecessary.
- at the same time, an open-minded, informed, and willing participation by members of the church in the mutual enrichment of both forms of the Roman Rite, as a contribution in our era to the historical evolution of that rite and of its "liturgical forms which the Church, guided by the Holy Spirit, develops in time and space" (*Sacramentum Caritatis* 12).
- new energy and commitment on the part of pastors, scholars, artists, and others to the patient work of a new liturgical movement, in service to the church and its liturgy.

Each of these potential positive outcomes could be described and explored at greater length, but a pertinent prior question concerns what it will take for any of them to be realized at all. I suggest we can find pointers to an answer in the address given by Kathleen Hughes at the 2010 annual conference of the National Association of Pastoral Musicians. In the address, titled "Hope and Harmony," she briefly reviewed contemporary events in society and church, highlighted the gains brought by the postconciliar liturgical reforms, offered a balanced assessment of the pros and cons of its implementation, and concluded with a look forward, proposing (with reference to the work of Mark Searle) a theological framework for understanding the liturgy and then identifying nine concrete steps toward a better liturgical future. Each of the nine proposed steps reflects pastoral sense and wisdom and is well worth serious consideration.

Her seventh step is cited as the third epigraph at the head of this chapter. Her counsel that we "actively develop generous hearts" regarding the liturgical preferences of others echoes Pope Benedict's call to "generously open our heart" to one another.[2] And when others took alarm at the publication of SP, interpreting it negatively, her decision to respond with the judgment, "Let a thousand flowers bloom," very much reflects the spirit in which this book has been written, the spirit it proposes for the most fruitful reading and reception of that papal document, and a key to the answer to what it will take to realize its positive potential in the life and liturgy of the church.

The proposal here is that this spirit can be adopted, if one chooses to adopt it—just as Hughes also says, as her ninth step, that "living in hope is itself a matter of choice."[3] The decision whether to make this choice to receive *Summorum Pontificum* appreciatively and in hope carries consequences, for the actual impact of the document in the life of the church will be determined not only by what it says but by how it is received. If SP has genuine potential for good, the decision to interpret and receive it negatively, as retrogressive and a cause of division, will only contribute to its becoming a cause of division, and thus to impede the emergence of that potential good; this negative choice can become a self-fulfilling prophecy. An appreciative reading makes it more possible for that

[2] CGF 8. Compare Alcuin Reid's appeal for "liturgical charity," in Reid, "The Genius of the Roman Rite. Part 6—After *Summorum Pontificum*: a New Era for the Roman Rite," *Music and Liturgy* 36, no. 4 (February 2011): 6–10, at 9. Reid later added: "Above all . . . it is to be hoped that," as a result of SP and through its implementation, "no-one will consider themselves alienated from the Body of Christ because they wish to worship according to a liturgy of the Church that they know and love, be it ancient or modern" (9).

[3] Hughes, "Hope and Harmony," page 8. So also it is ultimately a matter of choice whether one will "*actively* develop generous hearts" (emphasis added). A related and relevant finding from the field of social psychology is that the choice to cultivate empathy for the other, as this book has encouraged, can be "triggered consciously," if one is motivated to do so; see the first epigraph to this chapter, by Jean Decety (reference at note 1).

potential good to emerge, whether one expects it confidently, or uncertainly, or even thinks it unlikely; the good, if it is there, will be discovered best, or perhaps only, through an appreciative reception and response.

The prudent response, then, is to choose to be appreciative. For those inclined against permitting the traditional liturgy this could mean the following: implement SP's provisions generously; teach the document appropriately and supportively; welcome its supporters warmly; participate in extraordinary form celebrations at least occasionally; and talk SP up rather than down. For those inclined toward the traditional liturgy this could mean: prove Pope Benedict right to maintain SP will neither cause divisions nor detract from Vatican II; join willingly in and contribute positively to postconciliar parish life; participate in the church's ordinary form celebrations at least occasionally, or even regularly; talk Vatican II up rather than down. Practicing such mutually supportive behavior, grounded in corresponding attitudes, is how such goods as inner reconciliation in the heart of the church will be achieved, if at all. And so the working hypothesis of this book has been: Let us give the two documents a chance, so as to discover and foster what positive potential they have.

"Mutually supportive behavior, grounded in corresponding attitudes." In this process those "corresponding attitudes" of mutual acceptance and support are all-important if the behavior is to be genuine and truly effective. This includes attitudes toward the different *ritual forms* and their underlying spirituality, and toward the *persons* attached to those forms and spiritualities.

We see an example of the appropriate attitude toward ritual forms in an essay by Clement McNaspy on liturgical music published the year the liturgy constitution was approved. With renewal very much in the air, and sensing in his own day a turning of the tide from one liturgical era to another, McNaspy nonetheless took the long view and wrote:

> We should be prepared to accept an impermanent vector, depending on the strength of the several tugging forces. Our generation, facing its need for a more socially oriented spirituality, has stressed the participational, communitarian, gregarious poles of worship. Another, perhaps, reacting against crude conformity and oversocialization, may find it necessary to refocus on the interior, the personalist, the

I-Thou (as opposed to the We emphasis). The mystic, transrational, sacral stress may prove, at one time, to be more appropriate in one century than in another, when light, clarity, rationality seem more in order.[4]

These words, I think, can speak to us today—whether because we sense them being fulfilled, or because we resonate to the post-modern note of "impermanence." In either case McNaspy is right to recognize two things: (1) that there are in each age "several tugging forces" of the kind described, forces of quite differing character—if only because there are in every age persons of quite differing character—and also (2) that no one set of forces is enduringly preferable, as though all others were inherently inferior. Rather, one or another can alternately come into prominence, each becoming appropriate when the temper of the times or the needs of people change accordingly.

Or perhaps we should say, even more challengingly, that McNaspy is right to recognize that the church in each era would do well to make room for the various and sometimes even conflicting forces, for those forces are not merely abstract principles to oppose or defend, but represent and can carry the living faith, convictions, and desires of persons of goodwill seeking a pathway of fidelity to God. And so McNaspy went on to counsel inclusiveness and balance, in words that echo phrases from *Sacrosanctum Concilium* 2 (and *Lumen Gentium* 8): "[A]ll of these ingredients [the 'forces' described in the preceding citation] will always be at work, and we impoverish our religious attitudes if we jettison any of them in favor of its opposite. For if the Church is one and many, local and universal, divine and human, transcendent and immanent, eschatological and incarnational, it goes without saying that the forms of her worship will reflect this complexity."[5]

Pope Benedict, I think, would affirm this vision and maintain it was an impoverishment simply to "jettison" the *usus antiquior*; he would then describe SP as an attempt to right the balance and render

[4] Clement J. McNaspy, "The Sacral in Liturgical Music," in *The Revival of the Liturgy*, ed. Frederick R. McManus (New York: Herder and Herder, 1963), 163–90, at 184.

[5] Ibid., 184–85.

the liturgy more capable of reflecting the church's "complexity," an inclusive, fruitfully tensive richness. At the same time, however, let me suggest that Pope Benedict would also insist on a certain clarification of fundamental importance: that these forces naming our ways of experiencing or even organizing the liturgy—mystic, sacral, participational, communitarian, and so on—are all subordinate to the reality and primacy of God's action in the liturgy, which must be foremost in the awareness of worshipers and be reflected in the language of the celebration (words, gestures, music, art, vesture, etc.). He would then maintain that this is not always evident in the church's liturgical celebrations at present (that is, in the era of his papacy),[6] and that SP is intended to aid in the effort to make it more evident. Adopting today the attitude McNaspy once recommended would further this work of balancing and enriching the liturgy.

As regards cultivating an attitude of acceptance and support toward the *persons* attached to the "other" ritual form, this can be a challenge for those on both sides. What Pope Benedict did in SP, as Michael Kunzler describes it, was to attempt to serve the all-important good of unity in the church by granting this "broad-minded permission" for celebration of the *usus antiquior*.[7] Kunzler points toward a double consequence—that those who favor that traditional form of worship no longer are and should no longer be marginalized in the church, by the attitudes or practices of others; and that they, in their turn, should not self-marginalize themselves, considering themselves "the only true church" or calling into ques-

[6] John Baldovin makes a similar observation in his "*Sacrosanctum Concilium* and the Reform of the Liturgy: Forty-Five Years Later," *Studia Liturgica* 39 (2009): 145–57, at 156. After affirming great good in the reformed liturgy and discounting some objections of critics who find that liturgy "less reverent," he nonetheless goes on to say, "I think it can be admitted that sometimes our liturgies have veered more in the direction of entertainment or even self-congratulation. What is often lost in this conversation is the conviction—the very Catholic conviction—that God is actually at work in the liturgy; that . . . the liturgy is in the first place a marvelous gift of God." That the liturgy is more God's action than ours is a cornerstone of Pope Benedict's understanding of liturgy.

[7] Michael Kunzler, *Die 'Tridentinische' Messe: Aufbruch oder Rückschritt?* (Paderborn: Bonifatius, 2008), 99 (*großzügigen Erlaubnis*).

tion the validity or inherent worth of the reformed liturgy or the good faith of those who accept it.[8]

Guidance in this challenging process for both sides can be found in the "spirituality of communion" described by John Paul II in his apostolic letter at the end of the Jubilee Year and the beginning of the new millennium, *Novo Millennio Ineunte*. He identified four components of this spirituality, each of which can contribute to Pope Benedict's project of internal reconciliation in the church between those who find themselves divided over liturgical differences.

1. First, "a spirituality of communion indicates above all the heart's contemplation of the mystery of the Trinity dwelling in us, and whose light we must also be able to see shining on the face of the brothers and sisters around us."[9] The mystery of the Trinity, and specifically the indwelling Trinity, grounds this spirituality and has direct consequences for how we look upon one another and what we choose to see when we do. To recognize the light of the Trinity "shining on the face" of those viewed as quite mistaken in liturgical matters or even as a threat to the wellbeing of the church is meant, in this spirituality of communion, to capacitate a transformation of one's attitudes toward them. The transformation does not require agreement over liturgical forms but does call for relinquishing antipathy and aversion and cultivating respect and even love for the other, as one in whom the Trinity dwells.

   It should be emphasized this is meant equally for those who prefer either form of the Roman Rite and are inclined to disparage the other. The spirituality of communion applies to all, and for SP to bear fruit, those in both camps need to receive John Paul's words as intended directly for themselves, as they consider and encounter those in the other camp. This is how "camps" break down and communion builds up; it happens

[8] Kunzler, *Die 'Tridentinische' Messe*, 99–100 (*die einzig wahre Kirche*, 100).

[9] John Paul II, *Novo Millennio Ineunte* 43. All passages in the following paragraphs pertaining to the spirituality of communion are drawn from this section of NMI.

on both sides, or communion is not realized. This pertains as well to the other three elements of this spirituality—they apply across the board.

2. Second, "a spirituality of communion also means an ability to think of our brothers and sisters in faith within the profound unity of the Mystical Body, and therefore as 'those who are part of me.'" The ability to think of the other in a certain way can be chosen and cultivated, the choice motivated by a recognition of "profound unity" with the other, grounded in the theological mystery of the Mystical Body of Christ, of which both are members. Those who are *other* because of their liturgical or theological views are now considered "part of me" because they are also part of the Body of Christ, in whom we are one. Again, differences need not be overlooked but they no longer define the relationship; rather, Christ does. In the resultant spirit of unity, we become more willing and able "to sense their desires and attend to their needs." When this extends to their liturgical desires and needs, the context for Benedict's hoped-for reconciliation is being realized. As the work of reconciliation unfolds, each can even become inclined "to offer [the other] deep and genuine friendship." Such is the potential of relationships cultivated in the spirituality of communion.

3. Third, "a spirituality of communion implies also the ability to see what is positive in others, to welcome it and prize it as a gift from God: not only as a gift for the brother or sister who has received it, but also as a 'gift for me.'" The capacity to be developed here is that of seeing—which may take practice in looking for—and welcoming "what is positive in others," including the richness to be found in their preferred liturgical form, newly re-envisioned now as a "gift for me." This recommendation can resemble what is known in the Ignatian spiritual tradition as *agere contra*, doing what is contrary to one's natural inclinations as a pathway to spiritual growth. Here it refers to looking for and finding some feature(s) of the non-preferred form of the Roman Rite to receive as a gift for oneself—something formerly unappreciated or even disparaged that one becomes able, knowingly and consciously, to receive

with special appreciation and (precisely because received as a gift) with gratitude.[10]

4. "A spirituality of communion means, finally, to know how to 'make room' for our brothers and sisters, bearing 'each other's burdens' (Gal 6:2) and resisting the selfish temptations that constantly beset us and provoke competition [and] distrust." Cultivating the spiritual capacity to make room for brothers and sisters and their chosen form of worship—making room for all forms of worship the church allows—is what Pope Benedict urged and exhorted the church to do (CGF 8). What FE burdens might this invite FO adherents to be willing to bear? The disapproval or even scorn of FO colleagues who as yet do not accept and perhaps still belittle the extraordinary form and its adherents? What FO burdens might FE adherents need to be willing to share in? Perhaps FO celebrations still marked by deformations that all wish removed, until such time as they fade through liturgical education or the influence of mutual enrichment? Or perhaps even the pain or frustration of FO adherents at what appears to be a pulling back from the vitality brought to the church and the liturgy by the council?

Adopting this spirituality would help one acquire that attitude of acceptance and support for those "brothers and sisters" with differing liturgical preferences and values. This, in turn, would serve Pope Benedict's goal of fostering a reconciliation that is not only

[10] Such a development could take place, for example, through a "describe in detail" exercise, perhaps as part of an educational study of the history of the Mass. As Ellen J. Langer observed, if we try to describe someone (or in our case, something) in great detail, even if we do not like the person (or thing), we will eventually find something positive to say. This will likely not reverse our negative feelings, but it can open a door toward some measure of informed and new appreciation. Imagine FO adherents doing such a "describe-in-detail" exercise regarding the extraordinary form (and its adherents)—and then vice versa, with FE adherents doing the same regarding the ordinary form (and its adherents). Might such an exercise make possible what John Paul invites—that each discover in the other something to recognize as a legitimate gift for that person, and to receive also as a "gift for me"? See Langer, *Mindfulness* (Reading, MA: Addison-Wesley, 1989), 65–66.

liturgical, pertaining to ritual forms in the practice of the church, but also ecclesial, pertaining to persons living together in the communion of the church—that is to say, it would serve his care for the church and its liturgy.

❐❐❐

What the experiment of reading *Summorum Pontificum* in a predominantly appreciative spirit has revealed is for each reader attempting the experiment to say. My sense is that reading the document this way and implementing it accordingly creates the potential to strengthen in the life of the church today the experience and reality of the Eucharist—celebrated ordinarily in the ordinary form, also freely available in the extraordinary form—as "a sacrament of love, a sign of unity, a bond of charity."[11] And if mutual charity in the church, adopted as the way of receiving and implementing SP, becomes the fruit of this papal initiative—a fruit that will take diligent cultivating, but that can be cultivated, with an appreciative spirit—then the future of the liturgical renewal, and thus of the life of the church, will only be enriched thereby.

Interestingly, it is this very quality of charity that Father Joseph Ratzinger, just months after the close of the Second Vatican Council, named as key to the postconciliar liturgical renewal. What he said then can still show the way forward today.

> The liturgical reform calls for a very generous measure of tolerance within the Church, which in the given situation is only another way of saying that it calls for a great measure of Christian charity. And the fact that this charity is often so little to be found is perhaps the real crisis for liturgical renewal in our midst. The "bearing with one another" of which Saint Paul speaks, the diffusion of charity of which we read in Saint Augustine—it is these alone that can create the setting within which the revival of Christian worship can grow in maturity and achieve its true flowering. For the real divine worship of Christianity consists in charity.[12]

[11] SC 47 (*Sacramentum pietatis, signum unitatis, vinculum caritatis*).

[12] Joseph Ratzinger, "Catholicism after the Council," *The Furrow* 18 (1967): 3–23, at 13.

Bibliography

Adam, Adolph. *Foundations of Liturgy: An Introduction to Its History and Practice*. Collegeville, MN: Liturgical Press, 1992.

Aillet, Marc. *The Old Mass and the New: Explaining the Motu Proprio* Summorum Pontificum *of Pope Benedict XVI*. Translated by Henry Taylor. San Francisco: Ignatius Press, 2010.

Anderson, Allan. *An Introduction to Pentecostalism: Global Charismatic Christianity*. Cambridge: Cambridge University Press, 2004.

Austin, Gerard. "*Theosis* and Eschatology." *Liturgical Ministry* 19 (Winter 2010): 1–8.

Baldovin, John F. "'Lo, the Full Final Sacrifice': On the Seriousness of Christian Liturgy." *Antiphon* 7 (2002): 10–17.

———. "Pastoral Liturgical Reflections on the Study," in Madden, ed., *The Awakening Church*, 98–114.

———. "Reflections on *Summorum Pontificum*." *Worship* 83 (2009): 98–112.

———. *Reforming the Liturgy: A Response to the Critics*. Collegeville, MN: Liturgical Press, 2008.

———. "*Sacrosanctum Concilium* and the Reform of the Liturgy: Forty-Five Years Later." *Studia Liturgica* 39 (2009): 145–57.

Barrett, David B., George T. Kurian, and Todd M. Johnson, eds. *World Christian Encyclopedia: A Comparative Survey of Churches and Religions in the Modern World*. 2nd ed. Oxford: Oxford University Press, 2001.

Beal, John P., James A. Coriden, and Thomas J. Green, eds. *New Commentary on the Code of Canon Law*. Commissioned by the Canon Law Society of America. New York: Paulist Press, 2000.

Bede. *A History of the English Church and People*. Translated by Leo Sherley-Price. Revised by R. E. Latham. Baltimore: Penguin, 1968.

Bell, Catherine. "The Authority of Ritual Experts." In *Foundations in Ritual Studies: A Reader for Students of Christian Worship*, edited by Paul Bradshaw and John Melloh, 176–98. Grand Rapids, MI: Baker Academic, 2007. Originally published in *Studia Liturgica* 23 (1993): 98–120.

Benedict XVI (see also Ratzinger, Joseph). "Address of His Holiness Benedict XVI: Meeting with French Episcopal Conference" (September 14, 2008). http://www.vatican.va/holy_father/benedict_xvi/speeches/2008/september/documents/hf_ben-xvi_spe_20080914_lourdes-vescovi_en.html.

———. "Address of His Holiness Benedict XVI: Meeting with Representatives from the World of Culture" (September 12, 2008). http://www.vatican.va/holy_father/benedict_xvi/speeches/2008/september/documents/hf_ben-xvi_spe_20080912_parigi-cultura_en.html.

———. *Con Grande Fiducia:* "Epistula. Ad Episcopos Catholicae Ecclesiae Ritus Romani." *Acta Apostolicae Sedis* 99 (2007): 795–99.

———. *Ecclesiae Unitatem*: Apostolic Letter "Motu Proprio" of the Supreme Pontiff Benedict XVI concerning the Pontifical Commission *Ecclesia Dei* (July 2, 2009). http://www.vatican.va/holy_father/benedict_xvi/apost_letters/documents/hf_ben-xvi_apl_20090702_ecclesiae-unitatem_en.html.

———. "Expergiscere." "Address of His Holiness Benedict XVI to the Roman Curia Offering Them His Christmas Greetings" (December 22, 2005). *Acta Apostolicae Sedis* 98, no. 1 (2006): 40–53. Also http://www.vatican.va/holy_father/benedict_xvi/speeches/2005/december/documents/hf_ben_xvi_spe_20051222_roman-curia_en.html.

———. "Interview of the Holy Father Benedict XVI during the Flight to France" (September 12, 2008). http://www.vatican.va/holy_father/benedict_xvi/speeches/2008/september/documents/hf_ben-xvi_spe_20080912_francia-interview_en.html.

———. *Jesus, the Apostles, and the Early Church: General Audiences 15 March 2006–14 February 2007*. English translation by *L'Osservatore Romano.* © 2007 by Libreria Editrice Vaticana, Vatican City. San Francisco: Ignatius Press, 2007.

———. "Letter Accompanying Motu Proprio on the Tridentine Mass." *Origins* 37, no. 9 (July 19, 2007): 132–34.

———. "Letter of His Holiness Benedict XVI to Seminarians" (October 18, 2010). http://www.vatican.va/holy_father/benedict_xvi/letters/2010/documents/hf_ben-xvi_let_20101018_seminaristi_en.html.

———. "Letter of His Holiness Pope Benedict XVI to the Bishops of the Catholic Church Concerning the Remission of the Excommunication of the Four Bishops Consecrated by Archbishop Lefebvre" (March 10, 2009). http://www.vatican.va/holy_father/benedict_xvi/letters/2009/documents/hf_ben-xvi_let_20090310_remissione-scomunica_en.html.

———. *Light of the World: The Pope, the Church, and the Signs of the Times: A Conversation with Peter Seewald*. Translated by Michael J. Miller and Adrian J. Walker. San Francisco: Ignatius Press, 2010.

———. *Sacramentum Caritatis: Sacrament of Charity*. Vatican translation. Libreria Editrice Vaticana, Vatican City. Boston: Pauline Books & Media, 2007.

———. *Summorum Pontificum*: "Litterae Apostolicae 'Motu Proprio' Datae. II. De usu extraordinario antiquae formae Ritus Romani." *Acta Apostolicae Sedis* 99 (2007): 777–81.

———. "Video Message of His Holiness Pope Benedict XVI for the Closing of the Fiftieth International Eucharistic Congress in Dublin" (June 17, 2012). http://www.vatican.va/holy_father/benedict_xvi/messages/pont-messages/2012/documents/hf_ben-xvi_mes_20120617_50cong-euc-dublino_en.html.

Bishop, Edmund. *Liturgia Historica: Papers on the Liturgy and Religious Life of the Western Church*. Oxford: Oxford University Press, 1918.

Bonagura, David G. "The Future of the Roman Rite: Reading Benedict in the Light of Ratzinger." *Antiphon* 13 (2009): 228–46.
Brewer, Marilynn B. *Intergroup Relations*. 2nd ed. Buckingham and Philadelphia: Open University Press, 2003.
Brown, Rupert. "Relative Deprivation (RD)." In *The Blackwell Encyclopedia of Social Psychology*, edited by Anthony S. R. Manstead and Miles Hewstone, 475–77. Oxford: Blackwell Reference, 1995.
Bruguès, Jean-Louis. "L'eucharistie et l'urgence du mystère." *Nouvelle Revue Theologique* 130 (2008): 3–25.
Bugnini, Annibale. *The Reform of the Liturgy 1948–1975*. Translated by Matthew J. O'Connell. Collegeville, MN: Liturgical Press, 1990.
Bux, Nicola. *Benedict XVI's Reform: The Liturgy between Innovation and Tradition*. Translated by Joseph Trabbic. San Francisco: Ignatius Press, 2012.
Bux, Nicola, and S. Vitiello. "Was the Old Rite Abrogated?" *Mass of Ages* (February 2008), as on the web site of The Latin Mass Society of England and Wales. http://www.lms.org.uk/resources/articles-on-the-mass/was_the_old_rite_abrogated.
Cabié, Robert. *The Eucharist*. Translated by Matthew J. O'Connell. Collegeville, MN: Liturgical Press, 1986.
Cahoy, William, ed. *In the Name of the Church: Vocation and Authorization of Lay Ecclesial Ministry*. Collegeville, MN: Liturgical Press, 2011.
Caldecott, Stratford, ed. *Beyond the Prosaic: Renewing the Liturgical Movement*. Edinburgh: T&T Clark, 1998.
Carroll, Jackson W. *God's Potters: Pastoral Leadership and the Shaping of Congregations*. Grand Rapids, MI: Eerdmans, 2006.
Catechism of the Catholic Church. 2nd ed. English translation of the *Catechism of the Catholic Church* for the United States of America. United States Catholic Conference, Inc.–Libreria Editrice Vaticana, 1994. English translation of the *Catechism of the Catholic Church: Modifications from the Editio Typica*. United States Catholic Conference, Inc.—Libreria Editrice Vaticana, 1997.
Chauvet, Louis-Marie. "Are the Words of the Liturgy Worn Out? What Diagnosis? What Pastoral Approach?" *Worship* 84 (2010): 25–37.
———. *Symbol and Sacrament: A Sacramental Reinterpretation of Christian Existence*. Translated by Patrick Madigan and Madeleine Beaumont. Collegeville, MN: Liturgical Press, 1995.
Chesterton, G. K. *Orthodoxy*. Garden City, NY: Image / Doubleday, 1959.
"Chronicle: A Minisynod on Liturgical Reform." *Worship* 59 (1985): 72–81.
Chupungco, Anscar J. "History of the Roman Liturgy until the Fifteenth Century." In *Handbook for Liturgical Studies*. Vol. 1, *Introduction to the Liturgy*, edited by Anscar J. Chupungco, 131–51. Collegeville, MN; Liturgical Press, 1997.
———, ed. *Handbook for Liturgical Studies*. Vol. 1, *Introduction to the Liturgy*. Collegeville, MN: Liturgical Press, 1997.
Collins, Mary. *Worship: Renewal to Practice*. Washington, DC: The Pastoral Press, 1987.

Collins, Patrick W. *Bodying Forth: Aesthetic Liturgy*. New York: Paulist Press, 1992.

Congar, Yves. *Tradition and Traditions: An Historical and Theological Essay*. New York: Macmillan, 1963.

Congregation for the Doctrine of the Faith. *Donum Veritatis*: Instruction on the Ecclesial Vocation of the Theologian (May 24, 1990). http://www.vatican.va/roman_curia/congregations/cfaith/documents/rc_con_cfaith_doc_19900524_theologian-vocation_en.html.

Conrad, Sven. "Renewal of the Liturgy in the Spirit of Tradition: Perspectives with a View towards the Liturgical Development of the West." *Antiphon* 14 (2010): 95–136.

Constitution on the Sacred Liturgy. Collegeville, MN: Liturgical Press, n.d. [1963].

Cowan, Michael A. "Sacramental Moments: Appreciative Awareness in the Iron Cage." In *Alternative Futures for Worship*. Vol. 1, *General Introduction*, edited by Regis A. Duffy, 35–61. Collegeville, MN: Liturgical Press, 1987.

Cowdrey, H. E. J. "Pope Gregory VII (1073–1085) and the Liturgy." *Journal of Theological Studies* 58 (2004): 55–83.

Crichton, J. D. *Christian Celebration: The Mass*. London: Geoffrey Chapman Publishers, 1971.

———. *Lights in Darkness: Forerunners of the Liturgical Movement*. Collegeville, MN: Liturgical Press, 1996.

———. "Worshipping with Awe and Reverence." *Priests and People* 9 (1995): 451–55.

Crouan, Denis. *The History and the Future of the Roman Liturgy*. San Francisco: Ignatius Press, 2005.

———. *The Liturgy Betrayed*. San Francisco: Ignatius Press, 2000.

Danneels, Godfried. "Liturgy Forty Years after the Council: High Point or Recession?" *The Jurist* 69 (2009): 190–207.

Dawson, Christopher. *Religion and the Rise of Western Culture*. Garden City, New York: Image/Doubleday, 1958.

Day, Dorothy. *Loaves and Fishes*. Maryknoll, NY: Orbis Books, 1997 [1963].

De Clerck, Paul. "La participation active: Perspectives historico-liturgiques, de Pie X à Vatican II." In *The Active Participation Revisited: La participation active 100 ans après Pie X et 40 ans après Vatican II*, edited by Jozef Lamberts, 13–31. Leuven: Peeters, 2004.

———. "La réforme liturgique: ce qui reste à faire." *Questions Liturgiques: Studies in Liturgy* 91 (2010): 64–75.

Decety, Jean. "Perspective Taking as the Royal Avenue to Empathy." In *Other Minds: How Humans Bridge the Divide between Self and Others*, edited by Bertram F. Malle and Sara D. Hodges, 143–57. New York: Guilford Press, 2005.

Diekmann, Godfrey. "Worship." In *Theology of Renewal Proceedings of the Congress on the Theology of the Renewal of the Church: Centenary of Canada, 1867–1967*. Vol. 2, *Renewal of Religious Structures*, edited by L. K. Shook, 88–99. New York: Herder and Herder, 1968.

Diocese of Rzeszów (Poland). Letter to the Pontifical Commission "Ecclesia Dei" (January 5, 2010) and Response of the Commission (Prot. N. 13/2007, January 20, 2010). http://www.nowyruchliturgiczny.pl/2010/02/komisja-ecclesia-dei-odpowiada-na.html.

Dobszay, László. *The Bugnini-Liturgy and the Reform of the Reform*. Front Royal, VA: Catholic Church Music Associates, 2003.

———. *The Restoration and Organic Development of the Roman Rite*. Introduced and edited by Laurence Paul Hemming. London: T&T Clark International, 2010.

Dovidio, John F., Samuel L. Gaertner, and Tamar Saguy. "Another View of 'We': Majority and Minority Group Perspectives on a Common Ingroup Identity." *European Review of Social Psychology* 18 (2007): 296–320.

———. "Commonality and the Complexity of 'We': Social Attitudes and Social Change." *Personality and Social Psychology Review* 13 (2009): 3–20.

Drew, Mark. "The Spirit or the Letter? Vatican II and Liturgical Reform." In *Beyond the Prosaic: Renewing the Liturgical Movement*, edited by Stratford Caldecott, 49–67. Edinburgh: T&T Clark, 1998.

Driscoll, Michael. "The Conversion of the Nations." In Wainwright and Wester-field Tucker, *The Oxford History of Christian Worship*, 175–215.

Duffy, Eamon. "Postscript: *Turning East*." *Priests and People* 9, no. 11 (1995): 448.

Duffy, Regis A., ed. *Alternative Futures for Worship*. Vol. 1, *General Introduction*. Collegeville, MN: Liturgical Press, 1987.

Ellard, Gerald. "Pius Tenth and the New Liturgy." *Orate Fratres* 1 (1927): 241–46.

Emminghaus, Johannes H. *The Eucharist: Essence, Form, Celebration*. Revised and edited by Theodor Maas-Edwerd. Collegeville, MN: Liturgical Press, 1997.

Faggioli, Massimo. *True Reform: Liturgy and Ecclesiology in* Sacrosanctum Concilium. Collegeville, MN: Liturgical Press, 2012.

Fellay, Bernard. "Statement of Bishop Fellay to SSPX Members and Friends" (January 22, 2001). http://archives.sspx.org/sspx_and_rome/statement_of_bishop_fellay_jan22_01.htm.

———. "Superior General's Letter to Friends and Benefactors #73" (October 23, 2008). http://www.sspx.org/superior_generals_news/sup_gen_ltr_73.pdf.

Ferrone, Rita. "Anti-Jewish Elements in the Extraordinary Form." *Worship* 84 (2010): 498–513.

———. "A Step Backward." *Commonweal* 134, no. 14 (August 17, 2007): 13–15.

Finigan, Timothy. "'Mutual Enrichment' in Theory and Practice." *Usus Antiquior* 2 (2011): 61–68.

Finocchiaro, Antonio. "Problematiche aperte nel *Web* sul Motu Proprio *Summorum Pontificum*: Posizioni e valutazioni." *Rivista Liturgica* 94 (2007): 947–75.

Fiorenza, Francis Schüssler. "From Theologian to Pope: A Personal View Back, Past the Public Portrayals." *Harvard Divinity Bulletin* 33, no. 2 (Autumn 2005). http://www.hds.harvard.edu/news/bulletin_mag/articles/33-2_fiorenza.html.

Flanagan, Kieran. *Sociology and Liturgy: Re-presentations of the Holy*. London: Macmillan, 1991.

Foley, Edward, Nathan D. Mitchell, and Joanne M. Pierce, eds. *A Commentary on the General Instruction of the Roman Missal: Developed under the Auspices of the Catholic Academy of Liturgy and Cosponsored by the Federation of Diocesan Liturgical Commissions*. Collegeville, MN: Liturgical Press, 2007.

Folsom, Cassian. "Gestures Accompanying the Words of Consecration in the History of the *Ordo Missae*." In *The Veneration and Administration of the Eucharist*, translated and edited by members of CIEL UK, 75–94. Southampton: The Saint Austin Press, 1997.

———. "Roman Rite or Roman Rites?" In *Looking Again at the Question of the Liturgy with Cardinal Ratzinger*, edited by Alcuin Reid, 58–81. Farnborough: Saint Michael's Abbey Press, 2003.

Fortescue, Adrian, J. B. O'Connell, and Alcuin Reid. *The Ceremonies of the Roman Rite Described*. 15th ed. London: Burns & Oates, 2009.

Franklin, R. W. "Chronicle: The Liturgical Schism." *Worship* 62 (1988): 448–51.

Gamber, Klaus. *The Modern Rite: Collected Essays on the Reform of the Liturgy*. Translated by Henry Taylor. Farnborough, UK: Saint Michael's Abbey Press, 2002.

———. *The Reform of the Roman Liturgy: Its Problems and Background*. Translated by Klaus D. Grimm. San Juan Capistrano, CA: Una Voce Press, 1993.

Geffroy, Christophe. *Benoît XVI et "la paix liturgique."* Paris: Les Éditions du Cerf, 2008.

Gelineau, Joseph. *The Liturgy Today and Tomorrow*. Translated by Dinah Livingstone. New York: Paulist, 1978.

Gerhards, Albert. "'Die Sorge der Päpste': Das Motu Proprio Benedikts XVI. zur Wiederzulassung der alten Liturgie." *Herder Korrespondenz* 61 (2007): 398–403.

Giampietro, Nicola. *The Development of the Liturgical Reform: As Seen by Cardinal Ferdinando Antonelli from 1948 to 1970*. Fort Collins, CO: Roman Catholic Books, 2009.

Giraudo, Cesare. "La costituzione 'Sacrosanctum Concilium': il primo grande dono del Vaticano II." *La Civiltà Cattolica* (2003/IV): 521–33.

———. "La Liturgia nel Solco della Traditione: Riflessioni in Margine al *Motu Proprio* 'Summorum Pontificum.'" *Rivista Liturgica* 95 (2008): 253–72.

Glare, P. G. W., ed. *Oxford Latin Dictionary*. Oxford: Oxford University Press, 1982.

Glatz, Carol. "Allowing Girl Servers Ended Prejudice, Inequality, Says Vatican Paper." *Catholic News Service* (August 9, 2010). http://www.catholicnews.com/data/stories/cns/1003218.htm.

Glendinning, Chad. "Adopting Pre-Conciliar Liturgical Practices in the Celebration of the Ordinary Form of the Mass." In *Roman Replies and CLSA Advisory Opinions 2009*, edited by Sharon A. Ewart and Siobhan M. Verbeek, 61–67. Washington, DC: Canon Law Society of America, 2009.

———. "The Significance of the Liturgical Reforms Prior to the Second Vatican Council in Light of *Summorum Pontificum*." *Studia Canonica* 44 (2010): 293–342.

———. "Was the 1962 *Missale Romanum* Abrogated? A Canonical Analysis in Light of *Summorum Pontificum*." *Worship* 85 (2011): 15–37.

Gribbin, Anselm J. *Pope Benedict XVI and the Liturgy: Understanding Recent Liturgical Developments*. Leominster, UK: Gracewing, 2011.

Grillo, Andrea. "Paolo VI, Pio V e la realtà virtuale: A proposito del Motu Proprio 'Summorum Pontificum.'" www.statusecclesiae.net.

Griswold, Wendy. *Cultures and Societies in a Changing World*. Thousand Oaks, CA: Pine Forge Press, 1994.

Groome, Thomas H., and Michael J. Daley, eds. *Reclaiming Catholicism: Treasures Old and New*. Maryknoll, NY: Orbis Books, 2010.

Harrison, Brian. "Postconciliar Eucharistic Liturgy: Planning a 'Reform of the Reform.'" In Thomas Kocik, *Reform of the Reform?* 151–93. San Francisco: Ignatius Press, 2003.

Haunerland, Winfried. "Ein Ritus in zwei Ausdrucksformen? Hintergründe und Perspektiven zur Liturgiefeier nach dem Motu proprio 'Summorum Pontificum.'" *Liturgische Jahrbuch* 58 (2008): 179–203.

Hayburn, Robert F. *Papal Legislation on Sacred Music 95 A.D. to 1977 A.D.* Collegeville, MN: Liturgical Press, 1979.

Heaney, Seamus. *The Redress of Poetry*. New York: Farrar, Straus and Giroux, 1995.

Heft, James L., ed. *Passing on the Faith: Transforming Traditions for the Next Generation of Jews, Christians, and Muslims*. New York: Fordham University Press, 2006.

Heinz, Andreas. "Ars Celebrandi: Überlegungen zur Kunst, die Liturgie der Kirche zu feiern." *Questions Liturgiques—Studies in Liturgy* 83 (2002): 107–26.

———. "Les recherches liturgiques dans le monde germanique." *La Maison-Dieu* 253 (March 2008): 121–28.

Hemming, Laurence Paul. *Benedict XVI: Fellow Worker for the Truth. An Introduction to His Life and Thought*. London: Burns & Oates, 2005.

Hen, Yitzhak. *The Royal Patronage of Liturgy in Frankish Gaul to the Death of Charles the Bald (877)*. London: Henry Bradshaw Society, Boydell Press, 2001.

Hope, D. M., revised by G. Woolfenden. "The Medieval Western Rites." In Jones and others, *The Study of Liturgy*, 264–85.

Howell, Clifford. "From Trent to Vatican II." In Jones and others, *The Study of Liturgy*, 285–94.

Huels, John. *Liturgy and Law: Liturgical Law in the System of Roman Catholic Canon Law*. Montréal: Wilson and Lafleur, 2006.

———. "Reconciling the Old with the New: Canonical Questions on *Summorum Pontificum*." *The Jurist* 68 (2008): 92–113.

———. "Towards Redefining the Notion of 'Office' in Canon Law." *The Jurist* 70 (2010): 396–433.

Hughes, Kathleen. "Hope and Harmony." Keynote Address at the 2010 Annual Convention of the National Association of Pastoral Musicians. http://www.npm.org/Articles/Hope&Harmony.pdf.

Hünermann, Peter. "The Ignored 'Text': On the Interpretation of the Second Vatican Council." In *Vatican II: A Forgotten Future*, Concilium 2005/4, edited by Alberto Melloni and Christoph Theobald, 118–36. London: SCM Press, 2005.

International Commission on English in the Liturgy. *Documents on the Liturgy 1963–1979: Conciliar, Papal, and Curial Texts*. Collegeville, MN: Liturgical Press, 1982.

Irwin, Kevin W. "Authentic Worship in Spirit and in Truth." *Pastoral Music* 33, no. 1 (October 2008): 51–60.

———. *Context and Text: Method in Liturgical Theology*. Collegeville, MN: Liturgical Press, 1992.

———. "Getting Past the Liturgy Wars: Reform at the Service of Renewal." *Church* 16, no. 3 (Fall 2000): 5–10.

Jackson, Pamela. *An Abundance of Graces: Reflections on* Sacrosanctum Concilium. Chicago: Hillenbrand Books / Liturgy Training Publications, 2004.

Jeffery, Peter. *Translating Tradition: A Chant Historian Reads* Liturgiam Authenticam. Collegeville, MN: Liturgical Press, 2005.

———. "Widening Our Hearts." *Commonweal* 134, no. 14 (August 17, 2007): 10–13.

John XXIII. *Rubricarum Instructum*. In *Papal Teachings: The Liturgy*, 565–68.

John Paul II. "Address of the Holy Father Pope John Paul II to the Bishops of the Episcopal Conference of the United States of America (Washington, Oregon, Idaho, Montana and Alaska)" (October 9, 1998). http://www.vatican.va/holy_father/john_paul_ii/speeches/1998/october/documents/hf_jp-ii_spe_19981009_ad-limina-usa-2_en.html.

———. "Discorso di Giovanni Paulo II in occasione della commemorazione ufficiale della costituzione 'Sacrosanctum Concilium'" (October 27, 1984). http://www.vatican.va/holy_father/john_paul_ii/speeches/1984/october/documents/hf_jp-ii_spe_19841027_commemorazione-sacrosanctum-concilium_it.html.

———. *Dominicae Cenae*: Letter of the Supreme Pontiff John Paul II to All the Bishops of the World on the Mystery and Worship of the Eucharist (February 24, 1980). http://www.vatican.va/holy_father/john_paul_ii/letters/documents/hf_jp-ii_let_24021980_dominicae-cenae_en.html.

———. *Ecclesia Dei*: Apostolic Letter of the Supreme Pontiff John Paul II Given Motu Proprio (July 2, 1988). http://www.vatican.va/holy_father/john_paul_ii/motu_proprio/documents/hf_jp-ii_motu-proprio_02071988_ecclesia dei_en.html.

———. *Ecclesia de Eucharistia*: Encyclical Letter of His Holiness Pope John Paul II to the Bishops Priests and Deacons Men and Women in the Consecrated Life and All the Lay Faithful on the Eucharist and Its Relationship to the Church (April 17, 2003). http://www.vatican.va/holy_father/special_features/encyclicals/documents/hf_jp-ii_enc_20030417_ecclesia_eucharistia_en.html.

———. *Mane Nobiscum Domine*: Apostolic Letter of the Holy Father John Paul II to the Bishops Clergy and Faithful for the Year of the Eucharist (October 7, 2004). http://www.vatican.va/holy_father/john_paul_ii/apost_letters/documents/hf_jp-ii_apl_20041008_mane-nobiscum-domine_en.html.

———. *Novo Millennio Ineunte*: Apostolic Letter of His Holiness Pope John Paul II to the Bishops Clergy and Lay Faithful at the Close of the Great Jubilee of the Year 2000 (January 6, 2001). http://www.vatican.va/holy_father/john_paul_ii/apost_letters/documents/hf_jp-ii_apl_20010106_novo-millennio-ineunte_en.html.

———. *Vicesimus Quintus Annus*: Apostolic Letter of the Supreme Pontiff John Paul II on the 25th Anniversary of the Promulgation of the Conciliar Constitution "*Sacrosanctum Concilium*" on the Sacred Liturgy (December 4, 1988). http://www.vatican.va/holy_father/john_paul_ii/apost_letters/documents/hf_jp-ii_apl_04121988_vicesimus-quintus-annus_en.html.

John of Taizé. "A Spiritual Crossroads of Europe: The Taizé Community's Adventure with the Young." In *Passing on the Faith: Transforming Traditions for the Next Generation of Jews, Christians, and Muslims*, edited by James L. Heft, 147–61. New York: Fordham University Press, 2006.

Johnson, Todd M., David B. Barrett, and Peter F. Crossing. "Christianity 2010: A View from the New *Atlas of Global Christianity*." *International Bulletin of Missionary Research* 34 (2010): 29.

Johnston, William H. "Pope Benedict XVI on the Postconciliar Liturgical Reform: An Essay in Interpretation." *Antiphon* 17, no. 2 (2013): 118–38.

Jones, Cheslyn, Geoffrey Wainwright, Edward Yarnold, and Paul Bradshaw, eds. *The Study of Liturgy*. Rev. ed. New York: Oxford University Press, 1992.

Jones, L. Gregory, and Kevin R. Armstrong. *Resurrecting Excellence: Shaping Faithful Christian Ministry*. Grand Rapids, MI: Eerdmans, 2006.

Jungmann, Joseph A. "Constitution on the Sacred Liturgy." In *Commentary on the Documents of Vatican II*. Vol. 1, edited by Herbert Vorgrimler, 1–87. New York: Herder and Herder, 1967.

———. *The Mass of the Roman Rite: Its Origins and Development (Missarum Sollemnia)*. 2 vols. Translated by Francis A. Brunner. New York: Benziger Brothers, 1951, 1955.

Kaczynski, Reiner. "Angriff auf die Liturgiekonstitution? Anmerkungen zu einer neuen Übersetzer-Instruktion." *Stimmen der Zeit* 219 (2001): 651–68.

———. "Theologischer Kommentar zur Konstitution über die heilige Liturgie *Sacrosanctum Concilium*." In *Herders Theologischer Kommentar zum Zweiten*

Vatikanischen Konzil, edited by Peter Hünerman and Bernd Jochen Hilberath, Band 2, 1–227. Freiburg im Breisgau: Herder, 2004.

Kasper, Walter. *Theology and Church*. New York: Crossroad, 1989.

Kavanagh, Aidan. *Elements of Rite: A Handbook of Liturgical Style*. New York: Pueblo Publishing, 1982.

———. "How Rite Develops: Some Laws Intrinsic to Liturgical Evolution." *Worship* 41 (1967): 334–47.

———. "Liturgical Needs for Today and Tomorrow." *Worship* 43 (1969): 488–95.

———. "Reflections on the Study from the Viewpoint of Liturgical History." In *The Awakening Church: 25 Years of Liturgical Renewal*, edited by Lawrence J. Madden, 83–97. Collegeville, MN: Liturgical Press, 1992.

———. "What Is Participation?—Or, Participation Revisited." *Doctrine and Life* 23 (1973): 343–53.

Keifer, Ralph A. "Squalor on Sunday." *Worship* 44 (1970): 292–96.

———. *To Give Thanks to the Lord: General Instruction of the Roman Missal, with Commentary for Musicians and Priests*. Washington, DC: National Association of Pastoral Musicians, 1980.

Kilmartin, Edward J. "Theology of the Sacraments: Toward a New Understanding of the Chief Rites of the Church of Jesus Christ." In *Alternative Futures for Worship*. Vol. 1, *General Introduction*, edited by Regis A. Duffy, 123–75. Collegeville, MN: Liturgical Press, 1987.

Klauser, Theodor. *A Short History of the Western Liturgy: An Account and Some Reflections*. Translated by John Halliburton. London: Oxford University Press, 1969.

Kocik, Thomas M. *The Reform of the Reform? A Liturgical Debate: Reform or Return*. San Francisco: Ignatius Press, 2003.

Kollmorgen, Gregor. "Important Clarifications from Ecclesia Dei." *New Liturgical Movement* (February 15, 2010). http://www.newliturgicalmovement.org/2010/02/important-clarifications-from-ecclesia.html.

Kunzler, Michael. *Liturgie sein. Entwurf einer Ars celebrandi*. Paderborn: Bonifatius, 2007.

———. *Die 'Tridentinische' Messe: Aufbruch oder Rückschritt?* Paderborn: Bonifatius, 2008.

Lamberts, Jozef, ed. *The Active Participation Revisited. La participation active 100 ans après Pie X et 40 ans après Vatican II*. Leuven: Peeters, 2004.

Langer, Ellen J. *Mindfulness*. Reading, MA: Addison-Wesley Publishing Company, 1989.

———. "Mindfulness/Mindlessness." In *The Blackwell Encyclopedia of Social Psychology*, edited by Anthony S. R. Manstead and Miles Hewstone, 388–90. Oxford: Blackwell Reference, 1995.

———. "Mindfulness Versus Positive Evaluation." In *Oxford Handbook of Positive Psychology*, edited by C. R. Snyder and Shane J. Lopez, 279–93. Oxford: Oxford University Press, 2009.

———. *The Power of Mindful Learning*. Reading, MA: Addison-Wesley Publishing Company, 1997.
Langer, Ellen J., and Mihnea Moldoveanu. "The Construct of Mindfulness." *Journal of Social Issues* 56, (2000): 1–9.
"Liturgical Briefs." *Worship* 33 (1959): 116–22.
Loew, Josef. "The New Instruction." *Worship* 33 (1958): 2–13.
Lucas, Daria. "Active Participation in the Liturgy according to Thomas Aquinas." *Assembly* 34 (2008): 6–16.
Lüdecke, Norbert. "Canonical Remarks on the Motu Proprio *Summorum Pontificum*." Translated by Gary N. Deckant and Gunhild von der Bank. *Antiphon* 13 (2009): 193–227.
———. "Kanonistische Anmerkungen zum Motu Proprio *Summorum Pontificum*." *Liturgische Jahrbuch* 58 (2008): 3–34.
Madden, Lawrence J., ed. *The Awakening Church: 25 Years of Liturgical Renewal*. Collegeville, MN: Liturgical Press, 1992.
Mannion, M. Francis. "The Catholicity of the Liturgy: Shaping a New Agenda." In Caldecott, *Beyond the Prosaic*, 11–48. Also in Mannion, *Masterworks of God: Essays in Liturgical Theory and Practice*, 202–35. Chicago: Hillenbrand Books / Liturgy Training Publications, 2004.
Manstead, Anthony S. R., and Miles Hewstone, eds. *The Blackwell Encyclopedia of Social Psychology*. Oxford: Blackwell Reference, 1995.
Marianist Education Working Group. "Habits of Inquiry and Reflection: A Report on Education in the Catholic and Marianist Traditions at the University of Dayton" (May 5, 2006). http://www.udayton.edu/artssciences/about/images/Habits_of_Inquiry.pdf.
McCoy, Alban. "Rites and Reality." *The Tablet* 263, no. 8782 (March 7, 2009): 12–13.
McDonnell, Kilian. "The Ratzinger/Kasper Debate: The Universal Church and Local Churches." *Theological Studies* 63 (2002): 227–50.
McGavin, Paul A. "Brackets and Footnotes: A Way toward Mutual Enrichment." *Antiphon* 14 (2010): 273–84.
McManus, Frederick R. *Sacramental Liturgy*. New York: Herder and Herder, 1967.
McPartlan, Paul. "The Local Church and the Universal Church: Zizioulas and the Ratzinger–Kasper Debate." *International Journal for the Study of the Christian Church* 4 (2004): 21–33.
Melloni, Alberto, and Christoph Theobald, eds. *Vatican II: A Forgotten Future*. Concilium 2005/4. London: SCM Press, 2005.
Metzger, Marcel. *History of the Liturgy: The Major Stages*. Collegeville, MN: Liturgical Press, 1997.
Michel, Virgil. "Christian Culture." *Orate Fratres* 13 (1939): 296–304.
———. *The Liturgy of the Church: According to the Roman Rite*. New York: Macmillan, 1937.
———. "The Liturgy the Basis of Social Regeneration." *Orate Fratres* 9 (1935): 536–45.

———. "The Scope of the Liturgical Movement." *Orate Fratres* 10 (1936): 485–90.

———. "Why Do We Do It?" *Orate Fratres* 9 (1934): 63–67.

Mitchell, Nathan D. "The Amen Corner: '*Summorum Pontificum*.'" *Worship* 81 (2007): 549–65.

Mitchell, Nathan D., and John F. Baldovin. "*Institutio Generalis Missalis Romani* and the Class of Liturgical Documents to Which It Belongs." In Foley and others, *A Commentary on the General Instruction of the Roman Missal*, 1–27.

Moroney, James P., ed. *Liturgy: Active Participation in the Divine Life*. Major Addresses from the 1989 Meeting of the Diocesan Liturgical Commissions. Collegeville. MN: Liturgical Press, 1990.

Moynihan, Robert. "The Return of the Latin Mass." *Inside the Vatican* 18, no. 5 (May 2010): 30–33, 35.

Mullahy, Bernard L. "Pastor Angelicus: Pius XII." In *Participation in the Mass: 20th North American Liturgical Week*. University of Notre Dame, August 23–26, 1959, 3–17. Washington, DC: Liturgical Conference, 1960.

Nebel, P. Johannes. "Die 'ordentliche' und die 'außerordentliche' Form des römischen Messritus. Versuch einer Orientierungshilfe zum tieferen Verstehen beider Formen." *Forum Katholische Theologie* 25 (2009): 173–203.

Nichols, Aidan. *Looking at the Liturgy: A Critical View of Its Contemporary Form*. San Francisco: Ignatius Press, 1996.

———. "Salutary Dissatisfaction: An English View of 'Reforming the Reform.'" In Kocik, *The Reform of the Reform?* 195–210.

Nolan, Hugh J., ed. *Pastoral Letters of the United States Catholic Bishops*. Vol. 3, 1962–74. Washington, DC: United States Catholic Conference, 1983.

Noll, Mark A. *Turning Points: Decisive Moments in the History of Christianity*. Grand Rapids, MI: Baker Books, 1997.

O'Collins, Gerald, and Mario Farrugia. *Catholicism: The Story of Catholic Christianity*. Oxford: Oxford University Press, 2003.

O'Connor, Flannery. "The Fiction Writer and His Country." In O'Connor, *Mystery and Manners*, 25–35. New York: Farrar Straus and Giroux, 1961.

Olsen, Glenn W. "Why We Need Christopher Dawson." *Communio* 35 (2008): 115–44.

O'Malley, Timothy P. "Re-reading *Orate Fratres*: The American Liturgical Movement Is Born (1926–27)." *Oblation: Catechesis, Liturgy, and the New Evangelization* (blog post; September 20, 2012). http://blogs.nd.edu/oblation/2012/09/20/re-reading-orate-fratres-the-american-liturgical-movement-is-born-1926-27.

O'Neill, Colman E. "The Theological Meaning of *Actuosa Participatio* in the Liturgy." In *Sacred Music and Liturgy Reform after Vatican II*, edited by Johannes Overath, 89–108. Rome: Consociatio Internationalis Musicae Sacrae, 1969.

Overath, Johannes, ed. *Sacred Music and Liturgy Reform after Vatican II*. Proceedings of the Fifth International Church Music Congress, Chicago-Milwaukee, August 21–28, 1966. Rome: Consociatio Internationalis Musicae Sacrae, 1969.

"The Oxford Declaration on Liturgy." In Caldecott, *Beyond the Prosaic*, 163–65. Also at http://www.secondspring.co.uk/spirituality/declaration.htm.

Papal Teachings: The Liturgy. Selected and arranged by the Benedictine Monks of Solesmes. Translated by the Daughters of St. Paul. Boston: St. Paul Editions, 1962.

Pecklers, Keith F. *The Genius of the Roman Rite: On the Reception and Implementation of the New Missal*. Collegeville, MN: Liturgical Press, 2009.

———. "History of the Roman Liturgy from the Sixteenth until the Twentieth Centuries." In *Handbook for Liturgical Studies*. Vol. 1, *Introduction to the Liturgy*, edited by Anscar J. Chupungco, 153–78. Collegeville, MN; Liturgical Press, 1997.

———. "Importance and Dignity of the Eucharistic Celebration." In Foley and others, *A Commentary on the General Instruction of the Roman Missal*, 99–112.

———. *The Unread Vision: The Liturgical Movement in the United States of America: 1926–1955*. Collegeville, MN: Liturgical Press, 1998.

———. *Worship: A Primer in Christian Ritual*. Collegeville, MN: Liturgical Press, 2005.

"PCED Clarification on the Motu Proprio." *LMS Chairman: The Chairman's Blog* (February 19, 2010; Latin Mass Society of England and Wales). http://www.lmschairman.org/2010/02/pced-clarification-on-motu-proprio.html.

Pieper, Josef. "Prudence." In *The Four Cardinal Virtues*, 3–40. Notre Dame, IN: University of Notre Dame Press, 1967.

Pietrusza, David. *Sursum Corda: Documents and Readings on the Traditional Latin Mass from the Council of Trent to Benedict XVI's Motu Proprio*. Printed in the United States of America, 2008.

Pius X. *Abhinc Duos Annos*. In *Papal Teachings: The Liturgy*, 226–27.

———. "Letter *Il desiderio*, December 8, 1903, to Cardinal Respighi." In *Papal Teachings: The Liturgy*, 188–93.

———. *Tra le Sollecitudini*. In *Papal Teachings: The Liturgy*, 177–87.

Pius XI. *Divini Cultus Sanctitatem*. *Acta Apostolicae Sedis* 21, no. 2 (1929): 33–41. English translation in *Papal Teachings: The Liturgy*, 244–54.

Pius XII. *Mediator Dei*. *Acta Apostolicae Sedis* 39 (1947): 521–95. English translation in Pamela Jackson, *An Abundance of Graces: Reflections on* Sacrosanctum Concilium, 124–78.

Pontifical Commission *Ecclesia Dei*. *Universae Ecclesiae* (April 30, 2011). http://www.vatican.va/roman_curia/pontifical_commissions/ecclsdei/documents/rc_com_ecclsdei_doc_20110430_istr-universae-ecclesiae_en.html.

Poterak, Kurt. "Gnostic Traditionalists and Liturgical Singing." *Sacred Music* 136, no. 3 (Fall 2009): 72–73.

———. "Whither *Summorum Pontificum*?" *Sacred Music* 135, no. 1 (Spring 2008): 72–73.

Power, David N., and Catherine Vincie. "Theological and Pastoral Reflections." In Foley and others, *A Commentary on the General Instruction of the Roman Missal*, 46–72.

Rapp, Catherine Teresa. *De Cura pro Mortuis Gerenda Sancti Augustini: Text, Translation, Introduction and Commentary*. Master of Arts Thesis, Department of Ancient Languages, University of Notre Dame, 1931.

Ratzinger, Joseph (see also Benedict XVI). "40 Jahre Konstitution über die heilige Liturgie. Rückblick und Vorblick." *Liturgische Jahrbuch* 53 (2003): 209–21.

———. "Assessment and Future Prospects." Translated by Henry Taylor. In Reid, *Looking Again at the Question of the Liturgy with Cardinal Ratzinger*, 145–53.

———. *Called to Communion: Understanding the Church Today*. Translated by Adrian Walker. San Francisco: Ignatius Press, 1996.

———. "Cardinal Ratzinger's Remarks Regarding the Lefebvre Schism." Address given on July 13, 1988. Accessed at http://www.catholicculture.org/culture/library/view.cfm?id=3032&repos=1&subrepos=&searchid=292734.

———. "Catholicism after the Council." *The Furrow* 18 (1967): 3–23.

———. "The Church Has Never Abolished Orthodox Liturgies." *Inside the Vatican* 6, no. 10 (December 1998): 58–59.

———. "Dix ans après." Address given on October 24, 1998. Original French text available online at http://lacriseintegriste.typepad.fr/weblog/1998/10/conf%C3%A9rence-du-cardinal-ratzinger-pour-les-10-ans-du-motu-proprio-ecclesia-dei.html; English translation: "The Church Has Never Abolished Orthodox Liturgies," *Inside the Vatican*, Year 6, no. 10 (December 1998): 58–59.

———. "Europe's Crisis of Culture." In *The Essential Pope Benedict XVI: His Central Writings and Speeches*, edited by John F. Thornton and Susan B. Varenne, 325–36. New York: HarperCollins, 2007.

———. *The Feast of Faith: Approaches to a Theology of the Liturgy*. Translated by Graham Harrison. San Francisco: Ignatius Press, 1986.

———. *God Is Near Us: The Eucharist, the Heart of Life*. Edited by Stephan Otto Horn and Vinzenz Pfnür. Translated by Henry Taylor. San Francisco: Ignatius Press, 2003.

———. *God and the World: A Conversation with Peter Seewald*. Translated by Henry Taylor. San Francisco: Ignatius Press, 2002.

———. *Jesus of Nazareth: From the Baptism in the Jordan to the Transfiguration*. Translated by Adrian J. Walker. New York: Doubleday, 2007.

———. "Liturgie—wandelbar oder unwandelbar? Fragen an Joseph Ratzinger." In *Theologie der Liturgie*, 613–26.

———. *Milestones: Memoirs 1927–1977*. Translated from the German by Erasmo Leiva-Merikakis. San Francisco: Ignatius Press, n.d. (Italian edition 1997, German edition 1998).

———. *A New Song for the Lord: Faith in Christ and Liturgy Today*. Translated by Martha M. Matesich. New York: Crossroad, 1996.

———. *Pilgrim Fellowship of Faith: The Church as Communion*. Edited by Stephan Otto Horn and Vinzenz Pfnür. Translated by Henry Taylor. San Francisco: Ignatius Press, 2005.

———. "Preface" to Alcuin Reid, *The Organic Development of the Liturgy*, 9–13. 2nd ed. San Francisco: Ignatius Press, 2005.
———. "Response to Father Gy," *Antiphon* 11, no. 1 (2007): 98–102.
———. *The Ratzinger Reader*. Edited by Lieven Boeve and Gerard Mannion. New York: T&T Clark International, 2010.
———. *Salt of the Earth: The Church at the End of the Millennium. An Interview with Peter Seewald*. Translated by Adrian Walker. San Francisco: Ignatius Press, 1997.
———. "The Second Vatican Council: The First Session." *The Furrow* 14 (1963): 267–88.
———. *The Spirit of the Liturgy*. Translated by John Saward. San Francisco: Ignatius Press, 2005.
———. *Theological Highlights of Vatican II*. New York: Paulist Press Deus Book, 1966.
———. *Theologie der Liturgie: Die sakramentale Begründung christlicher Existenz*. Gesammelte Schriften, Band 11. Edited by Gerhard Ludwig Müller. Freiburg im Breisgau: Herder, 2008.
———. "Um die Erneuerung der Liturgie. Antwort auf Reiner Kaczynski." *Stimmen der Zeit* 219 (2001): 837–42.
———. "Zum Gedenken an Klaus Gamber." In *Theologie der Liturgie*, 633–35.
Ratzinger, Joseph, and Vittorio Messori. *The Ratzinger Report: An Exclusive Interview on the State of the Church*. Translated by Salvator Attanasio and Graham Harrison. San Francisco: Ignatius Press, 1985.
Read, Gordon. "Motu Proprio Summorum Pontificum." *Newsletter: Canon Law Society of Great Britain and Ireland*, no. 151 (September 2007): 9–21.
Regan, Patrick. *Advent to Pentecost: Comparing the Seasons in the Ordinary and Extraordinary Forms of the Roman Rite*. Collegeville, MN: Liturgical Press, 2012.
———. "Liturgy and the Experience of Celebration." *Worship* 47 (1973): 592–600.
Rehak, Martin. *Die außerordentliche Gebrauch der alten Form des römischen Ritus: kirchenrechtlichen Skizzen zum Motu Proprio* Summorum Pontificum *vom 07.07.2007*. St. Ottilien: EOS-Verlag, 2009.
Reid, Alcuin. "The Genius of the Roman Rite. Part 6—After *Summorum Pontificum*: A New Era for the Roman Rite." *Music and Liturgy* 36, no. 4, issue 340 (February 2011): 6–10.
———. "The Liturgical Reform of Pope Benedict XVI." In *Benedict XVI and the Sacred Liturgy*, edited by Neil J. Roy and Janet E. Rutherford, 156–80. Dublin: Four Courts Press, 2010.
———. *The Organic Development of the Liturgy: The Principles of Liturgical Reform and Their Relation to the Twentieth-Century Liturgical Movement Prior to the Second Vatican Council*. 2nd ed. San Francisco: Ignatius Press, 2005.
Reid, Alcuin, ed. *Looking Again at the Question of the Liturgy with Cardinal Ratzinger*. Proceedings of the July 2001 Fontgombault Liturgical Conference. Farnborough: Saint Michael's Abbey Press, 2003.
"Risposte del Cardinale Presidente della Pontificia Commissione 'Ecclesia Dei' a certi quesiti." www.clerus.org/clerus/dati/2008-10/24-20/castrillon

_rispost.html. English translation at http://qien.free.fr/2008/200810/20081028_response.certain.questions.1986.htm.
Robinson, Jonathon. *The Mass and Modernity: Walking to Heaven Backward*. San Francisco: Ignatius Press, 2005.
Robitaille, Lynda. "A Canonical Wish List for the Authorization of Lay Ecclesial Ministers." In Cahoy, *In the Name of the Church*, 102–33.
The Roman Missal, Third Edition. Washington, DC: United States Conference of Catholic Bishops, 2011.
Romano, John F. "The Fates of Liturgies: Towards a History of the First Roman *Ordo*." *Antiphon* 11 (2007): 43–77.
Rowland, Tracey. *Ratzinger's Faith: The Theology of Pope Benedict XVI*. Oxford: Oxford University Press, 2009.
Roy, Neil J., and Janet E. Rutherford, eds. *Benedict XVI and the Sacred Liturgy: Proceedings of the First Fota International Liturgy Conference, 2008*. Dublin: Four Courts Press, 2010.
Rudder, Christopher R. J., ed. *The Introductory Matters of the* Roman Missal *of 1962*. Columbus, OH, 2009.
Ruff, Anthony. *Sacred Music and Liturgical Reform: Treasures and Transformations*. Chicago: Hillenbrand Books / Liturgy Training Publications, 2007.
Sacred Congregation for Divine Worship and the Discipline of the Sacraments. "Responsa Officialia." *Notitiae* 35, nos. 7–8 (1999): 307–309.
Sánchez-Gil, Antonio S. "Gli innovativi profili canonici del motu proprio *Summorum Pontificum* sull'uso della liturgia romana anteriore alla riforma del 1970." *Ius Ecclesiae* 19 (2007): 689–708.
Schaefer, Mary, and Joanne M. Pierce. "Mass at Which Only One Minister Participates." In Foley and others, *A Commentary on the General Instruction of the Roman Missal*, 310–24.
Schillebeeckx, E. "Towards a Rediscovery of the Christian Sacraments: Ritualizing Religious Elements in Daily Life." In *Ordo: Bath, Word, Prayer, Table; A Liturgical Primer in Honor of Gordon W. Lathrop*, edited by Dirk G. Lange and Dwight W. Vogel, 6–34. Akron, OH: OSL Publications, 2005.
Schindler, David L. "Truth, Freedom, and Relativism in Western Democracies: Pope Benedict XVI's Contributions to *Without Roots*." *Communio* 32 (2005): 669–81.
Schmitt, Paul Joseph. "A Propos du Missel de Saint Pie V." *Notitiae* 16, no. 3, issue 164 (March 1980): 110–15.
Schumacher, William A., and Lynn Jarrell, eds. *Roman Replies and CLSA Advisory Opinions 1990*. Washington, DC: Canon Law Society of America, 1990.
Searle, Mark. *Called to Participate: Theological, Ritual, and Social Perspectives*, edited by Barbara Searle and Anne Y. Koester. Collegeville, MN: Liturgical Press, 2006.
———. "Culture." In *Liturgy: Active Participation in the Divine Life*, edited by James P. Moroney, 27–51. Collegeville, MN: Liturgical Press, 1990.

———. "Reflections on Liturgical Reform." In *Vision: The Scholarly Contributions of Mark Searle to Liturgical Renewal*, edited by Anne Y. Koester and Barbara Searle, 82–100. Collegeville, MN: Liturgical Press, 2004.

Skeris, Robert A. "Sarto, the 'Conservative Reformer'—100 Years of the *Motu Proprio* of Pope St. Pius X." *Sacred Music* 130, no. 4 (Winter 2003): 5–9.

Smith, Christopher. "Mutual Enrichment and the Reform of the Reform: A Game Plan?" *The Chant Café* (January 10, 2011), http://www.chantcafe.com/2011/01/mutual-enrichment-and-reform-of-reform_10.html.

Snyder, C. R., and Shane J. Lopez, eds. *Oxford Handbook of Positive Psychology*. Oxford: Oxford University Press, 2009.

Spadaro, Antonio. "A Big Heart Open to God: The Exclusive Interview with Pope Francis." *America* 209, no. 8 (September 30, 2013): 30. Also http://www.americamagazine.org/pope-interview.

Stelten, Leo F. *Dictionary of Ecclesiastical Latin*. Peabody, MA: Hendrickson Publishers, 1995.

Stravinskas, Peter. "Why I Oppose a Tridentine Prelature." *The Catholic World Report* (February 1992), as cited in Kocik, *The Reform of the Reform?*

Sweeney, James. "How Should We Remember Vatican II?" *New Blackfriars* 90, no. 1026 (2009): 251–60.

Taft, Robert F. *The Liturgy of the Hours in East and West: The Origins of the Divine Office and Its Meaning for Today*. 2nd rev. ed. Collegeville, MN: Liturgical Press, 1993.

Tanner, Norman P. *Decrees of the Ecumenical Councils*, 2 Vols. Washington, DC: Georgetown University Press, 1990.

Tattersall, Glen. "*Pasch* and *Eschaton* in *Ecclesia*: Joseph Ratzinger's Theology of the Liturgy." *The Priest* 11, no. 1 (2007): 12–15, 21, 24.

———. "*Summorum Pontificum*—A Commentary and Appreciation: 'And the Church will give thanks for Benedict XVI.'" *The Priest* 11, no. 2 (2007): 22–23, 27.

Tena, Pere. "Celebrar la liturgia después de una reforma." *Phase* 309 (2012): 227–43.

———. "El motu proprio 'Summorum Pontificum': Análisis y reflexiones." *Phase* 280 (2007): 275–88.

Thibodeau, Timothy. "Western Christendom." In Wainwright and Westerfield Tucker, *The Oxford History of Christian Worship*, 216–53.

Thirty-Five Years of the BCL Newsletter 1965–2000. Washington, DC: USCCB, 2004.

Thornton, John F., and Susan B. Varenne, eds. *The Essential Pope Benedict XVI: His Central Writings and Speeches*. New York: HarperCollins, 2007.

Twomey, D. Vincent. *Pope Benedict XVI: The Conscience of Our Age. A Theological Portrait*. San Francisco: Ignatius Press, 2007.

USCCB. *General Instruction of the Roman Missal*. Liturgy Documentary Series 2. Washington, DC: USCCB, 2003.

———. "Use of Vernacular at Mass" (1964). In *Pastoral Letters of the United States Catholic Bishops*, Vol. 3, 1962–74. Edited by Hugh J. Nolan, 35–44. Washington, DC: USCCB, 1983.
———. *Program of Priestly Formation*. 5th ed. Washington, DC: USCCB, 2006.
———. *Sing to the Lord*. Washington, DC: USCCB, 2007.
———. "The Theological Vision of *Sacrosanctum Concilium* and the Roman Missal." http://www.usccb.org/romanmissal/resources-reflections.shtml.
Van Dijk, Stephen J. P., and J. Hazelden Walker. *The Origins of the Modern Roman Liturgy: The Liturgy of the Papal Court and the Franciscan Order in the Thirteenth Century*. Westminster, MD: Newman, 1960.
Veltri, John. "Traditional Mass Never Forbidden." Digitally reprinted from February 1998 edition of *Catholic Family News*. Niagara Falls, NY. www.cfnews.org/tridmass.htm.
Vogel, Cyrille. *Medieval Liturgy: An Introduction to Its Sources*. Translated and revised by William G. Storey and Niels Krogh Rasmussen, with the assistance of John K. Brooks-Leonard. Washington, DC: Pastoral Press, 1986.
Von Hildebrand, Alice. "Present at the Demolition." In *The Latin Mass*, Summer 2001. http://www.latinmassmagazine.com/articles/articles_2001_su_Hildebran.html.
Wainwright, Geoffrey, and Karen B. Westerfield Tucker, eds. *The Oxford History of Christian Worship*. Oxford: Oxford University Press, 2006.
Weakland, Rembert G. "Liturgical Renewal: Two Latin Rites?" *America* 176, no. 20 (June 7–14, 1997): 12–15.
Weil, Simone. *Gravity and Grace*. New York: G.P. Putnam's Sons, 1952.
Weishaupt, Gero P. *Päpstliche Weichenstellungen: Das Motu Proprio* Summorum Pontificum *Benedikts XVI. und der Begleitbrief. Ein kirchenrechtlicher Kommentar*. http://kirchenrechtlicher-kommentar.gero-p-weishaupt.com.
Wells, Samuel. *Improvisation: The Drama of Christian Ethics*. Grand Rapids, MI: Brazos Press, 2004.
White, James F. *Roman Catholic Worship: Trent to Today*. 2nd ed. Collegeville, MN: Liturgical Press, 2003.
Witte, Henk. "Reform with the Help of Juxtapositions: A Challenge to the Interpretation of the Documents of Vatican II." *The Jurist* 71 (2011): 20–34.
Woodward, Kenneth L. *Making Saints: How the Catholic Church Determines Who Becomes a Saint, Who Doesn't, and Why*. New York: Simon & Schuster, 1996.
Zaleski, Carol. "Worshiping with Agatha Christie." *Christian Century* 124, issue 17 (August 21, 2007): 35.
Zerwick, Max, and Mary Grosvenor. *A Grammatical Analysis of the Greek New Testament*. Unabridged, rev. ed. in 1 vol. Rome: Biblical Institute Press, 1981.

Appendix

Summorum Pontificum

❐ ❐ ❐

De usu extraordinario antiquae formae Ritus Romani.

Summorum Pontificum cura ad hoc tempus usque semper fuit, ut Christi Ecclesia Divinae Maiestati cultum dignum offerret, « ad laudem et gloriam nominis Sui » et « ad utilitatem totius Ecclesiae Suae sanctae ».

Ab immemorabili tempore sicut etiam in futurum, principium servandum est « iuxta quod unaquaeque Ecclesia particularis concordare debet cum universali Ecclesia non solum quoad fidei doctrinam et signa sacramentalia, sed etiam quoad usus universaliter acceptos ab apostolica et continua traditione, qui servandi sunt non solum ut errores vitentur, verum etiam ad fidei integritatem tradendam, quia Ecclesiae lex orandi eius legi credendi respondet ».[1]

Inter Pontifices qui talem debitam curam adhibuerunt, nomen excellit sancti Gregorii Magni, qui tam fidem catholicam quam thesauros cultus ac culturae a Romanis in saeculis praecedentibus cumulatos novis Europae populis transmittendos curavit. Sacrae Liturgiae tam Missae Sacrificii quam Officii Divini formam, uti in Urbe celebrabatur, definiri conservarique iussit. Monachos quoque et moniales maxime fovit, qui sub Regula sancti Benedicti militantes, ubique simul cum Evangelii annuntiatione illam quoque saluberrimam Regulae sententiam vita sua illustrarunt, « ut operi Dei nihil praeponatur » (cap. 43). Tali modo sacra liturgia secundum morem Romanum non solum fidem et pietatem sed et culturam

[1] *Institutio generalis Missalis Romani*, Editio tertia, 2002, 397.

Summorum Pontificum

❒❒❒

On the Extraordinary Use of the Ancient Form of the Roman Rite

SP 1

It has always been the care of the Supreme Pontiffs up to our own day that the church of Christ offer worthy worship to the divine majesty, "for the praise and glory of his name" and "for the good of all his holy church."

SP 2

As from time immemorial, so also into the future, let the principle be observed "according to which each particular Church must be in accord with the universal Church not only regarding the doctrine of the faith and sacramental signs, but also as to the usages universally received from apostolic and unbroken tradition. These are to be kept not only so that errors may be avoided, but also so that the faith may be handed on in its integrity, since the Church's rule of prayer (lex orandi) corresponds to her rule of faith (lex credendi)."[1]

SP 3

Among the Pontiffs who have exercised such requisite concern, the name of Saint Gregory the Great stands out. He took care to transmit to the new peoples of Europe both the Catholic faith and the riches of worship and culture accumulated by the Romans during the preceding centuries. He made provision that the form of the sacred liturgy as celebrated in the city of Rome, both the sacrifice of the Mass and the Divine Office, be established and preserved. He greatly encouraged monks as well as nuns who, soldiering under the Rule of Saint Benedict, everywhere illustrated by their life, along with the preaching of the Gospel, that most salutary saying of the Rule, that "nothing is to be preferred to the work of God" (chap. 43). In this way the sacred liturgy according to the Roman custom made fruitful not only the faith and devotion but also the culture of many peoples. Indeed, it is known that the Latin liturgy

[1] *General Instruction of the Roman Missal*, 3rd ed. (2002), no. 397.

multarum gentium fecundavit. Constat utique liturgiam Latinam variis suis formis Ecclesiae in omnibus aetatis christianae saeculis permultos Sanctos in vita spirituali stimulasse atque tot populos in religionis virtute roborasse ac eorundem pietatem fecundasse.

Ut autem Sacra Liturgia hoc munus efficacius expleret, plures alii Romani Pontifices decursu saeculorum peculiarem sollicitudinem impenderunt, inter quos eminet Sanctus Pius V, qui magno cum studio pastorali, Concilio Tridentino exhortante, totum Ecclesiae cultum innovavit, librorum liturgicorum emendatorum et « ad normam Patrum instauratorum » editionem curavit eosque Ecclesiae Latinae usui dedit.

Inter Ritus Romani libros liturgicos patet eminere Missale Romanum, quod in Romana urbe succrevit, atque succedentibus saeculis gradatim formas assumpsit, quae cum illa in generationibus recentioribus vigente magnam habent similitudinem.

« Quod idem omnino propositum tempore progrediente Pontifices Romani sunt persecuti, cum novas ad aetates accommodaverunt aut ritus librosque liturgicos determinaverunt, ac deinde cum ineunte hoc nostro saeculo ampliorem iam complexi sunt redintegrationem ».[2] Sic vero egerunt Decessores nostri Clemens VIII, Urbanus VIII, sanctus Pius X,[3] Benedictus XV, Pius XII et beatus Ioannes XXIII.

Recentioribus autem temporibus, Concilium Vaticanum II desiderium expressit, ut debita observantia et reverentia erga cultum divinum denuo instauraretur ac necessitatibus nostrae aetatis aptaretur. Quo desiderio motus, Decessor noster Summus Pontifex Paulus VI libros liturgicos instauratos et partim innovatos anno 1970 Ecclesiae Latinae approbavit; qui ubique terrarum permultas in linguas

[2] Ioannes Paulus PP. II, Litt. ap. *Vicesimus quintus annus* (4 Decembris 1988), 3: *AAS* 81 (1989), 899.

[3] *Ibid.*

of the church in its various forms, in all the centuries of the Christian era, spurred on many saints in the spiritual life, and strengthened so many peoples in the virtue of religion and made their devotion fruitful.

SP 4

Moreover, so that the sacred liturgy might fulfill this role more efficaciously, many other Roman Pontiffs across the centuries manifested particular solicitude, among whom Saint Pius V stands out. With great pastoral zeal, and urged on by the Council of Trent, he renewed the whole worship of the church, saw to the publication of liturgical books corrected and "restored according to the norm of the Fathers," and provided them for the use of the Latin church.

SP 5

Among liturgical books of the Roman Rite, clearly the Roman Missal is preeminent. It grew in the city of Rome and over succeeding centuries gradually took on forms which have a great similarity with the one in force in more recent generations.

SP 6

"It was toward this same goal that succeeding Roman Pontiffs directed their energies during the subsequent centuries in order to ensure that the rite and liturgical books were brought up to date and when necessary clarified. From the beginning of this century they undertook a more general reform."[2] This, indeed, is what our predecessors carried out—Clement VIII, Urban VIII, Saint Pius X,[3] Benedict XV, Pius XII, and Blessed John XXIII.

SP 7

In more recent times, however, the Second Vatican Council expressed the desire that due respect and reverence for divine worship be renewed again and adapted to the needs of our age. Moved by this desire, our predecessor the Supreme Pontiff Paul VI approved in the year 1970 for the Latin Church liturgical books reformed [or: restored] and partly made new. These books, translated

[2] John Paul II, Apostolic Letter *Vicesimus Quintus Annus* (December 4, 1988) 3: *Acta Apostolicae Sedis* 81 (1989), 899.

[3] Ibid.

vulgares conversi, ab Episcopis atque a sacerdotibus et fidelibus libenter recepti sunt. Ioannes Paulus II, tertiam editionem typicam Missalis Romani recognovit. Sic Romani Pontifices operati sunt ut « hoc quasi aedificium liturgicum [...] rursus, dignitate splendidum et concinnitate» appareret.[4]

Aliquibus autem in regionibus haud pauci fideles antecedentibus formis liturgicis, quae eorum culturam et spiritum tam profunde imbuerant, tanto amore et affectu adhaeserunt et adhaerere pergunt, ut Summus Pontifex Ioannes Paulus II, horum fidelium pastorali cura motus, anno 1984 speciali Indulto « Quattuor abhinc annos », a Congregatione pro Cultu Divino exarato, facultatem concesserit utendi Missali Romano a beato Ioanne XXIII anno 1962 edito; anno autem 1988 Ioannes Paulus II iterum, litteris Apostolicis « Ecclesia Dei » Motu proprio datis, Episcopos exhortatus est ut talem facultatem late et generose in favorem omnium fidelium id petentium adhiberent.

Instantibus precibus horum fidelium iam a Praedecessore Nostro Ioanne Paulo II diu perpensis, auditis etiam a Nobis Patribus Cardinalibus in Consistorio die XXIII mensis Martii anni 2006 habito, omnibus mature perpensis, invocato Spiritu Sancto et Dei freti auxilio, praesentibus Litteris Apostolicis DECERNIMUS quae sequuntur:

Art. 1. Missale Romanum a Paulo VI promulgatum ordinaria expressio « Legis orandi » Ecclesiae catholicae ritus Latini est. Missale autem Romanum a S. Pio V promulgatum et a beato Ioanne XXIII denuo editum habeatur uti extraordinaria expressio eiusdem « Legis orandi » Ecclesiae et ob venerabilem et antiquum eius usum debito gaudeat honore. Hae duae expressiones « legis orandi »

[4] S. Pius PP. X, Litt. Ap. Motu proprio datae *Abhinc duos annos* (23 Octobris 1913): *AAS* 5 (1913), 449-450; cfr Ioannes Paulus II, Litt. ap. *Vicesimus quintus annus* (4 Decembris 1988), 3: *AAS* 81 (1989), 899.

into many vernacular languages throughout the world, were gladly received by the bishops, and by the priests and faithful. John Paul II gave recognition to the third typical edition of the Roman Missal. This is how the Roman Pontiffs have acted, so that "this liturgical edifice, so to speak . . ." should appear "again, resplendent with dignity and proportion."[4]

SP 8

In certain regions, however, some of the faithful—by no means few—adhered and continue to adhere to the prior liturgical forms, which so profoundly imbued their culture and spirit; for this reason the Supreme Pontiff John Paul II, moved with pastoral concern for these faithful, granted the faculty in 1984, in a special indult prepared by the Congregation for Divine Worship, "Quattuor Abhinc Annos," to use the Roman Missal edited by Blessed John XXIII in the year 1962. Further, in the year 1988 John Paul II once again, in his apostolic letter "Ecclesia Dei" given motu proprio, urged the bishops to make a wide and generous use of this faculty in favor of all the faithful who sought it.

SP 9

Having now for a long time pondered the pressing requests of those members of the faithful to our predecessor John Paul II, having listened also to the Father cardinals gathered by us in the consistory of March 23, 2006, having pondered all these matters fully, having invoked the Holy Spirit and relying on the help of God, with these apostolic letters WE DECREE the following.

SP, ARTICLE 1

The Roman Missal promulgated by Paul VI is the ordinary expression of the "lex orandi" of the Catholic Church of the Latin rite. The Roman Missal promulgated by Saint Pius V and reedited by Blessed John XXIII is to be regarded as the extraordinary expression of the same "lex orandi" of the church and is to enjoy due honor on account of its venerable and ancient usage. These two expressions

[4] Pope St. Pius X, Apostolic Letter motu proprio datae *Abhinc Duos Annos* (October 23, 1913): *Acta Apostolicae Sedis* 5 (1913), 449–50; cf. John Paul II, Apostolic Letter *Vicesimus Quintus Annus* (December 4, 1988) 3: *Acta Apostolicae Sedis* 81 (1989), 899.

Ecclesiae, minime vero inducent in divisionem « legis credendi » Ecclesiae; sunt enim duo usus unici ritus Romani.

Proinde Missae Sacrificium, iuxta editionem typicam Missalis Romani a beato Ioanne XXIII anno 1962 promulgatam et numquam abrogatam, uti formam extraordinariam Liturgiae Ecclesiae, celebrare licet. Condiciones vero a documentis antecedentibus « Quattuor abhinc annos » et « Ecclesia Dei » pro usu huius Missalis statutae, substituuntur ut sequitur:

Art. 2. In Missis sine populo celebratis, quilibet sacerdos catholicus ritus Latini, sive saecularis sive religiosus, uti potest aut Missali Romano a beato Papa Ioanne XXIII anno 1962 edito, aut Missali Romano a Summo Pontifice Paulo VI anno 1970 promulgato, et quidem qualibet die, excepto Triduo Sacro. Ad talem celebrationem secundum unum alterumve Missale, sacerdos nulla eget licentia, nec Sedis Apostolicae nec Ordinarii sui.

Art. 3. Si communitates Institutorum vitae consecratae atque Societatum vitae apostolicae iuris sive pontificii sive dioecesani quae in celebratione conventuali seu « communitatis » in oratoriis propriis celebrationem sanctae Missae iuxta editionem Missalis Romani anno 1962 promulgatam habere cupiunt, id eis licet. Si singula communitas aut totum Institutum vel Societas tales celebrationes saepe vel habitualiter vel permanenter perficere vult, res a Superioribus maioribus ad normam iuris et secundum leges et statuta particularia decernatur.

Art. 4. Ad celebrationes sanctae Missae de quibus supra in art. 2 admitti possunt, servatis de iure servandis, etiam christifideles qui sua sponte id petunt.

Art. 5, § 1. In paroeciis, ubi coetus fidelium traditioni liturgicae antecedenti adhaerentium stabiliter exsistit, parochus eorum petitiones ad celebrandam sanctam Missam iuxta ritum Missalis Romani anno 1962 editi, libenter suscipiat. Ipse videat ut harmonice con-

of the "lex orandi" of the church by no means introduce a division in the "lex credendi" of the church, for they are two uses of the one Roman rite.

Accordingly, it is permitted to celebrate the sacrifice of the Mass according to the typical edition promulgated by Blessed John XXIII in 1962 and never abrogated, as the extraordinary form of the liturgy of the church. The stipulations for use of this Missal established by the prior documents "Quattuor Abhinc Annos" and "Ecclesia Dei" are replaced as follows.

SP, ARTICLE 2

In Masses celebrated without the people, each Catholic priest of the Latin Rite, whether secular or religious, can use either the Roman Missal edited by Blessed John XXIII in 1962, or the Roman Missal promulgated by the Supreme Pontiff Paul VI in 1970, and on any day except the sacred Triduum. For such celebration, according to one or the other Missal, a priest needs no permission, either from the Apostolic See or from his ordinary.

SP, ARTICLE 3

If communities of institutes of consecrated life or societies of apostolic life, of either pontifical or diocesan right, desire to have the celebration of holy Mass according to the edition of the Roman Missal promulgated in 1962 in conventual or "communal" celebration in their own oratories, it is permitted them. If an individual community or an entire institute or society wishes to do such celebrations often or habitually or permanently, the matter is to be decided by the major superiors according to the rule of law and their own particular laws and statutes.

SP, ARTICLE 4

The faithful, moreover, who seek it on their own initiative can be admitted to celebrations of holy Mass described above in Art. 2, all relevant laws being observed.

SP, ARTICLE 5, SECTION 1

In parishes where a group of the faithful attached to the prior liturgical tradition exists stably, the pastor should willingly receive their requests to celebrate holy Mass according to the rite of the Roman Missal edited in 1962. Let him see to it that the good of these faith-

cordetur bonum horum fidelium cum ordinaria paroeciae pastorali cura, sub Episcopi regimine ad normam canonis 392, discordiam vitando et totius Ecclesiae unitatem fovendo.

§ 2. Celebratio secundum Missale beati Ioannis XXIII locum habere potest diebus ferialibus; dominicis autem et festis una etiam celebratio huiusmodi fieri potest.

§ 3. Fidelibus seu sacerdotibus id petentibus, parochus celebrationes, hac in forma extraordinaria, permittat etiam in adiunctis peculiaribus, uti sunt matrimonia, exsequiae aut celebrationes occasionales, verbi gratia peregrinationes.

§ 4. Sacerdotes Missali beati Ioannis XXIII utentes, idonei esse debent ac iure non impediti.

§ 5. In ecclesiis, quae non sunt nec paroeciales nec conventuales, Rectoris ecclesiae est concedere licentiam de qua supra.

Art. 6. In Missis iuxta Missale beati Ioannis XXIII celebratis cum populo, Lectiones proclamari possunt etiam lingua vernacula, utendo editionibus ab Apostolica Sede recognitis.

Art. 7. Ubi aliquis coetus fidelium laicorum, de quo in art. 5 § 1 petitam a parocho licentiam non obtinuerit, de re certiorem faciat Episcopum dioecesanum. Episcopus enixe rogatur ut eorum optatum exaudiat. Si ille ad huius modi celebrationem providere non vult res ad Pontificiam Commissionem « Ecclesia Dei » referatur.

Art. 8. Episcopus, qui vult providere huiusmodi petitionibus christifidelium laicorum, sed ob varias causas impeditur, rem Pontificiae Commissioni « Ecclesia Dei » committere potest, quae ei consilium et auxilium dabit.

ful harmoniously accords with the ordinary pastoral care of the parish, under the guidance of the bishop according to Canon 392, avoiding discord and fostering the unity of the whole church.

SP, ARTICLE 5, SECTION 2

Celebration according to the Missal of Blessed John XXIII can take place on weekdays; moreover on Sundays and feast days also one celebration of this kind can be held.

SP, ARTICLE 5, SECTION 3

For the faithful or priests who request it, let the pastor permit celebrations in this extraordinary form even in other particular circumstances such as marriages, funerals, or occasional celebrations, for example, pilgrimages.

SP, ARTICLE 5, SECTION 4

Priests using the Missal of Blessed John XXIII should be qualified and not impeded by law.

SP, ARTICLE 5, SECTION 5

In churches which are neither parish nor conventual churches, it is for the rector of the church to grant permission concerning the foregoing.

SP, ARTICLE 6

In Masses according to the Missal of Blessed John XXIII celebrated with the people, the readings can be proclaimed also in the vernacular, using editions recognized by the Apostolic See.

SP, ARTICLE 7

Where some group of the lay faithful mentioned in Art. 5 sec. 1 has not obtained the permission sought from the pastor, let it make the diocesan bishop aware of the matter. The bishop is earnestly requested to answer their wish. If he is not willing to provide for this kind of celebration, let the matter be referred to the Pontifical Commission "Ecclesia Dei."

SP, ARTICLE 8

A bishop who wishes to provide for such petitions of the lay Christian faithful but is impeded for various reasons can entrust the matter to the Pontifical Commission "Ecclesia Dei," which will give him advice and help.

Art. 9, § 1. Parochus item, omnibus bene perpensis, licentiam concedere potest utendi rituali antiquiore in administrandis sacramentis Baptismatis, Matrimonii, Paenitentiae et Unctionis Infirmorum, bono animarum id suadente.

§ 2. Ordinariis autem facultas conceditur celebrandi Confirmationis sacramentum utendo Pontificali Romano antiquo, bono animarum id suadente.

§ 3. Fas est clericis in sacris constitutis uti etiam Breviario Romano a beato Ioanne XXIII anno 1962 promulgato.

Art. 10. Fas est Ordinario loci, si opportunum iudicaverit, paroeciam personalem ad normam canonis 518 pro celebrationibus iuxta formam antiquiorem ritus Romani erigere aut rectorem vel cappellanum nominare, servatis de iure servandis.

Art. 11. Pontificia Commissio « Ecclesia Dei » a Ioanne Paulo II anno 1988 erecta,[5] munus suum adimplere pergit.

Quae Commissio formam, officia et normas agendi habeat, quae Romanus Pontifex ipsi attribuere voluerit.

Art. 12. Eadem Commissio, ultra facultates quibus iam gaudet, auctoritatem Sanctae Sedis exercebit, vigilando de observantia et applicatione harum dispositionum.

Quaecumque vero a Nobis hisce Litteris Apostolicis Motu proprio datis decreta sunt, ea omnia firma ac rata esse et a die decima quarta Septembris huius anni, in festo Exaltationis Sanctae Crucis, servari iubemus, contrariis quibuslibet rebus non obstantibus.

[5] Cfr Ioannes Paulus PP. II. Litt. ap. Motu proprio datae *Ecclesia Dei* (2 Iulii 1988), 6: *AAS* 80 (1988), 1498.

SP, ARTICLE 9, SECTION 1

The pastor, having pondered all things well, can grant permission to use the prior ritual in administering the sacraments of baptism, matrimony, penance, and anointing of the sick, if the good of souls recommends it.

SP, ARTICLE 9, SECTION 2

Moreover, the faculty is given to ordinaries to celebrate the sacrament of confirmation using the prior Roman Pontifical, if the good of souls recommends it.

SP, ARTICLE 9, SECTION 3

It is lawful for clerics constituted in sacred orders to use also the Roman Breviary promulgated by Blessed John XXIII in 1962.

SP, ARTICLE 10

It is lawful for the local ordinary, if he judges it opportune, to erect a personal parish, in accord with the norm of Canon 518, for celebration according to the prior form of the Roman rite, or appoint a rector or chaplain, all relevant laws being observed.

SP, ARTICLE 11

The Pontifical Commission "Ecclesia Dei" erected by John Paul II in 1988[5] continues to carry out its function.

This Commission is to have the form, duties, and procedural norms which the Roman Pontiff may wish to give it.

SP, ARTICLE 12

The same Commission, beyond the faculties it already enjoys, will exercise the authority of the Holy See in keeping watch regarding the observance and application of these dispositions.

We order everything decreed by us in these apostolic letters given Motu proprio to be established and ratified, and to be observed from the fourteenth day of September of this year, on the Feast of the Triumph of the Holy Cross, anything to the contrary notwithstanding.

[5] Cf. John Paul II, Litterae Apostolicae motu proprio datae *Ecclesia Dei* (July 2, 1988), 6: *Acta Apostolicae Sedis* 80 (1988) 1498.

Datum Romae, apud Sanctum Petrum, die septima mensis Iulii, anno Domini MMVII, Pontificatus Nostri tertio.

BENEDICTUS PP. XVI

Given at Rome, at Saint Peter's, on the seventh day of July in the year of our Lord 2007, the third of my pontificate.

POPE BENEDICT XVI

Con Grande Fiducia

❒ ❒ ❒

Ad Episcopos Catholicae Ecclesiae Ritus Romani.

Cari Fratelli nell'Episcopato,
con grande fiducia e speranza metto nelle vostre mani di Pastori il testo di una nuova Lettera Apostolica « Motu Proprio data » sull'uso della liturgia romana anteriore alla riforma effettuata nel 1970. Il documento è frutto di lunghe riflessioni, di molteplici consultazioni e di preghiera.

Notizie e giudizi fatti senza sufficiente informazione hanno creato non poca confusione. Ci sono reazioni molto divergenti tra loro che vanno da un'accettazione gioiosa ad un'opposizione dura, per un progetto il cui contenuto in realtà non era conosciuto.

A questo documento si opponevano più direttamente due timori, che vorrei affrontare un po' più da vicino in questa lettera.

In primo luogo, c'è il timore che qui venga intaccata l'Autorità del Concilio Vaticano II e che una delle sue decisioni essenziali — la riforma liturgica — venga messa in dubbio. Tale timore è infondato. Al riguardo bisogna innanzitutto dire che il Messale, pubblicato in duplice edizione da Paolo VI e poi riedito una terza volta con l'approvazione di Giovanni Paolo II, ovviamente è e rimane la forma normale — la *forma ordinaria* — della Liturgia Eucaristica. L'ultima stesura del *Missale Romanum*, anteriore al Concilio, che è stata pubblicata con l'autorità di Papa Giovanni XXIII nel 1962 e utilizzata durante il Concilio, potrà, invece, essere usata come *forma extraordinaria* della Celebrazione liturgica. Non è appropriato parlare di queste due stesure del Messale Romano come se fossero « due Riti ». Si tratta, piuttosto, di un uso duplice dell'unico e medesimo Rito. Quanto all'uso del Messale del 1962, come *forma extraordinaria* della Liturgia della Messa, vorrei attirare l'attenzione sul fatto che questo Messale non fu mai giuridicamente abrogato e, di conseguenza, in linea di principio, restò sempre permesso.

Con Grande Fiducia

❒❒❒

To the Bishops of the Catholic Church of the Roman Rite

CGF 1
Dear brothers in the episcopacy, with great trust and hope I put in your hands as pastors the text of a new apostolic letter "motu proprio data" on the use of the Roman liturgy prior to the reform made effective in 1970. The document is the fruit of long reflection, many consultations, and prayer.

CGF 2
News reports and judgments made without sufficient information have created not a little confusion. There are very diverse reactions ranging from joyful acceptance to harsh opposition, concerning a project whose contents were in reality not known.

CGF 3
To this document two fears most directly opposed themselves, which I would like to confront a little more closely in this letter.

CGF 4
In the first place, there is the fear that here the authority of the Second Vatican Council could be harmed and that one of its essential decisions—the liturgical reform—could be cast into doubt. Such fear is unfounded. In this regard it must first of all be said that the Missal published in two editions by Paul VI and then republished a third time with the approval of John Paul II obviously is and remains the normal form—the *forma ordinaria*—of the Eucharistic liturgy. The last version of the *Roman Missal* before the council which was published with the authority of Pope John XXIII in 1962 and used during the council, will be able to be used, instead, as the *forma extraordinaria* of the liturgical celebration. It is not appropriate to speak of these two versions of the Roman Missal as if they were "two rites." We are dealing rather with a twofold use of one and the same rite.

Al momento dell'introduzione del nuovo Messale, non è sembrato necessario di emanare norme proprie per l'uso possibile del Messale anteriore. Probabilmente si è supposto che si sarebbe trattato di pochi casi singoli che si sarebbero risolti, caso per caso, sul posto. Dopo, però, si è presto dimostrato che non pochi rimanevano fortemente legati a questo uso del Rito romano che, fin dall'infanzia, era per loro diventato familiare. Ciò avvenne, innanzitutto, nei Paesi in cui il movimento liturgico aveva donato a molte persone una cospicua formazione liturgica e una profonda, intima familiarità con la forma anteriore della Celebrazione liturgica. Tutti sappiamo che, nel movimento guidato dall'Arcivescovo Lefebvre, la fedeltà al Messale antico divenne un contrassegno esterno; le ragioni di questa spaccatura, che qui nasceva, si trovavano però più in profondità. Molte persone, che accettavano chiaramente il carattere vincolante del Concilio Vaticano II e che erano fedeli al Papa e ai Vescovi, desideravano tuttavia anche ritrovare la forma, a loro cara, della sacra Liturgia; questo avvenne anzitutto perché in molti luoghi non si celebrava in modo fedele alle prescrizioni del nuovo Messale, ma esso addirittura veniva inteso come un'autorizzazione o perfino come un obbligo alla creatività, la quale portò spesso a deformazioni della Liturgia al limite del sopportabile. Parlo per esperienza, perché ho vissuto anch'io quel periodo con tutte le sue attese e confusioni. E ho visto quanto profondamente siano state ferite, dalle deformazioni arbitrarie della Liturgia, persone che erano totalmente radicate nella fede della Chiesa.

Papa Giovanni Paolo II si vide, perciò, obbligato a dare, con il Motu Proprio « *Ecclesia Dei* » del 2 luglio 1988, un quadro normativo per l'uso del Messale del 1962, che però non conteneva prescrizioni dettagliate, ma faceva appello, in modo più generale, alla generosità dei Vescovi verso le « giuste aspirazioni » di quei fedeli che richiedevano quest'uso del Rito Romano. In quel momento il Papa

As for the use of the Missal of 1962 as the *forma extraordinaria* of the liturgy of the Mass, I would like to draw attention to the fact that this Missal was not ever juridically abrogated and, consequently, as a matter of principle remained always permitted. When the new Missal was introduced, it did not seem necessary to issue specific norms for the possible use of the prior Missal. Probably it was supposed it would be a matter of a few individual cases that would be resolved case by case on the local level.

After, however, it soon became clear that not a few remained strongly attached to that use of the Roman Rite which from childhood had become familiar to them. This happened first of all in countries in which the liturgical movement had given many people a remarkable liturgical formation and a profound, intimate familiarity with the prior form of the liturgical celebration.

We all know that in the movement led by Archbishop Lefebvre, fidelity to the old Mass became an external sign; the reasons for the split which began here, however, are found in deeper matters.

Many people who clearly accepted the binding character of the Second Vatican Council and were faithful to the pope and the bishops nonetheless also desired to find again the form of the sacred liturgy dear to them. This happened first of all because in many places there were celebrations unfaithful to the prescriptions of the new Missal; indeed it even came to be taken to authorize or even require creativity, which often led to deformations of the liturgy, to the limit of what could be endured. I speak from experience, for I myself also went through that period with all its expectations and confusions. And I have seen how profoundly wounded, by arbitrary deformations of the liturgy, were persons who were totally rooted in the faith of the church.

CGF 5

This is why Pope John Paul II saw himself obliged to provide, with his *motu proprio "Ecclesia Dei"* of July 2, 1988, a normative framework for the use of the Missal of 1962—a framework however which did not contain detailed provisions but made an appeal in a more general way to the generosity of bishops toward the "just aspirations" of those faithful who requested this use of the Roman

voleva, così, aiutare soprattutto la Fraternità San Pio X a ritrovare la piena unità con il Successore di Pietro, cercando di guarire una ferita sentita sempre più dolorosamente. Purtroppo questa riconciliazione finora non è riuscita; tuttavia una serie di comunità hanno utilizzato con gratitudine le possibilità di questo Motu Proprio. Difficile è rimasta, invece, la questione dell'uso del Messale del 1962 al di fuori di questi gruppi, per i quali mancavano precise norme giuridiche, anzitutto perché spesso i Vescovi, in questi casi, temevano che l'autorità del Concilio fosse messa in dubbio. Subito dopo il Concilio Vaticano II si poteva supporre che la richiesta dell'uso del Messale del 1962 si limitasse alla generazione più anziana che era cresciuta con esso, ma nel frattempo è emerso chiaramente che anche giovani persone scoprono questa forma liturgica, si sentono attirate da essa e vi trovano una forma, particolarmente appropriata per loro, di incontro con il Mistero della Santissima Eucaristia. Così è sorto un bisogno di un regolamento giuridico più chiaro che, al tempo del Motu Proprio del 1988, non era prevedibile; queste Norme intendono anche liberare i Vescovi dal dover sempre di nuovo valutare come sia da rispondere alle diverse situazioni.

In secondo luogo, nelle discussioni sull'atteso Motu Proprio, venne espresso il timore che una più ampia possibilità dell'uso del Messale del 1962 avrebbe portato a disordini o addirittura a spaccature nelle comunità parrocchiali. Anche questo timore non mi sembra realmente fondato. L'uso del Messale antico presuppone una certa misura di formazione liturgica e un accesso alla lingua latina; sia l'una che l'altra non si trovano tanto di frequente. Già da questi presupposti concreti si vede chiaramente che il nuovo Messale rimarrà, certamente, la forma ordinaria del Rito Romano, non soltanto a causa della normativa giuridica, ma anche della reale situazione in cui si trovano le comunità di fedeli.

È vero che non mancano esagerazioni e qualche volta aspetti sociali indebitamente vincolati all'attitudine di fedeli legati all'antica tradizione liturgica latina. La vostra carità e prudenza pastorale sarà

Rite again. At that time the pope wanted in this way to help above all the Society of St. Pius X to return to full unity with the successor of Peter, seeking to heal a wound felt ever more painfully. Unfortunately this reconciliation has not yet come to pass; nevertheless, a succession of communities has with gratitude made use of the possibilities of that *motu proprio*. Difficult, on the other hand, has remained the question of the use of the Missal of 1962 outside these groups for whom there were no specific juridical norms, above all because often the bishops in these cases feared that the authority of the council would have been placed in doubt. Immediately after the Second Vatican Council one could have supposed that requests for use of the Missal of 1962 would be limited to the older generation that had grown up with it, but in the meantime it has clearly emerged that young persons as well have discovered this liturgical form, feel themselves attracted by it, and have found there a form particularly appropriate for them to encounter the mystery of the most holy Eucharist. Thus a need has arisen for a clearer juridical regulation, which one could not have foreseen at the time of the *motu proprio* of 1988. These norms intend also to free the bishops from the need always to evaluate anew how to respond to diverse situations.

CGF 6
In the second place, in discussions on the anticipated *motu proprio*, the fear was expressed that a wider possibility for use of the 1962 Missal would lead to disturbances or even to divisions in parish communities. This fear, too, does not seem to me to be well founded. Use of the ancient Missal presupposes a certain degree of liturgical formation and a basic facility in the Latin language; neither the one nor the other is found very often. Already from these concrete presuppositions one sees clearly that the new Missal will certainly remain the ordinary form of the Roman Rite, not only because of the juridical norms but also because of the actual situation in which one finds communities of the faithful.

CGF 7
It is true that there have not been lacking exaggerations and at some times social aspects unduly linked to the attitude of the faithful bound to the ancient Latin liturgical tradition. Your love and

stimolo e guida per un perfezionamento. Del resto le due forme dell'uso del Rito Romano possono arricchirsi a vicenda: nel Messale antico potranno e dovranno essere inseriti nuovi santi e alcuni dei nuovi prefazi. La Commissione « Ecclesia Dei » in contatto con i diversi enti dedicati all'« usus antiquior » studierà le possibilità pratiche. Nella celebrazione della Messa secondo il Messale di Paolo VI potrà manifestarsi, in maniera più forte di quanto non lo è spesso finora, quella sacralità che attrae molti all'antico uso. La garanzia più sicura che il Messale di Paolo VI possa unire le comunità parrocchiali e venga da loro amato consiste nel celebrare con grande riverenza in conformità alle prescrizioni; ciò rende visibile la ricchezza spirituale e la profondità teologica di questo Messale.

Sono giunto, così, a quella ragione positiva che mi ha motivato ad aggiornare mediante questo Motu Proprio quello del 1988. Si tratta di giungere ad una riconciliazione interna nel seno della Chiesa. Guardando al passato, alle divisioni che nel corso dei secoli hanno lacerato il Corpo di Cristo, si ha continuamente l'impressione che, in momenti critici in cui la divisione stava nascendo, non è stato fatto il sufficiente da parte dei responsabili della Chiesa per conservare o conquistare la riconciliazione e l'unità; si ha l'impressione che le omissioni nella Chiesa abbiano avuto una loro parte di colpa nel fatto che queste divisioni si siano potute consolidare. Questo sguardo al passato oggi ci impone un obbligo: fare tutti gli sforzi, affinché a tutti quelli che hanno veramente il desiderio dell'unità, sia reso possibile di restare in quest'unità o di ritrovarla nuovamente. Mi viene in mente una frase della Seconda Lettera ai Corinzi, dove Paolo scrive: «La nostra bocca vi ha parlato francamente, Corinzi, e il nostro cuore si è tutto aperto per voi. Non siete davvero allo stretto in noi; è nei vostri cuori invece che siete allo stretto... Rendeteci il contraccambio, aprite anche voi il vostro cuore! » (2 *Cor* 6, 11-13). Paolo lo dice certo in un altro contesto, ma il suo invito può e deve toccare anche noi, proprio in questo tema.

pastoral prudence will be a stimulus and guide toward improvement. Moreover, the two forms of the use of the Roman Rite can be mutually enriching: new saints and some of the new prefaces can and should be inserted in the ancient Missal. The Commission "Ecclesia Dei" in contact with diverse entities dedicated to the *usus antiquior* will study the practical possibilities. The celebration of the Mass according to the Missal of Paul VI will be able to manifest, in a stronger way than has often been the case up to now, that sacrality that attracts many to the ancient usage. The surest guarantee that the Missal of Paul VI can unite parish communities and come to be loved by them consists in celebrating it with great reverence in conformity with the prescribed norms. This will make visible the spiritual riches and theological depth of this Missal.

CGF 8

I arrive then at that positive reason which has motivated me to update, through this *motu proprio*, that of 1988. It is a matter of reaching an internal reconciliation in the heart of the church. In looking back over the past at divisions that in the course of the centuries have torn apart the body of Christ, one continually has the impression that in critical moments in which the division was just beginning, not enough had been done on the part of those responsible for the church to keep or to gain reconciliation and unity. One has the impression that omissions in the church have had their share of blame in the fact that these divisions were able to harden. This look at the past imposes an obligation on us today: to make every effort so that all those who truly have the desire for unity be enabled to remain in that unity or to regain it anew. I am mindful of a phrase in the Second Letter to the Corinthians, where Paul writes: "Our mouth has spoken to you in all frankness, Corinthians, and our heart itself is wide open to you. You are truly not restricted by us; it is rather in your own hearts that you are restricted . . . . As recompense in kind, you also, in your turn, open your heart!" (2 Cor 6:11–13). Paul says this certainly in another context, but his invitation can and should touch us also, precisely on this theme. Let

Apriamo generosamente il nostro cuore e lasciamo entrare tutto ciò a cui la fede stessa offre spazio.

Non c'è nessuna contraddizione tra l'una e l'altra edizione del *Missale Romanum*. Nella storia della Liturgia c'è crescita e progresso, ma nessuna rottura. Ciò che per le generazioni anteriori era sacro, anche per noi resta sacro e grande, e non può essere improvvisamente del tutto proibito o, addirittura, giudicato dannoso. Ci fa bene a tutti conservare le ricchezze che sono cresciute nella fede e nella preghiera della Chiesa, e di dar loro il giusto posto. Ovviamente per vivere la piena comunione anche i sacerdoti delle Comunità aderenti all'uso antico non possono, in linea di principio, escludere la celebrazione secondo i libri nuovi. Non sarebbe infatti coerente con il riconoscimento del valore e della santità del nuovo rito l'esclusione totale dello stesso.

In conclusione, cari Confratelli, mi sta a cuore sottolineare che queste nuove norme non diminuiscono in nessun modo la vostra autorità e responsabilità, né sulla liturgia né sulla pastorale dei vostri fedeli. Ogni Vescovo, infatti, è il moderatore della liturgia nella propria diocesi.[1]

Nulla si toglie quindi all'autorità del Vescovo il cui ruolo, comunque, rimarrà quello di vigilare affinché tutto si svolga in pace e serenità. Se dovesse nascere qualche problema che il parroco non possa risolvere, l'Ordinario locale potrà sempre intervenire, in piena armonia, però, con quanto stabilito dalle nuove norme del Motu Proprio.

Inoltre, vi invito, cari Confratelli, a scrivere alla Santa Sede un resoconto sulle vostre esperienze, tre anni dopo l'entrata in vigore di

[1] Cfr Conc. Ecum. Vat. II, Cost. sulla sacra liturgia, *Sacrosanctum Concilium*, n. 22: « Sacrae Liturgiae moderatio ab Ecclesiae auctoritate unice pendet quae quidem est apud Apostolicam Sedem et, ad normam iuris, apud Episcopum ».

us generously open our heart and make space for all that the faith itself allows.

CGF 9
There is no contradiction between the one and the other edition of the *Roman Missal*. In the history of the liturgy there is growth and progress, but no rupture. What was sacred for prior generations remains sacred and great for us as well and cannot be all of a sudden entirely prohibited or even considered harmful. It is good for all of us to preserve the riches that have grown in the faith and prayer of the church and give them their rightful place. Obviously, to enjoy full communion also the priests of the Community adhering to the old usage cannot, as a matter of principle, exclude celebration according to the new books. A total exclusion of the new rite would in fact not be consistent with recognition of its value and holiness.

CGF 10
In conclusion, dear Brothers, it is very important to me to emphasize that these new norms do not diminish in any way your authority and responsibility, either for the liturgy or for the pastoral care of your faithful. Each bishop, in fact, is moderator of the liturgy in his own diocese.[1]

CGF 11
Nothing, then, is taken away from the authority of the bishop whose role in any case remains that of taking care that everything proceeds in peace and serenity. If some problem should arise that the parish priest is not able to resolve, the local ordinary can always intervene, in full harmony, however, with all that has been established by the new norms of the *motu proprio*.

CGF 12
Furthermore, I ask you, dear brothers, to write to the Holy See an account of your experiences, three years after this *motu proprio* takes

[1] Cf. Second Vatican Council, Constitution on the Sacred Liturgy, *Sacrosanctum Concilium* 22: "Regulation of the sacred liturgy depends solely on the authority of the Church, that is, on the Apostolic See and, as laws may determine, on the bishop."

questo Motu Proprio. Se veramente fossero venute alla luce serie difficoltà, potranno essere cercate vie per trovare rimedio.

Cari Fratelli, con animo grato e fiducioso, affido al vostro cuore di Pastori queste pagine e le norme del Motu Proprio. Siamo sempre memori delle parole dell'Apostolo Paolo dirette ai presbiteri di Efeso: « Vegliate su voi stessi e su tutto il gregge, in mezzo al quale lo Spirito Santo vi ha posti come Vescovi a pascere la Chiesa di Dio, che egli si è acquistata con il suo sangue » (*Atti* 20, 28).

Affido alla potente intercessione di Maria, Madre della Chiesa, queste nuove norme e di cuore imparto la mia Benedizione Apostolica a Voi, cari Confratelli, ai parroci delle vostre diocesi, e a tutti i sacerdoti, vostri collaboratori, come anche a tutti i vostri fedeli.

Dato presso San Pietro, il 7 luglio 2007.

BENEDICTUS PP. XVI

effect. If truly serious difficulties come to light, ways can be sought to find a remedy.

CGF 13

Dear brothers, with grateful and trusting thoughts I entrust to your hearts as pastors these pages and the norms of the *motu proprio*. Let us always be mindful of the words of the Apostle Paul to the presbyters of Ephesus: "Take heed to yourselves and to all the flock, in which the Holy Spirit has made you overseers, to care for the church of God which he obtained for himself with his own blood" (Acts 20:28).

CGF 14

I entrust to the powerful intercession of Mary, Mother of the Church, these new norms and with all my heart impart my apostolic blessing to you, dear brothers, to the parish priests in your dioceses, to all the priests, your coworkers, as also to all your faithful.

Given at Saint Peter's, July 7, 2007

POPE BENEDICT XVI

Index

Bold text indicates pages on which primary commentary can be found.